Making San Francisco American

Making San Francisco American

Cultural Frontiers in the Urban West, 1846–1906

Barbara Berglund

UNIVERSITY PRESS OF KANSAS

Parts of Chapter 3 were originally published as "Chinatown's Tourist
Terrain: Representation and Racialization in Nineteenth-Century
San Francisco," *American Studies* 46, 2 (Summer 2005): 5–36.
Parts of Chapter 5 were originally published as " 'The Days of Old,
the Days of Gold, the Days of '49': Identity, History, and Memory
at the California Midwinter International Exposition, 1894,"
Public Historian 25, 4 (Fall 2003): 25–49.

Published by the University Press of Kansas (Lawrence, Kansas 66045),
which was organized by the Kansas Board of Regents and is operated and
funded by Emporia State University, Fort Hays State University, Kansas
State University, Pittsburg State University, the University of Kansas,
and Wichita State University

Library of Congress Cataloging-in-Publication Data
Berglund, Barbara.
Making San Francisco American : cultural frontiers in the urban West,
1846–1906 / Barbara Berglund.
   p. cm.
Includes bibliographical references and index.
ISBN 978–0–7006–1530–8 (cloth : alk. paper)
1. San Francisco (Calif.)—Social life and customs—19th century.
2. San Francisco (Calif.)—Social life and customs—20th century.
3. City and town life—California—San Francisco—History.
4. Elite (Social sciences)—California—San Francisco—History.
5. Social control—California—San Francisco—History.
6. Assimilation (Sociology)—California—San Francisco—History.
7. National characteristics, American—History. 8. Political culture—
California—San Francisco—History. 9. San Francisco (Calif.)—Social
conditions. 10. San Francisco (Calif.)—Ethnic relations. I. Title.
  F869.S35B47 2007
  306.09794'6109034—dc22   2007015902

British Library Cataloguing-in-Publication Data is available.

Printed in the United States of America

10 9 8 7 6 5 4 3 2 1

To San Franciscans—Past, Present, and Future

Contents

Preface

Growing up in San Francisco, I never liked gold rush history. There was too much lore about miners and big-hearted dance-hall girls, frontier justice, saucy newspaper editors, and the rise to power of mining and railroad elites. The stories all seemed to swirl around the same key events and figures—like Emperor Norton, Belle Cora, the Broderick-Terry duel, Vigilance Committees, and the Big Four. There's nothing intrinsically wrong with those stories but, from my vantage point, they just weren't that interesting. So there is a certain amount of irony in the fact that I've written this book. Or maybe not, given that what I hope to have accomplished here is to have written a different kind of history about the growth and development of San Francisco: one that moves beyond familiar stories and into a new and different way of conceptualizing the city that I will always regard as my home.

Instead of stemming from an early fascination with gold rush history, I actually think the germ of this book was planted in all the time I spent riding the bus—first as a city kid trekking to school and roaming with friends, later as a car-less urban dweller and working commuter. Because, when I rode the bus, I watched the parade of people around me and wondered about their stories—about who they were, where they came from, and where they were going. Public transportation is an amazing cultural frontier. You pay your fare, climb aboard, and for the length of your ride, you are allowed glimpses into moments of other people's lives—people that you might never otherwise interact with. If you are a careful observer you have the opportunity to take in what your fellow riders wear, read, and carry; whom they talk to and what they say; where they get on, where they get off. You might not know regular riders' names but you may have a pretty good idea of where they work and live. You might even have an interesting, if fleeting, conversation, meet someone new, or witness an altercation. Granted, if you bury your head in a book, stare out the window, or just don't pay attention, you can miss all of that. But that wasn't my modus operandi. For me, what was going on inside the bus was usually the fun part—however weird, wonderful, uneventful, or disturbing the interactions between passengers on a particular ride might be. I fell in love with observation. And when I began this love affair, in San Francisco in the 1970s, the city was a pretty colorful place so there was a lot to take in. I credit those long-ago bus rides with starting me down the path of wanting to know how the world I observed was put together—and that dovetailed with wanting to know how my city had been put together.

But there were other things besides my innumerable bus rides that had a hand in leading to writing this book. Things that in a legendarily cosmopolitan and tolerant city made me incredibly conscious of how differences rooted in race, class, and gender intersected with social power. I rode the city bus to a school across town because my parents opposed busing, which started the year I began first grade. They'd worked hard to buy a modest house in a neighborhood on the west side of Twin Peaks with good schools close by. Sending me to a school in the Mission District, a poorer neighborhood, with schools that were less good and people who were less white was unacceptable to them. As a result, I ended up a nominally Protestant student in a Catholic school far from my home neighborhood for all but one year of elementary and high school. I memorized all the prayers, prepared for all the sacraments, but since I never actually made them, I sat in the pew—with the Russian Orthodox and Chinese kids—when everyone else went to communion. During a couple of early elementary school summers, I had a blast going to Cameron House day camp in Chinatown. I knew that as a big white kid, I sort of stood out, but I had such a good time singing camp songs and going on urban adventures that I barely noticed. It was where one of my best friends from my neighborhood was going, so it was where I went, too. But my parents drew the line at me going to Chinese school—that my Chinese friends would have to do without me.

In a strange twist of fate, in 1976, the year that I didn't go to Catholic school, I went to a public junior high school literally next door to where I would have been bussed. Other neighborhood friends were going there, I wanted to be with them, and since I was accepted into the gifted program, my parents accepted my desire for change. That year, I found my way to disco, learned how to cut class and explore the Mission and the Castro, and aspired to be a chola. I got as far as the Ben Davis pants and remember experimenting with lots of hairspray and eyeliner, but my awkward junior high self couldn't quite pull off that kind of artful style. The next year, despite or because of all the life-altering educational experiences I'd had inside and outside the class-room, I opted to go back to Catholic school. While reconnecting with my friends there that I had known since first grade, I learned that acceptance hinged on giving up disco and soul and reclaiming rock-n-roll. Sitting in a friend's downstairs room learning to get comfortable with the initially ear-splitting sounds of Led Zeppelin and Rush instead of the smooth tunes of the Commodores and Earth, Wind & Fire was a serious lesson in relearning the tropes of urban whiteness.

In high school, I was taught by nuns who embraced social justice, who taught me about feminism, the evils of apartheid, and how to boycott Nestle. But tables in the cafeteria often self-segregated along racial lines, and the prevailing under-standing was that a pregnant schoolmate had been asked to leave as she began to show—even though she had ostensibly done the right thing. I knew boys who proclaimed W.P.O.D., which didn't mean "White Punks on Dope," as the Kinks suggested, but "White Power or Death," and who adorned their trucks with Confederate flags and called their steel-toed boots "nigger stompers." Racist jokes and anti-immigrant sentiment were part and parcel of my everyday life. It wasn't until I was in my mid-20s that I entered a house in Pacific Heights. And then I joked to my friends that I was attending the fancy party I'd been invited to by a college friend as a representative of San Francisco's working class. I was, after all, the daughter of a teamster, had just recently been driven to try out grad school at San Francisco State by the bleakness of a four-year-long series of secre-tarial jobs, and I was wearing $10 Payless Shoe Source shoes.

I've included these biographical snippets in order to give you a sense of the personal stake I have in the story that follows. The city I grew up in was cosmopolitan and tolerant, but at the same time it was also bigoted, angry, and fearful of its own diversity. The story of San Francisco's nineteenth-century past that I offer here is my contribution to figuring out how it got that way. When I attended the bash in Pacific Heights, I was at the beginning of my journey of becoming a historian. That training, as well as my undergraduate study of sociology at UC Santa Cruz and my skills of observation, well-honed from years of bus riding, has given me the kind of tools that I hope have al-lowed me to capture the contradictions and wrinkles, beauty and ugliness, ex-ceptionalism and sameness of San Francisco's history. I should mention that if you had asked me that night in Pacific Heights what I wanted to focus my his-torical studies on, I seriously doubt that I would have ever said anything about local history. Women's history, sure. Immigration history, maybe. Something that revealed how power worked in society, even better. But I never intended initially to focus my research on San Francisco.

Yet by that evening I suspect that I may have begun to develop my attraction to cultural history. And it was cultural history that brought me to the history of my home town. As I explored that burgeoning field, I found myself reading all sorts of wonderful books about theaters, saloons, dance halls, amusement parks, blackface minstrelsy, bare-knuckle prize fighting, and myriad other nineteenth-century cultural practices. The vast majority looked at the rest of the nation from a New York City–centered viewpoint. Painfully few paid any attention to the premier city of the nineteenth-century West—San Francisco. When push came to shove, and I needed to pick a research paper topic in one of my first graduate seminars at the University of Michigan, I realized I knew San Francisco's urban terrain much better than I could ever hope to know New York's. As a San Franciscan, I knew that New York wasn't really the center of the universe. And I also firmly believed that San Francisco's cultural history, despite those who told me I wouldn't find material because of the destruction of the 1906 fire and earthquake, was a story just waiting to be told. Soon I would stumble into the history of the American West—it took me a while to realize that San Francisco was part of that history, which I still somehow associated with rural spaces and cowboys and Indians—and the insights of that field allowed me to figure out how to connect San Francisco's local story into a larger story of nation-making and empire-building.

This book, which has grown from a life lived mostly in urban settings and many years spent in school, looks at nineteenth-century San Francisco through the lens of the classic frontier questions that ask how a society was organized and a new American place formed, but with a twist. Instead of the more traditional realms of law and politics, the focus here is on cultural spaces—like restaurants, hotels, and boardinghouses; places of amusement; Chinatown's tourist terrain; and fairs and expositions. I looked to these places as a historian, in part because, as an urbanite, these were the kinds of places where I came face-to-face with other people—where I made sense of who they were, and who I was. In the history I've written, I use these places, which I call *cultural frontiers*, to illuminate how race, class, and gender relations were hammered out in the course of everyday life. In nineteenth-century San Francisco, establishing nationally dominant forms of race, class, and gender hierarchies was an essential part of making the recently acquired, heavily immigrant city into a recognizably American place, and cultural frontiers functioned as key arenas of this process. Implicit in offering this new, differently focused narrative of San Francisco's history is a recognition of the power of stories and that stories are embedded in structures of power. My hope is that taking a journey back into an exploration of the stories generated on San Francisco's nineteenth-century cultural frontiers will spur greater mindfulness about the power of twenty-first-century cultural frontiers that continue to shape the meanings we make about the human diversity that surrounds us.

Acknowledgments

This book's lengthy gestation has been enriched by the scholarly insights, professional guidance, friendship, and financial support of a number of individuals and institutions that I am delighted to have the opportunity to acknowledge here. Let me begin by thanking the Mellon Foundation and the Rackham Graduate School at the University of Michigan for generous fellowships and grants that funded the research trips and long days of writing that brought this project to fruition at the dissertation stage. For the priceless gift of a year-long fellowship that provided me with the time to write and think— to do the revisions necessary to turn my dissertation into this book—I am indebted to the generosity of the Howard R. Lamar Center for the Study of Frontiers and Borders at Yale University. For a highly productive and enjoyable month of research and intellectual community, thanks also goes to the Huntington Library for support in the form of a Fletcher Jones Foundation Research Fellowship. I am also grateful to the archivists, librarians, and staff of the Bancroft and Doe Libraries at the University of California at Berkeley, the California Historical Society, the San Francisco Public Library, the California State Library, the Harlan Hatcher Graduate Library at the University of Michigan, and the Beinecke Library at Yale University.

It has been my good fortune to have come into contact with dedicated professors and advisors throughout my years as both a graduate and undergraduate student. My first encounter with academics was as an undergraduate at the University of California at Santa Cruz. Thanks to Candace West and Bettina Aptheker for inspiring me to choose this path. At San Francisco State University, Barbara Loomis, Paul Longmore, Bob Cherny, Tani Barlow, Sally Scully, and Bill Issel took a wayward sociologist and turned her into a historian. At the University of Michigan, my dissertation committee—María Montoya, Jay Cook, Rebecca Zurier, and Richard Cándida Smith—challenged, supported, and encouraged me. This project had its start in David Scobey's cultural history seminar and, in many respects, what I learned from him there has influenced not only the way this project began, but the way it developed and matured. Towards the end of my time at Michigan, I benefited tremendously from Phil Deloria's insights and intellectual generosity. Carroll Smith-Rosenberg, Fernando Coronil, Gina Morantz-Sanchez, and Carol Karlsen also influenced me in ways that helped shape this project. University of Michigan history department staff members Lorna Alstetter and Sheila Williams deserve oodles of recognition and thanks for their good humor and skillful navigation of university bureaucracy.

I have also been fortunate enough to find support, mentorship, and generally wise friends beyond the institutions where I received my formal training. Thanks to David Wrobel for taking an early and lasting interest in me and my work. To Howard Lamar, John Mack Faragher, Jay Gitlin, and George Miles, I'm grateful for their roles in helping me find my way to and around Yale. I was lucky enough to be in-residence there with Martha Sandweiss—someone I already knew to be an inspiring scholar who has become an incredible mentor and friend. She and Ann Fabian, who both read and commented upon chapters of my manuscript, taught me so much about writing and how to tell stories. For their comments and advice on panels, in print, and in less formal settings, thanks also go to Virginia Scharff, Peter Boag, David Rich Lewis, David Igler, and Anne Hyde.

Nancy Jackson, in her role as acquisitions editor for the University Press of Kansas, had the vision to see my dissertation as something of a diamond-in-the-rough. The mark of her editorial finesse is on just about every page of this book. Fred Woodward and Kalyani Fernando brought the manuscript successfully through its final stages. Special thanks to Susan Schott, for her marketing expertise; to Susan McRory for steering me through the production process; and to Martha Whitt, a careful and graceful copyeditor.

When I began teaching at the University of South Florida in Tampa in 2003, I found myself surrounded by an incredibly smart, funny, and supportive community of colleagues. They have helped me adjust to life in the tropics, to navigate my first years of teaching, and to stay sane as I've made my way towards tenure. For that, as well as for just generally making coming to work fun, thanks go to Giovanna Benadusi, Fraser Otanelli, Bob Ingalls, David Johnson, LuAnn Jones, Phil Levy, Case Boterbloem, Tamara Zwick, Julie Langford-Johnson, Bill Cummings, Golfo Alexopolis, William and Suzanne Murray, John Belohlavek, Paul Dosal, and the late Ward Stavig. In the office, Sylvia Wood and Judy Drawdy always seem to have a kind word and find a way to make things easier. Outside of the history department, other friendships that have had their genesis in the USF community have enriched the last four years in innumerable ways. Thanks to Dan Weiskopf, Mary Thurman, Maria Cizmic, Andrew Berish, Jacqueline Messing, Carolyn Eichner, Kennan Ferguson, and Frank Guridy.

For the decade it's been with me, I've carried this project through numerous parts of the country, several institutions, and more than a couple phases of my life. Throughout, I have been sustained by a stellar community of friends who have shared ideas, brainstormed, commiserated, and celebrated over many meals, cups of coffee, beers, glasses of wine, and telephone lines. At Michigan, I had the good fortune to befriend two amazing women, Alexandra Stern and April Mayes, who have been there through it all. For keeping it real during my years at Michigan and beyond, thanks also to David Salmanson, Lori Lorenz, Mike Niklaus, Ellen and Dennis Hartigan-O'Connor, Anna Lawrence, Dan Bass, Alice Ritscherle, Pablo Mitchell, Chris Talbot, Andrew Needham, Alyssa Picard, Judy and Mike Daubenmier, Terri Koreck, Alexander Shashko, Kate Masur, Libby Garland, Leslie Paris, Jeff Filipiak, Tom Romero, Andrew Goss, Pax Bobrow, Alex Navarro, Chloe Burke, Patrick Carroll, and Josephine Rood. For making me feel welcome during my year in New Haven, thanks to Amy Scott, Scott Gac, Nicole Neatby, Adam Arenson, Kat Charron, Dan Lanpher, Roxanne Willis, and members of the Writing History group. For sticking it out for the long haul I thank Danielle and Ella Driscoll, Martin Meeker, Linda Melville, Matt Glickman, Ned Mitchell, Dan Granja, Kristine Tellefsen, and Melanie von der Schulenburg. I am indebted to Gabriela Arredondo, Ernesto Chavez, Doug Sackman, Kathleen Brosnan, Matt Bokovoy, and Ben Johnson for providing intellectual camaraderie and general good cheer at conferences and other visits all over the country.

The support, understanding, and generosity of my family have also been invaluable. To my mother, Joyce Berglund, there are really no words to convey the depth of my gratitude for being such a loving and devoted, yet thoroughly human mom. My father, James Berglund, died soon after I received notification that I'd been admitted to UC Santa Cruz. Although he probably could never have imagined that I would have embraced the value he placed on education to this degree, he knew I'd started down the path that has led me here and I think he would have been proud of where I've ended up. My adopted family, the Norton-Landgraf clan—Mary, Dave, and Rob Landgraf; Barbara Walczak; Jack Norton; Lisa and Curtis Clark and, by extension,

Marilyn Thieme—have just never stopped welcoming me with open arms. Marge Norton, my adopted grandma, has been a wise, loving, and caring force in my life since I was a teenager. That's when I met her granddaughter, Lisa, who since those early years has been like a sister to me. I really got to know Marge, though, when she housed me every time I came into San Francisco to do research for this project, often for months at a time. She not only opened her home to me, but also her heart, kept me laughing with funny stories and gave me lots of great advice from her ninety-plus years of accumulated wisdom. My father- and mother-in-law, Hubert and Laurel Dubb, and my uncle-in-law, Lee Gordon, accepted me from the start, and that has meant a lot. Steve Dubb, my most wonderful partner in life's many adventures and editor extraordinaire, has my heartfelt thanks and all of my love for being my friend, for believing in me, and for reading every word.

Introduction:
Ordering the Disorderly City:
Nation-Making on Cultural Ground

The mass migration inspired by the California gold rush of 1849 reverberated in communities across the nation and around the world. In San Francisco, the rush to the gold fields precipitated the emergence not only of a new American city but also a new urban society on the far western edge of the United States' landed empire. The rapid growth and diverse populace of San Francisco, a place in formation, inhabited by a people in formation, gave it both exciting and unsettling qualities. The racial, ethnic, and religious diversity of its population—in combination with its overwhelming maleness—astounded and often disturbed nineteenth-century observers. In this emerging society, race, gender, and class relations diverged markedly from the familiar and seemingly well-ordered patterns that prevailed elsewhere. Its international, polyglot assemblage quickly earned it a lasting reputation for disorder rooted in the promiscuous mixture of peoples and cultures that sat in an uneasy tension with strivings for social order.[1]

Indeed, San Francisco's nascent elite frequently sought to downplay and to control its unruly population. In elite hands, the dominant narrative of the city's history became one of the triumph of order over disorder. In 1883, writer James O'Meara recounted this story in an article published in the *Overland Monthly*. He explained that "from out of an unparalleled confusion and incongruity of race and class, by the due process of intelligence, wholesome conduct, and perseverance, the wild city of the tumultuous gold-hunting period has become a home of affluence, of society and fashion, of enterprise and sound prosperity, of wholesome laws and general good order."[2] There was more than an element of truth in O'Meara's depiction of the city's past and present that linked progress with attaining control of race and class relations. As the century advanced and San Francisco developed into an urban metropolis—the jewel in the crown of America's western empire—social fluidity declined and a social order more in step with nationally dominant hierarchies became increasingly prevalent. Yet conflict and disorder rooted in the organization of race, class, and gender remained pivotal. Celebratory narratives like O'Meara's always existed in dialogue with, and often in an attempt to silence, contradictory realities and competing visions.

Combining the characteristics of a city on the western frontier and a cosmopolitan port of entry, San Francisco emerged as a place where peoples pushed and pulled by multiple migratory trajectories encountered each other and established relations along a continuum ranging from conflict, coercion, and exploitation to friendship, sexual liaison, and marriage.[3] Tensions inherent in powerful nineteenth-century dichotomies—civilization and barbarism, purity and mixture, inclusion and exclusion, excess and austerity—shaped the contours of everyday life. San Franciscans negotiated those tensions on the city's cultural frontiers—its restaurants, hotels and boardinghouses, places of amusement, annual fairs, and long-running expositions—central components in what made up the rhythms of city life.[4] Unlike institutions—such as churches, schools, and hospitals—cultural frontiers were firmly embedded in the market relations that gave rise to popular and consumer cultures. Unlike streets or parks, all were semipublic commercial spaces in that they limited the public that occupied them by virtue of their commercial nature—for example, the price of admission, the cost of a meal, or the types of service workers employed. Given the potential of these types of cultural spaces to serve as potent, often double-edged symbols of urbane civilization or frontier barbarism, observers often evaluated their quality and quantity as reflections of the city's progress or decline. As meeting grounds on which residents worked, ate, lived, and played, cultural frontiers functioned as vital terrain on which people came face to face with one another and enunciated varied and competing racialized, gendered, and class-based views of themselves and those around them. In the context of the city's newness, rapid growth, diversity, and social fluidity, they served as sites of mixture and segregation in which notions of self and other were articulated. The ways San Franciscans understood their differences and translated them into social hierarchies on the city's cultural frontiers is the untold story behind the dominant narrative of nineteenth-century San Francisco—

of ordering the disorderly city. It is the story of how San Francisco became an American place.[5]

Accounts during the gold rush years stressed that the society taking shape in San Francisco was anything but ordinary. New arrivals often found themselves so awestruck that they described their initial encounters with the city as experiences that pushed them far beyond the boundaries of their ordinary existences. "They seemed suspended between two worlds," wrote one observer of newcomers to the city in 1854; "the one they had known, loved and enjoyed was left for the one they were just merging into." A few years earlier, journalist Bayard Taylor, chronicling his experiences in the city in 1849, recorded similar sentiments. "Every newcomer in San Francisco is overtaken with a sense of complete bewilderment. The mind, however it may be prepared for an astonishing condition of affairs, cannot immediately push aside its old instincts of value and ideas of business. . . . there is a period when it wears neither the old or new phase, but the vanishing images of one and the growing perceptions of the other are blended in painful and misty confusion." Intrepid explorer and trader Richard Henry Dana, appraising the scale of transformation he witnessed between 1835 and 1859, wrote, "When I reflected on what I once was and saw here, and what now surrounded me, I could scarcely keep my hold on reality at all, or the genuineness of anything, and seemed to myself like one who had moved in 'worlds not realized.'"[6]

Part of what made early San Francisco so unusual was the disjuncture between social class and occupation as well as a lack of expected social deference. As *The Annals of San Francisco*, a chronicle of the city through the early 1850s, explained, "The great recognized orders of society were tumbled topsy-turvy. Doctors and dentists became draymen, or barbers, or shoeblacks; lawyers, brokers, and clerks, turned waiters, or auctioneers, or perhaps butchers; merchants tried laboring and lumping, while laborers and lumpers changed to merchants . . . All things seemed in the utmost disorder." Bayard Taylor observed similar class disarray during the time he spent in the city in 1849, but he appeared much more pleased by what he exuberantly characterized as "the practical equality of all the members of a community" that made California "the most democratic country in the world." "Dress," he wrote, "was no gauge of respectability, and no honest occupation, however menial in its character, affected a man's standing. Lawyers, physicians and ex-professors dug cellars, drove ox-teams, sawed wood and carried luggage; while men who had been Army privates, sailors, cooks or day laborers were at the head of profitable establishments and not infrequently assisted in some of the minor details of Government." Taylor concluded that "a man who would consider his fellow beneath him, on account of his appearance or occupation, would have had some difficulty in living peaceably in California."[7]

Chroniclers also regularly found themselves moved to reflect upon the level of racial and ethnic diversity on San Francisco streets. Bayard Taylor recorded his impressions about the remarkable array of people—as well as the architectural disorder—he encountered upon his arrival. "On every side stood buildings of all kinds, begun or half-finished," he wrote, "the greater part of them mere canvas sheds . . . with all kinds of signs, in all languages." "The streets," he explained, "were full of people, hurrying to and fro, and of as diverse and bizarre a character as the houses: Yankees of every possible variety, native Californians in *sarapes* and sombreros, Chilians, Sonorians, Kanakas from Hawaii, Chinese with long tails, Malays armed with their everlasting creeses, and others in whose embrowned and bearded visages it was impossible to recognize any especial nationality." Twenty-two-year-old Englishman Frank Marryat provided a visual representation of "the men of all nations" who flocked to San Francisco in *High and Dry*, one of twenty-six engravings that illustrated his memoir of his extraordinary experiences in California in the early 1850s. In the far left of the foreground of this typical street scene stand two Chinese men, wearing straw hats, elbow-to-elbow with bearded Euro-Americans in their red miners' shirts. Close by, a dark-skinned man, possibly African American, stands with his arm raised. In the left corner, a man astride a horse, sporting a broad-brimmed hat, talks to another wearing a poncho, both likely Latin Americans. In the background, Marryat depicted a bustling block, complete with some important early cultural frontiers—like the Eagle Saloon and Niantic Hotel—that San Franciscans of the early 1850s poured into when not congregating out on city streets (see figure 1).[8]

Demographics also reflected the city's exceptional racial and ethnic diversity, imbalanced sex ratios, and social fluidity. In 1850, half of the residents claimed foreign places of birth while the same could be said for only one in ten nationally. In 1860, the city's population of foreign-born remained about the same, putting it in third place among America's immigrant centers. By the end of the 1860s, those born in Ireland, Germany, China, and Italy accounted for one of every three San Franciscans.[9] By the 1870s, Chinese immigrants made up nearly 8 percent of San Francisco's inhabitants.[10] Latinos, primarily Californios, Mexicans, Chileans, and Peruvians, were a significant presence

Figure 1. *High and Dry*. Frank Marryat, artist, 1855. San Francisco's heterogeneous residents in the foreground, its cultural frontiers in the background. (Robert B. Honeyman, Jr., Collection of Early California and Western American Pictorial Material, Bancroft Library, University of California, Berkeley)

throughout this period. Census figures for 1870, 1880, and 1890 showed that San Francisco had a higher percentage of foreign-born residents than any other major American city during these decades—exceeding New York and Boston in the east as well Chicago, Milwaukee, Detroit, and Cleveland in the Midwest. Only Fall River, Lowell, and Lawrence—Massachusetts mill towns with a large immigrant work force—had higher proportions of foreign-born residents.[11] African Americans, most from New England and Middle Atlantic states like their Euro-American counterparts, constituted a relatively small but significant proportion of the population. Native Americans made up an even smaller part of the population; their numbers decreased as the overall population of San Francisco increased.[12] Amidst this racial and ethnic diversity, by the mid-1860s, women had increased their share of the population to about 40 percent. Throughout the nineteenth century, social fluidity and mobility were prominent features of San Francisco's emergent society at both ends of the economic continuum. Among the working classes arriving between 1850 and 1870, only one in ten stayed in the city for three decades; three out of four left within eight years of arriving. Tellingly, when the names of the 120 wealthiest residents of the city were published in 1871 only three of the 509 rich men listed in 1851 reappeared.[13]

While San Francisco's social fluidity and racial and ethnic diversity were reflected in the city's demography and widely commented upon by both city residents and travelers just passing through, few observers remarked upon the fact that the people who came to San Francisco during the gold rush years entered a newly conquered part of America's growing landed empire. Demography also failed to capture the significance of this component of the new city. Typically, those who noted conquest's role in San Francisco's emergent society simply made a brief reference—as did French engineer Louis Laurent Simonin in 1859—to Mexicans as "the dispossessed master of California." Yet, up until July 9, 1846, the place that would become the American city of San Francisco existed as the Mexican pueblo of Yerba Buena. On that day, Captain John Montgomery claimed Yerba Buena for the United States. In conquering the pueblo, Montgomery and his troops engaged in no military violence and encountered no outright resistance. Having forewarned William A. Leidesdorff, the American vice-consul, the day before, Montgomery and his troops landed their boats in the mud flats, made their way through the sandy corridors that passed for streets, hoisted the American flag over the plaza, read an official declaration of conquest, and occupied the town, its mission, and presidio. Yerba Buena had never garnered much favor among Spaniards, Mexicans, Californios, or Americans. It spanned only a few blocks dotted with adobes and simple frame structures. By 1845 both its mission and presidio were barely functional and its population stood at about 150.[14]

Once physically ensconced, the Americans officially redesignated the plaza Portsmouth Square in honor of the ship that brought the invading forces. Soon, the military appointed mayor renamed the pueblo "San Francisco" in an attempt to draw settlers to the sandy, foggy, and windswept peninsula by capitalizing on the reputation of its fine natural harbor. Between 1845 and 1848, the arrival of about 200 Mormons, combined with the U.S. troops stationed there, served to stimulate trade and increase the population. By the end of the Mexican-American War in 1848, the Treaty of Guadalupe Hidalgo confirmed the United States' conquest, and San Francisco's population had grown to around 900 people—an international mix of merchants and commercial entrepreneurs, Mormons, Indians, Africans, Hawaiians, Mexicans, and Californios. This made it a substantial enough settlement to attract both goldseekers and their commerce after 1849. By 1850, San Francisco had

Figure 2. San Francisco, 1855. The world poured in with the gold rush, and the new American city's population soared from 900 in 1848 to 35,000 in 1850. (Robert B. Honeyman, Jr., Collection of Early California and Western American Pictorial Material, Bancroft Library, University of California, Berkeley)

emerged as an important point of departure for the mines and the commercial entrepôt for the region; its population soared to 35,000 (see figure 2).[15]

Word of the discovery of gold at Sutter's Mill sounded the death-knell for the former pueblo's community. After the initial acquisition of Yerba Buena, the process of incorporating San Francisco into the national fabric did not fall neatly into such tried-and-true categories of empire-building as the establishment of settler colonialism or the imposition of imperial bureaucracies. In San Francisco, an immigrant society whose members hailed from nations all over the world—more than a colony of settlers dispatched to secure the imperial dominance of the United States—displaced the indigenous Native American, Mexican, and Californio populations. At the state level, the politicians who formed California's initial governing bodies were better characterized as men-on-the-make than imperial bureaucrats. Yet giving some semblance of nationally recognizable order to the state's diverse population—a mix of immigrants; American migrants; and Mexicans, Californios, and Native Americans—fell as one of their first orders of business. In 1849, California's State Constitution decreed that Mexicans could be granted citizenship because they fell under the rubric of the category "white" whereas Native Americans were considered nonwhite and thus could not be citizens. A few years later, in 1854, the California Supreme Court in *People v. Hall* denied citizenship to Chinese immigrants by decreeing that they "were generically 'Indians' and therefore, nonwhite."

Through such measures, politicians and legislators handily divided the state's diverse population into nonwhite and white groups—the former devoid of civic power, the latter created through a process in which ethnic differences among varied foreign and native-born European-American groups were over-shadowed by the benefits of the construction of a collective white identity.[16]

As an ongoing process of incorporation and hierarchy-building with its genesis in the imperial impulse, nation-making in San Francisco occurred across time and on several different fronts. The military conquest of Yerba Buena was the first, easiest, and most clear-cut stage. Following that, nation-making shifted to two distinct but interconnected arenas—one of law and politics, the other of culture. At the level of law and politics, elites drove the process and met with success early on. Establishing legislative and political order, however, was a much tidier process than *cultural ordering*—inscribing the same race, class, and gender-based hierarchies on the city's cultural frontiers where the politics of everyday life occurred. Here elites also had to contend with the daily activities of ordinary San Franciscans who, independent of elite visions, constantly engaged in the creation of civic order as they asserted, contested, or transgressed race, class, and gender identities in the rituals of urban life. But it was precisely these varied and competing interests that made the stakes so high. In a place like nineteenth-century San Francisco, the arm of the state could only reach so far. Cultural frontiers, as much, if not more than, the legislature or voting booth, served as central sites where social power[17]—asserted through class, race, and gender identities—was deployed and civic order negotiated. These identities—at the level of one's self-identity, the identity of a social group, and especially the social construction of the categories of identity themselves, such as "Chinese man" or "white woman"—set the terms from which city residents fashioned social hierarchies. The categories of identity forged on the city's cultural frontiers—functioning in tandem with those delineated in the legislative and political arena—were the foundations upon which the newly conquered city's emergent social order were built.[18] In San Francisco, the market—the force catalyzing the production and consumption of cultural forms—was as significant as the state in structuring the power relations that suffused everyday life.[19]

The concept of the frontier has had a long history of deep connections to processes of empire-building and nation-making. Frederick Jackson Turner theorized the frontier as the crucible that forged characteristics central to the making of both the American people and the American nation.

He also identified the frontier as the process through which Euro-Americans conquered the American West and built a landed empire. In Turner's vision, the frontier existed as an east-to-west moving line that mapped settlers' progress across the continent. It marked the meeting point between savagery and civilization where hardy pioneers confronted Native Americans and the environment and established distinctly American places characterized by a spirit of individualism and democratic institutions. The concept of cultural frontiers shares in this lineage, but with some crucial differences. San Francisco's cultural frontiers also existed as less than neutral meeting grounds and operated as key sites of nation-making. Yet rather than following a single line of settlement, they dotted the urban landscape, their existence dependent on the needs and tastes of the populace. On San Francisco's cultural frontiers, when people from different nations, races, classes, and creeds met, a wide range of possibilities existed for the social ramifications of their encounters. But when San Franciscans sought to install the distinctly American social order that stood at the heart of the nation-making process on the city's cultural frontiers, it meant one that embodied nineteenth-century race, class, and gender norms as much or more than the democracy and individualism that Turner placed at the nation's core.[20]

Although regional differences existed in the contours of power, a distinctly American social order in the nineteenth century generally meant Euro-American dominance over people of color, patriarchy, and capitalism. While contrary to the stories of opportunity and equality that the nation likes to believe about itself, the hierarchies that followed from these forms of social and economic organization were central to making a place look and feel American. They permeated and shaped people's everyday lives in ways that democracy and individualism—most realizable for white men—could not. The urge to order San Francisco's diverse populace in familiar ways was present early on. For example, in 1859, Louis Laurent Simonin reflected upon "the most disparate and unusual costumes" he observed among the city's residents. In his description, he chose to list the various people he observed according to a loose but discernible Euro-centric racial hierarchy—organizing the social disorder around him by drawing upon customary schemas and applying them to the local scene. "First come the Americans in hurried rows," Simonin wrote. "The French, English, Irish, Germans and Italians are mixed with the Americans. . . . Then comes a strange mixture of Mexicans, the dispossessed master of California, proudly draped in serapes; Chileans covered by their brightly colored ponchos; Chinese men in round bonnets and silk pants and Chinese women strangely dressed; finally Negroes, for the most part dressed in tatters picked up here and there, and who stroll by while singing and dawdling in the streets."[21]

Simonin was fairly successful in identifying the outlines of the city's emergent racial order. He sensed the inclusive circle of whiteness open to those of European descent that, in San Francisco, drew Irish and Italian immigrants more quickly into ethnic white identities than in other cities like Boston or New York. He also identified those positioned at the bottom of society: Chinese immigrants and African Americans. Here, however, Simonin's impressions failed to fully capture social reality. While in most other American cities, African Americans did occupy the lowest rung in the racial order, in San Francisco that place was generally reserved for the Chinese. Chinese immigrants quickly outnumbered the relatively small population of African Americans. Because of their larger numbers and the racial ire directed at them by threatened white workers—reflected in the passage of foreign miners' taxes as early as 1850—the Chinese emerged as the group that bore the full brunt of white antipathy. The hostility directed at the Chinese actually made San Francisco a relatively friendly environment for African Americans throughout the nineteenth century. Moreover, the shared anti-Chinese sentiment that crossed class and ethnic lines helped give shape to San Francisco's circle of whiteness, uniting whites across lines that in other contexts often served to divide them.[22]

While the kind of social order that San Franciscans established was in full accord with nineteenth-century norms, the failure to examine how it came to be risks naturalizing a complicated, ongoing process that was particularly challenging given the city's anomalous population—its exceptional racial and ethnic diversity, imbalanced sex ratios, and social fluidity. Conquest alone did not make San Francisco into an American place. Recognizing this allows San Francisco's development to be seen as an integral part of America's national expansion and consolidation. At one level, the race-, class-, and gender-based categories of identity used to order the city were adaptations of ordering hierarchies deployed in eastern cities like New York. Tempered by local and regional conditions, these hierarchies determined inclusion in or exclusion from the body politic across the nation. Nation-making linked the processes of ordering in the East and West in a reciprocal interrelationship that together articulated hegemonic categories of American identity and defined the terms of successful conquest, assimilation, or acculturation. Revealing how race, gender, and class were understood and constructed in San Francisco, by both majority and minority groups, and the way these understandings and constructions changed over time, not only enriches but also traces the ties of the national story by connecting this local history to broader patterns of empire-building and nation-making. Charting the connections between empire-building, nation-making, and cultural ordering in San Francisco offers a new method for understanding both the immigrant society and the imperial practices that shaped the city. It also joins the usually disconnected histories of American San Francisco and Mexican and Spanish Yerba Buena by highlighting their shared lineage in processes of nationalism and imperialism.[23]

San Francisco's cultural frontiers evolved within the larger context of the rapidly growing city. The transformation of San Francisco from Mexican pueblo to American metropolis in less than fifty years brought the full measure of nineteenth-century pressures—urbanization, industrialization, immigration, and internal migration—to bear on the city and its inhabitants with particular force and speed. As early as 1856, the pace of San Francisco's development, its position as a site of capital accumulation, and its fortunate geography that made it a transportation hub had set it apart from its closest regional rivals, Sacramento and Stockton. Situated on the hilly, foggy, sandy, forty-seven-square-mile tip of a peninsula on the nation's west coast, throughout the nineteenth century its location separated it from cities of comparable pre-eminence by a distance of half a continent or more while its geography made it much smaller and more compact than other developing urban centers such as Chicago or New York. From the start, San Francisco's economy was distinguished by its commercial, rather than agricultural or industrial, nature. It was fueled by timely infusions of fresh capital from the resource rich, newly conquered areas to the north and east—first from gold and later from the Central Pacific railroad and the silver of the Comstock Lode. Although the city initially depended upon imported goods for most of life's necessities, its position as the point of departure for the mines and its emergence as the region's commercial entrepôt contributed to its development as an urban center of finance and consumption. As San Francisco evolved into an imperial city in its own right, it extracted food, taxes, labor, and other resources from its expansive hinterland which, in return, received access to an urban marketplace as well as military protection. The relationship between city and hinterland, however, was less than equitable. San Francisco's success was built on the economic domination of smaller cities and surrounding territories as well as on the exploitation of the natural environment on which its sustenance depended.[24]

Throughout the 1860s and 1870s, San Francisco continued to maintain some of the "instant city" traits of the gold rush years as well as the characteristics of the quintessential "walking city"—fairly compact in size, easily navigable on foot, with neighborhoods that combined workplaces and residences, in which its diverse inhabitants had regular, personal, face-to-face encounters. But the city was also in the midst of the transformation into an industrial metropolis—the opposite of a walking city in terms of its size, complexity, and social geographies. As the metropolis replaced the walking city, social and spatial segregation became increasingly prevalent forms of urban organization and had far-reaching implications for the way residents used and conceptualized public space. Residential, commercial, and entertainment districts became more clearly demarcated. Affluent suburbs, the neighborhoods of the middle class, and the crowded districts of the working class came to exist strictly apart from one another, and despite advances in transportation and communication, encounters among residents diminished. The process of transformation from a walking city to an industrial metropolis was aided and abetted by a variety of sources—the Civil War, the transcontinental railroad, the discovery of Nevada's Comstock Lode, technological innovations, and an expanding population— that also spurred growth, progress, and prosperity. During the 1860s, as manufacturing output's value quadrupled, capital investments in industry saw a tenfold increase, and the growing numbers of people employed in industrial jobs expanded to eighteen times greater than what it had been at the beginning of the decade to represent nearly half of the city's workforce. Economic depression in the 1870s catalyzed long-simmering racism and made anti-Chinese agitation by white laborers a central theme of city politics. By then, San Francisco's population had reached almost 138,000 and the city had emerged as an industrial as well as a commercial and financial center (see figure 3).[25]

From the 1880s through 1906—the year of the earthquake and fire that devastated the city—these economic and demographic trends, hand-in-hand with patterns of increasing spatial and social segregation, continued and developed. Despite cyclic economic highs and lows, manufacturing and commercial enterprises flourished and the city advanced to rank ninth in the nation in terms of both population and industrial output. By 1890, San Francisco's population numbered nearly 300,000 and the city possessed proportionally

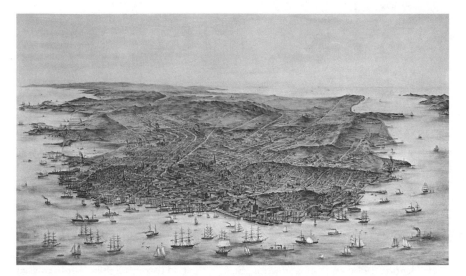

Figure 3. San Francisco, 1868. During the 1860s, the city developed into an industrial metropolis. By 1870, its population neared 150,000. (Yale Collection of Western Americana, Beinecke Rare Book and Manuscript Library)

more foreign-born residents than any other American city. In terms of gender, the ratios of seven men for every five women in the 1880s and 1890s—which put women at about 45 percent of the population—were much closer to national norms than the three-to-two ratio that prevailed in the 1860s or the nearly eleven-to-one ratio at the height of the gold rush. San Franciscans responded to the increase in the density of settlement that followed population growth by doubling the city's inhabited area in the 1880s.[26]

At the same time, despite its increasingly cosmopolitan veneer, social divisions rooted in class and ethnic differences became more acute and racial hostilities more severe. Precipitated, in part, by labor agitation on the West Coast, in 1882 the nation passed the Chinese Exclusion Act—largely a product of class tensions between whites for which Chinese immigrants became scapegoats—which, following renewals and extensions in 1888 and 1892, indefinitely banned immigration of Chinese workers beginning in 1902. In city politics, these years reflected both the climate of increasing class conflict and a new style of elite control. In particular, in the 1890s, political elites sought to temper class strife by weaving together the interests of upwardly mobile ethnic working-class voters and a younger generation of merchants and capitalists. Elected to the mayoralty in 1896, banker James Phelan typified the new

Figure 4. San Francisco, 1905. By 1890, the city ranked ninth in the nation in terms of both population and industrial output. By 1900, it was home to 340,000. (San Francisco Historical Photograph Collection, San Francisco History Center, San Francisco Public Library)

style of businessmen reformers—a sharp contrast to the city's long-standing culture of political bosses and personal politics. While Phelan himself would be voted out of office in 1901 after opposing a strike of over 1,500 teamsters and waterfront workers, by 1907 he and his allies had regained control of San Francisco's governing board of supervisors, establishing a mode of political dominance—grounded in coalition-building and a corporate style—that would endure well into the twentieth century (see figure 4).[27]

Snapshots of the micro-workings of power on five key cultural frontiers—restaurants, hotels and boardinghouses; places of amusement; Chinatown's tourist terrain; the Mechanics' Institute's annual fairs; and the California Midwinter International Exposition—brings a new level of understanding to these developments by illuminating the intersection of nation-making and culture in nineteenth-century San Francisco. The story told here begins with the freewheeling disorder of the gold rush and ends just over four decades later at the Midwinter Fair's '49 Mining Camp Exhibit, where, through cultural ordering, local elites reconfigured and transformed the chaos of those years into a nostalgic version of California history that sought to assuage race-, class-, and gender-based anxieties in the present by emphasizing white male dominance and downplaying the economic dislocations associated with industrial capitalism. In between the actual gold rush and its representation, the process of cultural ordering is traced, for example, in how the desire for containment and mixture simultaneously collided in the promiscuous vice district, the Barbary Coast; how ideas about class and race clashed in labor disputes at the tony Palace Hotel; how the combination of titillation and morality exhibited at Pacific Museum of Anatomy and Science responded to concerns about appropriate gender and sexual identities; and how an emerging Chinatown tourism was intricately bound up with anti-immigration discourses. Each site or constellation of sites reveals a story of how race, gender, and class were understood and constructed in the city, shaping the resulting social order. Each is placed in the context of the macro processes of urbanization, capitalist development, and immigration that transformed the city from pueblo to metropolis during this period. Together, the following chapters tell a story of how the ordering processes that occurred on cultural ground in post–gold rush San Francisco were every bit as far-reaching, profound, and integral to nation-making as the military and political conquest of the late 1840s.

CHAPTER ONE

Living in the City:
Everyday Cultures of
Restaurants, Hotels, and Boardinghouses

Nineteenth-century San Franciscans took up residence in hotels and board-inghouses and dined publicly—in restaurants, hotel dining rooms, or "free lunch" saloons—in far greater numbers than their contemporaries. As local historian John Hittell remarked in 1878, "Ever since the gold discovery the home life of San Francisco has been different from that of any other city." San Francisco's rapid growth, shortage of housing, high rents for available homes, lack of domestic servants, and heavily male and often transient population re-sulted in a local proclivity for public dining and hotel and boardinghouse liv-ing that was so notable that census officials remarked on it as late as 1880.[1] Middle-class, elite, and working-class families; miners; tourists; bachelors and single women; businessmen; prostitutes; sailors; socialites; politicians; foreign dignitaries; and many others stayed in hotels and boardinghouses—variously ranked for respectability—for days, weeks, months, or even years. Hotel din-ing rooms fed registered guests as well as those who just came for the food. By 1875, San Francisco possessed options for accommodation that ranged from ramshackle hostelries to the Palace Hotel—touted as the largest and most luxurious hotel in the world. Hand-in-hand with the development of the city's hostelries, the number of restaurants mushroomed with the gold rush. By 1849, eateries had opened all over town and served the food of a variety of nationalities. "In the matter of dining, the tastes of all nations can be grat-ified here," wrote journalist and travel writer Bayard Taylor on his visit to the city that year. "There are French restaurants on the plaza and on Dupont street; an extensive German establishment on Pacific street; the Fonda Peru-ana; the Italian Confectionery; and three Chinese houses denoted by their long three-cornered flags of yellow silk." At the city's American-style restaurants, hungry San Franciscans "who delighted in corn-bread, buckwheat cakes, pickles, grease, molasses, applesauce, and pumpkin pie, could gratify their taste to the fullest extent."[2] By 1875, journalist Samuel Williams could glowingly explain to readers of *Scribner's Monthly* that "San Francisco is famed for its restaurants. In no city in America are these establishments so numerous in proportion to the population. They number between two and three hundred and it is safe to say that at least thirty thousand people take their meals at them. They are of all grades and prices from the 'Poodle Dog,' Martin's and Maison Dorée, where a meal costs from $1.50 to $20—down to the Miners' Restaurant, where it costs only forty cents."[3]

The hotel, boardinghouse, and restaurant cultures that emerged in nineteenth-century San Francisco were situated within a broader national context that had just begun to assign meaning to these increasingly common urban spaces. In 1865, for example, in an article titled "Restaurants and Their Function," the *Nation* carefully explained to its readers the larger purpose these establishments served in American society. "The restaurant is a potent civilizer," the magazine told its readers, "The restaurant is progress. The restaurant is as important a branch of that modern material civilization of which we brag so heartily as the railroad or the telegraph. . . . As mere accidental conveniences or as places of self-indulgence they would be unworthy of our consideration. . . . The use of the restaurant is to raise the standard of good living. It cannot be set too high." In the nineteenth century, "civilization" emerged as a powerful conceptualization of social order that, in a word, signaled the sort of technical progress and class relations associated with industrial capitalism, white—especially Anglo-Saxon—superiority, and a gendered order based on distinct differences and inequalities between men and women. Drawing upon popular currents in natural history and political economy, adherents posited that human races moved up an evolutionary scale from savagery through barbarism to a state of advanced civilization. Yet since it was generally believed that only the white races had evolved to the civilized stage, it was no coincidence that, in the United States, the marks of civilization mirrored the dominant characteristics and values of middle-class and elite white Euro-Americans.[4]

Across the nation, the number and sophistication of restaurants and hostelries in urban areas increased rapidly after 1850. Their growing presence reflected the changing relationship between home and work that accompanied the transition to a wage-based economy as well as the development of new forms of transportation that enhanced the ease and speed of travel for both business and pleasure. In these sites, rituals previously contained within the realm of private life, such as eating and sleeping, increasingly intersected with often unfamiliar if not foreign cuisines; a new, promiscuous urban public sphere; and novel commercial forms of leisure and consumption. Among nascent middle classes and elites, new urban spaces such as restaurants, hotels, and boardinghouses conjured up much of the same kind of excitement and anxiety provoked by the more dramatic social, political, and economic changes that rocked America in the nineteenth century—and which San Francisco's boomtown climate only exaggerated. Unabashed delight in abundance, be it of the table or the expanding national marketplace, ran up against fears of the corrupting potential of excess and luxury. Qualms about the blurring of social boundaries existed in uncomfortable juxtaposition with the hopeful promise of restaurants' civilizing potential. Worries surfaced about how eating, sleeping, or even sitting in close proximity to one's social inferiors might subvert class distinctions and lead to a radical and disturbing kind of leveling. Those who feared the kinds of changes set in motion by the expansion of the franchise, mounting class tensions, and growing immigration found themselves particularly susceptible to such unease. The promiscuous public spaces and new commercial areas—of which restaurants, hotels, and boardinghouses were such a vital part—also generated social anxieties. There the significance and meaning of the appearances of others and even of the public spaces themselves were no longer transparent—but were in fact often multiple and shifting, sometimes downright deceptive. Among nineteenth-century middle classes and elites, the resultant uncertain ability to read and order others at a glance, coupled with considerable anxiety over being gazed upon and read, possibly wrongly, by anonymous strangers emerged as a deeply troubling social phenomenon.[5]

Out of these concerns emerged an intense preoccupation with the maintenance of proper standards of etiquette, the perils of rudeness, and the dread of embarrassment. As part of an intricate process of simultaneously regulating society and marking one's place in the social order, displaying good manners, both in public and private, increasingly helped to consolidate middle-class and elite identities. For the uninitiated, mastering these practices was no easy task. Good manners meant concealing and controlling bodily processes, restraining unseemly emotional displays, and deftly maneuvering numerous appliances.

As a result, the production of and appetite for literature that provided instruction in etiquette—and thus made gentility, civility, and respectability purchasable and learnable styles—boomed in the nineteenth century. While on one hand, proper etiquette could be deployed to mark off the "better sort" from the remainder of humanity, on the other hand there was the explicitly expressed hope, as evoked by the *Nation* in "Restaurants and Their Function," that the broad-based transmission of such attributes would give order to social interactions by spreading civility and curb what were thought of as the excesses of democracy.[6]

For newcomers to San Francisco, especially in the 1840s and 1850s, there was little room for squeamishness about dining in restaurants or living in hotels and boardinghouses and no time to learn how to properly engage in these activities. By necessity, the multitude of middle-class anxieties around shared public space needed, at least temporarily, to be held in abeyance. While middle-class sensibilities were by no means entirely absent during the city's first two decades, they were regularly besieged and disrupted by the diversity, social fluidity, and rough-and-tumble environs of early San Francisco. This state of affairs was aided and abetted by the fact that during these years money emerged as a particularly potent marker of status, at times overshadowing the traditional classifications of people according to class, religion, political affiliation, educational attainment, or nationality. Although money increasingly greased the wheels of social mobility throughout the nation, the newness of San Francisco's society and the volatility of wealth derived from both gold and finance capitalism exacerbated its power and effect. Six major fires between 1849 and 1851, in which entire districts were destroyed and rebuilt, made even the city's social geography unstable and tenuous.[7]

Newcomers who poured into San Francisco with the gold rush initially found themselves in a city with an infrastructure and amenities stretched to their limits but also expanding rapidly to meet growing demand. As of August 1847, serving the city's 800 or so residents were "41 places of business, including two hotels, one apothecary, three bakeries, three butchers, and seven grocery stores." By the end of April 1848, about the time the gold seekers began to arrive, the town had grown a bit and contained, according to one early history, "nearly two hundred buildings . . . one hundred and thirty-five finished dwelling-houses, ten unfinished houses of the same class, twelve stores and warehouses, and thirty-five shanties." Some of the earliest, notable hotels included the City Hotel, "a building of adobe a story and a half high, on the south-west corner of Clay and Kearny;" Vioget's House, which would later gain renown as the Portsmouth House; the Parker House, erected in 1848; and, built a year later, the fashionable "St. Francis, a three-story wooden structure, on the south-west corner of Clay and Dupont" (see figure 5).[8]

Some hostelries had restaurants attached and more than a few sported gambling saloons. Some were "jerry-built bunkhouses . . . with gambling halls and restaurants on the first floor" that were "ironically called Astor House, Irving House, Tremont House"—after some of the finest hotels in the nation. Others, like the Niantic, depicted by Frank Marryat in *High and Dry*, were wrought from clipper ships abandoned by eager gold seekers and "dragged ashore" and "wedged between ports." According to historian Hubert Howe Bancroft, during the height of the rush, "Any shed was considered fit for a lodging-house." In some of the hotels, rooms were "merely 2 1/2 ft. x 6 ft. cubicles with walls of calico, or of canvas, decorated with colored papers." But, by the second half of 1849, coexisting with these crude conditions were establishments that offered relative luxury. The growth of the city was so rapid and the development of its amenities so impressive, that Bayard Taylor, returning after a four-month absence, was moved to declare, "Of all the marvelous phases of the history of the Present, the growth of San Francisco is the one which will most tax the belief of the Future." "Then," he reminisced, "the gold-seeking sojourner lodged in muslin rooms and canvas garrets, with a philosophic lack of furniture. Now, lofty hotels, gaudy with verandas and balconies, were met with in all quarters, furnished with home luxury, and aristocratic restaurants presented daily their long bills of fare, rich with the choicest technicalities of the Parisian cuisine." By 1853, the city boasted "626 brick or stone buildings . . . 160 hotels and public houses with a descriptive name, 66 restaurants and coffee saloons, [and] 63 bakeries."[9] While initially developed out of necessity, restaurants, hotels, and boardinghouses quickly became important and seemingly concrete signs of San Francisco's development—heartening symbols of civilization on this frontier boomtown's emerging urban landscape.

Yet at the same time as the growth of the city's hostelries and eateries appeared to offer proof of desirable forms of progress, throughout the period extending from the initial rush for gold through the 1850s, such spaces—from the lowliest to the finest—more often than not operated as cultural frontiers ripe with possibilities for forms of social mixture, general disorder, and bad manners aberrant enough to be regularly remarked upon, sometimes vilified,

Figure 5. The City Hotel, one of San Francisco's earliest hostelries, ca. 1849. The crowds of men around it suggest its centrality to city life. (San Francisco Historical Photograph Collection, San Francisco History Center, San Francisco Public Library)

and periodically celebrated. William Shaw, an Englishman who arrived in San Francisco from Australia in 1849, penned a particularly detailed recollection of his time in the city that shed light on how the primitive conditions in some of the city's hostelries put racially diverse men in uncharacteristically close proximity. He described the "lodging houses in San Francisco" as "long barn-like tenements." "The one I sometimes resorted to," he related, "was about sixty feet long by twenty in width; it had no windows, and the walls, roof, and floor, were formed of planks, through the seams of which rain dripped through. Along the sides were two rows of 'bunks,' or wooden shelving, and at the end was some boarding, serving as a bar for liquors." Shaw explained that "from about ten till twelve at night men flocked in with their blankets around them—for no mattress or bedding was furnished by this establishment." The price of one dollar entitled a man to a place to sleep. If the night happened to be wet, "upwards of eighty people would be packed together: Yankees, Africans, Chinamen, Chilians, all huddled together on the ground" (see figure 6).[10]

Figure 6. San Francisco's diverse inhabitants outside of the Pacific Hotel, ca. 1849. During these early years, residents of various races and ethnicities also encountered one another inside local hostelries, where they frequently found themselves sharing the available ramshackle accommodations. (San Francisco Historical Photograph Collection, San Francisco History Center, San Francisco Public Library)

Although Shaw concluded that "the sleeping accommodation—if such a term may be used—was wretched in St. Francisco," he weighed in much more favorably on the quality and quantity of "places of refreshment." He found it remarkable that the fare was of "the most heterogeneous kind" as well as that "dishes of the most incongruous characters" were "placed on the table at the same time: boiled and roast meats, fresh and salt, potted meats, curries, stews, fish, rice, cheese, frijolis, and molasses" were "served up on small dishes, and ranged indiscriminately on the table." In his listing of heterogeneous and incongruous dishes, Shaw identified standard European-American fare served alongside curries, a designation often given to Chinese food, and "frijolis," a misspelling of *frijoles*, the beans that formed a staple of the Mexican diet. Mexicans, Chinese, and Euro-Americans made up three of the most visible racial groups in the city—their mixture on the table presenting to Shaw an image as striking, yet as ordinary, as their mingling in a hostelry or on city streets.

Shaw also revealed how taking meals in the city had become a daily ritual, complete with its own loose form of organization. "At certain hours in the day," he wrote, "the beating of gongs and ringing of bells from all quarters, announce the feeding time at the various refectories; at this signal a rush is made to the tables." This rush to the tables—combined with the tobacco chewing, teeth-picking, and questionable sanitation that followed—were all marks of very bad manners. "It is not uncommon," he wrote, "to see your neighbor coolly abstract a quid from his jaw, placing it for the time being in his waistcoat pocket, or hat, or sometimes beside his plate, even." In the "fierce attack on the eatables" that ensued, in which each diner helped himself "indiscriminately," the lucky man was one who had "a quick eye and a long arm." Upon completion of their meals, "the satiated" picked their "teeth with a fork" and, in the rapid turnover of replenishing tables "for a second party," the "greasy knives" that remained were simply given a quick wipe before being replaced.[11] Shaw's account left little doubt that in this fluid social world, notions of proper table etiquette had quickly fallen by the wayside—a surefire sign that in these early years, San Francisco's restaurants were not exactly operating as the kind of "potent civilizers" *The Nation* article had extolled.

Partaking in the climate of promiscuous social mixture in the city's eateries and hostelries was not confined to male adventurers, contained by class position, or peculiar to the rank of a particular establishment. Amelia Ransome Neville, a nineteen-year-old American, arrived in the city in 1856, accompanied by her parents and her new husband, who had served as a captain in the British army. Five years earlier she had visited England and been presented to Queen Victoria. In San Francisco, where she was to make her home for the next fifty years, she and her family quickly made a place for themselves among the nascent elite. For their first few years in the city, Amelia and her family lived initially in the International Hotel and later in the Oriental Hotel. Both were built in 1851 and were two of the finest, most expensive, and most respectable hotels in the city during the 1850s. The International was, in fact, the city's first brick hostelry. Of her initial experience of hotel living, her fellow boarders, and public dining in San Francisco she later wrote:

Meals at the International were on "the American plan" and not at all bad. Long tables were each adorned with a center line of pies, the line broken by an occasional jelly cake in a high glass dish with a glass cover. Facing me sat a stout elderly woman in a low-neck red velvet dress with a diamond necklace and fingers literally covered with rings. It was the custom for gamblers to invest their winnings in diamonds rather than hoard them in a bank. Diamonds could be seen, while bank savings were a total loss so far as display was concerned. The lady had been lucky, or perhaps it was her husband. Next to the red velvet lady, a tall young man tilted back and forth in his chair while he waited for dinner to appear . . . Presently his chair came down with a snap and he reached across the table to take a slab of pie. Then he tilted back again and ate pie from his fingers until the roast beef arrived. Who could have guessed that in time he would be a very courtly diplomat, the American minister to Japan?[12]

Clearly there was a lot going on at Amelia's table at the International Hotel, along with pies, jelly cakes, and roast beef, that had to do with social mixture, the performance of identities, the presence or absence of proper etiquette, and the assertion of status and class. The "American plan" meant that meals were included in the price of one's room, were served in a dining hall at set times during the day, and the various and usually abundant dishes from which one could choose were generally all brought to the table at one time and both carved, if needed, and served by the proprietor or even the guests themselves. This style of dining was eventually replaced by the "European plan" whereby the guest paid only for a room and meals were taken outside the hotel in independent restaurants. It was also in sharp contrast to the growing trend among refined diners for "a la Russe" dining in which carving and serving took place out of view, the handling of food was minimized, a clear line was drawn between servants and diners, and meals were regulated through an orderly series of courses.[13]

It is possible that Amelia Neville, having just spent time in Europe, was familiar with this emergent form of what constituted the height of civilized dining. For William Shaw as well, familiarity with dining "a la Russe" may have made the incongruities and heterogeneities he witnessed at table a few years earlier particularly notable. It is also probable that, for Amelia, sharing a table with the likes of the "lady" in red, who was depicted as possibly either a madam or a gambler's moll—but definitely not a "proper lady"—was a novel experience. Yet the lady in red, dripping in diamonds, had what it took to gain entry into the dining room of the International Hotel. What she had in money, which she exhibited with flamboyance, made up for what she lacked in respectability. Amelia also knew, being well versed in proper etiquette, that

Figure 7. The International Hotel, ca. 1859. Originally built in 1851, the International Hotel was the city's first brick hostelry. It quickly gained a reputation as an elegant, respectable resort favored by the nascent elite as well as the newly rich. (Yale Collection of Western Americana, Beinecke Rare Book and Manuscript Library)

the tilting posture evidenced by the young man who later became a courtly diplomat was not only bad manners but also generally associated with lower-class men. The fact that this young man's physical carriage made his status hard to read—leaving his identity open to misinterpretation and making him seem something that he was not—was exactly why good manners and proper etiquette were deemed so important and why public spaces like restaurants could put such fear into the hearts of order-craving nineteenth-century elites and middle classes. This level of informality in the dining room of one of San Francisco's best hotels was more than enough to make any advocate of proper etiquette shudder (see figure 7).[14]

Other newcomers recorded their experiences of the city's eateries and hostelries in ways that demonstrated how the most ordinary interactions on these important early cultural frontiers could both showcase disorder and assert emerging social hierarchies. John Henry Brown, the manager of the City Hotel and co-owner of the Parker House, told of the "grand ball" and "bountiful supper" that was held to celebrate the opening of the Parker House. Not only was it "free to all" but the "invitations were general in those days," he recalled, with "no distinction as regards persons, Jack was considered as good as his master." Bayard Taylor related a race- and class-infused introduction to the city. He recalled how, upon disembarkation, he and his traveling companion "scrambled up through piles of luggage, and among the crowd collected to witness our arrival, picked out two Mexicans to carry our trunks to a hotel." In terms of San Francisco's emergent racial order, it was not surprising that recently conquered Mexican men would assume servile tasks. However, in the context of the gold rush economy, doing this undesirable but necessary work often proved surprisingly lucrative. After Taylor's "luggage was deposited on one of the rear porticos" he paid the porters "two dollars each." A sum he characterized as "so immense in comparison to the service rendered that there was no longer any doubt of our having actually landed in California." Unfortunately for Taylor there were no available rooms at his first choice establishment, John Brown's Parker House, so he was escorted across the plaza to the hotelier's other establishment, the City Hotel, where he "obtained a room with two beds at $25 per week, meals being in addition $20 per week." When he asked the landlord whether he could send a porter for the trunks that had been left at the other hotel, Taylor was told "there is none belonging to the house . . . every man is his own porter here." Forced to bow to the pressure of gold rush–imposed social egalitarianism, Taylor returned to the Parker House, hoisted a heavy trunk upon his shoulder, picked up his valise, and made his way back to his quarters at the City Hotel. Both the lack of class distinction at the ball and the dearth and dearness of menial laborers served as markers of the prevailing societal disorder among what the *Annals of San Francisco* termed the city's "strange mixed population."[15]

Regular patronage of Chinese restaurants by white San Franciscans provided another register of social mixture tinged with emerging hierarchies during these early years. From the start, the Chinese faced racial hostility and discrimination and would quickly be positioned on the bottom of the city's racial order. Yet during the first few years after the gold rush, white patrons not only praised Chinese eateries for providing especially cheap and tasty food, they also possessed a culinary curiosity that was not laced with the especially negative racializations that would come to characterize descriptions of their experiences within the next decade. While they sometimes noted the unfamiliarity of the cuisine or registered suspicion about its ingredients in ways that highlighted perceived differences between Euro-American and Chinese cultures, their accounts revealed that Chinese restaurants were a part of the everyday fabric of city life, places not yet relegated to a spatially segregated tourist terrain. Bayard Taylor informatively explained that "Kong-Sung's house is near the water; Whang-Tong's in Sacramento Street, and Tong-Ling's in Jackson street. There the grave celestials serve up their chow-chow and curry, besides many genuine English dishes; their tea and coffee cannot be surpassed." Pioneer journalist and writer James O'Meara recalled that, "Chinese restaurants were largely patronized by the mass, where one could purchase a package of twenty-one tickets, each good for a meal, breakfast, dinner, or supper, for $20, or get a fair single meal for $1.50." He added that "it was not always easy to ascertain just what it was he was feasting upon, but the average customer was more bent upon quantity than quality; and no matter for what he called, the Chinese waiter, who did not understand a word of any language but his own, was sure to return with a plate fairly filled with something hot, that satisfied the appetite." James J. Ayers, who would become one of the first editors of the *San Francisco Call*, recollected that "the best restaurants . . . were kept by Chinese, and the poorest and dearest by Americans."[16]

Not all boundaries or proprieties went unobserved in gold rush San Francisco, however. Lore abounds about the chivalry inspired by the presence of women—respectable and not—in the city's predominantly male society. When middle-class matron Sarah Royce, mother of philosopher and educator Josiah Royce, arrived in San Francisco in January 1850 after being flooded out of Sacramento, her hoteliers recognized her need, as a lady, for a level of privacy beyond what was usually offered and attempted to make some adjustments to add to her comfort. In her memoirs, Royce recalled her initial encounter with the Montgomery House. She described the exterior of the hotel as "covered on the outside partly with boards, and partly with canvas, diversified . . . with sheets of zinc, in places that particularly needed staying." Inside, on the right, there "was a small room, wholly without carpet, containing one table, and a very few chairs, and lighted by one window. This was the sitting room. The partition which separated it from the dining room behind it was of cloth. Across the little hall-way into which the front door opened, and directly opposite the sitting room door, was the bar room, a much larger apartment than the sitting room." For middle-class and elite Americans, the clear demarcation and separation of public and private activities in the home was of the utmost importance. Flimsy cloth partitions marking off one space from another would likely have been a source of concern. Moreover, the parlor, or sitting room, was the public face of the house—the locus of proper decorum and presentation of self. One as shabbily appointed as she described and as out-scaled in size and importance by the bar room—site of potential intemperance and vice—constituted egregious violations of the middle-class code.[17]

Ascending a stairway, Royce found herself in a narrow hall with "partitions on each side . . . wholly of cloth, and at distances of about four feet apart along the whole length of the hall." Inside these partitions were "two berths, one above the other . . . the only sleeping accommodations afforded." This was not what Sarah Royce, weary from travel, had expected. "I had supposed," she wrote, "that in two or three hours, I should be in a private room, resting, preparatory to arranging a home nest." Instead, she would stay at the Montgomery House for about a week before finding more suitable lodgings and finally, after a lengthy search, an available single-family dwelling. But, although the conditions at the Montgomery House affronted and challenged many of her middle-class conventions, she was generally impressed by the way boarders and management conducted themselves and, in particular, how they worked to insure herself and her daughter, Mary, the most privacy possible under the circumstances. "The landlord," she wrote, "thoughtfully proposed to the two lodgers who occupied the berths at the farther end of the hall, against the wall of the house, to give them up to us; thus placing us in the most private spot to be obtained, for which I was certainly grateful."[18]

Although Royce carefully maintained her privacy when she could, she did endure some environmentally mandated social mixture when "a rainy day or two" forced many of the boarders at the Montgomery House "to spend the whole day, crowded into the little comfortless sitting room or huddled . . . around the bar-room stove." She recalled that although "there were of course many there who were far from refined in manners . . . I received no rough or discourteous word from anybody; I witnessed no offensive behavior; and, whatever there was of drinking at the bar, I saw no drunkards, either at the bar-room stove or in the sitting room." More than once she was "very kindly invited to a warm seat at the stove with Mary" and she "never went there without finding room cheerfully made."[19] As Sarah Royce's account attests, even though the small number of women in the city put normative gender relations in serious disarray, societally dominant ideologies of white womanhood that viewed middle-class women as beings distinctly different from men—who, as naturally more pious, morally pure, and domestic but also intellectually inferior, submissive, and dependent, required special care and protection—were in good working order and perhaps even intensified under the strain.

Yet the fact of skewed sex ratios had material consequences—beyond hotel living and restaurant dining—that also effectively disrupted dearly held gender roles. While the idea that domestic tasks were women's work might have held sway, the reality of such a notion could not. According to Bayard Taylor, "every man was his own housekeeper, doing, in many instances, his own sweeping, cooking, washing, and mending. Many home-arts, learned rather by observation than experience, came conveniently into play." Taylor concluded that, under the circumstances, "he who cannot make a bed, cook a beefsteak, or sew up his own rips and rents, is unfit to be a citizen of California." F. P. Wierzbicki, a native of Poland, was not happy about this state of affairs. He wrote worriedly that, "In the midst of abundance of every kind women are very scarce; the domestic circle does not exist; domestic pleasures are wanting, and household duties are unfulfilled." He told readers of his *Guide to the Gold Fields*, "the greatest privations that a bachelor in this country is exposed to, consist in not being able to furnish himself with clean linen when he desires, as domestic service is too difficult to be kept here for want of working women." He lamented that in order to "induce some of the few women that are here to condescend to wash their linen for them" men "have to court them besides paying six dollars a dozen."[20]

Wierzbicki was not alone in his worry about the nonexistent "domestic circle." In 1854, a writer for *The Pioneer, or California Monthly Magazine*, identified only as A.H.B., wrote an article, "Impressions on Arriving in San Francisco," which captured the way hotel life was regarded by some as an ominous antithesis to a more normative domestic order grounded in single-family homes. A.H.B.—probably from a class position akin to Amelia Neville's and participating in a similar social scene that grew up around the city's more elite hotels—told readers about her observation of two types of couples "similarly circumstanced as regards station, perhaps not very opposite in sentiment, but differently situated." "The first," A.H.B. explained, "locate themselves at a large and fashionable hotel," become "acquainted with the gayest circles," and "launch out into all the foibles and extravagances of the day. In due time, they "see the folly, the frivolousness, aye, the wickedness, which streams around them, become dissatisfied with the place, themselves and their neighbors, and soon denounce the whole country as a cheat, the place as dangerous to good morals and altogether disgusting." The moral, domestic opposite to the hotel-dwellers were those who organized their lives "in a simpler way, perhaps in their own little homes." Within that sanctuary they would "find enough both to occupy and interest." They would "look for their enjoyment, not to the world at large, but to each other."[21]

Although Sarah Royce did not witness any bad behavior at the Montgomery House, the author of "Impressions on Arriving in San Francisco" clearly connected certain types of hotel living with becoming acquainted with a fast lifestyle, excessive consumption, and related forms of immorality. Moreover, in addition to the way hotel life represented the questionable respectability associated with disrupted domesticity, topsy-turvy gender relations, and unusual racial mixture, many hotels—because of the gambling saloons connected to them—gained notoriety as actual hotbeds of vice. The Parker House and the City Hotel, for example, sported public and private gaming rooms where both gambling and additional sorts of troubling social interactions took place. Hubert Howe Bancroft described the "promiscuous" crowd that gathered nightly at these establishments. "There were men in black clothes, immaculate linen, and shining silk hats, merchants, lawyers, and doctors, Chileans, and Mexicans; Irish laborers, Negroes, and Chinamen, some crowded around the tables intently watching the games, others lounging about, smoking, chewing, spitting, drinking, swearing." Bayard Taylor also observed the diverse society that congregated at the gambling saloons. "There are about eight tables in the room, all of which are thronged," he wrote in his description of the nightly scene. "Copper-hued Kanakas, Mexicans rolled in their serapes and Peruvians thrust through their ponchos, stand shoulder to shoulder with the brown and bearded miners." This climate of widespread disorderly mixture on the city's cultural frontiers would, however, not go unchallenged for long. Beginning in the late 1850s and continuing throughout the century, these years would be used as the benchmark that some San Franciscans—desirous of a social order more in keeping with nationally dominant hierarchies of gender, race, and class—would define themselves and their vision of the city against.[22] Even most of those who looked fondly upon the "wild West" legacy of the gold rush did so in a way that relegated it safely to the past of historical memory, making it little or no threat to the city's immediate future. Similarly, proponents of San Francisco's continuing cosmopolitanism tended to embrace the city's diversity hand-in-hand with strategies for containing it.[23]

In 1859, in an attempt to capture the essence of San Francisco's rapid growth and development, French visitor Louis Laurent Simonin character-ized the city as a great "mixture of luxury and decay." Interpreting disorder spatially, he was struck by the contrasts offered by the continuing coexistence of elegant homes, well-planned and maintained streets, "vast stores and im-mense signs; fast carriages filling the streets" and other marks of progress with "San Francisco of the early days." He drew his readers' attention to "a run down shanty next to the most sumptuous residence; a wooden sidewalk with missing planks through which a passerby might disappear completely; [and] other streets unpaved in many places." Yet these architectural and infrastruc-tural incongruities marked the beginning of the commercial and industrial growth of the 1860s and 1870s that signaled San Francisco's emergence as a regionally and nationally significant metropolis. This accelerated urban de-velopment prompted the construction of numerous fine restaurants and hos-telries. As they had during the gold rush years, these edifices served as cele-bratory emblems of the city's development and increasing civilization. But the heightened exclusivity of many of these new spaces made them cultural fron-tiers on which social hierarchies could be more effectively enacted and in-scribed. In this changing climate, the boundary between high status and low status establishments became less permeable and the variety of etiquette asso-ciated nationally with middle-class status began to do its work as a means of social exclusion. The primary transgressors of the boundary that separated high status from low status and respectable from risqué became young, unat-tached middle-class and elite males; some adventurous tourists; and workers who staffed upscale haunts.[24] This state of affairs prompted journalist Samuel Williams to report that "society has greatly changed for better within the past few years, but is still somewhat 'mixed.'" To his rather disappointed eyes, the "lines of class and caste" were still often "vague and shadowy."[25]

By this time, eating in restaurants and living in hotels had become deeply ingrained as part of the rhythm of everyday life. Published guides not only de-scribed the city's restaurants and hotels for tourists but also outlined the costs and feasibility of hotel and restaurant life for residents. The City Directory for 1864 enumerated 106 boardinghouses, 135 hotels, 172 lodgings, 7 coffee houses, and 73 restaurants. The aficionados of hotel and restaurant life were the still disproportionately high numbers of single men that inhabited the city during these years. "Were all the now single men in San Francisco to be married this month," remarked the author of an article in the *Overland Monthly* titled "Restaurant Life in San Francisco," "the restaurants would be insolvent, and half of the hotels would be compelled to close their doors." Yet families, too, still partook of hotel living. John Hittell told readers of his history of the city that many patrons of the fine new hotels that opened in the 1860s and 1870s—such as the Russ, the Lick, the Cosmopolitan, the Palace and the Baldwin—were middle-class if not elite "families who remain as permanent boarders from year to year." Of the city's eateries, B. E. Lloyd informed readers of his *Lights and Shades in San Francisco*, "there are chop-houses, coffeehouses, oyster 'grottoes,' lunch-rooms and restaurants in bewildering abundance in every street, lane or alley. . . . The French, the German, the Italian, the Spanish, the China, and the American nationalities, all have their respective eating-houses or restaurants. In respectability and the quality of the *cuisine*, they vary very much as to their locality." Under the heading, "Who Patronize Restaurants," Lloyd wrote, "Everybody. There is scarce a person in the city but that takes an occasional 'meal' at a restaurant. Those who have all the home-comforts in their residences, . . . clerks, bookkeepers, printer-boys, and young men engaged in all the various departments of business; young mechanics and laborers, and many of the working females, occupy hired furnished apartments and board at restaurants" and "small families often secure furnished apartments, convenient to an eating-house, so as to be rid of kitchen cares." "The restaurant," Lloyd concluded, "fosters the lodging-house and the lodging-house in turn furnishes the restaurants many patrons" (see figure 8).[26]

However, as restaurants, hotels, and boardinghouses continued to structure rituals of everyday life, they also became more important spaces for the assertion of identities at either end of the social scale—the elite and the abject. As these cultural frontiers gained significance in the construction of social norms and boundaries, they became ever more implicated in processes of cultural ordering. Restaurants, hotels, and boardinghouses frequently served as the settings for extraordinary disorderly occurrences such as abortions, robberies, assaults, rapes, assignations, suicides, and suspicious deaths. Press coverage of these events highlighted urban dangers and identified both particularly threatening and vulnerable individuals. In so doing, it mapped a terrain through hotels, boardinghouses, and restaurants that demarcated the respectable from the risqué or even immoral, often telling

Figure 8. San Francisco's nexus of boardinghouses and restaurants. In a city with rapid growth and a chronic shortage of housing, restaurants, hotels, and boardinghouses provided basic domestic sustenance—a place to live and food to eat—to large numbers of city residents on a daily basis throughout the nineteenth century. This photograph shows Market Street, at the corner of Montgomery, looking south, ca. 1860–1870. (The Lawrence and Houseworth Photography Albums, 1860–1870, Alice Phelan Sullivan Library at the Society of California Pioneers, San Francisco)

tales of the road to ruin, the perils of misguided youth in the big city, or sad stories of the urban desolation of people cut adrift from family or community ties. At the other end of the continuum, newspapers chronicled the hotel arrivals of the elite and the openings of new hotels that featured detailed descriptions of their opulent appointments. Two events—the trial of Andrew Jackson Stevenson for the rape of Martha MacDonald at the Cosmopolitan

Hotel in 1868 and the Palace Hotel's opening in 1875—illuminate the ways these cultural frontiers increasingly both delineated social hierarchies and policed their boundaries.[27]

The city's leading daily papers as well as the weekly *California Police Gazette* made the Stevenson-MacDonald case a prominently featured news story throughout the second half of January 1868. The details of the case were revealed in locally syndicated press coverage that included complete reports of trial testimony. The press generated such publicity about the case that crowds of people "swarmed the balcony and pressed the doors of the court room" in anxious anticipation of the unfolding local drama. The two main characters were Martha MacDonald, described on the first day of the trial as "a young woman, a little the rise of twenty-two years of age, of medium height, slight mould, and both in appearance and tone of voice evincing a delicate state of health" and Andrew J. Stevenson, in his fifty-fourth year and identified as "a well known citizen of San Francisco reported to be very wealthy; the proprietor of the large edifice at the corner of Montgomery and California streets." The story of the alleged rape contained components of the two discourses—one about urban disorder and danger; the other about order in the form of elite consolidation and prescriptive categories of identity—that were frequently situated in restaurants, hotels, and boardinghouses. Because the alleged rape happened in one of the city's more elegant hostelries—the Cosmopolitan Hotel—it highlighted the danger a space like an urban hotel, even a first-class one, could harbor for both the victim and the accused. The victim was vulnerable, because as a young, single woman of marginal middle-class status, she was a favored prey of sexually predatory men. By traveling and taking rooms at the Cosmopolitan without a proper chaperone—after all, hotels were often also the haunts of prostitutes—Martha's story fed into fears that hotels, because of the way they combined private acts with public space, could be dangerous places for a woman with sexual virtue to protect. The accused rapist—even though he was situated in a position of class privilege and economic power—was also vulnerable, as the defense would make clear, to the potential of false accusation and extortion by an avaricious young woman. Moreover, both MacDonald and Stevenson were open to the various but omnipresent risks involved in the fact that any of the people they fleetingly encountered in a place like the Cosmopolitan Hotel might be sporting counterfeit identities or have designs on their purse or virtue (see figure 9).[28]

Figure 9. The Cosmopolitan Hotel, ca. 1860–1870. The high-end hostelry where the young Scottish immigrant, Martha MacDonald, alleged that she had been raped by Andrew Jackson Stevenson, an elite businessman. The trial captured local attention throughout the second half of January 1868. (The Lawrence and Houseworth Photography Albums, 1860–1870, Alice Phelan Sullivan Library at the Society of California Pioneers, San Francisco)

Martha's testimony provided an account of her origins and the development of her relationship with Andrew Stevenson. She had immigrated from Scotland in 1861 to join her brother, James J. MacDonald, "who was in the mines." While traveling, she was "in the care of Mr. Ferry, a nephew of Mr. Bell of the firm of Falkner, Bell & Co.," and when she arrived in San Francisco she stayed at Mr. Bell's residence for a while before being sent to a "Mr. Searle's at San Juan." It seems that sometimes Martha was simply under the guardianship of these men and their families but that at other times she was in domestic service at some of the homes where she resided. After she arrived, it took some time to pin down the exact location of her brother. According to the *Call's* report, "Mr. Bell advertised in the *Evening Bulletin* to find the whereabouts of her brother and in the meantime she made inquiry whenever opportunity afforded." It was in her attempts to ascertain her brother's whereabouts that she first encountered Andrew Stevenson, contacting him at Mr. Bell's suggestion when she returned to San Francisco. At this initial meeting, Mr. Stevenson provided Martha with "the address of a brother of his, who was keeping store in Shasta, and to whom she proposed to write in the hope of finding a clew to her own brother." At this first encounter she had been appropriately chaperoned by Mrs. Bell. Martha "eventually learned that her brother was in Walla Walla, Oregon and went to him." It was not until 1866 that she would again encounter Andrew Jackson Stevenson.[29]

For Martha, the intervening years were marked by financial insecurity and illness. Initially, she "was placed by her brother at Bishop Scott's school, near Portland, Oregon, where she remained a few months, until her brother experienced a reverse in business." Martha then "left the school and endeavored to do something to assist him, so that she would not be a burden to him." It appears that she went to work for two different families in Portland during which time, on December 6, 1863, "she fell ill with inflammatory rheumatism." In the second week of January 1864 Martha was admitted to the hospital and it was not until June 1865 that she was "discharged cured." She testified that "the physicians had pronounced hers one of the worst cases of inflammatory rheumatism they had ever seen." Martha was sent by her brother to San Francisco for further medical treatment about "the 3rd or 4th of February, 1866," and upon her arrival she "took a room at the Cosmopolitan Hotel" where she remained for over a week.[30]

At the Cosmopolitan, Martha would have a series of encounters with Andrew Stevenson that would culminate in the alleged rape. As narrated by Martha, the story contrasted her innocence and lack of guile with Stevenson's cunning, premeditated deceit and sexual desire that, rebuffed, escalated to sexual violence. On her first day at the Cosmopolitan, "Mr. Stevenson came into the parlor and recognized her." Although "she did not at first recollect him" after "being reminded of her call . . . some years before when in search of her brother, she returned his salutation." After "a few inquiries concerning her brother and herself he remarked that she must be doing well to afford living at the Cosmopolitan Hotel." Martha replied that "she was well supplied with money by her brother." The "next day Stevenson came again into the parlor where she was, and addressed her familiarly, as if he had been acquainted with her a number of years." When he "came in again after lunch" he "invited her to accompany him to the theater or opera." Martha declined the invitation. Stevenson's response indicated that he was "rather displeased" with her refusal.[31]

The following day, at eleven o'clock, "Mr. Stevenson came to the parlor with a coat on his arm." He told Martha "that he was going out of town and that there were some illustrated papers in his room which she could get if she desired, when the chambermaid went to make up his room." When Martha called at his room some time later, the door was ajar and she received no reply when she knocked. Upon entering, however, Andrew Stevenson, "who was concealed behind the door, caught her from behind, around the waist and tried to use her violently." They struggled and Martha's dress was torn. Later in the evening, Stevenson found Martha in the parlor and "asked forgiveness a great many times." Martha refused, telling him, "No, you are a bad wicked man." Stevenson then made the first of what would be numerous declarations of his love for her, adding that "he would make her happy and buy her all she wanted if she would have him." Martha replied that "money could not buy her, nor make people happy." She then left Stevenson in the parlor and returned to her room to prepare for her departure the next day.[32]

Back at her room, Martha "had the chambermaid bring a warm bath . . . and after using it, had got into bed, leaving the door unlocked for the chambermaid to take out the bath, fearing that to leave it in her room all night would be bad for her rheumatism." At about ten o'clock, Martha was lying in bed "with her face to the wall, looking at a picture of her father in her hand" when she heard "a gentle knock at the door, supposed it was the chambermaid come for the bath, and said, 'Come in.'" When the person entering did not speak, she turned toward the door and saw Andrew Stevenson standing over her "ready to put his hand on her mouth." He said, "It's no use, Miss Mac-Donald, I love you passionately." In his hand Stevenson held a cloth soaked in chloroform. Aided by the drug's effect on Martha as well as his superior physical strength, Stevenson proceeded to get into Martha's bed "with all his clothes and his boots on" and rape her. Although the daily papers determined that Martha's description of "the struggle and his consummation of his intention" were "unfit for publication," the *California Police Gazette* was less inhibited. Martha told the court that "he had connection with me when he was on my person. . . . against my will and consent. I experienced violent pain in the region where his person came in contact with mine. . . . It was more painful than I can describe. The last thing I was conscious of was his getting out of bed. . . . I do not recollect anything more. . . . Never had connection with any man in my life except that time." Martha explained that the next morning she "was very sore and tired" and not able to leave her bed. She sent for a doctor who felt her pulse and gave her a prescription, but she "did not tell him what was the matter."[33]

Very soon after the attack, Martha returned to Oregon. She bounced from residence to residence, saw several doctors, and "had a child on the 10th day of November, at Mr. Caples's house in Portland." When the child was a few hours old, Mr. Caples and the doctor deposited it at a convent. As much as possible, Martha had kept her pregnancy and child a secret, as she feared her reputation would be ruined. Martha, however, had traveled to San Francisco in July 1866 prior to the birth of her child with the intention of returning to her sister in Scotland. Although her brother had covered the cost of her passage, she instead ultimately chose—for unexplained reasons—to return to Oregon instead. While in San Francisco, she again stayed at the Cosmopolitan Hotel and again saw Stevenson. But it was not until May 1867, after borrowing "thirty-five dollars of the clergy at Portland to pay expenses down," that she confronted him with news of her pregnancy, their child, and demanded some sort of financial compensation.[34]

Andrew Stevenson reacted with shock to the news of Martha's pregnancy. Martha related that she "had an interview with him afterward in his office" during which he offered her some money but she "threw it back at him, and said, 'Take your dirty money.'" Subsequently, Stevenson attempted to evade further contact so Martha "made inquiries for a good lawyer"—consulting and retaining the prominent Hall McAllister. During this time, Martha was near destitution and "without means except such as Mr. McAllister furnished her." She managed to meet with Stevenson and both of their lawyers so that "matters could be arranged without taking any advantage of him." Stevenson later testified that his lawyer had relayed to him that $1,500 was the amount required for settlement. Martha also filed charges—later dismissed in Police Court—against Stevenson for his alleged involvement in her abduction by two men in October 1867.[35]

From the outset, Andrew Jackson Stevenson's version of what happened painted a very different picture than Martha MacDonald's. His lawyer had asserted that "they would probably attack the character of plaintiff for virtue and also endeavor to prove that she had been an inmate of an insane asylum."

He also told the press that they "would probably endeavor to show that the prosecution was commenced for the purpose of extorting money, and that Miss MacDonald had adopted that means before, and further, that in regard to the present occurrences she had made various statements to different persons." Attacks on the alleged victim's reputation, mental health, and motive did constitute the basis of Stevenson's defense. Presented as an unimpeachable pillar of society, he categorically denied all charges. While he did admit to meeting Martha and then subsequently encountering her several times in the Cosmopolitan Hotel, he claimed that he "never was in her room in his life, at the Cosmopolitan, or any other place" and that he "never offered to marry her." In fact, "the thought never entered his head." His lawyers argued that Martha never had "inflammatory rheumatism" but instead was admitted to a psychiatric hospital "suffering under the symptoms of general mania" and the "delusion that persons were after her to do her violence." Under cross-examination, Martha responded that she was unaware of "any institution attached to the hospital" and admitted that "perhaps" she had been "regularly admitted into the Insane Asylum; but never heard until now." Not only did several doctors testify to her mental illness and paranoia, but the defense found that Martha had told similar stories of someone getting into her room, subduing her with chloroform, abusing her, and even impregnating her several times before. One doctor testified that he had feared discharging her from the hospital because he believed "she would get seduced, or bring some one into trouble."[36]

The arguments in the case had commenced January 18 and on January 28, 1868, "at about half past three the jury retired to consider their verdict." The *Call* reported that as of half past ten that evening the jury was "standing eight for acquittal and four for conviction." At five o'clock the next day, after thirteen hours of deliberation, the jury returned a verdict of not guilty. According to the *Alta*, "The testimony in the case had been very generally read and commented on by the public at large, and the verdict rendered was largely anticipated." Whether Stevenson committed the rape as Martha described is, despite the verdict, unknown. Whether she, delusional and paranoid, fabricated the attack or plotted the seduction herself for pecuniary gain is also open to speculation. What is clear is that the verdict of not guilty helped to define an elite class by showcasing that class's power as evidenced by Andrew Jackson Stevenson's victory over an apparent attempt at entrapment from below. Through the symbol of Martha MacDonald, it also delineated the kinds of women who could—or could not—occupy the category of respectable white womanhood and be worthy of the protections it afforded. If Stevenson did rape Martha MacDonald, the ruling sanctioned his desires—and his use of the privileges that came with being a rich and powerful man—to take advantage of a young, economically vulnerable woman. It also punished Martha for traveling and taking a room at a hotel without a proper chaperone and for bringing charges against her sexual assailant. In the end, the legal resolution of the Stevenson-MacDonald case made it into a cautionary tale about the tragedy that could befall a young woman who transgressed the boundaries of propriety. It also signaled that gender boundaries were becoming more rigid, especially when contrasted to San Francisco's earliest years when prostitutes made up such a significant proportion of its female residents that they were much less socially marginalized, and codes of gendered respectability were much more in flux, than in better-ordered cities.[37]

Material changes were also afoot in the city that sent similar kinds of messages about the increasing consolidation of the contours of power. In the second half of the 1870s, the main shopping and commercial area shifted—in response to the extension of Montgomery Street across Market and the planned building of a new city hall to the west—away from the vice district known as the Barbary Coast, the financial district, and many of the older hotels and restaurants. "With all the new prosperity and wealth of the seventies," observed Amelia Ransome Neville, "San Francisco changed greatly in appearance. Downtown was suddenly more metropolitan." It was in order to popularize this new area that the Palace Hotel—very ritzy, class-specific, and vitally important to the image of the city—was built in 1875. At the time that it opened, the Palace not only outshone the numerous first-class hotels that had been built in the 1860s, it was the largest, most modern, and most luxurious hotel in the world. Standing seven stories high and containing nearly 800 rooms capable of hosting 1,200 guests, it was huge by the standards of the day and dominated the city's skyline. The Palace took more than two years to build and occupied the entire block bounded by Market, New Montgomery, Jessie and Annie streets, covering an area of over 96,000 square feet. Thousands of workers were employed to erect it. When completed, it contained "three miles of hall and thirty miles of steam and gas pipe," and "nearly twenty-five millions of brick and three thousand tons of iron" were consumed in its construction. Its architects took extreme measures to protect the Palace from both fire and earthquake—an on-site system of artesian wells, storage tanks in

1802   Birdseye View of San Francisco, towards Palace Hotel and Nob Hill.   Photo., San Francisco

Figure 10. The Palace Hotel dominating the city's skyline, ca. 1890. At the time of its construction in 1875, the Palace was the largest, most luxurious hotel in the world. It had been built by William Ralston to showcase San Francisco's transition from a rough-and-tumble boomtown to a thoroughly civilized city. (I. W. Taber, photographer. Roy D. Graves Pictorial Collection, Bancroft Library, University of California, Berkeley)

the basement and on the roof, extra thick walls, and reinforcing iron. Thousands of bay windows lined the façade in vertical bands. The New Montgomery and Market Street sides featured space for eighteen retail stores. "Each had two entrances and two sets of show windows, one facing on the streets, the other on long galleries within the building; guests would thus enjoy the luxury of doing their shopping—or of merely admiring the displays—without the inconvenience of stepping outdoors." One promotional tract aptly described the Palace as an "architectural monarch" lifting "its colossal bulk above the very business and social centers of the Pacific Metropolis." "Amplitude, solidity, strength, and permanency," the account concluded, "reign in every part" (see figure 10).[38]

Impressive amenities—emblematic of modernity, progress, and civilization—graced the interior of the Palace. The *Springfield Daily Republican* headily enthused, "There are . . . five elevators, and seven grand staircases, fire escapes, fire alarm telegraphs, and a pneumatic dispatch tube for carrying messages and parcels to any point on the different floors." All of its spacious rooms had fifteen-foot ceilings, could be cooled, when necessary, by a novel air-conditioning system, and were furnished in the Eastlake style then in vogue. Highly polished and elaborately carved woodwork of mahogany, teak, rosewood, and ebony were used to finish both public and private spaces. The hotel's various lobbies, parlor, and reception rooms displayed "huge rugs specially woven in France" and artwork of California landscape painters. Ladies had a drawing room, reception room, and grillroom while "gents" had a reception room and the characteristically male spaces of the barbershop and billiards and bar room. French furniture—"fragile and be-fringed" decorated the ladies' reception room while more "masculine chambers" sported leather upholstered chairs. Three large courts supplied light and air to the interior rooms. The largest of these—the central court—faced the main entrance on the New Montgomery Street side. It featured a circular driveway that allowed arriving guests to be driven inside "and deposited on a marble-paved floor in the midst of a forest of potted trees and plants." Seven galleries, topped by a dome of opaque glass, extended upward on all sides (see figure 11).[39]

William Ralston, one of the city's leading capitalists, had self-consciously designed the Palace to symbolize San Francisco's transition from a raw mining camp and disordered boomtown to an established, civilized city. Originally from Ohio, Ralston had migrated to California in 1854, become a respected banker and speculator, and in 1864 founded the Bank of California. In the 1860s, he was one of a number of San Franciscans who began directing their accumulated profits from Nevada silver into the development of local manufacturing enterprises. In addition to financing the construction of the Palace Hotel and the Grand Hotel, as well as the development of the New Montgomery Street addition where both were located, over the years Ralston backed a remarkable number of ventures including the California Theater, the California Steam Navigation and California Drydock Companies, Buena Vista Winery, Consolidated Tobacco Company, Mission Woolen Mills, San Francisco and Pacific Sugar Refining Company, watch and furniture manufacturers, and a lock works. A bon vivant with a penchant for high living, Ralston had a well-deserved reputation for conspicuous consumption. Although he had been dead for two months when the Palace opened in October 1875, his role as a capitalist with an ordered vision was highly significant in terms of the development of his adopted city. For Ralston, a properly ordered city meant a socially segregated city. William

Figure 11. The Palace Hotel's Central Court. Its circular driveway allowed its elite guests to be driven inside and safely deposited, providing a barrier of privacy from the hustle, bustle, and potentially unwanted encounters of the city's streets. (Scenic Views in California and the Columbia River Gorge, Bancroft Library, University of California, Berkeley)

Sharon, a U.S. Senator from Nevada and an associate and a creditor, succeeded Ralston in the ownership of the hotel. Whether or not he shared Ralston's vision, he left the majority of his predecessor's plans for the Palace unchanged.[40]

Most fundamentally, the Palace Hotel distinguished and separated the elite from their social inferiors, both literally and symbolically. Not only was it a place designed to present an image of civilized San Francisco to all who read about it or stayed in it while traveling, it was also where the city's nascent elite came to assert themselves as leaders of the city and to simultaneously bolster their still precarious and sometimes recently attained class positions. According to Evelyn Wells, a chronicler of these decades, Leland Stanford inscribed "his name on the register as the first guest" and "Charles Crocker and his family were the first to enter the dining-room, followed by Collis P. Huntington and John W. Mackay." These individuals figured among San Francisco's most prominent elite. Stanford, Huntington, and Crocker were three of the Big Four—rich and famous for the part they played in building the Southern Pacific Railroad—and Mackay was a Comstock Lode millionaire. Mary Goodrich revealed in her history of the Palace that "Monday night was set aside for society. . . . It was a gala occasion; friends foregathered by habit or appointment and on the balconies or the beautiful colonnade, where Monday night promenade was in progress, there occurred many significant meetings." Even the Palace's location intensified its grandiosity—and that of its patrons—by presenting a towering contrast to the working-class neighborhood to its immediate south (see figure 12).[41]

One of the more lavish rituals of class consolidation at the Palace took the form of extravagant private banquets hosted and attended by San Francisco's elite. Quite often they were all-male fêtes. Bankers, railroad owners, steamship and mining magnates, lumbermen, and other prominent local empire builders used the hotel's best suites and dining rooms to wheel and deal. The city also hosted public celebrations for visiting dignitaries that were frequently followed by a private banquet at the Palace with select guests. In general, dining at the Palace was a sumptuous but formal affair that set the standard for what constituted refined dining in the city and beyond. The hotel featured a main dining room that was, at 150 feet in length, the largest in the West, a breakfast room, and private dining rooms on the second floor. Its kitchen and serving staff was the largest in the country. The food was prepared by the best chefs and was the epitome of gourmet French cuisine. Unlike the International Hotel's "American plan" in the 1850s, the Palace offered its guests enormous meals of almost innumerable, but clearly demarcated courses. It also offered its guests the option of taking their meals in the dining rooms of their suites, thus insuring their guests a kind of social privacy that was unavailable in the city's hostelries twenty years before.[42]

Figure 12. San Francisco gentlemen at the Palace Hotel. The city's leading capitalists used the hotel's lavish dining rooms, barrooms, and suites for wheeling and dealing. (San Francisco Historical Photograph Collection, San Francisco History Center, San Francisco Public Library)

During the Palace's first decade, it hosted a number of Civil War heroes who were fêted with citywide celebrations followed by private banquets. A banquet for General Philip Sheridan on October 14, 1875—just twelve days after the Palace opened its doors—was the hotel's first major public social event and "society appeared in full regalia." It was both a tribute to the general and a display of the city's increasingly civilized status. According to the *Call*, "it eclipsed in grandeur, in princely magnificence, all previous assemblages of this character in the city." Appropriately—since the Palace was a monument to San Francisco as an emblem of America's landed empire as well to the city's own regionally imperial position—Sheridan himself had been involved in western empire building. Twenty years before he had commanded a survey expedition between San Francisco and the Columbia River "for the proposed branch of the Pacific Railroad" and afterwards "held his troops among the Western Indians until the Civil War called him to other posts." General Sheridan's party was seated "at a flag bedecked table." "Three hundred brilliant gas jets illuminated the festive throng of black broadcloth and white neckties" and the seats for 216 guests were marked by place cards of solid silver that were theirs to take as commemorative favors. Diners were treated to rounds of jovial speech making and partook of eleven courses of French cuisine, several fine wines, and a variety of liqueurs in just over four hours. "The brilliant array of new silverware, glittering glasses, fruit and flowers added further fascination to the scene" and "the exhibition of pyramids of jellies and desserts enhanced the brilliance of the feast." Throughout the evening, the Fourth Artillery Band played in the grand court. "In the balcony above the open court," wrote Mary Goodrich, "the satin trains of California's society matrons swept the thickly carpeted promenade."[43]

Four years later, on September 20, 1879, Ulysses S. Grant arrived in San Francisco. During his stay, the city's elite wined and dined Grant inside and outside the Palace. Upon his arrival, San Franciscans turned out in force to welcome him. Streets were decorated and buildings were covered in bunting. As word spread that lookouts had caught sight of his approaching ship, tens of thousands of people thronged the streets and amassed on the hills overlooking the harbor. At the dock, Grant was met by an assortment of "civic authorities" along with "blaring bands and decorated carriages." In a "chariot with snow white horses" Grant was led on "a procession through arched and bannered Market Street to the Palace Hotel" where 200,000 people tried to crowd in for a sight of the former president. Police had succeeded in keeping the floor of the grand court clear, "but the six balconies were crowded to capacity." Banners and flowers festooned the galleries and the interior driveway. Celebration continued with more speeches, music, and ceremonies in which Grant received the keys to the city. Subsequently, this event was praised both for the warm welcome extended to Grant and for bringing the diverse and increasingly stratified San Francisco community together. Yet this mixture, especially at the Palace Hotel, was the exception to the rule. Although recognized by

San Franciscans as symbolizing an essential component of the increasingly civilized identity of the city, the Palace was an elite bastion that only occasionally opened its doors to the masses.[44]

The Palace's lavish celebrations, as well as its day-to-day operations, depended on the labor of its serving staff, which included nearly 200 African American waiters, porters, and chambermaids—the first to occupy such positions in a grand San Francisco hotel. At the banquet for General Sheridan, a writer for the *Call* had described this waitstaff as an "army of waiters in swallowtail coats and white Lislethread gloves, flitting noiselessly to and fro." For black men and women, many of whom were recruited from resort hotels in the East, work at the Palace offered good working conditions, relatively high wages, handsome tips, prestige within the black community, and the potential for further social mobility. White patrons generally praised the African American serving staff and regularly remarked that they enhanced the already genteel, civilized surroundings. Yet this response was only possible because of the way being served by African Americans reinforced the white racial dominance upon which notions of middle-class and elite civility and gentility were implicitly based. In their history of the Palace, Oscar Lewis and Carroll Hall revealed, using a quotation from an unattributed source, that the announcement to hire African Americans was met with widespread middle-class and elite approval because, "Whatever their shortcomings might be, Negro waiters were sure to be 'a vast improvement upon the impudent 'white trash' who have exchanged the hod for the napkin, but still retain the manners of their native hovels.'" In other words, some San Franciscans viewed African Americans as more appropriately servile—less "impudent" and better mannered both in terms of etiquette and attitude—than Irish American whites. These kinds of comparisons between blacks and Irish—that often favored the former—were common nationally during this period of heightened nativist sentiment. Yet in San Francisco, the small black population, the comparative ease by which the Irish were folded into the circle of white ethnics, and the huge amount of anti-immigrant ire directed at the Chinese tended to blunt these kinds of comments as well as much of the economically driven friction between Irish and blacks. As later events would reveal, however, at the Palace Hotel, such atypical tensions were precisely what were brewing beneath the surface. It also appears that fêting Union generals—who were credited with ending slavery—in this setting failed to arouse any sense of irony among the participants.[45]

Despite the iconic power of the Palace, the transformation of the city from a disordered boomtown to well-ordered American metropolis that the hotel symbolized was by no means absolute. Such elite-driven social visions coexisted, after all, with the city's unabashedly cosmopolitan population. In 1878, for example, *The San Francisco Illustrated Directory for Hotels and Steamers* advertised several boardinghouses that made the multilingual environment they offered a key selling point. At Normandie House, at 1205 Stockton, French, English, and Spanish were spoken. It offered guests "furnished rooms by the day, week, or month" at "50 cents to $1 per day or $10 to $30 per month." Robinson House—also known as La Casa Robinson—not only told readers of its ad that it featured "accommodating attendants who speak Spanish, French, and English" but ran its ad in both Spanish and English. Located at 810 Mission Street, this "private boardinghouse" offered "large sunny rooms, nicely furnished with every convenience of hot and cold water; fireplaces and large closets in each apartment; excellent bath rooms; sitting room, with the daily papers; parlor and piano; and excellent table furnished with the best the market affords." Yet both the Normandie House—on the edge of Chinatown and the Barbary Coast—and La Casa Robinson—in the working-class Mission district—were located in neighborhoods known for social mixture as well as vice and disorder. They were worlds away from the middle-class family retreats advertised in *The San Francisco Illustrated Directory*, that, like the Palace, made social segregation their selling point. The text of the ad for Abbotsford House, for example, read, "this Hotel, situated on Broadway between Larkin and Polk recommends itself to all on account of the desirability of its location." Not only was it in an entirely respectable neighborhood, but it was also "removed from the noise and turmoil of the city" yet "at the same time within easy reach of the principal centers of business." "Surrounded by pleasant shade trees and having beautiful gardens" it described itself as "a charming family resort."[46]

From the 1880s through the turn of the century, restaurants, hotels, and boardinghouses bore witness to hardening social divisions as an order increasingly in accord with nationally dominant hierarchies became more deeply inscribed on these cultural frontiers. Since segregation heralded San Francisco's progress toward attaining a civilized social order, the trend that emerged in the 1860s for mixture and heterogeneity to be associated not only with disorder but also with urban danger continued. Disorder was more frequently contained within spaces associated with vice, questionable morality, and the city's working-class and socially marginal residents.[47] Fine eateries and hostelries continued to serve as celebratory emblems of urban development in increasingly stratified terms. One indicator of this process can be seen in the fact that many tourist guides, middle-class and elite reminiscences, and early histories of these years tended to limit their focus to the city's finer eateries—many of which served French-inspired cuisine. Paeans were penned to places such as the Maison Riche, the Poodle Dog, Delmonico's, Tate's, the Palace Grill, Marchand's, Maison Tortoni, Bergez's, the Occidental, and the Mercantile Lunch.[48]

Daniel O'Connell's 1891 work, *The Inner Man: Good Things to Eat and Where to Get Them*, exemplified the increasingly exclusionary trend in San Francisco's restaurant culture. Within the first few pages of this 160-page guide, O'Connell, a prominent member of the all-male, elite Bohemian Club, proudly declared that "the progress in the refinements of the table has been most marked during the last decade." In the description that followed, all of the restaurants he featured were middle-class if not elite haunts and most were the domain of businessmen, although a few of these sex-segregated spaces were equipped with special areas for the occasional lady patron. Along with chapters such as "Setting the Table" and "The Art of Dinner Service and Carving—Some Hints about the Placing of Fish," which prescribed forms of etiquette associated with a high level of civilization, O'Connell also included the chapter "The Cuisine of Other Lands," which delineated some of the foodways practiced in Africa, Japan, China, and the Hawaiian Islands. Although he wrote about ancient Egypt to highlight the advanced stage of that civilization, his descriptions of African, Japanese, Chinese, and Hawaiian customs presented these cultures as savage opposites of civilized Euro-American practices. For example, in his description of African foodways, O'Connell emphasized the lack of complexity and segregation—markers of civilization in eating as well as in society. "The cooking is of a very inferior grade, the only spices used being salt and pepper," he wrote. "The kitchen utensils consist of common earthen or wooden ware. Very little time is spent in decorating the table. Knives, forks, napkins, etc., etc., are dispensed with. All victuals are served in large wooden vessels." In a later section he added, "Savages, who eat with their fingers, are always greedy and rapid eaters." Since some of the most prominent racial and ethnic groups in the city descended from Africa, China, Japan, and Hawaii, it seems likely that O'Connell's invocation of civilizing hierarchies to order San Francisco's heterogeneous population would not have been lost on contemporary readers.[49]

When writing on restaurant culture in the years after 1880 ventured into the realm of praiseworthy lesser eateries, such accounts generally suggested that the author was engaged in a little slumming. Journalist Will Irwin explained his happy discovery that, "Meals that were marvels were served in tumbledown little hotels." He described one of his favorite finds, the Hotel de France, where "the patrons were Frenchmen of poorer class, or young and poor clerks and journalists." The city's numerous ethnic eateries—Italian, Mexican, Japanese, Turkish, and German—also fell into this category and merited frequent accolades. Chinese restaurants often proved to be the exception to this rule, with accounts whose advice to investigate emphasized the strangeness of the Chinese more than their delicious cuisine—which by this time was frequently depicted as unpalatable if not polluted.[50] When in 1892, the *Overland Monthly* ran an article which, like those of thirty or forty years earlier, addressed the question, "How cheaply can a man live at restaurants and keep his health and strength?" the question might have been the same but passage of time made the answer quite different. The writer, Charles S. Greene, certainly had the appropriate credentials and expertise. He explained,

> The restaurants of San Francisco are pretty familiar to me; for I have long lived at them, and a restless spirit has driven me ever to seek new places, to wander from the best of them to the cheapest hash houses and bun shops, to try in turn American, French, Spanish, German, Italian, and even Chinese repasts. I have taken beans and coffee for ten cents sitting on a high stool at Blank's Beanery in the most lowly company, and have dined in the dining room of a great hotel where an orchestra played waltz tunes, and the ladies at the tables glittered with diamonds.[51]

Clearly he had paid his dues—traversing from high to low, indulging in haute cuisine as well as simple fare, and sampling the city's varied ethnic eateries. But the story he related about his experiences differed from those of earlier years in the greater attention it directed to class-specific eateries with patrons of corresponding class positions, rather than to high and low establishments, each harboring a wide variety of patrons, which had been characteristic of the gold rush years. Greene noted, for example, that restaurants had arisen that specifically catered to the needs of the working classes. "The cheapest place in the city," he wrote, "is in a neighborhood where there are many factory and sewing girls." This lunchroom, run by the YWCA, offered "many comforts, a piano, reading matter, etc." The girls could go to it during their lunch hour and could either bring their own food or could "obtain there bread, butter, soup, beans, milk, tea, coffee, or a sandwich at a cost of one cent for each." Greene was also not as enthusiastic as his predecessors about the still ubiquitous "free lunch" saloons. Since the city's earliest days, such establishments had been renowned for providing a midday repast for the cost of a drink. Although he found the food decent enough, his concern was that because "they do much to promote drinking habits . . . the trail of the serpent is all over these places." For him, the "free lunch" saloons, once a celebrated staple of the city's restaurant life, were now outside the realm of "legitimate eating places." Tellingly, the article was accompanied by a number of illustrations indicative of the changed climate. A picture of the courtyard café at the Palace Hotel, empty of patrons, was juxtaposed with stereotypical drawings of restaurant workers: an African American—perhaps one of the Palace's own, a German, an Italian, and a Frenchman—all accompanied by various captions in dialect. The African American waiter, for example, inquired, "Champagne, Sah?"[52]

Heightened concerns about respectability, anxieties about dining in public, and fears of urban danger were given voice in a story featured in the *Evening Bulletin*, "Noon Hour in the Café." In this article, writer Elinor Croudace presented a fly-on-the-wall account of the unnamed eatery and its patrons as they eavesdropped on conversations, attempted to read the social situations of the other customers, and became increasingly unsure about the respectability of the place. It began with a description of the café. "This is a swell place, an expensive place," Croudace told her readers. "It is decorated and lighted. The floors are of inlaid wood, the chandeliers of hammered brass, and the ceilings a tempting heaven, with Cupid, Psyche and Aurora sporting among the clouds and roses. In this café eating is a fine art." This, she explained, offering a class-inflected contrast, "is no vulgar hash-house, like the sty where pigs are sent to feed, where gnashing animal humanity throws itself . . . ; where the odor of pork and beans mingles nauseatingly with the air poisoned by hundreds of human beings crowded together in its small confines."[53]

At one table in the café were seated two men. At another, within earshot, were two young women. After overhearing apparent threats made by one of the men—who appeared prosperous but in fact was really ruined—to the other from whom he was trying to extract funds, the two young women became increasingly frightened about where they were and who they were with.

What seemed perfectly fine a few moments before quickly began to take on ominous qualities. With an awareness of the vulnerable nature of a respectable woman's reputation that suggested that the kind of lessons offered by Martha MacDonald thirty years before had been well-learned, the older one said to the younger, "It looked so attractive and pretty, but I think it is a wicked place. . . . Don't look around so much, people are noticing you . . . you and I are the only two women alone; every other one has a man with her. I was always told that it was horrid for men and women to be out together in the daytime, especially in a restaurant."[54]

Soon after theorizing that one of the other female diners was an actress—always a suspect category of womanhood—the two young women observed another woman entering the restaurant whom they found most admirable. She was "a handsome, middle-aged woman" in the company of her husband. Her clothes were "dark and plain" and bore "the marks of expenditure without stint." She carried herself "as if she had been used to the best all her life" and had an "air of feeling it a privilege to be herself and to have her connections." This woman, however, took a look around at the other patrons in the café and remarked to her companion, "Let us leave here and go to a better place. I notice this café is running down, becoming very common. Just look at those two girls with their atrocious millinery. That older one has been staring at me in the most underbred manner. I suppose, poor thing, she is not used to seeing ladies and gentlemen. But she should not be here. I understood that this place was select." Thus, in a moment of encounter, the girls who had positioned themselves as superior to the café's other patrons were viewed as inferior by a newcomer on the scene. This woman's final remark, moreover, conveyed that truly "select" places maintained the highest standards of exclusivity while only less tony haunts still contained considerable room for rubbing elbows with people who might be other than what they seemed.[55]

As San Francisco's eateries became ever more numerous—by 1906 there would be over 600 eateries listed in the city's *Classified Business Directory* that fed the city's residents on a daily basis—they employed more people as cooks, waiters, and waitresses. While the patrons various eateries served became increasingly stratified according to class, the staff—perhaps with the exception of chefs at the finest establishments—were generally from the working classes. But like the elite, workers in the city's hostelries and eateries were also more organized than in earlier years and expressed their own ideas about the social order of the city that sometimes clashed with elite aspirations. As Rudyard Kipling's account of his travels in 1889 attests, a certain level of class disorder—symbolized by a lack of deference on the part of white workers—was still prevalent enough in these later years to be remarked upon. "Money," he wrote, "will not buy you service in the West. When the hotel clerk . . . stoops to attend to your wants he does so whistling or humming, or picking his teeth, or in the pauses of conversations with someone he knows. These performances, I gather, are to show you that he is a free man and your equal." In addition, as an 1893 news item from the *Chronicle*, "Fought in a Pantry: An African Hammers a Chinese Cook" demonstrated, among the culinary workers behind the scenes there was still considerable room for social mixture along racial and ethnic lines. The report announced, "Another of those gory boarding-house race wars broke out in a fashionable private hotel on Jones Street near Sutter last Saturday morning. A long and sanguinary battle took place in a locked pantry between a descendent of Ham and son of old Confucius. While the battle raged a squad of valiant Caucasian waiter girls, armed with bread knives, stood outside the door and kept at bay the Mongolian friends of the suffering Celestial inside." In fact, during these years restaurants, hotels, and boardinghouses were the sites of numerous labor struggles in which white workers arrayed themselves in opposition not only to elite and employer interests but also to workers of color.[56]

During the favorable economic climate of the 1880s, the number of trade unions in the city increased from eighteen in 1878 to forty-five by 1883. Among the unions generated in this burst of activity was the Cooks' and Waiters' Anti-Coolie Association, organized in the late 1870s—years of intense anti-Chinese sentiment—for the purpose of protecting white workers from what they perceived to be the encroachments of the Chinese. Race, not immigrant status, drove the issue as the majority of culinary workers in late-nineteenth-century San Francisco were themselves foreign-born, predominantly German and Irish. Using figures obtained from "the secretary of the Waiters' Union from 1904 to 1907," historian Edward Eaves estimated the composition of that union as well as the Cooks' Union during the nineteenth century to be: "American 25%; Irish 20%; German 15%; French 10%; Scandinavian 10%; Slavonics 8%; and Miscellaneous 12%." Writing in 1925, he argued that the high percentage of foreign-born contributed to the radicalism of these organizations prior to 1906. But it also seems clear that the high proportion of members of European descent meant that they were able to increase their power as an organization by overcoming ethnic differences and coalescing around a common white identity vis-à-vis those groups—Chinese, African Americans, and possibly Mexicans and Latinos—excluded from that category and ostensibly the union. In forging this identity in relation to workers of color, these white workers articulated their own sense of appropriate racial hierarchies and contested elite formulations in ways that shaped how the cultural frontiers on which they worked figured into processes of cultural ordering. White workers, not employers or members of the elite, desired a white workforce.[57]

The founding members of the Cooks' and Waiters' Anti-Coolie Association engaged in a campaign of systematic recruitment, met with considerable success, and soon had a substantial following. Representatives from the association appealed to restaurant owners in terms that reminded them of their heavy reliance on working-class patronage and the financial losses they would face if such patrons boycotted their establishments in opposition to their continued employment of Chinese. This strong-arm approach worked. After successful organization of the city's restaurants, attention turned to its hotels. Again, organizers encountered little opposition, and the majority of the cooks and waiters at hotels joined with the Anti-Coolie Association.[58]

In the early 1880s, the Anti-Coolie Association changed its name to the Cooks and Waiters' Protective and Benevolent Union of the Pacific Coast. The union grew to nearly 1,500 members in the city, and while its central offices were in San Francisco, it also had branches in Seattle, Sacramento, Los Angeles, and other coastal cities. In 1887, the union launched a campaign to bring all restaurant owners into compliance with the union's goals. According to the *Alta*, the union's "committee visited most of the coffee houses and restaurants of the city during the day. They were successful in every case except one in inducing the proprietor to allow their employees to become members of the union." The exception was "H. Schultz," who kept a restaurant on 4th Street, opposed the union, and vowed not to employ a waiter who belonged. Edward Eaves found that the committee also encountered opposition at the Popular Restaurant on Geary Street where the proprietor staunchly refused to employ union men. At a meeting, the union decided that if the owners of noncompliant establishments would not agree to union demands, every union member, in restaurants all over the city, would walk off the job. This threat succeeded in securing promises from wayward owners that they would endorse union membership among their employees.[59]

Although the Cooks and Waiters' Union had dropped its explicitly racist intentions from its official title, it continued to pursue racist goals along with trade union ones. Nonwhites not only continued to be excluded from the union—but the organization also regularly forced workers of color from their jobs. On March 21, 1887 the *Alta* reported that "last week the union caused the proprietor of the Windsor House to discharge five Chinese employees under the threat of the displeasure of the union." The next day, the *Chronicle* noted that "under pressure of the union, a number of colored people were discharged at the Popular." Even after negotiating an agreement with employers that "provided for an eleven hour day, a minimum wage scale of $50 per month and the employment of union men only," on May 1, 1887, the "aggressive side of the union" continued to place minor boycotts "on small houses that continued to employ Chinese help."[60]

Despite the impressive gains made by the union in improving the working conditions of its membership, by the end of 1888 the organization had been broken. A poor strategic decision to go out on a sympathy strike that was not supported by the city's Federated Trades and that violated an agreement with employers to give one day's notice before striking opened a wedge for restaurant owners eager to assert their opposition to the union. Since this violation had released restaurateurs from any binding arrangement, they formed the Restaurant Keepers' Association, which then offered striking men their jobs back under the same conditions as had existed previously but without the union—including racially mixed or nonwhite dominant workplaces. From 1888 until the turn of the century, culinary workers were largely without union protection and their working conditions deteriorated. But even a year after its official demise, the Cooks and Waiters' Union still had enough residual power to have a hand in effecting a change in the racial composition of the workers at the Palace Hotel.[61]

When the African American serving staff had been hired at the Palace in the mid-1870s, the economy was booming and jobs were relatively abundant. By the late 1880s, however, another depression was on the horizon and jobs of any kind were increasingly scarce. In this climate, while the Palace's elite patrons praised the black staff, some of San Francisco's white restaurant workers reacted to the employment of African Americans at the Palace with mounting hostility. For these white workers, the Palace's employment of African-Americans when white workers remained unemployed represented a challenge to the privileges they believed should derive from their position—as white men—atop the racial hierarchy.[62]

In 1888, Captain Samuel F. Thorn was named the manager of the Palace and undertook a massive reorganization of the hotel in an attempt to improve its financial situation. One of his more drastic measures was the dismissal of the majority of the black staff in 1889, following fourteen years of successful service. Twenty-six bellboys, seventeen porters and bootblacks, and some chambermaids were retained. These, not surprisingly, were the lower-status positions. The *Alta* attributed the dismissals to Thorn's demand that workers in the dining-room and kitchen be searched at the end of their shifts. "It is said," the paper reported, "that before the colored gentlemen knew of the order some of them, taken unaware, were caught carrying home tenderloin steaks, fruit, chickens and even silverware." The black workers denied the allegations and refused to serve dinner until Thorn ceased his harassment. That succeeded for that evening only. The next day white workers replaced the black staff at the Palace. One of the spokesmen for the African American workers stated: "We think the record of hotel management in the United States will substantiate us in our claim that colored help, male or female, has proved to be fully equal in honesty and fidelity to white help. . . . We will not, even in self-defense, make use of information in our possession that the white help employed in the Palace Hotel has been deficient in integrity." When white workers were accused of theft a few years later in 1893, "new checking procedures were instated," but no dismissals followed. In 1896, the remaining black bellmen and porters lost their jobs—again amidst allegations of theft—to whites willing to work for lower wages.[63]

Although there is no direct evidence connecting the Cooks and Waiters' Union to this turn of events, the organization certainly had a hand in creating the conditions under which they took place. Moreover, the firing of the black workers at the Palace fit with the outlook and tactics deployed previously by the union. In the early 1880s, members of the union had determined that working with blacks did not serve their interests as white waiters. This position only hardened when, during a strike in June 1886, a number of restaurant owners threatened to replace striking whites with blacks. Reminiscent of their approach in the late 1870s when the offending workers were mostly Chinese, the striking white workers blithely asked their employers if they expected to have African American patrons.[64] Following in these footsteps, white workers at the Palace had mounted a successful challenge to the hotel's employment practices that forced elites to shift their strategies of racial hierarchy building to contain unruliness among a racially divided working class. Yet whether black workers were hired to serve the elite or fired to assuage the bruised white manhood of workers, in both cases, despite their different class inflections, a social order based on white racial dominance—configured in accord with San Francisco's construction of whiteness that expansively embraced white ethnics—was reasserted and confirmed.

CHAPTER TWO

Playing in the City:
Vicious and Virtuous Amusement

Just as many nineteenth-century San Franciscans lived publicly—engaging in forms of hotel and restaurant living that brought rituals of private life into more public, commercial realms—so too they played publicly. As local historian John Hittell, writing in 1878, aptly noted, San Francisco had "devoted a considerable share of her attention to the pursuit of pleasure."[1] In the wake of the gold rush, numerous places of amusement of the sort typical to nineteenth-century cities quickly emerged and formed a nexus of cultural spaces that made the growing city a center of leisure, pleasure, and consumption. One of the first public entertainments in 1849 was a circus that performed in a vacant lot on Kearny Street near Clay. Within the next year, two other circuses offering similar shows of gymnastics, stunts, and trick riding opened in crude tent structures. Crowds of over a thousand spectators paid "three dollars for seats in the pit, five dollars for a box, and fifty-five dollars for private stalls" to watch these exhibitions. By the middle of 1850, a number of theaters had emerged—including Robinson & Edward's Dramatic Museum, the Italian Theater, and the famous Jenny Lind Theatre located above the Parker House. By 1853, San Franciscans eager for recreation in a more pastoral setting could visit Russ Garden—a "popular suburban retreat"—on the corner of Sixth and Harrison streets. By that time, among its places of amusement, the city boasted "five American theatres . . . a French theatre, a music hall for concerts, balls, lectures, exhibitions, . . . a gymnasium and two race courses." Along with these various types of fairly virtuous amusements, however, the city's residents also heartily engaged in more vicious pastimes, especially gambling. According to the *Annals of San Francisco*, "Gambling was . . .

the amusement—the grand occupation of many classes—apparently the life and soul of the place" and "the bar-room of every hotel and public house presented its tables to attract the idle, the eager, and the covetous." In the city's predominantly male society, the pleasure and companionship offered by the burgeoning cultures of saloons and prostitution was also widely sought.[2]

But San Francisco's places of amusement did not just entertain. From the start, they functioned as cultural frontiers on which San Franciscans in all their diversity mixed, mingled, and negotiated how to get along in everyday life. In the process, they built a new American place. Like restaurants, hotels, and boardinghouses, as market-driven entities, places of amusement were brought into being by different entrepreneurial elites and catered to varied constituencies. Sometimes the impresarios behind them were social elites ideologically aligned with men like William Ralston and embraced similar visions for the kind of ordering role the city's cultural frontiers should play. Many others were simply guided by what would draw a crowd and bring in the bucks. Some fell somewhere in between, embracing the social potential of their venues but using them as platforms to express ideas that hovered beyond the boundaries of the mainstream. As cultural forms that pulled people out of the home and into a potentially promiscuous, public, and commercial realm, the respectability of urban places of amusement regularly came under suspicion. At their core, like restaurants, hotels, and boardinghouses, they bespoke a modern sensibility marked by the kinds of socially fluid interactions opened up by the option of urban anonymity and statuses that could be purchased and changed. Whatever the intentions of their creators, in the years after the gold rush, prevailing attitudes frequently framed disorder in the city's places of amusement in terms of vice but also associated it with what was seen as inappropriate social mixture between men and women and among people of differing races and classes. Virtuous pastimes, such as educational amusements, often in the domesticated spaces of the city's pastoral retreats, embodied an urban order more consonant with nationally dominant social arrangements. Ranging from the virtuous to the vicious, places of amusement tended to be situated within conceptualizations of the city that positioned the disorder of a wild, western frontier city at one end of a continuum of possibility and a well-ordered yet urbane and cosmopolitan port city at the other. The Barbary Coast, Woodward's Gardens, and the Pacific Museum of Anatomy and Science all came into being in the 1860s. Each occupied a different position on the virtuous-to-vicious continuum. Excavating their rise and fall reveals some of the varied interests and agendas contained within the overall trajectory of nation-making on San Francisco's cultural ground.

The Barbary Coast was the name given to San Francisco's primary vice district in the 1860s. The press and popular historical imagination fashioned it as a place of play where vicious amusements—most notably gambling, drinking, and prostitution—abounded. While on one hand the Barbary Coast was regularly maligned as representing all things disorderly and uncivilized about the city, on the other it was lovingly mythologized as embodying the freedoms from restraint associated with the Wild West and celebrated for its reputation as a place of excess. For example, historian Herbert Asbury—writing in the early twentieth century—characterized the nineteenth-century Barbary Coast as "the scene of more viciousness and depravity, but which at the same time possessed more glamour, than any other area of vice and iniquity on the American continent." B. E. Lloyd described the Sunday night revelry there as "mockery and dissipation." Yet his depiction also evinced a typically prurient quality. Of Sunday night on the Barbary Coast, Lloyd wrote, "The lowest dens of infamy are brilliantly lighted up, and in the doors and by the windows the most debased of fallen women stand gaudily attired and beck and nod to viler men that promenade the walks in front." When local papers—whether the mainstream press or the more sensational *California Police Gazette*—ran articles about the Barbary Coast, they tended to follow a formula of combining salacious coverage with sufficient moral outrage as well as ample information for the curious about where one might go and what one might see. By geographically containing rather than eradicating the disorder of the Barbary Coast, San Franciscans could assert an image—in keeping with the city's emergence as a metropolis in the 1860s—of a well-ordered city that flirted with, yet existed apart from, its infamous vice district.[3]

Although vicious amusements flourished during the gold rush years, there was no particular district designated for vice. Much of the area that would later become the Barbary Coast was originally simply a part of the city's compact downtown. In the first year or so after conquest, Pacific Street—which would become the Barbary Coast's primary artery—was not only "the first street cut through the sand-hills behind Yerba Buena Cove" but also "the main highway to Portsmouth Square and the western part of town." As a harbinger of things to come, however, other parts of the area were inhabited by socially marginal groups. A community of Chilenos—including some prostitutes—

briefly lived "clustered along the waterfront at Broadway and Pacific Street, and on the slopes of Telegraph Hill." Soon the numerous immigrants from Australia displaced the Chilenos and replaced many of their tents and shanties with "flimsy wooden and brick buildings" and "opened lodging-houses, dance-halls, groggeries, and taverns." These Australians became known as the Sydney Ducks and gained a reputation for both disorder and criminality. The area in which they congregated was known as Sydney-Town for about ten years before it started to be called the Barbary Coast.[4]

By the early 1860s, Sydney-Town had been redesignated as the Barbary Coast and had been literally and symbolically transformed from an unsavory part of town into the city's primary vice district. It roughly occupied the territory bounded on the east by the waterfront and the Embarcadero; on the south by Clay and Commercial streets; on the west by Grant Avenue and Chinatown; and on the north by Broadway, occasionally spreading into the area around North Beach and Telegraph Hill. The heart of the Barbary Coast lay a few blocks inland and abutted Chinatown, comprising "the rectangular district limited by Broadway and Washington, Montgomery, and Stockton streets," which was cut through with numerous alleys with names like Murder Point, Bull Run, Moketown, and Dead Man's Alley. Pacific Street remained its main thoroughfare, crowded with dives, grog shops, dance halls, melodeons, concert saloons, a few cheap restaurants, low-end clothing retailers, and a couple of auction houses.[5]

In 1869, the *California Police Gazette* characterized Pacific Street as an "abominable locality" of "crime, lawlessness, and prostitution" in which "every phase of villainy and turpitude" was concentrated. But this article was not only concerned with vice per se. It described the surrounding neighborhood as "one heterogeneous mass, one inexplicable confusion." In it, one found "rum shops, old clothes shops, boarding houses for sailors, loafers, and thieves, filthy dens for all sorts of purposes, damp cellars, gutters full of filth and cabbage leaves, windows full of long white paper, rags, and short old bottles." Mixed within this terrain were "painted sepulchers, young and old, modern and ancient—May and December—some fat, some thin, some tall, some short, English, Irish, Scotch, Germans, Swedes, Jews, Americans, Chinese, from all parts of the world."[6] As this depiction made clear, the viciousness of the Barbary Coast encompassed not just the questionable morality of drink, gambling, and commercial sex but also the promiscuous mixture of

men and women, often of different races and classes. The kinds of transgressive mixture for which the Barbary Coast was most notorious ran along two
overlapping threads: commercial sexual interactions that traversed lines of
race, class, and sometimes gender and the cross-class nature of the male sporting crowd. While on one level these vicious types of mixture and disorder flew
in the face of the movement toward greater stratification on the city's cultural
frontiers, at the same time, their containment on the Barbary Coast signaled
cultural ordering's solidification. Not only did the Barbary Coast's naughti-
ness increasingly stand in contrast to the rest of the city but, by creating a specific area designated for vice, San Francisco was becoming more like other
American cities and less like the city of its legendary, disorderly past.

Leisure entrepreneurs designed the Barbary Coast primarily as a playground for the men "from all classes of society" who patronized its various
haunts. Writing of the "Pretty Waiter Girl Saloons, the *California Police Gazette* explained that it was not uncommon to "behold merchants, clerks, doctors, lawyers, laborers, and honest miners among the frequenters of these establishments." Such men were members of what was known in the nineteenth
century as "the sporting crowd." Hailing from a wide range of social classes,
ages, ethnicities, and occupations, these men forged a shared culture through
their pursuit of leisure and their devil-may-care attitude toward middle-class
respectability. This cross-class fraternity of predominantly but not exclusively
bachelors was organized in and around the patronage of pastimes such as
blood sports, gambling, pugilism, and prostitution on precisely the kinds of
cultural frontiers for which the Barbary Coast was known—saloons, billiard
parlors, gambling halls, brothels, and dance halls.[7]

Most of the city's brothels existed within or adjacent to the Barbary Coast's
boundaries.[8] Yet outright prostitution represented only one strain of the
neighborhood's sexual commerce. Its dance halls, melodeons, and concert saloons—which offered music, drink, and sexually charged entertainments—constituted a more ambiguous form of the sex trade. These venues typically consisted of "a low-ceilinged rectangular room, with a bar along one side, in the
center a cleared space for dancing, and at one end a platform whereon the performers cavorted and the musicians dispensed more or less melodious sounds."
Melodeons, unlike the dance halls and concert halls, were without dance floors
and "offered only liquor and theatrical diversion." The only females generally
permitted within were those working as waitresses—often referred to as "pretty
waiter girls"—and performers, both of whom were expected to push drinks and

were not discouraged from selling sex. Shows included "bawdy songs, skits, and dances, principally the cancan" but occasionally the fandango and they sometimes featured women displayed in poses deemed obscene. An 1869 report in the *California Police Gazette* estimated that "nearly five hundred girls" were "employed in the cellars of this city" and that some saloons maintained fifteen to twenty, but that generally five to eight was the average. The Mammoth, located on the corner of Kearny and Jackson streets, was a "well known concert and billiard saloon" that shared space with the Eagle Sample Rooms and Rose's Hotel. In 1868 the Mammoth ran advertisements in the *California Police Gazette*—which counted on Barbary Coast patrons as part of its reading public—to promote its reopening celebrations, which included a Grand Ball and Concert. Readers were enticed with assurances that "beautiful maidens from the 'Fader-land' will attend to the wants of visitors." Similarly, in its regular ads, Brooks' Exchange, at 824 Kearny Street between Washington and Jackson, promised "a free concert nightly, first-class billiard tables," and "fair maidens who might pass for Houris in the days of heathen mythology."[9]

Slightly tamer amusements were offered by "low variety and music halls" like "the Bella Union, the Olympic, the Pacific, Bert's New Idea Melodeon, the Adelphi, and Gilbert's Melodeon." These also catered to male audiences but did not offer dancing or pretty waiter girls. They did feature performances that, while not considered obscene, were presented with "freedom from constrained etiquette." According to the *California Police Gazette*, "Vulgar talk and actions on the stage bring down the house and each person among the performers strives to outrival the others in dirty, smutty language." These places of amusement charged admission and discouraged outright prostitution but "as elsewhere on the Coast, the female performers were required to sell drinks between their appearances on stage." Women's performances frequently shared billing with minstrel shows, putting race and gender on a collision course and suggesting some of the limits of racial mixture on the Barbary Coast. On August 22, 1868, for example, the *California Police Gazette* advertised the shows at the New Olympic on Clay and Kearny streets. The theater was presenting "Miss Carrie Byrkel, The Swedish Nightingale" along with "The Popular Ethiopian Comedians, Messrs. Kelly and Holly." This extremely popular form of amusement featured white men in the roles of stereotypical black figures, speaking in dialect and wearing dark make-up. Through these performances, whites registered their fear and distaste for black culture by denigrating it and at the same time appropriated some of its

appealing characteristics. By constructing a vision of a black culture supposedly saturated with loose sexuality and a lackadaisical attitude toward regular
work, minstrels—in addition to tapping into prevailing racist attitudes—also
struck a resonant chord with an audience frequently at odds with both Victorian morality and a capitalist work ethic (see figure 13).[10]

Cockfights, dogfights, and the conviviality of saloons also brought men together. On Commercial Street, "three doors above Kearny," visitors to the
Barbary Coast would find J. B. Reed's cockpit—described as a "place for sport,
and sports." Advertisements boasted, "Every Saturday evening matches are
fought between the best game in the state according to the established rules
and, for variation, dog fights are interspersed through the performances. A bar
is kept in the best style where the different beverages, known to man, may be
obtained at reasonable rates." Nearby, on the northwest corner of Kearny and
Commercial streets, the Pony Express Saloon also specialized in drink and
dogfights and generated publicity for some fights up to three weeks in advance.
Other places more simply advertised themselves as friendly places to socialize,
get a drink, and grab a bite to eat. The Fashion Saloon—a favorite among
"military men"—was located on the northeast corner of Washington and
Montgomery streets and featured "choice wines, liquors, lunch, cigars, oysters
in every style, pigs' feet, eggs, rarebits, &c., &c., &c., with the fascinating
'James George' to dispense the liquids." At A. J. Brower's establishment at 712
Washington Street near Kearny, patrons "found at all times, the best of wines,
liquors, and cigars" as well as "a hot lunch every day at 11 o'clock am."[11]

The sporting crowd that patronized Barbary Coast resorts was an urban
phenomenon. In the years before the Civil War, droves of young men migrated from the countryside to cities in search of economic opportunities.
Some, already there, found themselves cast out of artisan households and into
wage-work as the pace of industrialization increased. Within this context,
warnings about the dangers of city life emanated from the pulpit and the
popular press. Yet the notable presence of middle-class clerks and students
among the sports that authorities found so worrisome indicated that a significant number of young men found the absence of traditional familial oversight
liberating rather than frightening. Distance from the East, the newness and
fluidity of society, and the inordinate proportion of unattached men made
conditions in San Francisco exaggerations of those in eastern cities. In other
words, if you wanted to get away from traditional ties and responsibilities, San
Francisco was the place where you could, ostensibly, do so with impunity.

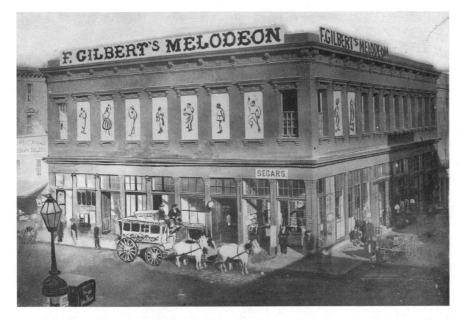

Figure 13. Gilbert's Melodeon, 1860. Located at Clay and Kearny streets, it offered music, drink, and sexually charged entertainment geared toward the city's sporting crowd. (San Francisco Historical Photograph Collection, San Francisco History Center, San Francisco Public Library)

Yet even in San Francisco, the visits of seemingly respectable white men from the middle classes to the Barbary Coast garnered particular attention in the city's press. Perhaps this kind of coverage represented resistance on the part of journalists to the shenanigans of hypocritical ordering elites. Or it may have meant that the constraints of the East really were not so far away after all. In an 1869 feature article on the Barbary Coast, the *Chronicle* reported this scene from the Bella Union. "In the next box are seated three or four young men of respectable family connections, said connections dozing away in their residences on Rincon Hill and elsewhere, under the hallucination that their worthy scions are attending a levee of the Young Men's Christian Association." A year earlier, the *California Police Gazette* ran an article that escorted readers on a nighttime trek through the Barbary Coast and also reported spotting middle-class men indulging in its pleasures. "See those three men sitting at tables in different parts of the room busily engaged chatting with 'pretty waiter girls.' They are clerks. He with dark curly side whiskers, *a la mutton chop*, expects to be a partner in a large concern on California street.

The other two get big salaries, but it is well known that they spend more money than they get in that way." The same year that paper also ran an exposé of the city's "Pretty Waiter Girl Saloons" accompanied by an engraving of an interior of such an establishment. It told readers that, "Wives whose husbands are in the habit of remaining out late of nights, by scrutinizing the engraving closely, will perhaps be enabled to ascertain where their lords are in the habit of being detained on 'business.'"[12]

In the Barbary Coast's culture of commercial sex, women—as pretty waiter girls, entertainers, and prostitutes—comprised the workforce and their bodies were one of the primary commodities consumed. The women who worked and lived on the Barbary Coast constituted a racially, ethnically, and economically diverse group. They embodied social disorder in terms of both their transgression of sexual boundaries and their heterogeneity. "Unlike most cities," explained Don Hugo, the author of a series of articles on San Francisco's demimonde, "where prostitutes are selected from among their own people, of the same race, complexion, and habits, we have here representatives of all the nations of the world." He found that the Euro-American, Spanish, and French women he identified as waiter girls and performers often lived in lodging houses on Dupont, Broadway, and Pacific streets where they shared suites or "large and commodious rooms, with double bed and other neat furniture." Although many boarded at restaurants, he explained that those who had "a kitchen contiguous to their rooms" were "fond of inviting each other to breakfast" where sometimes as many as six congregated over coffee. The living arrangements of these women formed part of a social geography of commercial sex that vacillated between racial and ethnic segregation and mixture. In Chinatown, for example, which bled into the Barbary Coast and shared its culture of gambling and sexual commerce, some parlor houses featured Chinese women exclusively while others showcased white women. On the Barbary Coast, while some blocks were known for the prevalence of black, Latina, French, or Jewish women, others were characterized by the mixture of such groups. Yet those with the most racial and ethnic mixture—such as the cribs "occupied by women of all colors and nationalities" that lined Morton Street— gained a reputation for being among the most vicious.[13]

As this suggests, even as the Barbary Coast frequently operated as both a racially and sexually transgressive space, it was by no means free from San Francisco's dominant racial hierarchies. In fact, at times it both reflected and reinforced them. Chinese, Japanese, Latina, and black women often found themselves excluded from the higher paying, more desirable parlor houses and many were relegated to the lower paying and least desirable cribs. Parlor houses offered anonymity to patrons, relative comfort and safety to the women who worked in them, as well as a twisted sense of respectability in their mimicking of middle-class homes. Cribs—rooms twelve feet wide and fourteen feet long constructed either as stand-alone shacks or as cubicles in buildings containing facilities for as many three hundred women—were the most prevalent option. While sporting culture fostered cross-class camaraderie among men, boundaries—some of which were about money, some about race—did exist that framed the way patrons pursued commercial sex. Men with money could afford, if they wished, the services of women who worked in elegant parlor houses. Yet money alone might not be enough as some parlor houses refused the patronage of men of certain races or ethnicities. Some even employed black maids and used their presence to signal the house's racial exclusivity in much the same way that black workers functioned at the Palace Hotel. Less financially flush men had the option of turning to streetwalkers, who took their clientele to cheap boarding-houses, or the many women who worked in the cribs, who had the least control over whom to accept or refuse as a patron.[14]

Although white males patronized Barbary Coast prostitutes of a wide variety of races and ethnicities, Chinese prostitution represented a particularly highly charged arena of commercial sex that intersected with racial ordering. The importation of Chinese women for prostitution began in the 1850s. By the 1870s, officials estimated the number of Chinese prostitutes in the city to be between 1,500 and 2,000. Prior to the Chinese Exclusion Act of 1882, little was done to regulate their importation. Kidnapped, lured, or acquired for as little as $50 by procurers in China, in the United States Chinese women bound for prostitution could be resold for as much as $1,000 in the 1870s. In San Francisco they frequently lived as virtual slaves, serving out contracts of indenture that they did not understand and that were nearly impossible to fulfill. With lives filled with physical and mental trauma, few outlived their terms of service.[15]

Chinese prostitution flourished in a larger social context in which the Chinese occupied the position of the most despised racial minority in San Francisco—by whites and members of other groups as well. White men patronized Chinese prostitutes despite their membership in a group considered to be racially inferior and their widespread characterization as pollutants—diseased, malodorous, and filthy. Don Hugo characterized Chinese prostitutes as "miserable, degraded and wretched beings"—hardly exotic beauties. To him, it was "beyond comprehension" that such "disgusting creatures were visited and patronized by white men" who, he nevertheless conceded, made up the bulk of their clientele. In 1868, another article in the *California Police Gazette* described the alleys along which Chinese prostitutes lived as full of "filth and horrible smells" and attributed the spread of venereal disease throughout the state to San Francisco's "Chinese dens." The author positioned Chinese prostitutes as a physical and moral danger to virtuous white manhood as well as the domestic realm of the American home and hearth. He asked, "How many young men, who have, after years of toil and privations in the mountains. . . . come to this city to take the steamer for the States, thinking to enjoy with the loved ones at home all the fond contemplated pleasures they had for so many years hoped for, wandered into these dens in a moment of thoughtlessness, and been ruined body and soul?"[16]

That same year, another article on "Chinese Immigration" used the figure of a diseased prostitute—emblematic of the barbarity of Chinese culture—to articulate opposition to Chinese immigration. The author explained that, "A few days ago, a Chinese woman (if they may be called by that sacred name, for they all appear to be degraded, groveling prostitutes) was found on Pacific street, in a horrible diseased condition, ready to die, heartlessly cast forth by her countrymen, who were no longer able to barter her person for gold." He used this woman to contrast innate Chinese "cruelty" with American civility, since while the Chinese had left her to die, Police Chief Crowley—the representative of the American state—had ordered her "conveyed to the hospital" for care. The writer then noted that, despite such evidence of the Chinese character, there existed "a numerous class of people who advocate the immigration of this vile race." Leaping to the logic that Chinese workers meant depressed wages or the absence of jobs for whites, he explained that supporting Chinese immigration meant discouraging "Caucasian" settlement because whites were "unable to live and compete with the Mongolian."[17]

Chinese women brought to the United States to work as prostitutes by Chinese men found themselves caught in a densely tangled web of the race and gender politics of both Chinese and American cultures. Because of perceived gender and class inequalities, in a community where Chinese women were scarce, Chinese men sold the bodies of lower-class Chinese women to white men for profit. Their home culture devalued them sufficiently because of their class and gender to allow them to be prostituted. The American culture that they entered into racialized them as less than white women but enough of a woman—as sexual object—to be used by white men to act out their need for racial dominance over Chinese men in sexual terms. Surely, many white men had sex with Chinese prostitutes out of desire, but it is also likely that such desire was infused with the assertion of social power. In ways not dissimilar from the sexual use of black women's bodies by white men in the American South, sex between white men and Chinese prostitutes, however complicated by desire or affection, would have been difficult to extract from the larger social context of relations of power structured along race and gender lines.[18]

Throughout the nineteenth century, most efforts by civic authorities to regulate the Barbary Coast were haphazard at best. Until late in the century, city officials did little to counter its reputation as "the general rendezvous of debauchery on the Pacific Coast." The city licensed gambling establishments until 1855 and since all that was required for a license was the payment of a fee, they were liberally dispensed and gaming flourished. In 1854, the state of California passed an antigambling law, but it was not systematically enforced, resulted in the closure of just a few small gambling houses, and was repealed in 1859. In 1869, the city enacted an ordinance that prohibited the employment of women in melodeons, dance halls, and concert saloons. Although considerable fanfare surrounded its passage, little effort was ever made to enforce it. A similar ordinance was enacted in 1876. It outlawed the presence of women in drinking cellars or saloons between six in the evening and six in the morning. Despite the fact that establishments found in violation faced closure, on the Barbary Coast it was as if such a regulation never existed. Three years later, in 1879, Charles Warren Stoddard, a well-known San Francisco journalist then writing for the *Chronicle*, fueled a public outcry over the purported obscenity of the leg-baring cancan. One dancer, Mabel Stanley, was arrested for indecent exposure, tried, and fined. When officials relaxed their vigilance soon after, the dancers resumed the cancan. In 1892, legislation passed that banned the sale of liquor in theaters, effectively closing the Bella Union and many like places of amusement. The changes spawned by this law undergirded an 1897 *Call* story titled "Barbary Coast Fast Becoming a Relic of the Past" that contended that the Barbary Coast's heyday had been in the 1860s and that its reputation was more about what it had been than what it currently was. In the years after the 1906 earthquake and fire, the district was reduced to what the *San Francisco News*, in a 1934 retrospective on the Barbary Coast, called a "slummer's Coney Island." Nevertheless, it was not until the first decades of the twentieth century that the Barbary Coast truly met its demise—a casualty of changing attitudes toward vicious amusements represented by the moralistic fury unleashed by the Red Light Abatement Act of 1914.[19]

Around the same time that the *San Francisco News* was featuring articles on the legend and lore of the Barbary Coast, the *San Francisco Chronicle* received a letter from W. A. Wynne requesting an appropriate memorialization of a very different but no less popular nineteenth-century place of amusement, Woodward's Gardens. Wynne wanted "the committee" in charge "of placing markers on the site of historical places" to put one "on the west side of Mission street, opposite Erie, between Duboce avenue and Fourteenth street"— the site of "the main entrance and, until the late eighties, the only entrance to Woodward's Gardens." Woodward's Gardens deserved this honor, Wynne explained, because "in the seventies and eighties" it "was the most popular amusement place in the city." Nostalgia may have fueled Wynne's desire for a memorial but it did not color his assessment of Woodward's Gardens centrality to city life. The *Pacific Rural Press* reported in 1871—just as Woodward's Gardens was entering its heyday—that it was "an important and indispensable feature" of the city that was "visited daily by large numbers of residents and sojourners."[20]

In contrast to the Barbary Coast, Woodward's Gardens rose to prominence as an eminently respectable resort occupying over four acres on the outskirts of town at Mission and Fourteenth streets. For those upright members of the middle and working classes whose tastes ran to something tamer than the Barbary Coast and more affordable than a night at the theater, Woodward's Gardens fit the bill. The creation of hotelier, collector, and leisure entrepreneur Robert B. Woodward, it successfully combined the features of a pastoral retreat, museum, zoo, aquarium, and amusement park. From the time of its establishment in 1866 to 1893, when it closed its doors, it was one of the city's most popular places of recreation among both locals and tourists. In his 1876 guidebook, *Lights and Shades of San Francisco*, B. E. Lloyd expressed his opinion that Woodward's Gardens was "without rival on the Pacific Coast." "For diversity of attractions," he explained, it was "not inferior to some of the celebrated parks in cities whose age in decades outnumber San Francisco's years." In fact, Woodward's Gardens promoted itself and was frequently referred to as the West's equivalent to New York's

Figure 14. Woodward's Gardens. A pastoral retreat that successfully combined the features of a museum, zoo, aquarium, amusement park, and picnic ground, it was one of the city's favorite places of recreation from 1866 to 1893. (Alice Phelan Sullivan Library at the Society of California Pioneers, San Francisco)

grand pastoral accomplishment, Central Park. As an ad for Woodward's Gardens on the back cover of the resort's own *Illustrated Guide and Catalogue* for 1873 exclaimed, "The Central Park of the Pacific embracing a marine aquarium, museum, art galleries, conservatories, menagerie, whale pond, amphitheatre, and skating rink—The Eden of the West!—Unequaled and Unrivaled on the American Continent."[21] Such a comparison to Central Park reflected Woodward's Gardens' symbolic importance for San Franciscans anxious about crafting an image of their city centered around civilized respectability rather than the social disorder characteristic of a frontier boomtown (see figure 14).

Prior to embarking on his career as a leisure entrepreneur, Robert B. Woodward owned the What Cheer House, a temperance and men-only hotel on Sacramento and Leidesdorff streets just below Montgomery, in the heart of the city. His position as a temperance advocate who offered a surprisingly proper sex-segregated space in the bawdy, liquor-infused early years of the gold rush sheds light on the kind of ordered social vision he espoused. By the mid-1860s, the What Cheer House was one of the largest hotels in the city. It had 1,000 rooms and served 3,000 meals per day, many to men who lived or labored nearby. Its popularity rested on its combination of good value, re-spectability, cleanliness, and a number of pleasant amenities, such as its library and bootblack stand, both of which were free and open to the public.[22]

The profits from the What Cheer House allowed Woodward to assert himself as one of the city's emergent elite and to develop a collecting habit. He traveled to Europe at least twice to enhance his holdings. In 1861, he en-listed the help of painters Albert Bierstadt and Virgil Williams in assembling his artistic collection, which included "marble statues of classical figures, and ornately framed copies, with some originals, of the old Italian masters"—all of which were transported by way of the newly completed Central Pacific Rail-road. In 1866, Woodward imported the nucleus of his museum's natural his-tory collection from "Verreux's establishment in Paris." The property that would become Woodward's Gardens—which had previously been the estate of the early Western explorer and empire-builder John C. Frémont—was Woodward's private residence for just over five years but it was in this home that he initially acquired and displayed his collection. The improvements he made to the property were regularly and favorably remarked upon, and pas-sersby routinely peeked into the gates to try to catch a glimpse of the most re-cent developments. As the *Pacific Rural Press* explained, "The beautiful plants and strange trees, the fine buildings with their novel architecture, the ponds and mossy rocks, the roar of the wild beasts, excited the curiosity of persons, to the most of whom the picket fence formed an impassable barrier." Woodward's granddaughter, Ethel Malone Brown, recalled, "He added gar-dens and fountains; a picture gallery, and a steam-heated conservatory,—all revolutionary in those days; even a grapery."[23]

While on his 1866 European trip, Woodward received a message from California requesting the use of his grounds for a Sanitary Fund benefit. Woodward consented, having already developed a reputation for hospitality and for allowing his friends free use of his estate. This request and his re-sponse to it that ultimately culminated in the establishment of Woodward's Gardens may have signaled Woodward's legitimacy among the city's elite and perhaps even confirmed his membership in this increasingly selective class. As an hotelier turned leisure entrepreneur, Woodward's elite status would never be as secure as the real estate developers, financiers, and mining and railroad tycoons who were emerging on the scene. Whether Woodward was pushed, pulled, or acted on his own volition, in May of the same year, Woodward's es-tate "was opened formally to the people of the city as Woodward's Gardens,—

with a gate, and a gate-keeper, and an entrance fee of 25¢ for grown-ups and 10¢ for children."[24]

The four acres of gardens formed a primary attraction in and of themselves. They were what made Woodward's Gardens so attractive for picnicking and promenading and gave it the qualities of a domesticated, pastoral retreat designed to offer an escape from city living. The *Pacific Rural Press* described gardens containing "level ground and elevations" with walks that were "graveled and meandering" and grass that was "dotted with every variety of flowering vines and shrubs, with trees of different climes." Its lake was "decorated with a margin of lilies and by large colored globes of glass, mounted on posts." Marble sculptures of "Pandora, Jupiter, Bacchas, Venus, Ceres, Terpsichore, Psyche and the 'Dancing girl,'" were tucked into "quiet nooks" while "benches and chairs" invited visitors to rest. Located on San Francisco's outskirts, Woodward's Gardens was not only geographically removed from the city, it was a different space altogether, purposely crafted to lift people outside of the urban experience. Unlike the Barbary Coast, which was suffused with connotations of urban danger and vice, the sculpted, tamed nature of Woodward's Gardens resonated with health, virtue, and wholesomeness. The well-ordered manner in which nature was arranged at Woodward's Gardens was explicitly created to present a morally uplifting contrast to the troubling social and spatial chaos characteristic of rapidly growing nineteenth-century cities. Across the nation planners such as Frederick Law Olmsted, the designer of New York's Central Park, promoted the building of parks for their ability to act as urban antidotes. Although Golden Gate Park was San Francisco's first large-scale urban park, the land it occupied was not acquired until 1870 and it would not really resemble a park for another ten years. In the meantime, in the context of San Francisco's overall climate in which the foundation of respectability—the middle-class household—was under persistent threat by unbalanced sex ratios and an inadequate number of single-family homes, Woodward's Gardens filled an important ordering role as the city's primary rural retreat (see figure 15).[25]

Woodward's Gardens not only offered a changed spatial experience for its visitors—replacing for a time a disordered city with a harmonious natural landscape—it also sought to change the visitors themselves. Woodward's Gardens was designed to impart uplift through educational amusements as well as through the morally restorative qualities of its pastoral environment. Its motto, after all was, "Education, Recreation, and Amusement the Aim!"[26]

Figure 15. Women and children enjoying Woodward's Gardens' pastoral setting and natural wonders—which included both live and taxidermied specimens. (Alice Phelan Sullivan Library at the Society of California Pioneers, San Francisco)

Observers regularly praised the expansive diversity of the collection of art, plants, and creatures of both land and sea that Woodward displayed. Woodward's former home became a museum where the curator, Mr. F. Gruber, a taxidermist, "near-scientist," and the compiler of the resort's guides and catalogues, gave occasional lectures and presided over the extensive natural history collections. This included the "The Zoologicon," described by Ethel Brown as, "a revolving platform with stuffed animals against appropriate backgrounds, and divided into four parts—Europe, Asia, Africa, and America." The *Pacific Rural Press* enthused that the Art Gallery contained "some seventy oil-paintings of merit and two marble busts" and the adjoining Museum of Miscellanies featured "a collection of birds and birds' eggs, one of upwards of a thousand coins of all ages and nations, idols, weapons, minerals, and hundreds of other articles." The library held "1,600 volumes, many of them very rare and costly."[27] The Gardens' happy jumble fit with the tendencies of museums across the country in the first half of the nineteenth century, before a countervailing trend that made many establishments more exclusive in terms of both their patrons and their collections took hold.[28]

Woodward's zoo—located on about an acre of land that also housed an amphitheater—was connected to the gardens by an underground passageway that ran under Fourteenth Street. His collection of animals was unrivaled on the West Coast and featured "various kinds from all countries and zones." Some of the tamer creatures roamed the grounds, where they mingled with taxidermied specimens. In cages and pens, visitors found a veritable menagerie. As the *Pacific Rural Press* explained, "California grizzlies, Oregon panthers, Mexican panthers, South American Jaguars, and Bengal tigers. . . . Deer and elk, badgers, raccoons, and marmots, foxes, weasels, ant-eaters, opossums, black and brown bears, monkeys of all sizes, and very many other animals live in close proximity. Pheasants, turkeys, quails, ducks, geese and chickens, eagles, sparrows, cranes, doves and canaries, of various breeds and hues and from countries remote and near, are confined in cages." In addition to its very popular "seal ponds," Woodward's Gardens had a bona fide aquarium. According to the *Illustrated Guide and Catalogue* for 1879, the aquarium made its debut on July 4, 1873, and occupied "the entire lower portion of a fine structure 110 feet long and 40 feet wide." Its fresh and saltwater tanks housed such creatures as salmon, halibut, sturgeon, Chinese carp, stingrays, sharks, crustaceans, sea anemones, and starfish.[29]

Woodward arrayed his collections in accordance with the belief that opportunities for education through simple observation would be the most effective in winning over patrons' hearts and minds. For example, the *Illustrated Guide and Catalogue of Woodward's Gardens* for 1879 happily reported upon the educational value of the aquarium. "It has created a taste for deep-sea studies," readers were told, "by giving delight to the eye and stimulating, through the medium of recreation, the spirit of scientific inquiry. It has brought a subject of profoundest interest within the practical reach of the humblest student."[30] For patrons who wanted to learn even more about the various components of Woodward's collection, educational guides and catalogues were

available at a cost of ten cents. While these guides provided patrons with typically useful things like maps of the grounds and information about where to
find lost children, the text was also quite densely packed with information
relative to the life sciences. For example, under the category, "Order. 8—Rodentia—Hare, Rabbit, Squirrel, Rat, and Mouse," readers of the *Illustrated
Guide and Catalogue* for 1875 found the following: "Sub. Fam. Castorinae—
Beavers—The genus *Aplodontia* of the rodentia is represented by the sewellel,
showtl, or nutria, and belongs to the rarer animals of California; it is destitute
of cheek pouches. The body is thick and short, clothed with fur like that of a
musk rat, but neither so long or so fine. The tail is very short, and almost concealed by fur. These animals form small societies, and live in burrows." The
information provided about the beaver continued for another seventeen lines,
most of which were devoted to the process by which they built dams. In keeping with Woodward's Gardens penchant for domesticating the wild, the account concluded by informing readers that, "Beavers may be easily tamed."[31]

As this example makes clear, Woodward's Gardens' educational guides
categorized and described its exhibits in the fashion typical to the nineteenth-
century science of evolutionary biology. While this type of science explicitly
expressed ideas about order in the natural world, it provided the basis for
ideas about social order as well. Methods of animal classification combined
with evolutionary theories to hierarchically rank races of people as well as animals during this period. The resultant understandings were arrayed along a
continuum that generally positioned white, industrializing societies as superior and darker, more primitive cultures as inferior. They fueled assumptions
about the innate racial characteristics of a population as well as how a given
society would develop over time. Ideas about what constituted a civilized,
well-ordered city leaned heavily on these kinds of conceptualizations of the
natural world harnessed to further social purposes.[32]

At Woodward's Gardens, evolutionary thinking was not confined to its
animal exhibits. According to F. L. McKenney, in his 1913 article for the
Chronicle, one of Woodward's "most daring and delightful undertakings" involved bringing to the Gardens "the tribe of Warm Springs Indians shortly
after the Modoc war of 1872" who had "assisted the troops in the conflict
with their savage brothers." A large part of the attraction of these and the numerous other Native Americans that Woodward exhibited had to do with the
fact that although they once represented the "wild" they now represented
order as they had been safely and effectively domesticated through military

conquest. These Native Americans served as symbols of both American national dominance in the West and the white racial dominance that accompanied it. In the ways it showcased Native Americans, Woodward's Gardens instructed its visitors—many of whom were children—in the operative racial hierarchies of the region. McKenney noted that the children who thronged Woodward's Gardens on May Day "never tired of gazing from a respectable distance at the wild looking aborigines in their war paint and feathers and were held by the fascination of terror when the Indians started up one of their tribal dances to the accompaniment of their weird music."[33]

As motivated as he was by the desire to disseminate his vision of social order through educational amusements, Woodward was also very much a showman. In fact, in ways not dissimilar from the comparisons made between Woodward's Gardens and Central Park, Woodward gained a reputation as "the Barnum of the West." His natural history collection, for example, featured serious specimens as well as its share of "curiosities and monstrosities of all kinds, alive and dead." The gardens featured the Circular Boat, a popular ride, and the amphitheater near the zoo provided a space for the exhibition of such things as "equestrian sports," "Roman chariot races," and "hurdle and foot races." The Grand Pavilion served as "a play-house, a dance-hall, and a skating-rink." As Ethel Malone Brown recalled, this was the space in which "Gilbert and Sullivan carolled gayly forth in Pinafore, Pirates of Penzance and the Mikado" and where "the famous French tight-rope walker, Blondin, cooked and ate his omelet while balanced over the heads of the awestruck hundreds." In 1875, the *Alta* ran an advertisement for Woodward's Gardens that described the array of amusing attractions visitors could expect. "At Woodward's Gardens," the ad read, "Capt. McDonald's trained Indians in their lightning drill and extraordinary acrobatic feats, Saturday and Sunday; also Professor Rice in his marvelous mind reading, the bear pit, trained bears, a monster boa constrictor and anaconda, baby elephant and glassblowing." Yet despite Woodward's ties and stylistic resemblance to Barnum, issues of fraud and controversy that surrounded the latter did not surround the former. Across the board, San Franciscans instead lauded Woodward and his gardens even when, for example, the Mendocino rattlesnake with forty rattles he exhibited turned out to be man-made. The value of the space he created as both a wholesome amusement and an ordering venue became more urgent and apparent amidst the disorder of San Francisco than in the Eastern cities where Barnum was frequently viewed more as a threat to rather than an enforcer of social order.[34]

Woodward's respectability, as well as the way elites embraced his vision of social order, was visible in Woodward's Gardens' position as a destination for illustrious visitors to the city. Ulysses S. Grant, for example, paid the resort, as well as the Palace Hotel, a visit. Respectability also emanated from the way Woodward inaugurated the completion of his "mammoth pavilion" in 1871. According to the *Alta*, he invited all "the Sabbath Schools of the city to be present at the ceremony" and distributed "upwards of eleven thousand tickets for children alone." The exercises included a prayer by Rev. Dr. Woodbridge and the singing of songs like "the 'Lord's Prayer' 'Praise God' and 'Shall We Gather At the River.'"[35] Another part of what made Woodward's Gardens respectable had to do with the way Woodward ran the resort. As at the What Cheer House, no hard alcohol was served in any of the refreshment stands at Woodward's Gardens. As the *Illustrated Guide and Catalogue of Woodward's Gardens* for 1873 explained, "No spirituous liquors can be obtained here, but a good quality of all kinds of wine, beer, etc. can be had." The credentials of Woodward's manager in the 1870s, Harry Andrews, indicated that he not only shared his employer's temperance views but was also involved with other aspects of social reform and embodied the kind of respectability associated with lifting oneself up by the proverbial bootstraps. For B. E. Lloyd, these qualifications were important enough to relate to readers of his guidebook. "Fifteen years ago," he explained in 1876, "he was a newsboy in the streets of San Francisco. From this occupation he drifted into a position in the *Alta California's* office, and four years later became manager of the Pacific Hygienan Home, where he remained three years, and in the meantime edited and published the *Pacific Hygienist*. He also edited the *Temperance Mirror* and the *Pacific Skate Roll*."[36]

In addition to refraining from the consumption of intoxicating spirits, patrons had to abide by a few other rules and regulations. The *Illustrated Guide and Catalogue* explained, "On entering from Mission street. . . . To the right and left of him, at no matter what season of the year, he will find a beautiful growth of green grass, plants, flowers, and trees. Before going further he should bear in mind the following injunctions: *Do not Smoke in the Buildings! Do not pick the Flowers! Do not tease the Animals.*" Woodward established these rules and regulations as part of his effort to create the well-ordered place of amusement that the *Illustrated Guide and Catalogue* for 1879 described. Perhaps he would not have needed these strictures had visitors been better behaved. But promotional material would surely have made those inclined to mischief feel in the minority as well as the possible targets of vigilante justice. "As long as the gardens exist no deaths by accident, no fire, or disturbances of any kind have occurred on the grounds; . . . the visitors protect the property as if it were their own. . . . None of the shrubbery or flowers are allowed by them to be broken off or anything defaced, and none of the animals molested. . . . every citizen looks to this institution with pride and pleasure." As a result, with regard to the safety of youngsters visiting the resort, readers were assured that, "Nothing is left undone to guard against accidents; no chance is left for a child to get hurt. Parents have become so assured of it, they bring their children and leave them in the gardens for the day without any protectors."[37]

If patronage is any indication, large numbers of San Franciscans responded positively to the ordered paradise created at Woodward's Gardens. While the record is silent with regard to patrons of color, it is clear that the resort was a cross-class favorite. As F. L. McKenney explained is his 1913 article for the *Chronicle*, "How large a place Woodward's Gardens . . . occupied in the old life of the city is graphically shown in many accounts of picnics and celebrations held there. May day, Fourth of July, the Fourteenth of July, and, in fact, all big holidays, the reception to General Grant in 1879, and other notables were all staged at the gardens."[38] Yet although San Franciscans maintained their devotion to Woodward's Gardens throughout most of 1880s, in the later years of that decade its popularity began to diminish and it was virtually defunct in the years before it closed its doors in 1893. After Robert Woodward's death in 1879, his heirs failed to maintain the property and it fell into an increasingly unappealing state of disrepair. By 1896, the same crowd that patronized Woodward's Gardens would likely be found at Sutro Baths, an elaborate three-acre complex opened that year on the edge of the Pacific featuring fresh and salt water swimming pools set at varying temperatures along with diving boards, slides, and trapezes. Sutro Baths' promotion of youthful athleticism and physicality stood in contrast to Woodward's Gardens culture of serene picnicking. The former offered a physical corrective to urban ills that appealed to a new ideal of strenuous masculinity and also tapped into changing notions of womanhood that had begun to embrace exercise, the outdoors, and education. The latter held to the restorative power of a pastoral place that fit more with the gendered ideals that had made the middle-class home and the domestic arrangements that it contained sacrosanct. Yet while each was the product of a different historical moment, both were organized around the desire to perpetuate uplift and wholesomeness in the face of the moral corrosion of city life. Both establishments also shared a penchant for a style of eclecticism that, by the time Sutro Baths opened, was falling out of favor. Although the pools served as the primary attraction, Sutro Baths offered the same hodge-podge of educational amusements as Woodward's Gardens in its natural history exhibits, art galleries, and stage shows. Nationally, the trend was toward museum collections constructed around a much narrower definition of what constituted art and museums themselves being relegated to the sacralized realm of high culture offering only carefully controlled access to the hoi polloi. San Francisco's first bona fide art museum, the de Young, opened in Golden Gate Park just after the 1894 Midwinter Fair in what had been that extravaganza's Fine Arts Building. While the fact that Woodward's Gardens belonged to an older style of amusement may have contributed somewhat to its decreasing popularity, without the vision and energy of Robert Woodward it may also have simply run the course of its commercial viability. Woodward's Gardens had served the city well and its social message still had enough relevance at the turn of the century that it had been picked up, tweaked, and outfitted by Sutro in snazzier packaging for a new generation of San Francisco moderns.[39]

In 1913, another of San Francisco's places of amusement that had grown to prominence in the 1860s closed its doors. For over fifty years, Dr. Louis Jordan's Pacific Museum of Anatomy and Science had published pamphlets, offered lectures as well as medical treatment, and exhibited the human body—both pure, uncorrupted bodies and bodies ravaged by vice—for the purpose of turning men away from dissolute living and the evils of masturbation. On a continuum of respectability it held a position somewhere in between the viciousness of the Barbary Coast and the virtue of Woodward's Gardens. While it had always existed on the fringes of legitimacy because of the way it played on sexual curiosity and the promise of explicit exhibits and discussion, it also promoted itself as a didactic moral and scientific corrective to the excesses of the Barbary Coast. Many of the city's guidebooks advertised and endorsed the museum alongside entirely respectable places like Woodward's Gardens.[40] Yet its advertisements, in addition to appearing in numerous mainstream newspapers, also regularly appeared in the *California Police Gazette* since it targeted patrons of the Barbary Coast as its potential clientele. Although these often displayed the sexually charged heading— "For Gentlemen Only—Visit Nature Unveiled"—framed by two small skeletons, they also featured promotional text that claimed that Jordan ought to be "considered a public benefactor" because of how his museum taught the young "temperance in all things" and warned them "to beware of vice and lead a life of virtue."[41]

The climate that tolerated such ambiguity came to an end in 1913 when Jordan's Museum became a target of the State Medical Board's fight against "fake specialists and medical museums." This was not the first time allegations of quackery had been leveled against the Pacific Museum. In 1874, Henry Gibbons, the editor of the *Pacific Medical and Scientific Journal*, published an article denouncing Jordan, his practices, and his establishment. But the State Medical Board had the power to do more than just rail against Jordan. It successfully charged the museum's proprietor—initially identified as Gideon M. Freeman and later as Paul Oesting—with running a museum that "duped and robbed" patrons. According to expert testimony from two Stanford University doctors, it featured exhibits that were "mislabeled or . . . exaggerated to inspire fear among the visitors and get them to patronize the quacks who operated a medical department in connection with the institution." In the State Medical Board's opinion, the Pacific Museum was a "menace to clean living, health, decency and public morals." Since it was "the only 'anatomical museum' still in operation, being protected by a license," the board took the position that it was time to revoke the museum's license and petitioned the court accordingly.[42]

The attorney for the Medical Board marshaled what the *Examiner* called "nearly a score of victims of the quacks" including "James Holland, 17 years old, an orphan and a schoolboy." Holland's story was tailor-made for their case. Having recently arrived in the city from Sonoma, "where he had saved $50 earned at hard labor to pay for his education," Holland testified that "he made a casual visit to the Jordan Museum and was caught at the door by the outside man and advised to see a 'doctor.'" In the course of examining him, the "'doctor' who proved to be a man called Gleason" who had since fled to Spokane "asked the boy how much money he had." Upon learning that Holland had $45, Gleason demanded $35 for the treatment, including some medicine, which Holland by this time believed he required. Later, Holland paid $25 in advance for an operation. After deciding not to have the procedure performed, he tried to get his money back "but was handled roughly, and at last told that 'the old doctor had gone on a vacation.'" Holland "had since discovered there was nothing wrong with him" and claimed "that he had been frightened by the quacks from the first." Testimony such as Holland's resulted in stiff punishment for Paul Oesting. Despite "pleas of reform and ill health," a year and a half later he was sentenced "to serve one year in the Alameda County Jail and pay a fine of $500." According to the press coverage in the *Examiner*, the "defendant collapsed as he left the court room."[43]

By the time of the Pacific Museum's closure in 1913, it was likely that, given typical life expectancies, a Dr. Jordan no longer existed. Yet even in 1914 and 1915 a listing for "L. Jordan, Inc. Physicians" could be found in the city directory, an indication that Jordan's agents continued to practice their form of medicine, using his name recognition, despite the museum's demise. In fact, by that time, Dr. Jordan had long maintained an international reputation that made his name a nineteenth-century brand synonymous with salacious exhibits and the treatment of sexual maladies. "Jordan" was attached to a veritable chain of museums with similar philosophies, exhibits, and publications that flourished in London, New York, Philadelphia, Boston, Melbourne, Boston, and New Orleans, as well as in San Francisco. And there were almost as many Jordans as there were museums: Robert Jacob Jordan, Henry J. Jordan, Philip J. Jordan, R. J. Jordain, Luis J. Jordan, and Louis J. Jordan. Their seemingly interchangeable identities and questionable medical degrees baffled contemporaries and continue to confuse historians. Robert Jacob and Henry Jacob may have been cousins, Henry and Louis may have been brothers, some names may have been aliases for the same man, and Louis Jordan may have been an alias of Louis Kahn, the proprietor of Kahn's Museum of Anatomy in New York City. Whatever their relationship and however many Jordans there actually were, charges of quackery routinely dogged them all and sometimes closed their establishments down. But whether out of the strength of their convictions or the remunerative nature of their cause, their tendency was to persevere in the face of such adversity.[44]

E. Graeme Robertson, writing in the 1950s, characterized what resulted from the Jordans' various establishments as "an international vice racket." Perhaps. But it seems that even if some patients felt like victims and came to the conclusion that the treatments offered were a sham, others believed that they were helped by the remedies a particular Dr. Jordan, or one of his associates, prescribed. Clearly the Jordans played on prevailing fears about sexual disease and dysfunction. The popularity of their museums and publications suggest the rampant nature of insecurities about sexual performance and concerns about the possible damage that could result from disease or masturbation. Many of the young men, and sometimes young women, who took sexual risks in the context of the freedom of the big cities in which the Jordans plied their trade wanted reassurance that no permanent harm would result from their transgressions. They also sought, on a more basic level, sexual knowledge. While the quality of medical treatment may have been questionable, the understanding of sexuality put forward in the museums' largely interchangeable catalogues and Dr. Louis Jordan's widely circulated tract, *The Philosophy of Marriage*, was at the progressive end of what was available in the context of prevailing thought and tended to generate information that was more helpful than harmful.

As a result, at the same time that the Jordans created museums filled with potentially titillating images that bespoke a variety of sexual practices, they also—through the philosophy of sexuality embodied by their museums and popularized in their publications—charted a path of reintegration into normative, heterosexual marital sexuality for the diseased or deviant. In doing so, they created cultural institutions that simultaneously expanded the bounds of sexuality, contained deviant practices, and supported dominant normative arrangements. Yet, in San Francisco, despite the Pacific Museum's promotion of marriage, stable families, and sexual moderation—as well its ability to remain salient enough to garner patronage to stay in business for fifty years—the establishment ultimately found itself caught in the crossfire of the growing professionalization of medicine, a powerful local antiprostitution crusade, and the continued mainstream resistance to openness about the subject of sex.

The various Jordan museums were fixtures of nineteenth-century cities with growing and fluid populations. San Francisco, in terms of its geographic isolation and disproportionate numbers of young, unattached men, had typical urban social problems—but on an amplified scale. In addition to establishing venues in London and the major cities along the eastern seaboard, the Jordans were smart to see a market for their museums in rough-and-tumble frontier port cities like San Francisco, Melbourne, and New Orleans. Yet while in Melbourne charges of quackery and a failed libel suit to reclaim his reputation sent H. J. Jordan running by the early 1870s, the L. J. Jordan museum in San Francisco was one of the most enduring even though it was known for featuring some of the most over-the-top exhibits of all the Jordan venues. In San Francisco, the same young men, unmoored from family and lured to the sex for sale on the Barbary Coast, came to Jordan for repair. As Don Hugo explained in his *California Police Gazette* feature on "The Demi-Monde of San Francisco," he had it "from the best medical authority, from physicians who make the treatment of secret diseases a specialty, that seven-eighths of the number of cases" that came "under their treatment" were "engendered by communication with Chinese prostitutes and . . . equally degraded Spanish and white women." In this sense, the Pacific Museum of Anatomy and Science functioned as a restorative space—not unlike Woodward's Gardens and other parks, rural retreats, and playgrounds that city planners across the nation advocated at this time. But the morally uplifting qualities offered by such pastoral settings were more feminized and domestic than the thoroughly urban ills associated with sporting culture's embrace of an unfettered male sexuality that Jordan sought to assuage.[45]

Throughout its existence, Jordan's Pacific Museum was not only advertised widely but it was also prominently located on three of the city's main thoroughfares—streets that many San Franciscans traversed regularly. That it was not hidden away on a back alley or in the vice district meant that residents would not only be accustomed to regularly seeing the venue but also that people entering and exiting it could also be easily seen by passersby. Until the mid-1870s, the museum occupied the Eureka Theater building, in the heart of the shopping and commercial district, at 318 Montgomery Street, between California and Pine. In 1876, the museum's publications announced that the establishment had "removed to Kearny Street" between Bush and Sutter—essentially around the corner. By 1882, it had moved to 751 Market Street—still centrally located in an area that was fast becoming a part of the city's burgeoning downtown. Louis Jordan also kept an office for private consultations at 211 Geary Street, between Stockton and Powell, in proximity to both the Market and Montgomery Street venues but also, like the locations of all his museums, not too far from the Barbary Coast. He identified himself with medical qualifications that have only been confirmed for Robert J. Jordan as a "member of the Royal College of Surgeons, London; Doctor of Medicine, Edinburgh, and Demonstrator of Anatomy and Surgery" with a specialty in "the anatomy, physiology and pathology of the generative organs" and "sexual disability." An ad in the 1882 edition of the *Guidebook and Street Manual of San Francisco* that featured a full page ad for "Dr. Jordon & Co." attributed to him and his fellows the discovery of "a Great Remedy for Painful Itchings, Boils and . . . Pimples on the Face, etc., Ulcers, Cramps, Disease of the Skin, Nose, Mouth, Scalp, and Loss of Hair, Lumps and Painful Swellings of Glands, Bad Dreams, Loss of Sleep and Power." A book would be sent to those interested in obtaining more information "on Receipt of 25 cents."[46]

An idea of what visitors encountered at the Pacific Museum of Anatomy and Science can be gleaned from an illustration of its interior featured in its publications. Along the walls hung huge pictures of human skeletons as well as nude, male bodies in various poses. In cases distributed around the sides of the room, Jordan exhibited actual bodies or their parts—sometimes these were the real thing suspended in a preservative solution; sometimes they were models that Jordan had acquired or made. Running down the center of the room, visitors encountered a collection of bodies lying in a long row, two to three across, displayed on slabs or in casket-like boxes. Depicted were two skeletons, two small mummified beings lying side by side, one woman's body naked at least to the waist, and the body of another woman, naked, and surgically cut open on the thigh and in the abdominal region so as to display its interior physiology. At the back of the room, in front of the windows, stood a podium from which Jordan—or one of his associates—delivered an "instructive lecture" nightly at eight o'clock. It was flanked by two models of the nude female form placed on pedestals, which gave them a statuary effect. In a half circle behind the podium about a dozen specimens were contained by glass domes. Around the room, approximately fifteen male patrons intently peered into the cases or gazed up at the walls (see figure 16).[47]

Unlike the majority of other medical experts who penned sexual advice literature, Louis Jordan—in the form of his Pacific Museum of Anatomy and Science—created a venue that was "open daily from 9 a.m. to 10 p.m., Sundays 5 till 8 p.m." and was filled with exhibits that literally embodied his ideas. Jordan's museum did its didactic work through the display and juxtaposition of oppositional forms. While most of its exhibits were of the human body and its various parts, it featured both healthy bodies and vice-ridden bodies as well as some bodies that were simply deemed freakish. The idea seemed to be that the act of seeing the price of vice, in a scientific and sanitized setting, would be enough—along with some basic sexual education—to change the ways of the reprobate. In the introduction to his *Handbook and Descriptive Catalogue*, which served as a guide to visitors by explaining the museum's holdings and also served as a platform for his sexual philosophy, Jordan informed his patrons that "the following magnificent collection . . . is designed to afford the public an opportunity of acquainting themselves how they live, move, and have their being." The phrase "have their being" was a euphemism for reproductive processes. "The Pacific Museum of Anatomy and Science," he explained, was "intended to promote the knowledge and morality of the general

Figure 16. Inside the Pacific Museum of Anatomy and Science. Dr. Louis Jordan and his associates designed this museum to turn young men away from dissolute living and the evils of masturbation. (Bancroft Library, University of California, Berkeley)

public—to act as a beacon to the young, who, ignorant of the dangers attending upon many of their thoughtless actions, are too prone, in their youthful impetuosity, to cultivate tastes and habits injurious and prejudicial at all times." Whether because Jordan knew that he was pushing at the boundaries of respectability and felt it necessary to reassure patrons of his propriety or whether he was actually signaling to those interested in the salacious that his museum was where they would find it, the introduction to his handbook explained that he had taken the "greatest care . . . in the arrangement of the collection to exclude anything calculated to shock." And probably because of past charges of quackery he also made assurances that "every model in the vast collection has been prepared with the most rigid adherence to fidelity and truth in all the complicated and anatomical details."[48]

At its core, Jordan's museum expressed his belief that one could not "tamper with the laws of Nature with impunity." As he explained, just "as the virtuous and temperate man is endowed with Nature's choicest blessings," a man of "loose and immoral habits" would incur nature's displeasure as manifest in "the various infirmities" that followed from "diverging from the paths of rectitude and virtue." In Jordan's schema, while redemption was possible, there were high costs if deviance from human sexuality's natural order—heterosexuality channeled into the institution of marriage—was left unchecked. *The Handbook and Descriptive Catalogue* organized and individually numbered his wide-ranging array of specimens into three broad categories: "A Series of Elegant and Elaborate Natural Preparations of the Human Species," "Botanical and Floral Anatomy," and the "Pathological Room." However, this schema was adhered to only loosely. For example, in the first section, descriptions of models of the anatomy of the human eye were places alongside those of the hands and feet of a woman who had an extra finger on each of the former and eight toes on each of the latter. These were not far from "a series of valuable and rare natural Foetal preparations illustrating almost every form of malformation, incomplete development, and monstrosity"—which the *Catalogue* attributed to the "vicious habits or practices" of the parents.[49]

Jordan's Pathological Room—with its epigraph "The wages of Sin is Death"—expanded on this theme. Here the majority of the 104 specimens consisted of physical maladies attributed to masturbation or venereal disease. While some of the exhibits in this section featured rather mundane body parts—arms, eyes, legs, hands—others displayed diseased genitalia. This aspect of Jordan's museum certainly did not contribute to its reputation as a respectable resort. Item 919, for example, was labeled, "Model, showing the introduction of the Speculum in the vagina, thus detecting chancres near the mouth of the womb." Item 926 was described as "Showing Penis, Bladder, etc., with testicle decayed, from self-abuse." Item 960 was the embodiment of Jordan's epigram. It featured a model of the "Appearance of the Face, after death, from self-abuse."[50]

Jordan had designed the Pacific Museum of Anatomy and Science in order to profitably proselytize his views on sexual health. While already fairly explicit in the museum's catalogue, he delineated his ideas even more forcefully in his 1865 tract, *The Philosophy of Marriage*. Following the medical orthodoxy of the time, Jordan identified masturbation with disease, misunderstood the female reproductive system, and viewed a carefully constructed and controlled heterosexuality ultimately channeled into marriage as the natural foundation of a stable social order. But he deviated from this typical path in that he endorsed the frank and open discussion of intimate matters and believed that sex and sexual desires, when appropriately exercised in a marital union, were integral to overall health. Despite his overblown claims of being the sole publisher of accessible sexual advice literature, such literature flourished during the nineteenth century. In part, this was because the reorganization of society that came with the transition from an agrarian way of life to an urban and industrial one affected the way people understood sexuality, as well as where they turned for sexual advice. Increasingly, a new breed of medical professionals came to fill the regulatory role once held by parents, the church, and the local community.[51]

Like Jordan, many writers of sexual advice literature stressed the physical and mental risks of uncontrolled masturbation. Often influenced by the idea that the body constituted a closed energy system, whose resources were depleted by each use, these authors took the position that excessive sexual indulgence could endanger one's health.[52] During the nineteenth century, the theory that masturbation caused disease and insanity supplanted older views that had labeled it as a taboo simply because of its nonprocreative nature. Benjamin Rush in the 1810s, Sylvester Graham and Reverend John Todd in the 1830s, and John Kellogg in the late nineteenth century were just a few of the new class of medical experts who adopted the position that masturbation posed a danger to physical and mental health and published advice tracts that advocated sexual self-control. In terms of his views on the importance of marital sexuality, the path of moderation that Jordan advocated placed him on the permissive side of the continuum. He was worlds away from the extreme positions of some writers—like Graham, Todd, and Kellogg—who regarded all sexual pleasure as potentially dangerous. He was actually leaning toward the view of marital sexuality that would gain increasing popularity in the later nineteenth century that held that sexuality was an important means of enhancing the spiritual connection between a husband and wife.[53]

The Philosophy of Marriage began with a detailed discussion of the structure and function of the male and female "generative organs" to remedy what Jordan believed to be a general lack of knowledge about basic biological functions. He explained that while "the philosophy of marriage, in its widest sense, would doubtless include the social, moral, mental, physical and religious aspects of the bond" since "the physical" was "the basis of the rest"—this justified his emphasis. After providing his readers with a basic sexual education, Jordan revealed both the high esteem in which he held the institution of marriage and his theories about the source of marital discord. He told his readers, the "end and purpose of marriage is high and holy, the institution itself

heaven appointed, and its vows and obligations the most sacred and binding."
However, Jordan also recognized that reality often fell short of this abstract
ideal. "In its practical every-day conditions," he qualified, "misery and woe
but too frequently follow in its footsteps; wretchedness is often its near companion, and distress and grief occasionally cling to it as though they formed a
part of its nature." For Jordan, a physician specializing in "the diseases of organs having a more important relation to this contract than any others," the
reason for these problems was not "difficult to divine"—it was sex.[54]

A good marital sex life, Jordan argued, was integral to the overall health of
the husband, the wife, their relationship, and the offspring resulting from the
union. In a place like nineteenth-century San Francisco, where longstanding
skewed sex ratios had made many view the formation of stable family units—
essential to the establishment of a well-ordered society—with heightened ur-
gency, this kind of message would have had a wide, interested audience. "To
have healthy offspring," Jordan explained, it was "necessary that the bodily
frame should have full vigor, and should be in that condition that sexual intercourse should be a necessity for health, that its performance should so far
from leaving a weakening or exhaustive feeling, impart a sense of lightness
and relief, of a kind of full health comparable to that which . . . we enjoy after
indulging in the luxury of a bath." His ideas also clearly had a eugenic
thrust—evidence that he had no problem helping nature along to further particular social ends. He suggested to his readers that they scrutinize potential
mates carefully. "Those who contemplate matrimony," Jordan advised,
"should also remember that diseases and defects of all kinds are hereditary."
While he believed that marital sexuality was important, he also cautioned
against too much of a good thing, recommending a path of moderation and
self-control that involved engaging in conjugal duties about twice a week.[55]

In Jordan's schema, sexual health was precarious. It was easily and often
unknowingly endangered—even among the "honest, temperate and virtuous." On one hand, this precariousness opened the door to his formula for redemption and reintegration. On the other, it necessitated those contemplat-
ing marriage to be examined—ostensibly by a specialist like himself—to make
sure that no sexual dysfunction was present. He explained—perhaps in the
process assuaging the anxieties of potential new patients—that "one of the
most numerous of the classes of patients" who consulted him were those who
"unsuspective of their disability, have contracted matrimony, and have afterwards found that they could neither enjoy the pleasures of the nuptial couch,

nor secure the frutification which is its greatest glory." Most often, according to Jordan, the sources of such sexual problems could be found in the physical and psychological maladies attributed to masturbation and "promiscuous sexual intercourse." Although he advocated early and thorough treatment of sexually transmitted diseases such as syphilis and gonorrhea, Jordan was most concerned about the effects of masturbation, which he believed caused "most of the functional disorders of the generative organs" and "the great prevalence of sexual debility." He laid a vast array of physical and psychological ailments at the feet of self-abuse that ranged from "melancholy and dejected appearance" to "loss of nervous power," impotence, or even death. According to Jordan, the diseases arising from "this habit" were "neither few nor small."[56]

Jordan packed *The Philosophy of Marriage* with illustrative cases of sexual disease and dysfunction that he had successfully cured as well as stories of patients who, through his methods, had found sexual redemption and reintegration. Since he treated numerous patients via correspondence, he had a store of letters from which to draw. All of the published cases involved the treatment of men in their twenties. In each, any clues that might reveal "the individuality of the parties themselves had been carefully eliminated." Some were "the verbatim statements of the patients themselves" while other letters were paraphrased by Jordan.[57]

While he never disclosed the nature of his remedies, the example of one such letter illuminates the kinds of entreaties he received, the range of symptoms attributed to masturbation, and Jordan's belief in the need for open and honest sexual education. Case 987—he assigned numbers to all of his cases—told the story of a young man who had come to the conclusion as a teenager that masturbation "was a positive good, since it was a means to him of avoiding the sin of fornication." Within about two years, however, "he began to look pale and emaciated, his appetite fell off, he experienced severe pain in the back part of the head, and in the testes and loins, seminal emissions frequently occurred, and he was fast becoming a shadow of his former self." The "family medical man" diagnosed "general debility" and recommended a "change of air and tonic medicines." However, because "the root of the disease had escaped attention," the patient "experienced no relief," and "at length the young man began to notice a great change in his genital organs." According to Jordan's presentation, "It was whilst in this state, that in the course of his reading he came across the 'Confessions of Jean Jacques Rousseau,' which completely opened his eyes, and he now saw clearly the nature of the horrible vice he had for so many years indulged in." Jordan quoted the young man as writing, "Oh, that my father, or some one else, had conversed with me on matters of this kind. . . . it would have prevented all this suffering. But no: all such subjects were prohibited from being mentioned."[58]

Jordan, in fact, found the social silence around sexual issues so dangerous that he devoted an entire chapter of *The Philosophy of Marriage* to what he termed "false delicacy." He took this position because of his beliefs about the way sexual problems interfered with normative marital relations. Jordan chastised the public for its reticence, urging sufferers of sexual dysfunction to "emancipate themselves" by seeking treatment. He also forcefully admonished the medical profession for taking less than seriously the study of "sexual physiology." Not only were "the sufferers themselves ignorant," Jordan explained, "but those who should have been able to instruct and relieve them" were "scarcely less devoid of the knowledge essential for that purpose." Jordan decried the fact that because false delicacy had become such a powerful prejudice that "men of some eminence . . . have actually propounded the doctrine, that because the worst, most wide-spread, and most ruinous of human diseases is for the most part the result of a vice, it should not be investigated and discussed and relieved, like other diseases."[59] He also railed against the tendency of available published work to be either too scientific for a wide audience or "the worse than ignorant lucubrations of the charlatan, who fattens upon the fears which he creates by his misrepresentations."

Ironically, this characterization of a charlatan turned out to be precisely the brush with which the State Medical Board painted Jordan and his associates in 1913. Yet accepting this assessment at face value is far too simple. When the California State Medical Society created the State Medical Board in 1876, it formed an agency designed to dispense medical discipline from within the profession's ranks. By 1913, the board symbolized both medicine's growing professionalization and the increasingly narrow range of practitioners it deemed could legitimately claim medical expertise. That year, the board dismantled its system of maintaining representatives from different schools of medicine—allopathic, homeopathic, osteopathic, and naturopathic—in favor of a board comprised solely of allopathic practitioners. This move followed recent national recommendations by the American Medical Association to eliminate all nonallopathic—what it considered to be nonscientific—schools of medicine. Under that directive, the board used its power to put many nonallopathic practitioners out of business by declaring them quacks and deploying a variety of disciplinary measures, including the revocation of licenses. It was within this context that the board went after the Pacific Museum.[60]

Not only were the medical credentials and practices of Jordan and his associates suspect, but Jordan's writings also openly and loudly critiqued the medical establishment's approach to sexual maladies. In 1913, Jordan's concerns about "false delicacy," initially written in the 1860s, still had relevance. Although reformers involved in efforts to change the nature of prostitution and stamp out venereal disease advocated greater frankness in the discussion of sexual matters as a preventative measure, some mainstream gynecologists still took the stance that speaking about venereal disease in public was not only unseemly but vicious. Adherents to this attitude also existed among the general public. In 1906, when the *Ladies Home Journal* published a series of articles on venereal disease, it lost seventy-five thousand subscribers.[61]

The closing of Jordan's museum not only coincided with a narrowing of the way legitimate medical practitioners were defined and an ongoing disinclination to openly discuss sexuality, but also with a powerful antiprostitution campaign that, while national in scope, had particularly serious implications for San Francisco. This effort, which changed prostitution from a necessary evil to be tolerated to a social evil to be eradicated, served as a staging ground for the kinds of changes underway in the practice of medicine and evinced the ways sexuality was emerging as a new kind of arena of state regulation and control.[62] It was marked by the sort of professionalization—and in this case medicalization—of reform that was a hallmark of many Progressive era causes. 1913, in addition to being the year of the Medical Board's reorganization and the demise of Jordan's museum, was also the year of the state legislature's passage of the Red Light Abatement Act and the opening of a Municipal Clinic in San Francisco to screen prostitutes for venereal disease. The Red Light Abatement Act targeted the owners of property in which illicit activities occurred. With the goal of eliminating prostitution, its thrust was decidedly different from the tightening regulation that had begun in the 1890s and the segregated red-light district that had been established in 1909.[63] Spearheaded by a coalition of newly enfranchised, reform-minded club-women, religious leaders, and some civic groups, the city's political elite less than wholeheartedly endorsed the measure. In fact, eleven of the twelve San Francisco legislators voted against it.[64] Nevertheless, in succeeding years, officials enforced the act stringently enough to deliver a truly crushing blow to the Barbary Coast's sexual commerce for the first time in San Francisco's history—inadvertently increasing the prevalence of streetwalkers in other parts of the city.[65] Although the Municipal Clinic was only in existence for six months, its establishment signaled the way anti-prostitution zeal dovetailed with new kinds of medical expertise and how such a union was turning what were once regarded as moral problems into public health concerns.[66]

Jordan's museum and publications clearly had a reform agenda of their own. They sought to cure the sexual deviant—whether a masturbator, a fornicator, or someone who had contracted a venereal disease—and redirect him into heterosexual marriage. Yet the Jordan empire was no match for the reformers who sought to exert control over it. Jordan saw people with sexual problems as simply derailed and wanted to get them back on the right track. Through his various treatments, he offered a return route to normalcy for those who had strayed. In many respects, he was a product of the school of thought that regarded prostitution and related sexual transgressions as necessary evils to be tolerated—at least in the short run. While he did not advocate the use of prostitutes, he also did not spend much time condemning them. That was simply not his crusade. By providing remedies for sexual maladies, he lowered the personal risks of the behavior that caused them, rather than trying to stop those practices entirely. Yet by the early twentieth century, as campaigns to wipe out prostitution were gaining favor, Jordan's brand of toleration was becoming increasingly passé. In the wake of Progressive era crusades, in a relatively short span of time, crackdowns on vice had diminished the Pacific Museum's potential clientele, those suffering from disease were directed to a new clinic for treatment, and the museum's proprietors were being charged with quackery and fraud. Instead of representing part of the solution, Jordan's museum was, by 1913, part of the problem.

The Pacific Museum's prosecution by the State Medical Board—preceded by decades of continual operation—pointed to deep changes in the social climate of the city that had occurred between the mid-1860s and 1913. Some of these changes were part of sweeping national trends. But they also had a distinct meaning in the local context of a very young city that, over the course of those years, had been transformed from a frontier boomtown into a major metropolis. When Jordan's museum emerged on the scene in the mid-1860s the city, with a population that would grow from 50,000 to 100,000 during that decade, was still shaking off the effects of the gold rush that had catapulted it into being. During these years, the Pacific Museum of Anatomy and Science's promotion of marriage, stable families, and sexual moderation furthered desirable forms of social order. Yet by the early decades of the twentieth century, San Francisco had a population exceeding 300,000 inhabitants, and a society organized along the lines of nationally dominant hierarchies had been firmly established. By then the museum's mix of titillation, moral treatises, and questionable medical practices had lost its appeal to authorities. Although the social problems that Jordan addressed remained, the solutions he offered seemed not only outdated but also more harmful than helpful in light of the possibilities offered by new, more professionally oriented regulatory regimes bolstered by an increasingly powerful state apparatus that no longer needed to rely on places like the Pacific Museum to compensate for its limited reach.

CHAPTER THREE

Making Race in the City:
Chinatown's Tourist Terrain

On May 18, 1886, a teenage girl identified only as E.G.H. arrived in San Francisco, one of many destinations on her trip through the West—perhaps with a Raymond Excursion Party—that had begun in Boston and included stops in Chicago, Kansas City, Santa Fe, Albuquerque, Los Angeles, Yosemite, and Mariposa. That day, from her "wonderful" accommodations at the city's luxurious Palace Hotel, she wrote to her "dear" Jay: "I am looking forward to my visit to Chinatown, where we are hoping to go in a day or two." Over the course of the next two weeks, E.G.H. made at least three trips into Chinatown, telling one recipient of her letters that she had "given as much time as possible to Chinatown" and was "fairly infatuated with the place."[1]

E.G.H.'s first foray into the neighborhood took place on her second evening in the city when she joined a "large party . . . made up to visit Chinatown." Upon reaching a certain corner the group was "suddenly joined by a Chinaman" named Chin Jun who—whether by accident or design—became their guide. Wearing the "costume of his country," including "a long pigtail hanging almost to his heels, with red silk braided in his hair," Chin Jun led this group of middle-class white American tourists "up a dark alley way to a Joss House," to the Chinese theater where they watched part of a play from seats in the gallery, and to a Chinese restaurant where they were "served with tea and sweetmeats, in true Celestial style." Although E.G.H. and her group "especially wanted" to see an opium den, Chin Jun refused, telling the group that it was simply too large. He spoke English "reasonably well," met their many questions with "a lovely smile," shared tea with E.G.H., and wrote his name for her in both English and Chinese as a souvenir. When Chin Jun was not leading white tourists around Chinatown, he worked as a clerk in a shop selling "fancy articles and curios" attractive to tourists. E.G.H. would encounter him again in this context and "make splendid bargains with him." In a letter relating her first Chinatown visit she declared, "I have lost my heart to Chin Jun."[2]

On her second visit, E.G.H was accompanied by Mrs. Law, a resident of the city whom she had been introduced to and who assured her that "she need not be afraid to go through Chinatown with her alone." Mrs. Law both knew the area and frequented it because of her association with friends doing missionary work in the neighborhood. Since E.G.H. was "quite ready to make any number of visits" to what she saw as a "curious and interesting place," she did not hesitate to accept Mrs. Law's offer and the two set off together. On their way they "passed through several dark and dirty alley ways, where men swarmed and stared," and as they traversed Chinatown's streets they "stopped to look at the curious things displayed in the markets." E.G.H. reflected that "as you walk through the streets of Chinatown you hardly realize yourself in America." During their excursion, E.G.H. paid another visit to a joss house where she learned more about Chinese religious practices than she had from Chin Jun, saw a woman with bound feet, heard tales of hidden gambling dens that made police raids so difficult, and went shopping—stopping at Chin Jun's store to purchase two Chinese musical instruments. Although E.G.H. noted that she "enjoyed this visit very much" she also indicated that she would "not be satisfied" until she had been to the opium dens.[3]

A few days later, E.G.H and four others "hired a detective" to take them "through Chinatown, and to the opium dens." Their guide took them "through streets and alley ways" and "down, down, along passageways, two feet wide, down another flight of stairs, along a narrow alley with doors opening into rooms not more than six feet square." In some of the rooms they passed they saw opium smokers reclining, in others they saw "Chinamen . . . eating their supper with chopsticks." At each encounter, the tourists nodded and said "Hello." At one point, the guide kicked open a door and led the group into a den "decorated with pictures and flowers" and occupied by "a Chinaman, with his pipe in hand." Although "somewhat under the influence of opium already" he greeted the tourists "pleasantly" and, at their request, provided a demonstration of the process of preparing and smoking opium. The group still desired to see "worse dens" so thanked the smoker and continued on, groping their way "through the filth and smell, upstairs, and then down again." It was not long before their guide forced open another door and the group was faced with a malodorous room crowded with people and animals. This sight prompted E.G.H. to reflect, "What is to be done with these Chinese is certainly a serious question. Forty-three thousand souls living in seven blocks!"[4]

E.G.H.'s account of her visits to Chinatown typified the kinds of tourist encounters that resulted from the fact that the most distinctly bounded ethnic enclave in nineteenth-century San Francisco—a product of virulent discrimination against Chinese immigrants—also functioned as a popular tourist destination for the city's visitors and a local place of amusement for its residents not unlike Woodward's Gardens, the Barbary Coast, or the Pacific Museum of Anatomy and Science. For the growing population of largely male laborers who made Chinatown their home, the neighborhood's community offered a relatively safe haven as well as networks of familiar people, institutions, goods, and services. As E.G.H.'s experience reveals, among the non-Chinese, Chinatown's appeal combined a number of overlapping impulses—the desire to see the exotic; the pull of an encounter with a different culture; the draw of slumming; and the attraction of experiencing, from a safe distance or with a police guide, racially charged urban dangers. This collision of the everyday cultures of an immigrant neighborhood and the tourist impulses of non-Chinese visitors—scripted through the literature of Chinatown tourism and the practices of Chinatown guides—made Chinatown into a cultural frontier that wielded considerable social power. The particular images of Chinatown that nineteenth-century tourists read about, reported upon, often expected to see, and as a result often saw, reflected and shaped the very idea of what "Chinese" meant in San Francisco. As a cultural frontier on which key components of San Francisco's racial order were articulated and solidified, Chinatown worked in tandem with larger legal and political developments, providing an arena where whites and Chinese encountered one another face-to-face and from which many whites came away with what they believed were social truths about this new immigrant group.[5]

Tourist literature's representations racialized the Chinese in terms of their unassimilability, their proclivity toward vice, the risks they posed to public health, and the threat they presented free white labor. These representations dovetailed with the logic of a developing local racial hierarchy that placed the Chinese on the lowest rung as well as with larger policy debates about Chinese immigration.[6] Across class lines, whites positioned the Chinese below

San Francisco's small population of blacks, the group that was typically positioned at the bottom of the racial ladder throughout much of the rest of the nation. As a result, "Chinese" and "white" rather than "black" and "white" emerged as the most potent racial opposites in the city, configuring its most highly charged racial divide. The way this process worked in San Francisco set important precedents for the nation as it was one of the first major American cities to incorporate a large Asian minority population. Moreover, while tourist literature's representations had particular significance within the locality of San Francisco, they also gave images of Chinatown and Chinese immigrants national and international circulation. E.G.H.'s account, for example, was published by a Boston press. Through these images, Chinese immigrants entered the racial imagination even in places where they had not settled and where people may have never actually seen an Asian person. As growing hostility in the West led increasing numbers of Chinese to settle and establish Chinatowns in cities such as New York and Boston, tourist literature generated templates of meaning that framed the way such developments would be received.

E.G.H. captured an incredibly wide range of the experiences available to and sought after by Chinatown tourists. She made sure to visit the four key sites of Chinatown's tourist terrain—restaurants, joss houses, opium dens, and theaters—and also took in some other popular, but nonetheless secondary, sights—women with bound feet, gambling dens, and shops. Like many tourists, her experiences occurred within nineteenth-century America's emergent Orientalism, which promoted a disdain for resident Asians but also a prurient fascination with a limited, largely manufactured, brand of Asian culture. The tension inherent in this kind of thinking about all things Oriental allowed E.G.H. to befriend Chin Jun and delight in Chinese food and wares while maintaining a perspective on Chinatown as utterly alien and believing her sojourn there would not be complete until she saw the Chinese displayed in stereotypically vicious pursuits.[7] Although representations of Chinatown more often than not worked to create a sense of insurmountable distance between Chinese and whites, the very presence of white tourists in Chinatown meant that on this cultural frontier real encounters between the two groups were taking place in ways that sometimes disrupted the dominant story—as the friendship between E.G.H. and Chin Jun attests—and at other times confirmed it. While Chinatown existed as a segregated space set apart from the rest of the city, its visitors and residents constantly negotiated a

Figure 17. White women walking through Chinatown. Chinatown quickly emerged as a curiosity and an organized site of urban tourism for city visitors as well as non-Chinese San Franciscans. (Chinese in California, Bancroft Library, University of California, Berkeley)

complicated dance of white social power and Chinese local knowledge that allowed both the tourist enterprise and the transgression of the racial boundaries that Chinatown represented to occur (see figure 17).

When E.G.H.'s letters were published in 1887, a year after her trip, they joined a rapidly expanding body of literature generated to feed the appetite of a reading public fascinated by San Francisco's Chinese population and eager either to play the armchair tourist or to use writings about Chinatown to make preparations for a visit of their own. Tourism boomed during the second half of the nineteenth century as developments in transportation and communication made travel easier and a middle class emerged flush with the financial resources, leisure time, and inclination to explore America. Organized tours, like the one that steered E.G.H. through the West, responded to this demand

and established itineraries of specific sites such as Chinatown, Yosemite, and Santa Fe—through which tourists came to understand the nation as well as their place in it. Whereas natural wonders and places of historical significance allowed tourists to define who they were and what they were a part of, the various peoples that became part of the tourist terrain—Mormons, Native Americans, Mexicans, and Chinese—were generally displayed and consumed in such a way as to reinforce their difference from and inferiority to the white tourists who gazed upon them. Writings about Chinatown emerged from within this larger context. Their depictions of the Chinese and Chinatown were shaped by the perceptions of various urban adventurers—often led by guides well versed in the tropes of the Chinatown experience—during forays into the neighborhood. In a circular relationship, for many readers—some of whom later became visitors—their perceptions and experiences of this cultural frontier were undoubtedly filtered through the tourist literature they consumed prior to their Chinatown excursion.[8]

The literature of Chinatown tourism constituted part of the urban exploration genre that generated popular and often luridly descriptive guides to nineteenth-century cities usually written from the point of view of a white, typically male spectator who traversed the city and recorded his voyeuristic observations with the kind of detached yet possessive authority that also characterized the consuming gaze of the typical tourist. It intersected stylistically with the reports of social reformers and policy makers; the studies of anthropologists and sociologists; as well as emergent forms of exposé journalism—none of which were averse to doubling as platforms for voicing opinions on pressing social issues. E.G.H.'s detailed descriptions of vice and crowding in Chinatown followed by a pronouncement about the Chinese question, in this context, were hardly unusual.[9]

Chinatown tourist literature took a wide variety of forms. It could be found in small travel guides devoted exclusively to the Chinatown experience, sections about Chinatown in larger guides of the city or state, articles in magazines published nationally as well as in England, local newspaper stories, books about the Chinese in California that included chapters on Chinatown, and reminiscences that recalled Old Chinatown just after the earthquake and fire of 1906. Both women and men authored these writings and both seemed to have been equally comfortable taking on the voice of the tourist gaze in their narrations of the standard tropes of the Chinatown experience. Writers included San Francisco residents who frequented the neighborhood, journalists and tourists, and religious men whose missionary impulses brought them to Chinatown.

While some writers explored Chinatown on their own, many, like E.G.H, relied on guides to protect them from overly dangerous encounters and to provide the kind of experience necessary for writing a piece that would satisfy both their own and their readers' desires for thoroughness and authenticity. Although Chinatown tourists frequently wanted to view an itinerary of predetermined sites, they did not necessarily seek out prepackaged experiences. Wandering through restaurants and joss houses, for example, they often encountered Chinese going about their everyday activities and many of what seemed like the most staged experiences often involved barging in on people and catching them unprepared for the tourist gaze.[10] Hired guides—whether drawn from the ranks of the city's police force, white men who had gone into business for themselves, or Chinese entrepreneurs—facilitated these experiences. They were not only widely available, but some advertised their services and much of the tourist literature encouraged their use.[11] The demand for Chinatown guides was fueled in part by tourist literature's frequent emphasis, often in quite dramatic language, of the risks involved when a tourist attempted to explore Chinatown alone, especially at night. Whether it was truly dangerous, a ploy designed to drum up business, or a by-product of the salaciousness of the urban exploration genre, the discourse was ubiquitous. W. H. Gleadell, in a piece written originally for *Gentleman's Magazine* and republished in the digest *Eclectic Magazine*, characteristically intoned, "Many places there are in this miniature China of San Francisco . . . to which no European has ever been admitted, or, if admitted, he has never survived to return to the world." Gleadell's recent tourist experience did allow him to concede that there were "certain parts" of Chinatown "which, at his own risk, the white man is free to traverse" but insisted that "in no case is it prudent to visit even these without the escort of a properly armed police officer well known on the Chinatown beat." Of salience for women adventurers, tourist literature refrained from casting Chinatown danger in sexualized terms. Characterizations of Chinese men as either objects of white women's desire or as lascivious predators that Chinatown fiction sometimes developed were largely absent from this ostensibly more realistic genre. In general, tourist literature tended to desexualize Chinese men in ways that opened the possibility for white women to hire them as guides and feel safe traversing the neighborhood with them.[12]

While many Chinatown guides were white men—sometimes but not always affiliated with the police—some were local Chinese, like E.G.H.'s guide, Chin Jun. Just as he seemed to have appeared out of nowhere, the product of a chance encounter—unlike white guides, who tended to be arranged by appointment—local writer Will Irwin described being led through Chinatown's legendary labyrinthine passages by a Chinese guide who announced both his presence and his intentions with the statement, "I take you." Another San Francisco resident, guidebook author William Bode, explained this tendency of white tourists to simply stumble upon Chinese guides in a way that suggests that participating in this nascent yet burgeoning tourist economy was a money-making opportunity not lost on local Chinese. He explained that, "Solicitations are made, at every crossing, to guide and conduct you to the various shrines and objects of curiosity, which abound here." Perhaps guiding tourists was lucrative enough to outweigh conforming to the stereotypes of the tourist terrain. Perhaps taking some control of the touring process away from white police allowed Chinese guides to disrupt, rather than reinforce, the racial stereotypes at the heart of tourists' expectations.[13]

For tourists, employing a Chinese guide meant having an experience on Chinatown's cultural frontier that was markedly different from simply wandering through Chinatown and gazing upon its Chinese inhabitants. It required engaging in a relationship with a Chinese person. Such a relationship was financial—the guide was hired to perform a service, it involved communication and conversation, it positioned the guide as the local expert, and it implied a certain amount of trust, given that the guide was leading the tourist into ostensibly dangerous areas. Granted, few tourists developed the kind of fondness for their guide that E.G.H. expressed for Chin Jun, but her experience presented one point on a continuum of possibility. Eleanor B. Caldwell's experience, captured in a piece that circulated in at least two national periodicals in the 1890s, offered another. She related that at the end of a long day touring Chinatown she stood on the balcony of a Chinese restaurant after taking a meal while her guide confided to her party "in a debonair way, and with remarkable English, his views of life and of his own career, the belief that he, 'John Chinaman,' might make a political leader if like Boss Buckley, he but owned a fine trade in the saloon line!" Caldwell scoffed at her guide's ambitions to become a player in local Democratic politics— highlighting in her tone the ridiculousness of such a proposition—and it

Figure 18. Balcony of the Chinese Restaurant, Dupont Street, San Francisco—perhaps like the one on which Eleanor Caldwell conversed with her guide. (I. W. Taber, photographer. Chinese in California, Bancroft Library, University of California, Berkeley)

was possible that her guide was making a joke by claiming for himself a completely absurd goal given the climate created by the Chinese Exclusion Act. Nevertheless, the two engaged in a conversation in which a Chinese man conveyed to a white woman his desire for a civic identity. Not only did this represent a level of discourse considerably beyond that required to explain Chinatown's sites to a party of tourists but it also presented a Chinese man as having aspirations like any other man—even if they were both belittled and denied (see figure 18).[14]

In gathering information for their joint effort of 1898, *Ten Drawings in Chinatown*, Ernest C. Peixotto and Robert Howe Fletcher also employed a Chinese guide. Apparently, despite the fact that both men were San Francisco residents and Peixotto was a well-known illustrator of Chinatown scenes, the two found themselves "making inappropriate inquiries in all sorts of strange places" during their "search through Chinatown for information and bric-a-brac." "It was in this way," they informed their readers, "while asking for silk in a tea store, that we accidentally made the acquaintance of Wong Sue." Wong Sue, one of a number of men in the shop, eventually came to the aid of Peixotto and Fletcher by acting as a translator for the two, who were struggling to communicate with the Chinese shopkeeper in English. Despite Wong Sue's initial hesitance, Fletcher recorded that, "His aid once having been tendered he proved very obliging and after explaining to us the nature of the shop we were in, volunteered to lead us to another where we could procure what we desired." The two white men, self-described as "Author and Artist," then proceeded to explain their purpose to Wong Sue. "We told him how Chinatown and the Chinese interested us and how odd and amusing many of their customs seemed to us . . . that we proposed to tell what was bad as well as good." Wong Sue listened silently, and then said: "I think maybe you tell the truth, that will be very good." So, Peixotto and Fletcher "started out to find the artistic truth of Chinatown under the guidance of the wise Wong Sue."[15]

From the start, Wong Sue's very willingness to serve as their guide—however initially reluctant he may have been—flew in the face of Peixotto and Fletcher's notions of the "Chinese character." "As a rule," they informed their readers, "the inhabitants of Chinatown are reserved, secretive, irresponsive and impenetrable in the presence of strangers. Each seems to have erected a little Chinese wall around his personality." But Peixotto and Fletcher did not see this reticence as entirely out of line given "the surveillance under which they live, the constant apprehension that the friendly stranger may at any moment throw open his coat and display a silver star, that dreaded emblem of law totally at variance with all their traditions and whose workings they do not comprehend." While dealing with an often hostile and corrupt police presence was an unfortunate fact of life in Chinatown, the notion that the Chinese in Chinatown were so bound to foreign tradition that they were unable to understand the procedures of American law enforcement was shown to be facetious when Wong Sue revealed a previously hidden facet of his identity. During their travels in Chinatown, Peixotto and Fletcher related to their readers that they "almost invariably enjoyed the distinction of being taken for country detectives." They knew that "every city detective and police officer" was known to the inhabitants of Chinatown but they also noticed that Wong Sue "seemed well known to the police." Images of Chinese criminals began to dance in their heads and they "began to wonder if our amiable guide was a 'high-binder' or professional murderer in disguise." Finally, Peixotto divulged their suspicions, "point blank." "What makes you think so?" asked Wong Sue calmly. Peixotto "explained that he seemed suspiciously well known to the officers of the law." "That," replied Wong Sue, "is because I'm a policeman, myself." And opening his blouse, sure enough, there was the star.[16]

In the tale they wove, Peixotto and Fletcher's encounter with Wong Sue effectively upended a number of their stereotypes about the Chinese. On one level, at least, they stood corrected. On another, however, their story further inscribed racializing stereotypes by making Wong Sue the exception that proved the rule. This double-edged quality, of reveling in some stereotypes about the Chinese even as they overturned others, also ran through Peixotto and Fletcher's clever inversion that gave Wong Sue access to a major source of power in Chinatown—the police—and made him part of the apparatus of surveillance rather than simply one of the regularly surveilled. That revealing himself to be an officer of the law was so surprising only made sense in a context in which that would seem as nearly as out of the ordinary as Eleanor B. Caldwell's guide aspiring to be the machine politician, "Boss Buckley." Yet, while all of these encounters—to varying degrees—revealed prevailing prejudices, nevertheless, at the base of all three was the fact that a middle-class white person and a Chinese person had spent the better part of a day conversing and roaming around together—something that was unlikely to happen outside the bounds of Chinatown's cultural frontier.

While Peixotto and Fletcher's account ultimately left a lot to be desired in terms of their understanding of the "Chinese character," they thoroughly succeeded in capturing the reality of the police presence in Chinatown. White visitors' use of police guides added another level of surveillance to the police presence already in the area. Tourists, after all, often chose police guides not just because of safety concerns but also for the knowledge of and access to Chinatown they could provide—a by-product of their constant presence. When tourist J. W. Ames visited Chinatown one evening in the company of a police guide, he described for readers of the article he wrote for *Lippincott's* the kind of rapport this Chinese-speaking officer had with the local community as they strolled down Jackson Street, effectively capturing both familiarity and a kind of deference that could just as likely be born of fear as admiration. "The sidewalks are thronged with passers, who all seem to know the officer," he wrote, "for they jump aside and bow with unfeigned respect. The officer now and then hails one, and sometimes pauses to carry on a short conversation." *Bancroft's Tourist Guide* also hinted at the inequality that permeated the tourist enterprise when it recommended a particular officer as a guide precisely because "his long experience" among the Chinese has "acquainted them with him to such a degree, that they allow him to enter and pass through their houses and rooms whence another might be shut out." That policemen were "allowed" into Chinese living spaces might have been part of a bargain struck between the tour guide and the toured upon in which each took a share of the profits or it might have been, more baldly, a product of police domination of the neighborhood. An account in London's *Cornhill Magazine* leaned bluntly toward the latter explanation, attributing the possibility of these kinds of intrusions to the fact that the Chinese had been "so thoroughly . . . cowed by the San Francisco police" that they were unable "to utter the faintest exclamation of annoyance." Even if reality tended toward some combination of Chinese agency and police power, the prevalence of these kinds of intrusions and the use of police guides meant that the power relations that existed between the police and the Chinese community framed this aspect of the tourist experience of Chinatown.[17]

Police guides, moreover, were known for deploying quite brutal, invasive, and generally disrespectful tactics that included kicking doors open, forcing their way into private living quarters, waking people from sleep, and shining bright lights into people's faces. Whether these encounters were staged or not, they made violence an expected part of the tourist experience in Chinatown. Local photographers capitalized on these expectations and sold souvenir photographs that claimed to "show the Chinaman taken by surprise, as the flash light illuminates his den." Photographer Henry R. Knapp packaged his series of such images in a three-inch square booklet, which made them easily portable and well suited for carrying in one's pocket or purse. The scenes he captured and captioned included the expected "Opium Den" and "Filling Opium Pipe," but the inclusion of "Old Blind Chinese Woman, Aged 77" and "Trimming His Corns" disclosed tourists' appetite for being let into private moments, not just vicious ones (see figures 19–22).[18]

Long-time San Franciscan Charles Warren Stoddard told a story of how when his "'special,' by the authority vested in him" demanded admittance to a particular closed door, "a group of coolies" who lived in the vicinity and had followed the tourists tried to divert his attention by assuring him that the place was vacant. The officer refused to leave, decided to employ force to open the door, and when he did, succeeded in revealing four sleeping men, "packed" into what Stoddard described as an "air-tight compartment" and "insensible" to the "hearty greeting" the tourists offered. W. H. Gleadell related invading the living quarters of an impoverished Chinese couple—upon his police guide's instruction—in order to be able to take in such a scene firsthand. The officer enticed him with the statement, "'Now, if you would really wish to see how some of the lower class of Chinese live, this is not a bad place for the purpose. Go down that stair, push open the door at the foot, and walk right in.'" Armed with his guide's permission and his own sense of entitlement, Gleadell persevered. He came upon a room in which he was "just able to stand upright" and "with the exception of a stove in one corner" and some straw matting that "answered the purpose of a bed" was otherwise "quite destitute of furniture." At "one end crouched a man, while a woman sat in the centre, and a wretched little cur groveled between them." Then, "after a general survey"—complete with commentary on the "loathsome squalor" of Chinatown that was so typical of the tourist literature—Gleadell inquired, "Who lives here?" The man replied simply, "Me, wife, and little dog."[19]

These two scenarios captured a series of extraordinarily revealing moments. In the first, Chinatown residents unsuccessfully tried to foil police efforts to gain entry into Chinese living quarters. A police guide used force to open a door and woke several sleeping Chinese men. The tourists he was leading then offered these men a greeting. In the second, a tourist—under the direction of a police guide—barged into the residence of a Chinese couple, made observations, and asked the occupants questions. And it is easy enough to add a third by revisiting E.G.H.'s final Chinatown visit in which her guide kicked open one door to reveal an opium smoker and forced open another to present a view of crowding and squalor—providing her with a very different kind of experience than her day with Chin Jun, who had refused to take her party to the opium dens. Although gazing upon other people and landscapes was part of any tourist experience, not all tourist experiences involved this kind of evaluation of a subordinate group by a dominant group. Even if these scenarios were staged and the local participants received some compensation from the guides for their role in these presentations of Chinatown, this does not diminish the social potency of these kinds of events. The violent invasions of the police guides, the boldness of a tourist like Gleadell, and the ways tourists scrutinized the Chinese and spoke to them could only be considered acceptable in a situation in which tourists viewed the toured upon as their inferiors. Chin Jun's refusal to take E.G.H. to an opium den and the attempt by

Figure 19–22. These images were packaged with others in a three-inch-square book-let designed to be easily portable, well suited for carrying in a pocket or purse. While "Opium Den" (top) and "Filling Opium Pipe" (bottom) presented expected tropes of the tourist terrain, "Old Blind Woman" (top) and "Trimming His Corns" (bottom)

revealed the desire of tourists to view—and the power of the photographer to capture—ostensibly private, domestic scenes as well as vicious ones. (Henry R. Knapp,
1889. Huntington Library)

bystanders to waylay the police from one of their raids also suggest that the degrading effects of these components of Chinatown's cultural frontier were not lost on neighborhood residents.

One chronicler of the Chinatown tourist experience, Reverend Otis Gibson, who had considerable knowledge of local practices from the vantage point of his long career as a missionary in the neighborhood, tried to draw tourists' attention away from the derogatory image of the Chinese being constructed for their consumption to the unfavorable image that such practices actually presented of white Americans and their culture. Gibson related an especially violent story of "one of these night excursions" in which a policeman, acting as a guide to a party of ministers, upon entering the living quarters of some of Chinatown's residents, "pulled away the apology for a curtain from before the miserable hole in which a poor Chinaman was peacefully sleeping." In order to give the ministers a better view, the police guide "then brought the full glare of his lamp upon the face of the sleeper." The man "feeling annoyed naturally growled his dissatisfaction." With that, the "policeman for the delectation of those *pious men* seized the poor fellow and brutally pounded and punched his head with his . . . fist." Gibson then concluded, tongue in cheek, "How our civilization must shine in the eyes of those poor underground Chinamen!"[20]

Gibson also explained to readers that there was a real problem with the way the "'special policemen'" were "always ready to take visitors through these dens, to show them 'the Chinese as they are.'" Visitors, as a result, would "go away and write up 'the Chinese in America,' giving as historical facts the impressions received from such a night adventure." Not only did Gibson openly "protest against this method of studying the Chinese Question"—the effects of which were rampant in the tourist literature—but he also played the devil's advocate with his readers. "Suppose the tables turned," he wrote, "and curious Chinamen escorted by some 'kind and intelligent policeman' should make a raid upon American bedrooms, about twelve or one o'clock at night, solely for the delectation of the Chinamen, and so that some Chinese correspondent could write sensational letters to the Pekin *Gazette*." "How," Gibson asked, "would the shoe fit on that foot? One might as well write up 'The Americans as They Are' from a visit to the Five Points in New York."[21]

Yet even without a police escort, tourists would go to great lengths to see the sights required to fulfill their Chinatown experience and some were not

Figure 23. Chinatown squad of the San Francisco Police Department, posing with sledgehammers and axes, 1895. Such men often worked as Chinatown guides, employing their hammers and axes to force their way into opium dens and living spaces for tourists' view. (San Francisco Historical Photograph Collection, San Francisco History Center, San Francisco Public Library)

averse to employing boldly invasive and downright rude tactics of their own. "It is about four o'clock in the afternoon; we pass through the dirty alley, lined on each side with a dirtier door in which a window sash forms the upper portion and low windows with panes of glass six by eight in size," reported one of the *Chronicle's* journalists. "We impudently peep through the first we come to." A story in the *Alta* related similar tourist behavior on the part of a young woman during Chinese New Year celebrations. "We followed the example of everyone else, and peered in at all the windows, or stood in the open doors, which was very rude of us, of course, but still we did it, until finally we were snubbed." J. Torrey Connor, a journalist who wrote up his experience for publication in the *Chautauquan*, related tagging along behind "a party of sightseers, at the heels of a professional guide," following them down a dark passage, and pushing open a door that had "been carelessly left ajar." [22]

In their visits to Chinatown, tourists—as they were led around by police guides and local Chinese and as they traipsed around on their own—participated in a range of activities that put them in different relationships with and proximities to Chinatown and its inhabitants. E.G.H. was not alone in being able to forge the kind of relationship with a Chinese person required to engage a Chinese guide, then to later be led around by a police officer who broke down the doors of local Chinese, and at other times to stroll and explore essentially on her own, perhaps also peering into windows as she went. Each way of taking in Chinatown brought with it varied experiences from which different meanings could be made about the place and its inhabitants. Yet as varied as the activities and ways of seeing were, they were powerfully framed by the literature of Chinatown tourism and the practices of Chinatown guides, which not only identified particular sights for tourists to see, but informed them what they were supposed to mean.

In the tourist literature, Chinese restaurants, for example, were portrayed as violating norms of public health as well as various food taboos; opium dens were used to conjure images of Chinese as particularly prone to vice; joss houses were described in ways that emphasized unassimilability and difference in the form of heathenism; and theaters were employed to illuminate issues about Chinese laborers and the backwardness of Chinese culture. The overall picture fortified the image of Chinese immigrants as utterly alien, insurmountably different, and from a culture that was considerably less evolutionarily elevated than that found in nineteenth-century America. The themes of unassimilability, contamination, labor competition, and vice were nodes around which the nineteenth-century image of "the Oriental" was structured in the dominant culture's imagination. Rather than constructing completely novel images of Chinese immigrants, tourist literature mobilized and elaborated upon themes already in circulation. In the decades prior to the gold rush, the Chinese immigrants who had come to the United States settled mainly on the Eastern seaboard and were generally viewed as exotic curiosities. The unprecedented numbers of Chinese immigrants that arrived in San Francisco prior to the Exclusion Act, however, could not be understood through definitions that linked difference with notions of visitors from a distant, far away land. Instead, they necessitated a more direct subordination through cultural ordering that positioned Chinese immigrants within the nation's operative racial hierarchies and was informed by representation of "the Oriental" as a permanent, threatening, and alien presence.[23]

One of the main ways Chinatown was represented in the tourist literature was as a foreign place. As early as 1859, Reverend J. C. Holbrook observed that there were "parts of two or three streets" in San Francisco where one could "get a very good idea of Canton." On her trip in 1886, E.G.H. had reflected that, "As you walk through the streets of Chinatown, you hardly realize yourself in America." Emphasizing that the Chinese community was in America, but not of America, reinforced notions of the Chinese as an unassimilable and alien people. Many writers, in fact, were so convinced in advance by tourist literature of the foreign-ness of the overall setting, they had a hard time assimilating the not-so-foreign aspects of Chinatown. As a result, tourist literature often downplayed things that pointed to the interpenetration of Chinese and American cultures—bilingualism and American style dress, for example—that might unsettle tourists' expectations. Yet when representations of Chinatown as a foreign place mobilized images associated with an exotic Orient, they lacked the comfort provided by distance. Whatever similarities authors of travel literature chose to draw, Chinatown was not Peking or Canton—a foreign land filled with foreign people visited briefly by the Euro-American tourist. Rather, Chinatown, as many accounts pointed out, was a segregated space located in the heart of an American city and the Chinese who inhabited it were not colorful foreigners "over there" but menacing aliens "over here."[24]

Layered on top of the representation of Chinatown as a foreign place—and just as prevalent—were unfavorable descriptions of the public health of Chinatown that focused particular attention on its overcrowding, unsanitary conditions, and malodorousness as well as its dark alleys and legendary underground passages in which it was imagined that all sorts of dirt and vice were hidden away. G. B. Densmore, author of the anti-immigration tract *The Chinese in California*, announced, both simply and typically: "The Chinese Quarter is very filthy. They have in the alleys and around their houses . . . old rags, slop-holes, excrement, and vile refuse animal matter. They are compelled by the police to clean up, or they would be buried in their own filth." That the crowding and lack of public sanitation in Chinatown were in large measure products of the poverty of its residents coupled with the denial of basic municipal services was of little interest. The discussions of the quality of public health in Chinatown found in the tourist literature were not exposés designed to bring middle-class aid to the neighborhood. Instead, the representations of Chinatown as a foreign place that was teeming, filthy, squalid, and smelly worked to racialize Chinese immigrants as literal pollutants—the social and cultural opposites of clean, virtuous, civilized white Americans. For many tourists, being an eyewitness to aspects of life in Chinatown that supported this representation of Chinese immigrants was not an accidental occurrence or something to be endured but actually a sought-after component of the tourist experience. When one journalist for the *Chronicle*, for example, paid a second visit to "the dens . . . located in the vicinity of Cooper's alley" in the company of "officer Woodruff," he seemed to revel in revealing that "the place seems even more disgusting than on our first visit; the stench more intolerable; the rough board flooring more uncertain and dangerous."[25]

While it might seem a little odd that after an enumeration of the dangerous public health conditions that existed in Chinatown, visitors would then be directed to go there and eat, this was, in many respects, precisely the point. Many accounts tended to stress the strangeness and difference of Chinese food and customs. In doing so, they often further developed the idea of the Chinese as dangerous alien contaminants by representing the Chinese diet as filled with polluted foods—or at least those unpalatable to Anglo-American tastes. In this configuration the Chinese were literally what they ate. "They eat things," Joseph Carey told readers of his guide, "which would be most repulsive to the epicurean taste of the Anglo-Saxon. Even lizards and rats and young dogs they will not refuse." Reverend Otis Gibson noted that many Chinese dishes "taste of rancid oil or strong butter," and local writer Josephine Clifford reported to her readers that while she did not want to "say anything mean against the Chinese" she did believe that "the funny little things . . . at the bottom of a deep earthen jar were rat's tails skinned." Both Carey and Clifford also stressed that appearances could be deceiving and that tourists, if they were not careful, might be misled into consuming polluted foods. Clifford, for example, rather incongruously noted that despite the supposedly unsavory products from which they were made, various Chinese edibles "came out as tempting morsels, square, round, diamond-shaped, octagonal, all covered with coating and icing in gay colors, and so tastefully laid out that had we seen them at a confectioner's on Market or Kearny street, we could not have resisted the wish to devour them." Nevertheless, while they may have been forewarned to the point of being terrified by the time they got there, tourists flocked to Chinatown's restaurants. As *Disturnell's Strangers' Guide* succinctly put it, Chinese restaurants were "often visited out of curiosity by white persons."[26]

A tourist could engage in several different kinds of activities, involving varying levels of participation, when it came to visiting a Chinese restaurant. Many tourists, like E.G.H., exercised caution and limited their consumption to tea and sweetmeats—"some small bean-meal cookies, a saucer of lichee nut, some salted almonds . . . candied strips of cocoanut, melon-rind and like delicacies"—which represented a sort of middle-ground between actually eating a full meal and simply watching Chinese people eat, two other popular alternatives. This allowed tourists to partake of some food and drink and to observe a tea-making process that—given how frequently it was described and commented upon—they found fascinating in its elaborateness. They also generally found the tea produced by this ritual to be delicious. As E.G.H. explained it, a waiter arrived table-side with "a large teacup on a carved wooden stand, with a saucer covering it" as well as a "smaller cup without a saucer" for each person. The larger cup was "filled with dry tea leaves" over which the waiter poured boiling water and after allowing it to steep "for a few seconds," "he dexterously poured the liquid off into the smaller cup, and it was ready for drinking." Yet even in this setting some tourists evinced a certain wariness about the strangeness and difference of the Chinese that they were experiencing through their foodways, even when they responded positively to the experience as a whole as well as to the items consumed. When Will Brooks, for example, related requesting the "boy" to bring him and his party "some tea and sweetmeats" he added that, "If he brings us cakes, we will not kill him; but we will not eat the cakes, lest they kill us." While Brooks might have stayed away from the cakes, he thoroughly enjoyed other aspects of the Chinese fare he tried, concluding that "in the preparation of ginger chow-chow, candied and pickled fruits, the Chinaman is a signal success. . . . They all taste good, and may be indulged in without much fear of after consequences."[27]

More adventurous tourists went beyond just having tea and sweetmeats and partook of a full meal in a Chinese restaurant. Mabel Craft—a local journalist, fiction writer, and collaborator with Chinatown photographer Arnold Genthe—who described Chinese cuisine as "appetizing after you have overcome your first repugnance," told readers that "if you want a regular Chinese dinner and give notice, a wonderful meal will be prepared." She cautioned, however, that "no one should try it except those of good digestion, for at first it is just a little trying" since the menu included such unfamiliar items as "varnished pig, shark's fins, Bird's nest soup, pickled duck's head, tea, and Sham-Shu or rice brandy." For these braver few, it was not just the food that would present a challenge but unfamiliar rules of etiquette as well. Reverend Otis Gibson provided his readers with some practical tips and general information to aid in navigating a meal at a Chinese restaurant. "The principal dishes," he told them, "are prepared and placed on the table within easy reach of all. Then each one drives his own chopsticks into the common dish and carries a piece to his mouth. This requires considerable skill and practice. Americans generally find 'many a slip between the cup and the lip.'" "If you get a bone in your mouth after getting all the meat off," he added, "just turn your head and drop the bone on the floor." For the less adept, Gibson noted, the "high-toned restaurants" that tourists frequented also kept on hand "knives, forks, plates, table-cloths, and napkins."[28]

Gibson also related to his readers his own experience of dining in a Chinese restaurant with out-of-town visitors—an experience familiar to many San Franciscans before and since. "In company with the Rev. Dr. Newman, Mrs. Newman, and Rev. Dr. Sutherland, of Washington City, and Dr. J. T. M'Lean, of San Francisco," he explained, "I once took a Chinese dinner at the restaurant on Jackson Street." He then described how members of his very respectable party liked their meal and gave some hint as to how each approached the novel event. "Dr. Newman took hold and ate like a hungry man, and when I thought he must be about filled, he astonished me by saying that the meats were excellent, and were it not that he had to deliver a lecture that evening, he would take hold and eat a good hardy dinner. Dr. Sutherland did not seem to relish things quite so well." His description that followed of Mrs. Newman's flexibility and resourcefulness was particularly striking given that middle-class women were so strongly associated with upholding proper etiquette. "Mrs. Newman," he wrote, "relishing some of the meats, and failing to get the pieces to her mouth with the chopsticks, wisely threw aside all conventional notions, used her fingers instead of chopsticks and, as the Californians would say, 'ate a square meal.'"[29]

Gibson's position as a Chinatown missionary certainly gave him unique insights into the neighborhood but his taking of a meal at a Chinese restaurant did not, by any means, make him an exceptional San Franciscan. During the gold rush, before there was even a specific area known as Chinatown, Chinese restaurants attracted wide patronage. In later years, locals not only stopped in for tea and sweetmeats as well as the occasional meal but Chinese elites also frequently used the occasion of a Chinese banquet to make political alliances with other local elites and officials. Typical attendees included members of the

press, the police, lawyers, judges, and politicians. Press coverage of such banquets generally gave them high praise, offering detailed descriptions of the
food that was served and noting the lavishness and expense of such affairs. As
one account in the *Alta* in 1864 reported, "The dinner for twenty people consisted of over one hundred dishes and could hardly have cost less than $1,000,
and may have cost double that sum." Yet, however favorable the overall reviews, the press also frequently felt compelled to make mention of the fact that
some of the food was so strange as to be "not at all gastronomically appreciated
by the guests."[30]

Now, if on a symbolic level, the Chinese were what they ate, what did it
mean when white visitors to Chinese restaurants ate Chinese food? While not
every account went so far as to suggest that rats and dogs were being served at
Chinese restaurants, the idea that many strange, unknown, and possibly taboo
and polluting things were served up in Chinese cooking was pervasive. Given
the fact that among nineteenth-century elites and middle classes, restaurants
and public dining were freighted with concerns about social purity and mixture, this was a highly charged arena. Food, food-tastes, and the rituals surrounding the consumption of food in both public and private were intricately
connected to, on both material and symbolic levels, the articulation of social
hierarchies. For white San Franciscans, eating French food, for example, carried with it the connotation of refinement, taste, and civility, while the eating
of Chinese food in Chinese restaurants resonated with very different kinds of
social meanings. Eating Chinese food in a Chinese restaurant might have
been experienced by some as furthering cultural understanding and softening
the social lines that congealed around racial differences. But, even in the best
of circumstances or with the best of intentions, taking in or simply observing
food that was unfamiliar and sometimes unpalatable also often reinforced the
otherness of the Chinese and the whiteness of the patrons that was at the core
of anti-Chinese sentiment. In effect, the frequent wariness—if not revul-
sion—with which whites approached consuming Chinese food echoed and reinforced the prevailing distaste for incorporating Chinese immigrants into
the American fold.[31]

For visitors to Chinatown who were not adventurous enough to partake of
refreshments at one of its restaurants—as well as for some who were but still
wanted to see more—the option also existed of experiencing Chinese eateries
by observing the ways Chinese people took a meal in them. Given the fact
that Chinatown was full of single workingmen who often rented rooms in

dormitory-like hotels, it is no wonder that numerous observers commented on the ubiquity of restaurants for ordinary folk. Many of these "cheap cellar places" were somewhat off the beaten path as far as the tourist trade—which gravitated toward the fancier eateries—was concerned and did not have much interest in the practices of merchants who often employed a cook to feed themselves and their staff from small kitchens in the rear of their establishments. William Doxey explained to readers of his guidebook that in the most humble restaurants "under the sidewalks or in basements" there were "wide benches and tables" for eating and "a series of shelves" for sleeping and usually, at the entrance, "a big cauldron steaming and scenting the air with a fishy smell."[32] Josephine Clifford related being led by her police guide into the basement of a house—described as a "respectable place"—which contained "a barber-shop, a restaurant, a pawnbroker's shop, an opium den, and a lodging house." Inside, sitting "at the round table in the restaurant," Clifford encountered "an enormously fat Chinaman busy with his rice and meat." Although this was clearly a space in which Chinese lived, socialized, and conducted business, her guide promptly asked the man to perform for the tourists he had in tow. What transpired next made it clear that while these kinds of excursions might have felt safer for some tourists—as they exempted them from any culinary obligations—it did not require the eating of Chinese food for restaurants and foodways to do racializing work. "'Hello, John,' the captain addressed him; 'let the ladies see you use your chopsticks.' 'All light,' he answered, laughing all over this broad, shining face; 'me eat licee with chopsticks.'" In language that gave the man animalistic qualities and emphasized his barbarous manners, Clifford declared, "Forthwith, he flung the 'licee' into his capacious maw with such rapidity that his cheeks were filled up and stood out like the pouch of a hamster who has been depredating on the nearest corn-crib." She and her group quickly "moved on for fear he should choke eating rice for our entertainment."[33]

While gazing upon Chinese in the "cheap cellar places" gave tourists a firsthand view of the working poor, elite eateries—generally located in upstairs apartments—were another favorite spot of observation that provided a somewhat different view of the Chinese and their environs. Accounts of these places, which were the kinds of restaurants that tourists typically frequented, often stressed the beauty of their appointments—offering a tone of appreciation that stood in contrast to the appraisals of lower-class eateries and the overriding emphasis on the strangeness of Chinese foodways. Charles

Keeler—local writer, artist, and naturalist—described one such restaurant he visited as "elegantly furnished with black teak-wood tables and carved chairs, inlaid with mother-of-pearl" and decorated with "carved open work screens." W. H. Gleadell recounted a scene in a more upscale Chinese restaurant and offered some insight into the way Chinese patrons reacted to white observers in their midst. He explained that he and his party "were conducted by our guide to a mammoth restaurant." "Attracted by the confused babel of noise proceeding from an upper-room," they made their way in that direction, making sure that they kept close to their guide. They found themselves "in a large square room in the midst of a mixed crowd of Chinese men and women, all chattering and shouting at one and the same time, and busily engaged in their evening meal." Most "were seated round a table, in the centre of which stood a huge bowl" from which "chop sticks were . . . dipped into and withdrawn from . . . all corners with rare dispatch." Gleadell and his companions "walked about quite unchallenged, and apparently quite unremarked, without arousing the slightest expression of curiosity or concern." It was, he wrote, "as though our presence were nobody's business but or own." Gleadell, perhaps, expected the Chinese to have viewed him as exotic or threatening as the Chinese were to him. Instead, it was quite possible that white visitors to Chinatown had become such a mundane occurrence that its residents found that it was safer and more convenient to simply avoid or ignore them when they could (see figure 24).[34]

Joss houses—or Chinese temples—were, like restaurants, routine stops on the Chinatown tourist's itinerary. Joss houses were mentioned as early as 1860 as sites of potential interest for whites curious about Chinese religious practices. Almost forty years later, William Doxey informed readers of his guide that "to many visitors, the joss-houses of Chinatown are the most interesting sights this oriental section of an occidental city includes." "The word joss," he went on to explain, "is a corruption of the Portuguese word deos (God); hence, idol." E.G.H. was interested enough in Chinese religious practices to visit joss houses twice, once in the company of Chin Jun, and once with Mrs. Law. Writing in the early 1880s, Disturnell revealed there were a number of joss houses for a tourist like E.G.H. to choose from and explore. "One of the largest and most expensively fitted up," he explained, is the Kong Chow, 512 Pine Street. . . . Other gorgeously fitted up temples are the Hop Wo, 751 Clay Street; Ning Yong, 230 Montgomery Avenue; Yeong Wo, 730 Sacramento Street; Yan Wo, St. Louis Alley; Tong Wah Meu, Jackson Street near Stockton;

Figure 24. Grand dining room of the Chinese Restaurant, Dupont Street, one of Chinatown's finer eateries. (I. W. Taber, photographer. Chinese in California, Bancroft Library, University of California, Berkeley)

and two, the Sam Yup and Tin How Meu, on Waverly Place between Clay and Washington Streets" (see figure 25).[35]

As white visitors encountered these places of worship, they fixated upon several components of Chinese religious practices as potent registers of the social, and sometimes racial, differences between whites and Chinese—frequently drawing stark contrasts between what they saw as civilized, Euro-American Christianity and the barbarous heathenism of the Chinese. This often began with descriptions of the interior spaces of Chinese places of worship that stressed the ways in which, in the words of Mabel Craft, joss houses were "superb in a garish way but to the last degree unchurchly according to occidental standards." Some of tourist literature's favorite words for describing what was found in the interiors of joss houses were "dingy," "grotesque," and "hideous." "They were all much alike," explained Iza Duffus Hardy, "dingy carpetless apartments up one or more flights of stairs." A. E. Browne,

Figure 25. Joss house. Like restaurants, opium dens, and theaters, joss houses—or Chinese temples—were routine stops on the Chinatown tourist itinerary. (I. W. Taber, photographer. Chinese in California, Roy D. Graves pictorial collection, Bancroft Library, University of California, Berkeley)

visiting San Francisco on a trip "across the Continent" with a Raymond and Whitcomb Party, recorded in her travel journal that while the shrines and altars were "ornamented by some very beautiful teak wood carvings . . . the images were unlike anything in human form and were grotesque and horrible." In an article he contributed to the *Overland Monthly*, D. E. Kessler described seeing "the looming figures of three mighty 'gods,' bizarre and bedizened with stiff brocades, their hideously carved, expressionless heads vaguely dim in the upper murky shadows" (see figure 26).[36]

The contrasts drawn between Chinese and Christian religion did not stop with observations about the differences in places of worship. Specific religious practices and tendencies also came under scrutiny. What was viewed as the stereotypically pervasive greed and venality of the Chinese that sullied their

Figure 26. The incense table in the Joss Temple of Lung Gong, 1887. Tourist literature generally displayed a lack of understanding of Chinese religious practices, characterizing them as barbarous heathenism. (I. W. Taber, photographer. Chinese in California, Bancroft Library, University of California, Berkeley)

religion was seen as especially egregious. When a writer for *Cornhill Magazine*
explained to his readers that "pious" Chinese were "expected, at certain periods, to feed 'Joss' by liberal offerings of food and drink," he also noted, conveniently overlooking the prevalence of the Christian collection plate, that
these "of course, ultimately go to the priests." This writer further related that
when he asked why the drinks were sold in glasses that held "little more than
a thimbleful" this question elicited "the truly Confucian reply, 'Fillee often,
payee often.'" J. W. Ames informed his readers that he had a hard time dis-
cerning whether the man he encountered in a joss house was "priest or proprietor." Although he was aware that the priests supported themselves and
their establishments through the sale of votive candles, incense, and other articles required by worshippers, he declared that from what he saw he believed
the religion of the Chinese was "simply a mercantile venture throughout."[37]

Within this formulation of the corruption of Chinese religious virtue by pecuniary impulses, the irony of the fact that it was the white tourists who were some of the liveliest participants in the commerce that took place in joss houses seemed lost on most observers. Even when it was not, however, the Chinese—not the tourists—bore the brunt of the criticism. The tourists might have been silly, but the Chinese—especially the priests—were represented as dangerously dishonest. J. W. Ames, so thoroughly convinced of the commercial nature of Chinese religion, told his readers that "if you like, barbarian as you are, you may purchase the whole establishment, idols, giants, screens, sacred bells and all"—the "shrewd old priestly fraud will gladly sell if you only offer enough." D. E. Kessler disclosed that to tourists—especially a "giggling coterie of ladies accompanied by an official white guide—joss sticks will be sold, prayers will be made for certain dollars, 'good luck' fetishes may be secured, [and] the future will be divulged . . . by the crafty, repellent priests in charge." While Kessler, like Ames, reserved greater criticism of the inclinations of the priests than the tourists, both also tapped into an undercurrent of hostility that they believed ran through these encounters. Ames referred to white tourists as "barbarians"—the term whites often used to refer to the way they believed the Chinese saw them. Kessler represented the Chinese priests as "the oily despisers of 'white devils'" who separated "the foreigner and his dollars" with "an inward glee and an outward subservience."[38]

Another feature of Chinese religious practices that seemed to really grab the attention of white observers was the fact that the Chinese had no clearly demarcated times for worship. As Mabel Craft explained to her readers, "no bell is rung, at no stated hour do the eyes of the worshippers turn toward a shrine. No congregation gathers for united praise and prayer, or sits to listen to an exposition of doctrine or duty." San Francisco resident, writer, and historian John S. Hittell described for readers of his guidebook what he called the "remarkable lack of reverence and formality" that characterized "the Chinese mode of worship." "They enter the temple as they would enter a lodging-house," he explained, "chatting and smoking, and with covered head." "Without uncovering, or ceasing their conversation," he continued, "they approach their favorite deity, go through the 'chin-chinning process' (bowing three times) . . . leave their offerings, . . . and go about their business without further ceremony."[39]

For Craft, Hittell, and many other observers, the meanings they took away from such religious practices—whether or not they truly understood what they were seeing—correlated directly to certain social and racial traits of the Chinese. "The religion of the Chinese is individualistic and intensely practical," Craft concluded, "like everything else about him."[40] Joseph Carey summed up the core thrust of white observations in joss houses when he wrote, "it is in religious services and ceremonies and beliefs that we get a true knowledge of a race or nation." According to his observations, the Chinese religion showed that the Chinese as a race were primitive, barbaric, and child-like when compared with American Christians. To drive this point home, Carey described an encounter with a joss house attendant "who was selling small, slender incense sticks" and who told him that "you could burn them to drive away the devil" and that they also happened to be "good to keep moths away." "Doubtless in the Chinese mind," he then told his readers, "there is a connection between moths and evil spirits." But, he explained, such "pueril-ities" belonged "to the childhood of the world and not to the beginning of the twentieth century."[41]

For men like Carey who had a special interest in spreading Christianity among the Chinese—he was a Doctor of Divinity—and others who worked directly among the Chinese and had made conversion their mission, the very existence of joss houses was a constant reminder that the missionaries' efforts had been largely unsuccessful and served as yet another sign of the supposed unassimilability of the Chinese to American ways. Chin Jun's reply to E.G.H. when she asked if he was a Christian—thinking perhaps that his reticence in answering her questions about Chinese religious practices had to do with the fact that he no longer performed them—was telling. Chin Jun "had been one for a month, but then gave it up." The reluctance of Chinese to convert to Christianity seems to have bred a certain amount of anxiety about reverse-conversions—in which Christian places and sometimes people were con-verted to Chinese ways. Some writers—in a strange twist on emergent yellow peril logic that conjured up images of the growing threat to the nation posed by ever-expanding numbers of Chinese immigrants—went so far as to express their fears that the strange religious practices of the Chinese would actually degrade the progress of Christianity or even worse, Christian civilization it-self. G. B. Densmore related his dismay—and what was nonetheless a patently false claim—that "where we have converted one Chinaman to Christianity, their influence has degraded ten white men to practical heathenism." Simi-larly, Reverend Otis Gibson, who actually did missionary work among the Chinese in San Francisco, decried the fact that "the Chinese have opened their heathen temples, and set up their heathen idols and altars in this Christian land; and instead of our converting their temples into Christian churches, they have absolutely changed one of the first Protestant churches of this city into a habitation for the heathen."[42]

The Chinese theater, like the restaurant and the joss house, was another frequent destination for Chinatown tourists. Like the church, the theater was a familiar institution to most Americans as it was an extremely popular form of amusement. This made it easy for tourists, when they visited the Chinese theater, to draw comparisons between the style, content, and audiences of Chinese and American venues. In the tourist literature, these comparisons resulted in reviews of Chinese theatrical performances that did not find much to recommend them and also generally concluded that a culture that produced such retarded theater had to be barbaric and antiquated itself. However, a trip to the theater was about much more than seeing the show on the stage. Like visiting a restaurant or a joss house, going to the theater provided tourists with another opportunity to observe the Chinese. But, whereas at a restaurant a tourist might observe a few diners or at a joss house see several worshippers coming and going, at the theater on a busy night, tourists shared the place with hundreds of Chinese. As Joseph Carey explained, "Here you see the Celestials *en masse*."[43]

Since tourist literature provided a wealth of practical information about where theaters were located, how much they cost, and the times of performances, it was not difficult for tourists to find these places whether they went on their own or with a guide. *Disturnell's Strangers' Guide* informed its readers that "there are two theaters—Tan Sung Fun, 623 Jackson Street; and the Bow Wah Ying, at 814 Washington Street. They are open every day from 2 o'clock p.m. until midnight. Price of admission fifty cents, boxes two dollars and a half." Local writer E. M. Green described a scenario that suggested that tourists were not only drawn to the Chinese theater but also to some degree encouraged to attend, if not welcomed. When he and his companions—who claimed they were "not sight-seers" and actually wanted to distance themselves from "the personally conducted"—entered one theater, they were initially both startled and repelled by a "huge white sheet bearing the legend 'Welcome Shriners.'" Why tourists were welcomed may have had something to do with the money that theater owners could make from them, especially since, as one account noted, theater revenues decreased along with Chinatown's population in the years after the Exclusion Act. For Chinese theater-goers, the price of admission at the opening of a performance was "half a dollar" but was gradually reduced as the evening advanced so that the late spectator paid for exactly as much as he saw. Many white theaters-goers, however, saw "over the box a notice in plain English, 'Admission fifty cents'" with no offer of a decreasing scale calibrated to the time of admission (see figure 27).[44]

In addition to providing general logistical information to help tourists navigate the Chinese theater experience, tourist literature also gave its readers a very clear picture of what to expect in terms of the performances that allowed them to arrive with an evaluative framework already in place for what they were about to see. Local writer B. E. Lloyd was not alone in being less than impressed with the Chinese theater and, like many others, was not the least bit shy about conveying this to his readers. "Viewing it from an American standpoint," he wrote, "the Chinese drama is in a very crude state." "The plays," W. H. Gleadell declared, "appear more than ludicrous to the uninitiated observer." "A Chinese play at its best," explained missionary Frederic Masters, "possesses few charms." Echoing the boredom, lack of interest, and inability to follow the plot reported by many tourists, Otis Gibson uncharitably remarked that, "Judged from an American stand-point, those who attend a Chinese theater ought to receive *a good salary paid in advance.*"[45]

Part of the problem, according to Gibson, was that while "the plays generally represent some historical train of events," they moved too slowly and did not "develop a plot with anything like the rapidity and dispatch which characterize our American and English plays." For French travel writer Lucien Biart, the unfamiliar pacing coupled with his lack of understanding proved to be his undoing. Although he had been led by curiosity to the Chinese theater, he told his readers that he left once he began "to feel uncomfortably inclined to yawn." "At first," he explained, "the costumes, the stage-scenery, the music, and the spectators had all interested me." But after watching for two hours what he described as "some awkward clowns making grimaces, brandishing their swords, defying and occasionally assaulting each other without . . . having the least idea of the reason of their incessant quarrels," he reported that he "began to detest the theatrical art—in the Chinese form of course." E.G.H. did something that seems to have been quite uncharacteristic of tourists at the theater—she asked a Chinese man "who, seeing we were strangers came and sat down by us," to explain the performance. He did, and usefully informed her, "He fight now—he want more soldiers—he sit down and write for

Figure 27. Interior of the Chinese Theater, Jackson Street. As it was across nineteenth-century America, the theater was a central form of entertainment in San Francisco's Chinese community. Chinatown tourists flocked there as well, although they generally did not care for the performances they saw. (I. W. Taber, photographer. Chinese in California, Bancroft Library, University of California, Berkeley)

more—they come—he fight—he dead." As a result, she and her party enjoyed the performance more than they would have otherwise although even the intrepid E.G.H. only lasted twenty minutes. Upon leaving, she admitted that she "was glad to get out of the pandemonium."[46]

Since tourists so rarely ever reported that these performances were enjoyable or even understandable, it seems likely that they went to the Chinese theater more to learn about Chinese culture than for entertainment. As E. M. Green noted, the "amusements of a people are great indicators." For many tourists, what they took away from the Chinese theater were lessons about Chinese qualities that were often cast in racial terms. Although Green discovered "a public as intelligent as their amusement" when he turned his attention to the audience, his favorable appraisal was unusual. More typical was journalist

Henry Burden McDowell's article for *Century Magazine*, which not only provided detailed information about how to interpret events on stage, but also revealed some of the ways the Chinese theater experience could translate into a racializing experience. According to McDowell, the "peculiar difference of manners, feeling, and national history" that kept "the Chinese people apart from the civilized world" resulted in a theatrical culture that bore "the unmistakable stamp of an arrested civilization." He then went on to suggest how this lack of development translated into Chinese racial traits that imbued them with moral qualities at odds with those of American society, believed to be at the height of the civilization process, evolutionarily speaking. McDowell explained, for example, that although "the Hong-Koi, or Chivalry plays might not be about chivalry as Americans understood it," the Chinese "were entitled" to use such terminology because of "the extreme rarity of the occasions on which one Chinaman helps another." The Chinese were not chivalrous, according to his thinking, because the "inherent selfishness as well as the superstition of the Chinese character excludes from it the active feeling of philanthropy." These qualities correlated with his interpretation of "the Hong Koi," which stressed that they dealt primarily with what he called "negative chivalry; not doing a man an injury when you might, and doing him a kindness when it is no very great inconvenience to yourself."[47]

Although white visitors to the Chinese theater were not terribly appreciative of its productions, they were very interested in observing its Chinese audience. "The body of the house is occupied by all sorts and conditions of 'the great unwashed,'" explained Frederic Masters, in a typical description of the general scene, "who sit with their hats on, their feet perhaps on the back of the next seat, and regale themselves during the performance with cigars, candies, *ma-tong*, peanuts, and sugar cane, which are vended about the house." The upper galleries were set apart for women and children. According to Masters, the women were separated by class and status with one gallery "for married women, mostly of the poorer class or the second wives of rich Chinese"; "the best gallery" for "the demi-monde class," who were recognizable by their "gaudy attire and rouged faces"; and the boxes "usually occupied by the 'golden lilies' or ladies with bound feet," who were the "first wives of the merchants and the local gentry." Otis Gibson reported that the women he saw in one gallery sat "with their feet elevated upon the balcony rail" and smoked and ate through the performance. The fact that the theater served as an important gathering place and site of sociability for the Chinese community was captured by several writers. Henry McDowell recalled being in a theater on Jackson Street one Saturday afternoon waiting for the show to start and observing "the young Chinamen . . . calling across the theater, exchanging jokes or the compliments of the season." Joseph Carey noted that the theater was "about the only place where they can meet on common ground, at least in large bodies."[48]

Observations of the audience, like the interpretations of Chinese theatrical performances, conveyed that prevailing racial logic played a role in how tourists understood what they were seeing. At the theater, tourists encountered the culture of Chinese laborers, who made up the bulk of the audiences, and whose image as a threat to the wages of white working men was a central component of anti-Chinese sentiment. Most accounts drew attention to the fact that the Chinese watched the performances in a state of inscrutable silence. The racialization of the Chinese as seemingly emotionless and thus unreadable was common in nineteenth-century America and, it appears, rather maddening to Euro-Americans desperate to "know" what these "strange" immigrants were about. As a writer for *Cornhill Magazine* explained, "No Chinese auditor ever exhibits any emotion. Neither pleasure nor disapprobation is ever expressed. For all apparent effect the actor produces he might be playing to an audience of ghosts." "During the most exciting performances on the stage," B. E. Lloyd explained, "there may be an occasional deep drawn sigh or a slight murmur of satisfaction in the audience; but however intense the interest in the play may be, there is never a burst of applause, commingled with the stamping of feet and clapping of hands." Josephine Clifford, in agreement with her fellow writers about the lack of response on the part of the audience, gave voice to what some may have feared lurked behind these unreadable countenances. She relayed that her police guide told her that if a performance deviated "from long established custom," the members of the audience would "set up the most vigorous yells, jump on the stage, beat the actors, pull up the benches, and destroy the gas-fixtures." Clifford remarked that, "Sitting there so perfectly still and impassive, with their 'Melican' hats jammed tight on their heads, no one would suspect the amount of fight and bloodthirstiness in the ugly souls of these Chinamen."[49]

While many white tourists were busy evaluating the Chinese they saw—both on stage and off—the Chinese, by often seating tourists on the theater's stage, positioned them in such a way that they were being observed as well. Chairs or campstools were provided for the visitors and from the descriptions in the tourist literature it was clear that at times the stage got a little crowded. A travel writer for *Outing* noted on the night of his visit, "A row of Americans extend on either side from the rear wall to the front of the stage." Joseph Carey and his party "felt quite at home on the stage at once" since "seated on either side . . . were many of our friends lay and clerical, men and women." A. E. Browne recalled that "after remaining about half an hour," she and her party "moved off to give place to another party of visitors"—suggesting that at times tourists had to queue up for a seat.[50]

While the tourist literature's accounts never hazarded a guess as to how the Chinese in the audience might have evaluated the tourists on the stage, several did record the way some Chinese responded to the presence of tourists. E.G.H. had revealed that a Chinese man came over to her group and volunteered to help them understand the play. But her account was unusual in the level of interaction that it recorded since most of the time what went on could best be described as mutual gazing, if that. Many tourists found that theater-goers, like restaurant patrons, evinced what they interpreted as an attitude of indifference—sometimes tinged with hostility, sometimes thoroughly benign. It was Mabel Craft's opinion that "the white spectator on the stage" did not "annoy his yellow brother in the least." To Joseph Carey it was "quite remarkable" that the Chinese "seemed to have neither ears nor eyes for their visitors." Yet he believed that although they "paid no attention to" the tourists, they nevertheless beheld them "with an indifference that almost bordered on contempt." W. H. Gleadell, however, detected neither "curiosity or resentment on the part of either the artistes or the spectators" from his seat "on the left hand side of the stage."[51]

Opium dens were undoubtedly the most sensational destinations on Chinatown's tourist terrain. While tourist literature's representations of them drew heavily on notions of a Chinese proclivity for vice, images of opium dens also suggested a kind of naughty deviance in that a visit put tourists in tempting proximity to a forbidden pleasure. Unlike restaurants, another arena of tourist consumption, in which visitors frequently recoiled—at least initially—at the food proffered, in opium dens it was the smokers who were disgusting, not the opium itself. Since the impulse to see Chinese opium smokers and their dens came from the desire to be both disgusted and tempted, such sights were simultaneously both repulsive and alluring to white middle-class sensibilities. On one level, representations of opium dens worked to differentiate the Chinese from white Americans. By virtue of the fact that tourist literature represented the Chinese as regular users of opium, it effectively configured them as lacking the kind of self-controls of mind and body that the nineteenth-century white middle class, in theory, was identified with and organized around. According to the *Chronicle*, for example, the "habit of opium smoking" was so prevalent among the Chinese that "the fumes of the insidious narcotic" poured forth throughout Chinatown "from basement and upper floor, from shop and office, from business house and private apartment." Yet while the idea that opium use set the Chinese apart was pervasive, on another level the tourist literature also revealed that it actually brought whites and Chinese together, both through the tourist enterprise and in their shared used of the drug.[52]

A desire to see the racially abject—the epitome of which was the opium smoker in his lair—compelled many tourists to seek out opium dens as part of their Chinatown excursion. Although E.G.H.'s guide, Chin Jun, claimed that the high number of people in her party prohibited him from taking them all to the dens, E.G.H. surmised that it actually had more to do with the fact that he "did not want to expose his countrymen" to their scrutiny. Given the fact that the kind of violent invasions commonly used by police guides were part and parcel of many opium den forays and given the way many tourists wrote about such experiences, Chin Jun had every reason to be reticent. Descriptions of opium dens tended to be organized around depictions of Chinese viciousness as well as Chinatown's crowding and filthiness. Tourist literature instructed tourists in advance that a visit to an opium den would allow them to venture into and behold some of Chinatown's most repellent sights. According to B. E. Lloyd, while a visitor to Chinatown "may have had his senses shocked by the savage noises that are heard in passing through the reeking alleys and lanes," he would not have "seen the most disgusting characteristic of the Chinese 'quarter'" until he was "within a well patronized opium den, and recovered from the shock experienced upon first entering." Iza Hardy, like many other writers, described the opium den her police guide led her to as "unlit, unventilated, very like the steerage cabin of an emigrant steamer, equally evil-odorous."[53]

For many tourists, however, just taking in the scene at an opium den was not enough. They also wanted to observe the den's inhabitants smoking opium. Josephine Clifford wrote about a performance of opium-smoking that was encouraged by the strong-arm tactics of her police guide. Her guide "commanded" one of the denizens, "Hurry up . . . now we want to see you fill

that pipe." This man, referred to generically as "John" replied "apologeti-
cally," "Opium no belly good . . . but me fixem pipe." With that, Clifford explained, "he drew a fat little jar toward him, of paste-like content" and in
"three or four whiffs" finished the pipeful. W. H. Gleadell wrote of entering
one opium den just as "a smoker was . . . commencing operations." He not
only observed the method and ritual of opium smoking but also, in vivid detail, recorded the process for his readers. Gleadell related that the smoker,
after "composing himself in a comfortable position on one of several couches
. . . took up the long wooden pipe provided by the establishment and carefully
examined it." Next, "taking up a long needle-like piece of steel" he "inserted it
in the ivory box and drew therefrom a small quantity of prepared opium."
Then, he "held this over the flame of the lamp"—because, as Gleadell explained, "the drug must be dried before it can be inhaled"—"carefully twist-
ing and turning it about until the heat had frizzled it up." Iza Hardy related
watching opium smokers "take a pinch of the dark jelly-like substance on a
wire and melt it over the lamp, then smear it over the aperture in the pipe, and
draw it with great deep breaths into the lungs."[54]

The intricate details of some of these descriptions suggest that they may
have not only functioned as one component of the lurid construction of a vicious Chinatown but also as instructional devices for the most adventurous.
The temptation to tourists was, at times, very real. W. H. Gleadell reported
that he not only began "to feel the effects of the opium-laden atmosphere" as
he watched the performance of opium smoking that he so carefully recorded
for his readers but that he and his companions were "very much pressed to try
a pipe ourselves." They "unanimously declined," and Gleadell reflected that
they were "deterred as much . . . by the fear of our surroundings as by the
sight of the white, sickly faces and glassy eyes of the smokers around us." Eleanor Caldwell was also invited to smoke opium. Her Chinese guide, who
may have been the same man she would later converse with about life and politics on a restaurant balcony, "twisted the opium on a little stick, burned it lovingly in a lamp, and depositing it in its receptacle at the side of the long
wooden tube, smoked a few whiffs, as exemplification." When the pipe was
passed in her direction, she and her companions did not decline. Instead they
"carefully wiped the mouth, and each took an inhalation." Caldwell was well
aware that her behavior was both transgressive and a little dangerous. She recalled that as she smoked, she saw "a Poe-like cat sitting on the edge of the
shelf" who "curved his back, as though the devil were expressing sympathy."[55]

While some Chinatown tourists who trekked down to the opium dens received offers to partake of the drug, others prompted different reactions from the people they saw and interacted with there. Eleanor Caldwell, in addition to being offered a smoke, reported that the men she observed were "lying in a trance, curled up," some with their backs toward her. One responded to her presence by leaning up on his elbow and looking at her in what she called "a dead-and-alive way . . . vacant of any comprehension." When she came upon another group of smokers in yet another den, her presence engendered a more hostile response. She described these men as "unhumanized beings, lolling in pale and imbecile torpor, or glaringly, gauntly resentful." Charles Warren Stoddard recalled not getting as much of a response as he would have liked from the smokers he encountered. When he initially addressed them he was "smiled at by delirious eyes." But as the drug took effect the smokers' heads sank "upon the pillows" and they no longer responded to his appeals, "even by a glance." A writer for *Cornhill Magazine*, however, reported a much livelier and sociable scenario in the opium den he entered in order "to purchase a pipe and smoking outfit" for his "curiosity case." Before he "had been in the place two minutes not an inch of standing room was unoccupied" and "every one who was able to speak any English volunteered advice and information" about what kind of pipe he should purchase.[56]

Chinese opium smokers clearly encountered more white tourists than they probably would have liked in the dens they frequented even if the displays of vice and depravity they presented were rewarded with money or drugs. Yet although tourist literature generally represented the typical opium smoker as Chinese and the typical white visitor as a tourist, a number also acknowledged that the Chinese were not the only opium smokers in Chinatown. Aside from the kind of incident in which Eleanor Caldwell and her friends each took a puff from an opium pipe, there were other white people, not tourists in the traditional sense, who frequented the dens. In many respects, because of the kind of social mixture and transgression of racial boundaries these white smokers represented, their activities far outweighed those of the Chinese in their scandalousness. Yet they too, in the ways they were written about and memorialized through photography, became part of Chinatown's tourist terrain. "White Women in Opium Den, Chinatown S.F.," one of the many photographs I. W. Taber produced for tourist consumption, depicted two white women—one smoking, the other asleep or unconscious—in the company of a leering Asian man. Although probably staged, this image mobilized notions of Chinatown's sexual danger prevalent in contemporary novels and short stories and powerfully activated imaginings of the licentiousness that could afflict young white women compromised by drugs (see figure 28).[57]

B. E. Lloyd explained to readers of his guide that "in some of the more secluded opium dens, and those kept under strict privacy by the proprietors," one would "find a number of young men and women—*not Chinese*—distributed about the room on lounges and beds in miscellaneous confusion, all under the influence of the drug." According to Lloyd, most of the women were of "the disreputable class," but the young men were "our respectable sons and brothers, who move in good society, and are of 'good repute.'" E. W. Wood, another San Franciscan "acquainted with the ins and outs" of Chinatown, testified that he discovered both "the sons and daughters of the wealthiest and most refined families . . . laying on the filthiest covered bunks along side of cracked and broken layouts, smoking and sleeping their lives away." An article in the *Chronicle* claimed, however, that the "most serious phase of the opium habit" in the city was the hold it had secured "upon the lower and more depraved classes of whites"—suggesting, when placed alongside the accounts of Lloyd and Wood, that opium use was a pastime that crossed class lines. As J. Connor Torrey sensationally put it, "Five thousand white slaves to the oriental drug in San Francisco, and the majority own to having taken the initial whiff in 'Chinatown.'"[58]

For whites interested in ingesting opium, neither finding the drug nor a place to consume it was particularly difficult. The enforcement of laws prohibiting "public opium-houses" was lax at best and private smoking among the Chinese was common enough that white guests in Chinese homes or businesses—or white tourists, like Eleanor Caldwell, in an opium den—were frequently invited to smoke. A story in the *Chronicle* that noted many of Chinatown's opium dens "were in the habit of providing the pipe for white people" was confirmed by one white visitor who, upon entering two different dens, was asked, "You wanchee smokee?" In one resort, this visitor "drew the fellow on so far as to induce him to bring a pipe and prepare to weigh 25 cents' worth of opium." The writer of this account also reported witnessing "an earthen-faced and haggard-looking young white man" approach "the basement of Wing Hing, 746 Commercial street" where there was "a great flaming advertisement in Chinese calling attention to the place as a smoking resort." The young man

Figure 28. White women in opium den. This image, probably staged, plays on widespread fears of Chinatown as a vicious place of sexual danger for white women, especially when combined with drug use. (I. W. Taber, photographer. Chinese in California, Bancroft Library, University of California, Berkeley)

"cast furtive glances on each side and then dashed down the steps." As one young woman, an actress and opium user, purportedly put it, "Then some one suggests a trip to Chinatown, and the opium-house obtains another customer. That's the way I drifted into them, and I must confess, I am not sorry for it either. It's a deal better than whiskey, and I had my choice of one or the other." If an interested party was not keen on visiting an opium den, a number of accounts pointed out that it was neither uncommon for retail stores in Chinatown to sell opium nor "to see young men and women stealing into Chinatown at night, entering an opium shop, and procuring half a dollar's worth of the lethal drug." Making it even easier was the fact that accounts in the San Francisco press that at some level were meant to function as exposés published huge lists of the names and addresses of both dens and retail outlets.[59]

Authors of Chinatown literature, in tandem with the practices of Chinatown guides, deftly charted paths that facilitated the navigation of
Chinatown's tourist terrain in ways that linked a visitor's experience of this
cultural frontier to an understanding of the Chinese as filthy, unassimilable,
vicious, and barbaric. They also often ventured a step further and used their
depictions as vehicles for articulating the morality and merits of the most
pressing social issue that pertained to their work: the "Chinese Question."
Throughout the second half of the nineteenth century, Chinese immigration
was a hotly debated issue in San Francisco and beyond. The vast majority of
the time, authors of Chinatown tourist literature answered the "Chinese
Question" in the negative. The not so subtle subtext of their arguments generally centered on whether or not Chinese immigrants were compatible with
the American body politic and revolved around issues of assimilability, public
health, labor competition, and vice—the same themes that were used to construct the "Oriental" in the popular imagination and which pervaded analyses
of tourist sites. The author of an article that ran in *Scribner's* put it bluntly but
typically, mobilizing themes of unassimilability and social pollution. "While
immigration is the life-blood of young nations," this writer explained, "there
is such a thing as blood-poisoning, and this is frequently occasioned by the
presence of some foreign substance." In this writer's opinion, "John" was
"that substance" because he was "utterly devoid of any quality of assimilation." A journalist who penned an article in *Outing* expressed his hostility to
Chinese immigration through his articulation of what had become widely
held beliefs about the threats the Chinese posed to free white labor. He explained, "The Chinese, with their great cunning, oust American labor. They
work at what would be starving wages to a white man, for a few years, then
leave for home with their hoarded earnings." Expressing his fears about the
risks Chinatown and Chinese immigrants posed to public health, J. Torrey
Connor warned that "when smallpox and other infectious diseases that germi-
nate in the filth of that malodorous quarter are raging, then, indeed do we
come to a full realization of the undesirability of our Mongolian neighbors."
Summing up tourist literature's overall sentiments, he added, "Unlike other
foreigners who come to our shores, the material from which 'good citizens'
are made is not to be found in this alien race."[60]

CHAPTER FOUR

Celebrating the City:
Labor, Progress, and the Promenade
at the Mechanics' Institute Fairs

On the morning of September 8, 1857, the Mechanics' Institute of San Francisco opened the doors of its specially constructed pavilion on Montgomery Street between Sutter and Post and revealed to those who ventured inside an Industrial Exhibition that showcased the fruits of "California genius and labor." The pavilion that held these representations of the state's progress took the "form of a Greek cross, with arms 60 feet wide by 180 long" and had "an elegant and airy dome sixty feet high" at its center. It was "composed of a wooden frame, with siding of green redwood, and a covering of strong canvass." Although designed as a temporary structure, according to the *Daily Alta California*, "from the heights about the city" the pavilion's bright linen covering, its graceful dome, and its overall size "as compared with others in the vicinity" created an eye-catchingly impressive edifice. Inside "festoons of bright green foliage" swept "in graceful curves along the delicate tracery of the upper framework." The dome's pillars were "decked with the brilliant flags of all civilized nations" and the walls were covered by "tasteful drapery, and elegant objects of art or mechanism." At the center of the dome hung "a large chandelier" with "a splendid marble fountain" rising beneath it.[1]

Fair-goers were treated to displays of 941 articles of locally made products, the work of California artists, live musical performances every night, and speeches that emphasized the state's overall progress as well as the dignity of the labor that furthered that end. Attendees took in the educational features of the exhibits—which received a bevy of prizes from fair officials—and also enjoyed the space for socializing and promenading created by the fair. In the evenings, the pavilion—bedecked with "splendid lights" and a "dense crowd

of visitors"—became "the great resort of all the beauty and fashion and intelligence of the city." Within the first ten days, the fair drew through its doors
no less than 10,000 patrons, garnering gross receipts sufficient to pay its expenses and to generate some revenue for the institute as well as local charities.
As another *Alta* report explained, the fair had succeeded in kindling "a feeling
of pride" among members of San Francisco's still young community by effectively demonstrating that the state was "rich in other elements than gold" and
that these would ensure continued prosperity long after the exhaustion of its
"mineral wealth."[2]

The fair's popularity, as well as the way it tapped into San Franciscans'
hopes and fears, proved a harbinger of things to come. The 1857 fair, far from
a one-time event, turned out to be the first of thirty-one industrial exhibitions
sponsored by the Mechanics' Institute held almost every year—usually for
about four weeks in late summer—from 1857 until 1899. During this time,
five different pavilions in an equivalent number of locations housed fairs that,
by the late 1870s, drew upwards of 10, 000 to 20,000 attendees per night. For
many San Franciscans, buying season tickets and going to the fair almost
every evening became a tradition. In 1868, one could do that for $3 as an indi-
vidual; $5 for "a gentleman and a lady"; and $1.50 for a child. A single day's
pass cost 50 cents for an adult and 25 cents for a child. For Lucy Pownall, a
high school student and devoted fair patron during the 1876, 1877, and 1878
seasons, the fairs—which she attended occasionally with family members but
usually with her male and female friends—had a central place in her budding
social life. On August 12, 1878, in a letter to her parents, who remained in Tu-
olomne County while she went to school in the city, Lucy revealed both her
enthusiasm and anticipation for the upcoming fair. She wrote, evincing the
sensibility of a middle-class young lady eager for the freedom to roam the
fairgrounds and socialize with her peers, "The Fair opens tomorrow and then
there will be a place of amusement for leisure hours." At the fair, Lucy sam-
pled the biscuits baked in "little stoves" given away by the Bower Bros., the
yeast-powder company; entered a raffle to win a piano; and ate ice cream. But
what she enjoyed the most was running into a number of her "school mates"
and generally taking in the "very large crowd." So that her parents could "get
some idea of the Fair" that was such an important part of her life, she made
sure to send them a copy of *The Argonaut Sketchbook*—a popular illustrated
chronicle of the fair's social world.[3]

Lucy Pownall would have agreed with the *Morning Call* writer who explained in 1882 that, although begun as an experiment, the Mechanics' Institute fairs had become "one of the features of our city life"—"a fixed institution" that "the public could not do well without." While over the years the number and types of displays shifted to reflect developments in technology, agriculture, industry, and manufacturing, the basic format of emphasizing local products, the honor of labor, the progress of California, and the mixture of educational exhibits with the sociability of the promenade remained essentially unchanged. In describing the plan of the 1868 exhibition to its readers, The *Mechanics Fair Daily Press* explained that as the visitor entered the door he would "find on his right hand, machinery and hardware in general, and on his left textile fabrics and lighter manufactures." The "front wings" were occupied by "musical instruments, drawings, and liquors . . . on the right hand, and by a restaurant on the left." The long traverse at the rear was devoted to art. In the galleries were "wines, confectionary, bookbinders productions, etc." The steam plow, a major technological innovation being featured that year, was "stabled outside" (see figure 29).[4]

Every fair was organized around the theme of progress—from the progress of the state and city in producing goods and innovations to the progress of individual citizens in educating themselves so they would be suited to fully participate in the civic economy. Orators at opening and closing ceremonies articulated a vision of class relations that emphasized the intrinsic harmony of different class interests and downplayed conflict. This outlook on economic relations, advocated by the Mechanics' Institute, also embraced a "producer ethic" that stressed the dignity of all labor and defined significant, complementary social positions for members of both the working and middle classes. In the elaborate pavilions erected to hold the fairs, people of varied classes, genders, and ethnicities mixed, promenaded, and became as much a part of the exhibit as the fruits of industrial progress. What emerged as the most noted forms of amusement were the largely middle-class rituals of heterosocial flirtation, courtship, and romance—reported upon as hopeful preludes to matrimony and a solid familial order. Year after year, at the same time that the Mechanics' Institute's fairs were displaying local manufactures, they also formed a cultural frontier that brought diverse San Franciscans together and disseminated a recipe for the way the family and the economy could be structured to create a city ordered according to quintessentially American variants

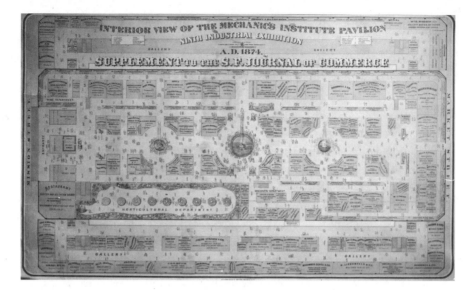

Figure 29. Interior view of the ninth Mechanics' Institute Fair, 1874. San Francisco's Mechanics' Institute regularly hosted these wildly popular fairs from 1857 to 1899. (Alice Phelan Sullivan Library at the Society of California Pioneers, San Francisco)

of capitalist, republican, and patriarchal values. Over their forty-two-year span, the Mechanics' Institute fairs functioned as high-profile ritual events that responded to what institute leaders viewed as the endemic social problems of imbalanced sex ratios, retarded family formation, social fluidity, and worker radicalism by promoting a vision of class harmony securely entwined with domesticity.

The Mechanics' Institute's vision of what constituted a well-ordered city had grown out of a reaction against the economic and social disorder of the gold rush years. It was guided by a desire to turn San Francisco's largely transient community built on the suspect economies of mining and speculation into a self-sufficient, stable, and identifiably American metropolis grounded in the sounder and more respectable economies of agriculture and, especially, manufactures. The Mechanics' Institute's founding had been a direct response to depressed economic conditions brought on by decreased yields from Sierra placers, the replacement of individual placer mining with corporate hydraulic mining, and declines in shipping and trading that had left half of the city's population unemployed. Organized to alleviate the economic downtown, the Mechanics' Institute sought to aid unemployed workers by providing technical and moral training and, in the process, to foster social order in the midst of fears about the havoc large numbers of unemployed men could wreak on the city's business climate. In other words, the Mechanics' Institute functioned to aid and abet the process of capital accumulation—it smoothed economic transitions, kept economic disorder at bay, fostered healthy competition, and provided worker training and education.[5] From the start its mission reflected its own double-edged nature—that it was for the working classes but organized, in most respects, by the middle classes and elite to create well-disciplined workers, to promote middle-class values, and to further social and economic advancement among the aspiring working class. Few middle classes were newer, born out of a more socially fluid context, or confronted with a working class more prone to unionization than nineteenth-century San Francisco's. The Mechanics' Institute became a key cultural institution through which this nascent middle class and elite could attempt to give order both to itself and the city's emerging society.[6]

The Mechanics' Institute had come into being on December 11, 1854, at a meeting of "a few earnest and not over-wealthy young men" in the Tax Collector's Office in the City Hall Building on Kearny Street. George K. Gluyas, a machinist and the builder of a local foundry, acted as its chair. The organizing committee—made up of "a stonemason, a foundryman, a carpenter, a commission merchant, and the owner of a sawmill who was also a contractor"—brought together artisans and businessmen in a cross-class and mixed-occupation combination that would become one of the institute's hallmarks. The constitution these men drafted for the new organization spelled out its intentions: "This Association shall be known as the 'Mechanics' Institute, of the City of San Francisco,' and shall have for its object the establishment of a library and reading room, the collection of a cabinet, scientific apparatus, works of art, and for other literary and scientific purposes." The city's newspapers not only published the meeting's proceedings but also commented favorably on the Mechanics' Institute's plans.[7]

Although the financial solvency of the Mechanics' Institute was uncertain for the first several years of its existence, more than enough San Franciscans purchased shares within its initial six months to afford the rent of "a $25-a-month room on the fourth floor of the Express Building on the northeast corner of Montgomery and California Streets." The institute's library holdings and the scope of its activities grew rapidly. On April 5, 1855, S. G. Bugbee presented the organization with its first four books—the Bible, the Constitution of the United States, the *Encyclopaedia of Architecture*, and *Curtis on Conveyancing*. The texts, emblems of Christian religion, American politics, and the building, buying, and selling of property, were apt harbingers of the organization's social and economic agenda. By the end of the year, it had collected one hundred volumes. In March 1856, at the Institute's first annual meeting, the president happily reported on the growth of the library collection to 487 volumes as well as its successful free lecture series at the Music Hall and the organization of a debating society among its members. By the early 1870s, the Mechanics' Institute was locally renowned for its "classes in mechanical drawing, applied mathematics, wood carving, iron work, and other technical subjects . . . its free lectures, and its chess club." By the turn of the century, it had over 4,000 members and its library was stocked with 135,000 books.[8]

As Ramon E. Wilson, Esq., emphasized in the address he gave at the opening of the 1886 fair, the Mechanics' Institute had maintained a long and proud history of being "indifferent to sects, creeds and parties." From the beginning, its members came from the varied class positions contained under the rubric of the category "mechanic." Many of its early members were drawn from the ranks of apprentices in various trades, and the organization's first *Constitution, By-Laws, Rules and Regulations* had declared that "all members eligible to office must be mechanics and citizens of San Francisco." But even then the term *mechanic* was fluid enough to include common laborers in search of education and, as the occupations of those present at the founding meeting indicated, a commission merchant, the builder of a foundry, and the owner of a sawmill. Edward Pollock, chosen to deliver the opening poem at the inauguration of the first fair in 1857, was "a house painter by trade and a lawyer by profession." By 1885, when the institute published an updated version of its constitution, membership was simply limited to "any person of good character" as defined by the Board of Trustees. Eligibility to the board did not require one to be a mechanic per se, but it did demand "devotion to progress in technical education and economic industries."[9]

In the early years of the Mechanics' Institute, some of the openness of the category "mechanic" could be attributed to the exigencies of gold-rush society. So much money could be made doing the work of a tradesman or laborer that stories abounded of lawyers, physicians, bookkeepers, and other professionals choosing to take on a very lucrative yet usually temporary type of downward mobility. But the fluidity that allowed a lawyer to claim instead the status of a mechanic—and made this status desirable—also reflected the

Mechanics' Institute's embrace of a conceptualization of society that venerated every producer and espoused the essential harmony of the interests of different classes. At the core of this "producer ethic" was the conviction that only those white men who created tangible forms of wealth—who farmed or mined the land, fished the seas, or produced goods in small workshops—had the virtue required to participate in creating and maintaining the nation's democratic republic. In the pantheon of republican idols, the mechanic took his place alongside the independent yeoman farmer as a potent symbol of American values. Not only did this honoring of labor represent a shift away from an older idea that held that while hard work might be necessary, there was little honor in it, but it made those who did not produce—who made a living from the work of others, whose work was relegated to the realm of speculation or ideology, or who were idle or impoverished—morally suspect. Yet even with these exclusions, like the concept of "the mechanic," the concept of "the producer" was elastic enough to embrace laborers as well as artisans and tradesmen (some of whom might be owners of workshops as well as employers of others), small to medium-sized merchants and manufacturers, and farmers of all stripes. Part of what allowed the producer ethic's inclusiveness was that it was not particularly critical of capitalism's acquisitiveness, economic individualism, or profit-mindedness. It did find that extreme economic inequality, in the form of the increasing gulf between haves and have-nots, went against the grain of the nation's democratic principles but did not see anything intrinsically wrong with making money or getting ahead. Since contained within the producer ethic was the idea of "the harmony of interests"— that different classes in society ultimately worked together for the good of the whole—in this schema's purest form, no preordained conflict of interest existed between workers and owners.[10]

From very early on, the elasticity of the term *mechanic*, the embrace of the producer ethic, and its espousal of the harmony of interests meant that the Mechanics' Institute had a broad membership that included workers; middle-class artisans, owners, and employers; and even the elite. But with class variety also came economic, social, and educational differences that signified a certain hierarchy of influence within the organization. Members of San Francisco's elite, for example, were involved in the production of the Mechanics' Institute fairs from their inception. James Lick, Thomas O. Larkin, and Samuel Brannan were awarded honorary membership during the planning of the first fair and readily took on advisory roles. Although Lick had roots as a piano maker and Brannan had worked as a journeyman printer, all three had made fortunes in the gold rush and were, by 1856, occupied as landowners, entrepreneurs, and financiers. For the first fair, Lick donated the use of the block of land he owned on Montgomery Street between Sutter and Post. Ten years later, when the Mechanics' Institute relocated its fair pavilion to the east side of Eighth Street between Market and Mission, real estate mogul Andrew B. McCreery felt so generously toward the institute that he only charged one dollar a year plus the payment of taxes to lease the site. To help pay for the new pavilion, projected to cost $107,000, William C. Ralston—the banker and developer of the Palace Hotel—advanced $5,000 that spurred the quick raising of an additional $52,630 within just a few days. While some of the support from wealthy men might have come from a sense of loyalty to their roots as mechanics, and some from a new sense of interest that emerged as they funneled more of their profits into the city's manufacturing enterprises, all were motivated to stand behind the Mechanic's Institute because they viewed its economic and social interests as commensurate with their own.[11]

Although the producer ethic was a vital part of the Mechanics' Institute from the start, its philosophy of the harmony of class interests was articulated most forcefully at the fairs beginning in the late 1860s—when manufacturing enterprises in the city were expanding and employing increasing numbers of workers. While the timing of San Francisco's settlement as well as its rapid development meant that there was no long-standing artisan tradition withering under the weight of industrial pressures, many of the men who migrated to San Francisco came with dreams of becoming Jacksonian-style independent proprietors—sometimes as tradesmen but often as miners in the goldfields. For some, embracing the identity of a mechanic in the city's industrializing context and forsaking what the Mechanics' Institute designated as the suspect economy of mining necessitated giving up dreams of economic independence. Just as the term *mechanic* was flexible enough to include members of the elite, it also could bend in the other direction to accommodate those who labored for wages. Although manufactures and factory production were, on one hand, viewed in a generally positive light because they symbolized progress, on the other, their increasing prominence signified the fact that the idea of California as a promised-land of economic independence was something realized by only a few and a dream that died hard for many more.

In general, periods that favored the growth of manufactures in San Francisco were not particularly kind to workers. The same conditions that favored labor—primarily labor scarcity, which kept wages high and made workers reluctant to accept industrial employment—actually hindered industrial development. Factory work tended to diminish worker control and the large number of available laborers that made manufacturing possible decreased the bargaining power when labor was both scarce and in demand. The Mechanics' Institute's mission to direct and shape a diverse, often transient, and growing population of workers by a somewhat backward looking but nonetheless potent discourse of harmonious class interests—at both its headquarters and its fairs—exerted a countervailing influence upon the growing threat increasingly disgruntled workers posed to economic and social order. At the same time that fair orators were advocating their vision of class harmony most forcefully, the spread of industrialization was actively creating a far more disharmonious reality. Conveniently, ideas about class harmony proved malleable enough to address the varied climates of labor-capital relations that ebbed and flowed throughout nineteenth-century San Francisco.[12]

Speaking at the opening exercises of the 1871 Mechanics' Institute fair, Hon. Milton S. Latham—the state's former governor and U.S. senator—voiced the central tenets of the harmony of interests in an address that was, according to the *Alta*, "throughout its course and at its termination, most warmly applauded." These kinds of ritual orations—regular events at the opening and closing of each fair—allowed for an articulation of the organization's values to a broad audience of listeners assembled on the cultural frontier that the Mechanics' Institute fairs created. Since the local press printed many of these speeches, their message also had the potential to reach an audience that extended far beyond fair attendees. Latham began by explaining that "the value of labor" was controlled by the principle of "supply and demand." He further elaborated that the more capital that was "introduced into a community, the greater the demand for labor." Consequently, "capital" was "the real friend of laboring men." At a time when the always prevalent and often radical but frequently fleeting local unions were becoming increasingly stable, Latham used this logic to take a clear anti-union stance, characterizing "combinations to arrest or suspend labor" as "mischievous in practice, and prejudicial in results" because they decreased "the funds for wages." Latham could oppose trade unions because he believed that there was "no natural conflict between capitalists and laboring men." Instead, they were "of equal necessity to each other's prosperity, capital being dependent on labor and labor on capital." He ended with a rather grand vision of progress through class cooperation in which he saw "capital and labor" with hands joined together "in harmony, steadily co-operating for each other's prosperity . . . increasing the comforts of our race, and enlarging the sphere of human happiness."[13]

Even the more fiery orations about the rights of labor given at the Mechanics' Institute fairs were positioned within the discourse of the harmony of interests. At the opening of the 1878 fair, W. J. Winans, Esq., decided to embrace—yet at the same time direct toward a harmonious conclusion—the prevailing strength of labor organization. He called on his audience to use "systematic combination and properly directed effort" to "elevate the condition, extend the usefulness, [and] promote the prosperity of the producing classes." "Organization," he declared, was "power." Yet these pro-union sentiments were not grounded in beliefs about any inherent antagonism between classes but rather in the hopes for greater harmony between them. "In sustaining the rights of labor," Winans continued, "you lift it up to a closer equality with capital" so that "the invidious and class distinctions of society are swept away, and the whole community is brought to stand upon a common platform."[14]

At the inaugural address of the 1888 fair, P. B. Cornwall—the Institute's president—combined the rights of labor with what he saw as its duty to stay firmly within the bounds of law, order, and the harmony of interests. Cornwall had made a fortune during the gold rush, was a member of California's first state assembly, and throughout his life continued to profitably invest in mining in both California and Washington as well as in other business concerns. By the time of his speech, many of the city's stable unions that had risen to prominence through the mid-1880s had fallen prey to a combination of an employer-led, city-wide open shop drive and national economic depression. "If capital infringes the law, we have the right to correct it," he explained. "If labor, misguided and criminal, attempts to overturn the laws, we, the majority, within the ranks of labor, must discipline and control it." According to Cornwall, riots were "never excusable;" anarchy was "a crime;" and communism was "indefensible." Then Cornwall went on to explain why the harmony of interests was a more valid point of view than that of class antagonism. "The cry against capital," he argued, was "not half a truth, because the greater bulk of the nation's vast wealth" was "owned and enjoyed by the working forces which created it." Labor was "the master," capital was "the indispensible, if not the always willing slave." But, tellingly, a little later into his speech, he revealed where the power and desire really lay. He admitted that as "proud as we are of labor, as dignified and honorable as we concede it to be, let none of us be so dishonest and hypocritical as not to admit that we would prefer to be millionaires rather than working mechanics."[15]

In fact, Cornwall's hyperbole notwithstanding, throughout the nineteenth century—whether workers were scarce or in demand—the Mechanics' Institute fairs used the producer ethic to put forth the view that labor was honorable and that laborers, because of the important contributions they made toward both economic and political progress, were dignified members of civic society. By emphasizing the significant role mechanics had to play in creating and maintaining an American society on the shores of the Pacific, speakers articulated a component of an identity for mechanics that had the potential to both control and empower. It empowered by offering adherents a stake in the community; it controlled by demanding limited challenges to the status quo. At the closing address of the city's second fair, Rev. A. H. Myers told those gathered to hear him speak that "the spirit of the age" demanded that they put away their "aristocratic notions" and recognize that "king" labor was "about to assume the government of this land." "Mechanics of San Francisco—citizens of California," he intoned, "you are engaged in the responsible and momentous work of founding a mighty empire." At the opening of the 1864 fair, Hon. John Conness explained that "the history of mankind" proved "that the foremost races of men" who had "controlled the civilized world, and who became great and prosperous, and impressed their ideas, habits, and civilization upon other races and peoples, were only foremost, great, and prosperous because a large proportion of their people were engaged in agriculture and the mechanic arts." Also stressing mechanics' political and economic significance to the process of building an American place, in his inaugural address at the 1885 fair, P. B. Cornwall told his audience that there were "no people in our country so much interested in the maintenance of our American system of national economy as the manufacturing and artisan classes throughout the land." He characterized them as "the bone and sinew of the nation," devoted to advancing "the prosperity of the country and the glory of the Republic."[16]

The educational mission of both the fairs and the institute itself was designed to harness and develop mechanics' potential as productive citizens for their own advancement as well as for the development of the city in which they lived. In the early years, mechanics were positioned—somewhat like farmers in other contexts—as bastions of moral and familial order and thus the advance guard of civilization on the California frontier. Not only did this fit within the harmony of interests and the producer ethic, but a society organized around happy, sober, and industrious mechanics' families would counter the Californio and indigenous barbarity that preceded American conquest, as well as the notorious debauched and disordered mining culture that succeeded it. In his opening address at the first fair, Henry F. Williams—identified in the press as "a carpenter and a member of the Institute"—spelled out the civilizing role he envisioned for California mechanics. He began by drawing his listeners' attention to how "we are indebted to the agriculturists and mechanics of our State for our present improved condition morally and socially" and contrasted this to the conditions brought about by a society of miners who "from time immemorial . . . have been distinguished for their laxity of morals." He reminded his audience that, "Our population was then composed chiefly of men, who were drawn hither by the glittering gold, and whose only desire, apparently, was to amass a fortune in the shortest possible time and leave our shores for distant lands never again to return." "How different the aspect," he continued, "when our fertile valleys began to fill up with farmers and their families,—when our cities, towns, and villages began to assume a character for stability by the permanent location there of artizans and tradesmen with their household gods, and all they held most dear."[17]

The Mechanics' Institute continued to reserve an elevated status to "artizans and tradesmen" in the progress of the state long past the point when their presence as permanent settlers with families was needed. Increasingly, mechanics were targeted for the role they could play in the developing metropolis as both workers and citizens if they were well educated and well trained. The Mechanics' Institute expected attendees to be actively involved in furthering their personal progress by taking advantage of the educational offerings of the fairs and the institute. The *Industrial Fair Gazette* defined the annual fairs as "the people's colleges" at which "farmers and mechanics" improved "their education" and from which they went forth "every year with an increase of useful knowledge." Going to the fairs, taking in the displays, and mingling with others not only filled mechanics with a sense of "the dignity and importance of their respective fields of operation" but also provided them with insights into how to make improvements that would "make the labors of the coming year lighter and more profitable." The *Industrial Fair Gazette* also explained to its readers that "in nearly all occupations" there was "a marked difference in the value of the labor" of a man who was illiterate and one who could "read and write." This editorial also noted that "a common laborer" who could "tell time by the clock" was "worth much more" than one without this skill. Although this may have had as much to do with the ability to adhere to new forms of work discipline as education, it nevertheless tied the acquisition of particular skills to one's ability to succeed in the labor market. Some tensions existed regarding the dependent status of wage workers in a republican society that embraced rhetoric that valued its citizens' independence, but for the most part the traits of a good worker in a capitalist economy were made to square with those of a good republican citizen.[18]

Of particular importance was how advances in scientific education contributed to the social and economic status of mechanics. "Nothing has done more to add dignity to the standing and calling of the mechanic," the *Mechanics' Fair Daily Press* intoned in 1869, "than the institution of Industrial Exhibitions. The wonderful creations of mechanical skill and ingenuity are admired everywhere." This was, in part, because science—in the form of technological advancements—had been an important factor in enabling national expansion and also because innovation tended to be equated with the highest levels of civilization. The mechanic, as a result, was "changed from a monotonous thoughtless machine, to a thinking, contriving being." Speaking at the opening of the first fair, Henry Williams had told his audience, "Ever bear in mind that the mechanic's duty is now something more than mere drudgery . . . he must combine science and art with labor and capital, to meet the exigencies of the times." Because of the high esteem in which skilled mechanics were now held, the occupation had become "honorable instead of discreditable" and was "no longer regarded as servile." In many respects, the promotion of science in the mechanic arts was part and parcel of the kind of self-progress that the Mechanics' Institute advocated for individual mechanics. But it also allowed upwardly mobile and more educated mechanics to disassociate themselves from manual work and assert an authoritative status over those less skilled while continuing to self-identify as mechanics. Ironically, however, it was at this time that both locally and nationally increasing numbers of mechanics were losing their crafts to the deskilled work processes of factory production and that the model of the successful inventor as a local artisan and tinkerer was giving way to that of the highly trained engineer with corporate backing.[19]

Although the promotion of science at times worked to highlight class differences among those who fell within the category of mechanic, the fairs also sought to connect the union of science and the mechanic arts to their vision of harmonious class relations. Rev. Dr. Scott, speaking at the advent of the first fair, delivered a careful explanation of the complementarity of the artisan and the scientist. "The Pavilion Palace is an exponent of the union of art with science," he told his audience. To alleviate any fears that one might be held in higher regard than the other he explained, in terms that resonated with the harmony of interests, "There is no jealousy between the laborer and the inventor of machines, nor any contention between art and science . . . The producer, the consumer and the trading-middle man, who brings the producer and the consumer together, are all members of one great family."[20] The seal designed to represent the Mechanics' Institute was indicative of the desire to show the happy union of the mechanic arts and science and to further elaborate the harmony of interests and its connection to economic progress. Soon after its appearance in 1858, the seal was described by the *Alta* as representing "a blacksmith and a man of science shaking hands." According to the reporter, "the latter holds a roll of paper in his hands, and has at his side a telescope and a globe, as the implements of scientific investigation, and a lyre and palette with brushes, as indicative of the fine arts. The blacksmith holds his hammer in his hand, and at his side are an anvil, a cog wheel, a plough, and a crane. Between the two figures is seen a bee-hive, with the little insects, which are the emblems of industry and economic foresight." In 1871, the *Industrial Fair Gazette* spoke of the fair as "the union of many minds and many hands.[21]

The conceptualization of progress promoted at the fairs included not only that of the individual citizen-worker, but also the city of San Francisco and the state of California. Progress was the key to the transition from the speculative and morally suspect economy of the gold rush to the stability and honor associated with the mechanic arts and agriculture.[22] It was also linked to notions of self-sufficiency. In the rhetoric of the Mechanics' Institute, the city and state needed to be freed from dependence on imports from Eastern states and other nations just as the citizen-worker needed to be independent and educated enough to maintain the civic virtue necessary to build and sustain a new republican society. Self-sufficiency required a fully functioning, diverse economy—not one dependent solely on mining. This, in turn, demanded certain kinds of social relations—a class, gender, and economic order that was consistent with the Mechanic Institute's vision. During his address, Reverend Dr.

Figure 30. Encouraging home industry, ca. 1870. The Mechanics' Institute's fairs promoted economic self-sufficiency as a symbol of the kind of social order it wanted to create in San Francisco. (Alice Phelan Sullivan Library at the Society of California Pioneers, San Francisco)

Scott dramatically identified the first fair as "our *Hejira,* whence we shall date our exodus from misrule, lawlessness and corruption, and from a servile dependence on other parts of the world." Although most forcefully articulated at the earliest fairs, concerns about self-sufficiency continued to be expressed through the late 1860s. The *Alta* described the 1868 fair as "evidence of the progress of mechanical and artistic industry, and of the independence of the State in manufactures of necessity and taste." Materially, home industries and California products continued to be honored in exhibits through the late 1870s (see figure 30).[23]

For San Franciscans anxious about social order in the face of a "wild west" reputation, the fairs served as especially important vehicles for demonstrating the city's advances in attaining a fully civilized state and becoming an American place—both to itself and to the rest of the nation. At the fairs, the displays of goods—the fruits of industrial progress—provided tangible evidence of the city and state's forward march. James A. Banks, in his inaugural address at the second Mechanics' Institute fair in 1858, explained to his audience that industrial fairs were "a most efficient means of marking the advancement of a people towards a high civilization . . . and in no State of the Union—in no quarter of the globe—are so many practical advantages to be derived from them as in our own young, vigorous and rich, but isolated, misrepresented and misunderstood California." Speaking in 1869, Irving Scott linked the progress of California to that of the nation, its republican experiment, and imperial expansion. "So rapid and marvellous has been this growth, that the mind scarce comprehends that half a continent has been reclaimed from savage rule, filled with people, interlaced with iron ways; and this, its outpost on the westward march, just nineteen years old, changing the current of exchange, dividing the world's commerce and carrying the banner of progress 'full high advanced.'"[24]

As Scott's comment about "savages" illustrates, ideas about the progress and advancing civilization of the city and the state often contained a racial component. During his address, James A. Banks, for example, touted the diversity of the labor force that had fueled California's growth but conspicuously overlooked the contributions not only of the Chinese but also Irish and Italians. "The skill of our mechanics is of no ordinary kind. It is not merely that of the tasteful Frenchman, the exact German, the careful and scientific Englishman, nor of the ingenious, venturesome Yankee, but a most favorable combination of them all." Whiteness—and the destiny of the white race—was also inscribed in the space of the fairs through goods and commodities. While this was expressed most explicitly in the early years of the fairs—when the fact that San Francisco was a recently conquered place was most actively felt—it was a part of the definitions of progress and civilization throughout the nineteenth century. Certain types of goods were equated with the progress of conquest and thus with the civilized state of the conquerors in contrast to the barbarity of the conquered. For example, in 1857, the *Alta* told a racialized story of progress in the context of its juxtaposition of some of the articles displayed at the fair. It began with a description of "an old California plow" that emphasized its simplicity and suggested it was from a more barbaric—that is, Spanish, time. "Thus one piece of wood, such as any American axeman could prepare in an hour, and a plate of iron, eight inches long by six wide made a Spanish plow. It is enough to make an ox weep." The piece then continued, "We can form some slight notion of the change in California, since the dominion of these plows, by turning into the department of furniture and seeing the display made by Jonas G. Clark, of sofas, chairs, and other articles, of the most elegant design and delicate finish, for furnishing the parlors of refined society." In terms of symbolic value, there was no question that parlor furniture—the epitome of middle-class status—conferred a more civilized designation than a "Spanish plow."[25] Rev. Dr. Scott, a local Presbyterian minister, invoked these same themes in an address delivered in the context of the first fair. "In the long years gone by before the American occupation of this coast," he explained, "there may have been savage and semi-barbarous fetes—scalp-dances, bull-fights, bear-fights, horse races, or a vernal lassoing of colts and calves for the branding but nothing—*never anything like an Industrial Exhibition . . .* in the order of progress."[26]

The role of the Mechanics' Institute fairs as places of amusement existed alongside—and sometimes in competition with—their goals to educate and demonstrate progress and self-sufficiency. The fairs, after all, served as a cultural frontier designed not to just teach lessons about class relations and social and technological advancements, but to do so in a celebratory context that brought people together to meet, socialize, and have fun. In 1865, the *Alta* gave expression to the tension that often existed between amusement and education. "As an entertainment, the Fair has been an institution with which we might well be satisfied. The brilliancy of the illumination in the evening, made by 1,200 gas lights, the excellent instrumental music, the play of the fountain, the elegant decoration and flowers, and the variety of faces and dresses presented by the moving throng, well repay a visit," the paper explained. "But the fair is also an educational institution," the *Alta* gently reminded its readers. "It collects the results of many branches of industry together, and places them where every one can see for himself." Several other accounts conveyed their impression that for many fair-goers, amusement overrode education as the primary attraction. "As an exhibition of home manufactures, home productions and foreign importations, it would be pretty hard to beat. But it is an absolute fact that not one-fourth of the people who visit the Pavilion know what all it contains," the *Industrial Fair Gazette* told its readers in 1871. "In fact, the goods and wares there exhibited do not constitute the attraction; to a few old fossils who are past the age of flirtations, and to country greens who never see anything outside of the city, the pumps and quartz mills, the salt and sugar, the soap and honey, present unusual attractions; but most persons go to see and be seen, to hear the music, to meet friends, make acquaintances, and to spend a pleasant evening." A writer for the *Call* likewise admitted in 1882 that, "Probably to the mass of visitors the fair is simply a show. It is an agreeable and well-conducted rendezvous, where people meet each other."[27]

But even though writers at the time often drew distinctions between fairs as educational institutions and as places of amusement, both functions not only bled into one another but also embodied many of the same tensions that were at the heart of the Mechanics' Institute's overall mission. The kinds of sociability ordained by the fairs juggled impulses to embrace the egalitarian tenets of republican democracy present in the logic of the harmony of interests but also to separate and distinguish the working classes from the middle classes and the elite in ways that reflected the social stratification that was accompanying capitalist expansion. These tensions were expressed in a column in the pages of the *Mechanics' Fair Daily Press* published during the second fair in 1858. On one hand the author invoked the egalitarian strains of republicanism, calling "the Pavilion" a "great catholic church, where we are all devotees, on a common footing, at that shrine of necessity which is called Industry." Within its walls there was "no aristocracy . . . no privileged class taking rank above another, nobody so great a fool to permit others to suspect that he feels himself in any manner above the level of the educated mass." At the Mechanics' Institute fairs, "owners of Spanish leagues" were indistinguishable from "an exhibitor of a hydraulic nozzle." As a result, "there could not be found in all the world a better representation of an intelligent republican community than that which we witness in the nightly frequenters of the Institute Pavilion." On the other hand, this same writer—not afraid to embrace contradiction—also told his readers that the fair was a cultural frontier on which social rank and class identities were asserted and displayed. He explained that although "social lines" were "not yet drawn with distinctiveness in California," they with their "attending ostracism" were an "inherent necessity" since "some kind of separation into classes" was "inevitable in the nature of man." In fact, this very process was underway at the fairs. Not only were "the elements of social rank and of California society of the future . . . all exhibited openly and unrestrainedly at the fair" but that was the reason, according to the writer, why so many of his readers—although they might not be "aware of it"—had been coming to the fair "night after night and looking at the people, instead of looking at inanimate things and machines."[28]

One important component of the amusement offered by the Mechanics' Institute fairs that shaped its social environment centered around the promenade—the organized display of the crowd for the purpose of watching and being watched. As the *Alta* declared in 1865, "As a place for lounging and promenading, the Pavilion has no rival." It also identified for its readers a site at the fair—the fountain—which would develop increasing renown as a place for watching the crowd. With "its numerous jets and its large basin . . . surrounded by chairs" it offered a perfect spot to "sit and observe the passing multitude." Four years later, in 1868, the same paper remarked that on any given day, "from the opening of the doors till the extenguishment of the gaslights, a surging multitude of men, women, and children promenaded the vast halls and galleries of the Pavilion." In 1869, the *Alta* identified "the galleries" as "favorite places of resort, where from a thousand to fifteen hundred persons may be observed each evening, seated or engaged in a promenade, the better to view the articles and people below." The account of the promenade featured in the literary creation *The Argonaut Sketchbook*—written collaboratively by Ambrose Bierce, Fred Somers, and several others involved in the publication of the weekly newspaper the *Argonaut*—that described the social goings on at the Mechanics' fair of 1878 highlighted the significance of crowd watching as an activity that both blurred social divisions and furthered them. The *Sketchbook* characterized the fair as "a huge, sheltered, promenade, where people pay 'four bits a head,' to wander about in space, and look at each other." It noted that the lower floor was a good place to start one's wanderings, but that the second story gallery—filled with "lighter exhibits" and reached by stairways at either end—was the more popular place to go. This upper story was so "extensively used as a promenade" that it became "something like a Parisian boulevard, or bazaar avenue." The *Sketchbook* also told its readers that "one of the interesting things to do" was "to sit down on one of the benches . . . and watch the indiscriminate throng as it circles about you." It explained that the "stream of curious faces" offered "a running commentary on the community at large." From your chair you would see "the proud aristocrat, and the humble plebian, side by side"—distinguished from one another yet brought together at the fair (see figures 31 and 32).[29]

The centrality of the promenade to the fair experience continued throughout the 1880s and 1890s. In 1882, the design of the new pavilion on Larkin Street was commended for taking the needs of promenaders into account. "The garden is so situated, under the main hall, as to be seen by promenaders without

Figure 31. Chairs positioned around the fountain for watching the crowd promenade at the Mechanics' Institute Fair, 1879. Seeing and being seen was an important part of every fair. (Carleton Watkins, photographer. Alice Phelan Sullivan Library at the Society of California Pioneers, San Francisco)

the trouble, as formerly, of having to pass through into an annex, and imparts a charming picture of harmony to the interior of the spacious structure." And, in 1891, the promenade was still such a central part of the Mechanics' fair experience that the *Call's* column on the opening of the twenty-sixth exhibition featured the section-heading "For Promenaders," which informed them that "the main aisle has also been widened to thirty-five feet, allowing space for several rows of chairs, thus obviating the great inconvenience found on previous occasions by promenaders, who love to linger around the band stand."[30]

Figure 32. The fountain, center, provided a gathering place amidst plenty at the Mechanics' Institute Fair, 1879. Socializing, often designed to promote the rituals of courtship, was as central to the fair as the fruits of industrial progress. (Alice Phelan Sullivan Library at the Society of California Pioneers, San Francisco)

Although the Mechanics' fair pavilions had ostensibly been designed as temples dedicated to the masculine realms of the honor of labor and the fruits of industrial progress, they were used by many fair-goers to pursue romantic encounters with the opposite sex. Although seemingly at odds, the prevalence of flirtation and courtship worked in tandem with the fairs' educational emphases as well as the Mechanic's Institute's moral mission. In fact, at the opening of the first fair, Rev. Dr. Scott had identified heterosocial mixture as one of the purposes he anticipated the fairs would serve. He expressed "the hope that the Fair, 'creation's loveliest fair,' will often shed the lustre of their eyes, the witchery of their radiant smiles on the faces of the honest sons of toil and trade under the shadow of their broad Pavilion." Scott saw this mingling of men and women as a potential prelude to marriage and the kind of familial order that implied. He hoped that one result of the "enlarged good-will and cordiality" inspired by the fair would be that "not a few stony hearts will be melted into the bonds that bind willing souls in wedded love."[31] Given the unbalanced sex ratios that characterized San Francisco's nineteenth-century population, just about any activity that might lead to the formation of stable family units was seen as a step in the direction of establishing a well-ordered city. Even as late as the 1880s and 1890s, there were still seven men for every five women in San Francisco, putting women at about 45 percent of the population. This was a significant change from the three-to-two ratio that prevailed in the 1860s, or the figures from the state survey of 1852 that put the ratio at six to one. As we have seen, images of San Francisco's mechanics as solid family men were often contrasted to those of unmarried miners and the disordered economy and domestic life they represented.[32]

As Scott had anticipated, the Mechanics' Institute fairs did indeed become cultural frontiers that fostered the mixture and mingling of San Franciscans young and old, male and female. They emerged as staging grounds for the largely—but not exclusively—middle-class social rituals of flirtation, courtship, and romance with hopes for matrimony frequently lurking in the background. For example, in 1868, the *Mechanics' Fair Daily Press* commented upon how much more attention young men were paying to the sewing machines being exhibited that were worked by young ladies as opposed to those being run by men. Wanting to better understand the intensity with which some of the young men were examining "the machinery moved by lady power," the authors asked "Jones"—described as "one of the most ardent students" of the machines—to explain the attraction. He informed them that "the young men were anxious to learn whether a connection could be made for attaining a washing, bread-making and cooking machine"—a clever euphemism for a wife—through their affiliation with the sewing machine girls. He also related that several of them were absolutely "prepared for such an addition."[33]

In 1871, the *Industrial Fair Gazette* reported upon a particularly hopeful scenario observed in "the brightly lighted salon of the Pavilion" in the form of "a young couple gazing abstractedly at the works of the Pacific Rolling Mill Company." "The young gentleman, aged about 23, was dressed in a neat suit of becoming black, with moustache, rather extended, and goatee to match. The young lady, aged about 17, was richly dressed in black, white and pink overskirt, pink bows and a jaunty little sailor hat, around which was a green gauze band." Having duly noted with approval the couple's properly styled attire, the piece then went on to describe the romantic countenance and appropriately feminine demeanor of the young lady that meshed with the prevailing white middle-class ideal of womanhood that valued piety, purity, submissiveness, and domesticity. The domestic values and family practices that grew out of this ideal not only structured the nascent nuclear family throughout the nineteenth century but also emerged as key components of a middle-class identity. "She coquettishly held in her right hand a small parasol which she had nervously twirled, while her beautiful blue eyes were dropped modestly to the floor, and a smile of half-seriousness shone upon her countenance, as she listened with 'pensive thought' to the ever-pleasing rose-colored story of Love." Next, the article moved to connect romantic love with civilized society and the civilizing power often associated with white middle-class women. "This same story of love has been whispered ever and anon to the confiding and listening daughters of Eve," the writer explained, "whose heavenly love purefies and cheers the rough heart of man in his lonely path-way down the rugged hill of life, and whose benign influence and sacred virtues have converted the world from a state of semi-barbarism into one of civilization and happiness." That this couple would take its rightful place in this progression was assured as was the important role of the Mechanics' Institute fair in their union. "When the above described young couple are linked together for life in the indissoluble bonds of matrimony (and we understand the 'happy day' is not far distant), may they, in after years, in retrospection, return and live over again the many happy hours of their 'love's young dream' so blissfully whiled away at the Eighth Industrial Fair."[34]

For men and women looking for romance or to practice the art of flirtation, the promenade was identified as an arena of special significance. In 1869, the *Mechanics' Fair Daily Press* reported that "the Bachelors' Club, thirty in number, promenaded the Pavilion Saturday evening in a body—perhaps for self-protection, remembering the old song—'When I goes out to promenade / I's looks so fine and gay, / I has to take the dogs along / To keep the gals at bay.'" Several years later, in 1871, the activities of some young men who were definitely not looking "to keep the gals at bay" made it into the pages of the *Industrial Fair Gazette*. "The ogling 'Army of Observation' have changed their theatre of attack on the fair sex from the left of the main entrance on the inside of the building," the paper reported. According to this journalist, these young men were not abiding by the rules of the promenade and were perhaps overstepping the bounds of propriety with the young ladies at the fair. "While this heterogenious admixture may not be unlawful," he wrote "it is not exactly in harmony with the laws, or more strictly, edicts of society and good breeding." He called on "the authorities" to "abate" this "nuisance."[35]

The city's young women also had a role to play on the promenade—one that revolved around observation and display. *The Argonaut Sketchbook* told its readers that in the early evening "a variegated tidal wave of beauty" made its way "through the corridors." "Singly, in pairs, in squads of three and four, the fair ones come sailing through the entrance vestibule, dressed in their best, and radiant with the most artistic touches of the toilet." Since there was "no particular attraction at the theatres" and "the trade winds" were "whirling the dust on the downtown sidewalks," they came to the fair "to see, and be seen." They arrived in "a pretty steady stream, and from every portion of the city" forming "a panorama of pretty faces, and gorgeous hats, and bonnets, and tastefully trimmed dresses, and smiles of all possible dimensions."[36]

Flirtations, courtship, and romance made up such an integral part of the fair experience that the various Mechanics' fair presses regularly reported stories of love lost and found in the pavilions. The *Industrial Fair Gazette* reported that "a young couple, evidently new beginners in the art of courting, were observed in the second tier, seated at the safe distance of about three feet apart, going through the various stages of flirting." Likely downplaying the appeal to observers, the *Gazette* took the position that "it was seriously interesting to themselves, but painfully unpleasant to disinterested spectators, of which there was more than one." In the same edition, that paper also noted, "Poor, dear, delightful, pretty Mr. Cm M–n was observed perambulating pensively through the Pavilion with the preoccupied and painful air of one who is in search of something valuable which he has lost. But alas! he did not find his missing treasure. His 'bright particular star' had another engagement." The authors of the *Argonaut Sketchbook* devoted considerable attention to describing "San Francisco's great social exhibit at the mechanics fair—flirting." They explained, "It is by no means a 'mechanic art,' yet it has its little inventions, and improvements, to display with each recurring season." They contended that it was "exceedingly interesting to watch the progress of the incipient flirtations." Moreover, according to their careful observations, "the pastime" was "not confined to the 'callow-brood,'" as "the old and the middle aged" were "as disgracefully reckless." They identified the art gallery as "one of the chosen places for the more sedate and discreet to flirt" and added that "the pictures are a most excellent excuse for sentimental conversations, it is quiet, and retired, very much different from the boulevard de gallerie outside, where the throng surges the thickest, and the stairs are cluttered with trail dresses, the air fragrant with Yosemite cologne, and the place filled with couples evidently enraptured in each other"[37]

Perfectly in keeping with the mission of the Mechanics' Institute, the way the *Industrial Fair Gazette* wrote about the promenade placed great emphasis on the potential for uplift and acceptance via the display of middle-class ideals and values. This was especially true in "Passing in Review," the title given to a column featured during the 1871 fair season. The title referred to the promenade as a place where people passed for the purpose of scrutinizing review. The column functioned as a gossip and society page for the promenaders, chronicling who was present at the fair, what they wore, what they were up to, and sometimes who they were with. Frequently, making it into "Passing in Review" was accompanied by a nod of social approval that confirmed certain demeanors and appearances as acceptable for members of the middle class. In this sense, "Passing in Review" worked as a mechanism of cultural ordering using social inclusion to consolidate class and gender identities. Take, for example, a typical excerpt from the column on August 23. "Miss Belle V–r–ya, a piquantte brunette, neatly clad in a black silk dress, with black silk overskirt, beautifully trimmed with black fringe, and one of the 'latest style' turban hats, looked very coquettish when she chanced to smile on some wan gentleman of her acquaintance—who were numerous—caught up by her fascinating glance." The columnists next turned their attention to "Mrs. Sallie L–k–n, late of Sacramento, who was in company and chatting gaily with the above young lady and others." She "was dressed in a wine-colored silk dress, with a blue silk overskirt, and wearing a dainty little bonnet. She looked charming as is her wont." Items from August 18 told its readers about budding romances. "Charley N– seemed happy in the company of Miss Nellie D–, whose deep blue eyes 'twinkled like diamonds in the sky' and he really wondered what they were, as they melted again into sweet tenderness . . . Miss Rosa—exchanged harmless glances of love with her beau ideal, George." Sometimes the column simply announced the presence of city notables at the fair. On August 28 it was reported that, "Joseph Sp–r, the well-known auctioneer, was seen going, going, for more than the third time, through the Pavilion." Two days earlier, the paper noted that, "The substantial Mr. W.W.M. and lady, of Santa Clara, made their first appearance, and seemed to enjoy the magnificent display at the Fair."[38]

But just as "Passing in Review" contributed to the construction of identities for middle-class San Franciscans through its framing of their appropriate participation in class-specific social rituals, it also functioned as an exclusionary device that marked who did not manifest the right sort of demeanor and appearance to be comfortably included among this emergent class. Some of these, although written as nineteenth-century "fashion don'ts," had definite class dimensions. Some were also rather mean-spirited. For example, "Passing in Review" told its readers, "Next most prominent was a young lady in blue—blue dress, blue sacque, blue parasol, blue gaiters, blue fan, jewelry tinted with blue, hat surmounted with blue, blue veil, and holding in her right hand, on which was a blue glove, a red rose-bud. She was leaning on the arm of her young red-faced gallant, who looked rather a little verdant—or green. Whether the rose-bud was intended as emblematic to him, referring to her own tender age, or merely as a contrast or 'relief' to her uniform outfit, we have no facility of knowing."

While it was clear that the young woman was dressed up, it was likely that she was exhibiting bad taste by sophisticated, middle-class standards but wearing an outfit that was, perhaps, perfectly appropriate among less elite San Franciscans. In the same column, the author also took to task a young, less than urbane man from the country who was not only out of sync with the fair's social rituals but was also ridiculed for his choice of companion. "Next on docket was a young man with fat, chubby face, bushy auburn hair . . . apparently from the rural districts, with hat in hand, and head proudly erect, as if at 'attention' on 'dress parade.' If his mother did not know he 'was out,' his aunt certainly did, for such we take to be the elderly lady with him, who doubtless was acting as his chaperone." A few days later, the column called attention to the awkward behavior of another young man. "One of those wax figures, who invariably stand on each side of the entrance in order to enforce that observance which they otherwise would not attract, unconsciously planted himself against the blackboard on which was chalked the musical program for the evening. This was about the only impression he made. His movements were watched with interest by several who attempted to 'read him,' doubtless thinking he was a 'standing advertisement' for some articles on exhibition, other than himself."[39]

"Passing in Review" and other fair publications, by highlighting groups that were excluded or marginalized, policed the boundaries of San Francisco's middle class. One news item drew attention to one group of San Franciscans that were left literally outside the fair's—and society's—boundaries. As a writer for the 1871 *Industrial Fair Gazette* explained, "Nearing the Pavilion door last evening we were accosted by a gamin on the wayside with, 'Mr. take me in?' Not wishing to encourage extravagance in the needy, we concluded that a boy who had no money would fare just about as well outside as on the inside of the building, and we charitably let him remain in status quo." By 1878, *Our Daily Circular* was complaining that it was not just "one or two that beset you nightly" but that such begging boys were so numerous that they forced fair-goers "to run the gauntlet for half a block." Another account in the 1871 *Industrial Fair Gazette* noted a woman who was not left out but thrown out. "Last night an apparently half-intoxicated woman named Maggie Meagher, was noticed taking a bottle of plum jelly—valued at about fifty cents—from the exhibition stand of the Pacific Honey Depot." She was arrested and "locked up, charged with petit larceny, and bailed in the sum of $10, which she forfeited." A couple weeks earlier, a writer for "Passing in Review" noted that "a few representatives of the demi-monde have put in an appearance at the fair, but so far as I have heard, have conducted themselves with sufficient regard to the external proprieties, not making themselves conspicuous either by their dress or in any other way." Impoverished children, poor women, or members of the demi-monde were not the only groups singled out for attention on this level. The Chinese, Jewish women, young working-class women, and tough types of young working-class men were also identified in ways that highlighted their existence outside the emergent social boundaries erected by San Francisco's middle class.[40]

In 1868, the *Mechanics' Fair Daily Press* ran two items that remarked upon the presence of Chinese fair-goers. One noted that "some fellow, more smart than honest" had sold to a Chinese attendee "one of the cards printed at the Fair for the Florence Sewing Machine as a card of admission to the Fair." Upon discovering this, "the Celestial" purportedly exclaimed, "Melican, him no belly good; him cheetie ebelly-boly tam!" The reporter related that it was "quite amusing to hear a Chinaman swear, but too bad to make them do so by cheating them." About a week later, the *Press* told readers the Chinese were "beginning to visit the Fair pretty numerously" and that those who visited were "very decent looking bodies" who seemed "to appreciate matters and things as well as anyone else." This account explained that "the character of the articles most interesting to them" was "suggestive" and explained that "a pen drawing of St. George and the Dragon detained one of them for a long time, whilst a group of them were seen discussing the merits of Liddell & Kaeding's fishing tackle." The first story tapped into the idea that the Chinese were such outsiders—regarded by most San Franciscans as the epitome of racial inferiority—that they could not even recognize a proper ticket and could therefore be easily duped. While their position as outsiders within this context was not particularly surprising, in some ways their attendance at the fair, related in the second anecdote, was. The fact that Chinese fair-goers were carefully observed and remarked upon was a sign of their difference from other San Franciscans as well as their typical exclusion from important political and social arenas. Their attendance at the fair—an important local event—may have been a bid for inclusion in the larger civic community. Or perhaps they attended out of curiosity, regarding their fellow San Franciscans and their various inventions and contraptions with as much interest as their fellow San Franciscans regarded them.[41]

Jewish women were featured as marginalized members of San Francisco's middle class in the pages of the *Argonaut Sketchbook*. As the title suggests, the *Argonaut Sketchbook* included drawings of scenes at the fair as well as of types of people present, likely done by local illustrator and artist Joseph D. Strong. "I don't know that it is exactly the correct thing to thus fix the features of people, but you will enjoy it nevertheless—especially the nasal features," the writer of the *Sketchbook's* text, Fred M. Somers, explained. "The Pavilion noses are some of them very funny, and plainly indicative of the fact that their ancestors once worshipped in the Temple. And the faces belonging to these noses, are often as expressive, as the noses themselves." He further revealed that, "When lighted up with joy, or expectancy, the fact is very apparent . . . and when the languishing look and soul exhausting glances has been repeatedly, generously, but! alas vainly bestowed, vacancy itself could not better tell the mournful tale, than does the pen and ink exhibit herewith presented." The drawing referred to showed a young woman with stereotypically Jewish features sitting alone on a bench, watching a man walking away from her. It represented an episode of failed flirtation and suggested that women of Jewish descent, possessing what were considered Jewish features, did not conform to what middle-class society considered attractive. It seems unlikely, given these sentiments, that Jewish women would have found themselves described in flattering terms in "Passing in Review."[42]

Working-class women at times clashed openly with their middle-class sisters at the fairs. Under the heading, "What Does It Mean?" the *Industrial*

Fair Gazette—curious about the identity of the young women referred to— reprinted a note that had been "written in a bold, free woman's hand" and "pinned in a conspicuous place in the Pavilion yesterday." It read, "If the young women who made the *kind* remarks in regard to my soiled hands will send me a box of 'Old Brown Windsor' and a pearl handled nail brush, I'll endeavor to relieve them of further anxiety. I would also suggest that if their own hands were soiled by honest toil, it would be to their credit. One of the latest style *chignons* will also be gratefully accepted." Apparently, the lessons about the dignity of labor propounded at the fairs had been lost on these young ladies.[43]

Tough types of young working-class men—frequently identified as hoodlums—inspired both fear and loathing among middle-class fair-goers. Accounts of their presence could be as benign as this one, which appeared on August 21, 1871, in the *Industrial Fair Gazette*. "'Ye ubiquitous Hoodlum' had rustled a couple of dollars, and was there in force with his Aramintas and Sarah Janes." They could also be much more hostile, as this item, published in the same paper several weeks later attests. "That ubiquitous biped and libel on the form of humanity, the Hoodlum, again showed his ill-mannered, uncouth and brutal innate disposition by indulging in obscene mimicry and vulgar remarks within the hearing of ladies who chanced to be passing . . . The uncultivated boors to whom, or rather, which, we especially refer, are well known characters, and frequent the California Market." The press also roundly ridiculed the hoodlums' "inexpressible impudence and contemptible foppery" and referred to them as an "army of invaders," emphasizing their inappropriate dress and demeanor as well as the fact that they were generally not welcome at the fair. It even singled out individual offenders, describing "one, in particular" as "dressed in black, with dyed hair and mustache . . . and round black skull cap." The account explained that his "prominent position in the center of an aisle leading to the fountain attracted the notice he so much coveted" as well as "the feelings of ridicule he so richly merited."[44]

The various fair presses not only policed the boundaries of the middle class but throughout the 1860s and 1870s, they also emerged as vehicles for prescribing appropriate behavior for middle-class women. During the summer of 1871, the *Industrial Fair Gazette* ran a series of columns that critiqued several "types" of women. Many had particular resonance in the fair's atmosphere of heterosocial mixture. For example, on August 11, 1871, the *Gazette* warned its readers of the "Vampire Woman." It intoned, "Beware the Vampire! Verdant youth-enamored and blinded senior—beware! She is fooling thee!" The warning continued, "The vampire woman is greedy of admiration—and of presents. She thirsts for masculine homage. . . . She strives to kindle a devotion which she will not reward, and to excite an affection she cannot return. She is calculating, mercenary, and heartless . . . Men are her prey." The writer further cautioned that "the vampire woman" belonged "to no particular social or intellectual grade." She could be a "'queen of society,' or an impecunious adventuress." She might wield her influence "at church fairs and charitable associations, or in the reunions of the *demi-monde*." But "whatever her social status" she had "her being not in the atmosphere of a *home*, but in the whirl of fashionable dissipation, or the glare and turmoil of publicity." Clearly, the problem with "Vampire Woman" was that she did not play by the rules. She took advantage of smitten men for gifts and admiration, usually without returning their affections. She was not appropriately domestic but instead was overly involved in fashionable society. Her behavior marked her as a public woman—a woman who, like prostitutes or other city women who were not always as respectable they appeared to be—symbolized the kind of urban dangers that might befall unwary middle-class men.[45]

A second type profiled in the *Industrial Fair Gazette* was the "Doll Woman." While she resembled the flip-side of the "Vampire Woman," fitting more within dominant constructions of white middle-class womanhood as pious, pure, domestic, and submissive, being so limited to these concerns was identified as the "Doll Woman's" downfall. "Society is depressed and frivolized by the influence of 'doll women,'" the *Gazette's* writer boldly declared. "If society makes dolls of women, it shuts them up in 'the domestic sphere,' and ridicules or declaims them out of every other sphere their intellect will inevitably become narrowed to fit the contracted dimensions of the sphere assigned them." The result of such imprisonment was that they became either "household drudges" or "the sphere of the butterflies of society." For the latter, "fashion and frivolity, dress and upholstery" were "the only field for the exercise of their powers." Next the writer went on to critique the heart of the promenade with the question. "Is it not too true, is it not every day becoming more and more apparent that what we call 'society' here in San Francisco, is nothing more than a field for senseless display?" The column concluded by asking its readers, "Do you doubt that women are capable of better things?" and then identified the relatively uncontroversial roles of "companion and help-meet" as proof that "even the women who do not thrust themselves before the public as agitators and reformers . . . need not . . . be 'doll women.'"[46]

A third type that was scrutinized by the *Industrial Fair Gazette* was "The Gad-Fly Woman." Again, the qualities associated with this type were particularly relevant in the context of the rituals of sociability that accompanied the promenade. And, like the critiqued leveled against the "Doll Woman," the critique of the "Gad-Fly Woman" had something of a feminist kick while at the same time having a regulatory component. The writer characterized the "Gad-Fly Woman" as "rather agreeable upon first acquaintance, but sometimes degenerates into a bore of the first quality." This, according to the writer, was because, "She is 'smart,' clever and good-hearted, but without large ideas or elevation of soul. She revels in the mere tattle or neighborhood gossip, and delights in retailing it from house to house." Worst of all, "She would not harm a mouse, but cherishes a cruel spite against the best and noblest of her own sex. She spits her weak venom against such women as Elizabeth Cady Stanton, whose greatness and goodness her busy little mind cannot take in."[47]

As the above examples suggest, the *Industrial Fair Gazette* took a mixed and at times contradictory but nevertheless often surprisingly positive view on issues related to women's rights. Many of its columns dealt with these issues. Considering the number of young women who attended the fairs and likely picked up free copies of the papers for perusal while sitting near the fountain to watch the crowd go by, it is probable that these columns that openly grappled with—but ultimately contained—new challenges to dominant images of womanhood were widely read. The *Gazette* went so far as to identify one of its "types" as the "Anti-Woman Woman," noting that, it is "among women that we find the most venomous opponents of 'Women's Rights.'" The column concluded with the widely held contention among women's rights activists that "much of the selfish, cold-blooded and heartless legislation of the day would be prevented by the infusion into it of the elements of womanly tenderness and woman's facile pity." The writer did confess a lack of certainty as to whether "this end would be promoted by admitting the waspish, spiteful, frivolous 'anti-woman' women to the suffrage." The *Gazette*, moreover, was not the only the fair press to take up women's issues. Contradictions about the status of women were also evident in the *Mechanics' Fair Daily Press* of the 1869 fair season. On one hand, it mocked women's rights advocates: "What's in a Name? Among the names of delegates from St. Louis to the Woman's Rights Convention at Chicago, are: Miss Letitia Snapper, Mrs. Sarah Cozzen, Mrs. Phoebe Nun, Miss Alice A. Snarling, and Miss Judith Singlepin. Such names are suggestive under such circumstances." Yet just a week later, the *Press* endorsed the Women's Cooperative Printing Union, noting that the work was "of artistic quality, and of the greatest variety of subjects." "It is gratifying to reflect that women," the piece continued, "are in this manner able to make themselves both useful and independent . . . it cannot be doubted that if they had the incentive and opportunities of men, there would be small occasion to pronounce the sex inferior." Within the span of one week, the *Press* stereotyped women's rights activists as grumpy old maids and advocated work in a traditionally masculine preserve—printing—so as to allow them to rise to a position of equality.[48]

Throughout the 1871 fair season, the *Industrial Fair Gazette* featured many articles in support of women's causes. It endorsed women's education, noting that its benefits went beyond individual women to society as a whole. "Everything that can be done by men to instruct, refine and ennoble woman should be done, for the reason that mothers educate their sons, and the more intellectual the mother the more intellectual the son, so that thus, one citing on the other, little by little the whole race is elevated." Clearly part of the reason the *Gazette* took such a scathing view of the various "types" of women it profiled was that all of them were too frivolous to value education. It also published a glowing review of the *Pioneer*, described as "one of the ablest papers devoted to the cause of Women's Rights that can be found in the United States." "The *Pioneer*," readers were told, "is edited with great spirit and vigor, and is the organ of all 'progressive ideas.' It is cordially hated by all bigoted 'conservatives,' which is proof of its power." It identified "men of the bat-and-owl school, who hoot and screech their clamorous protests against every threatened improvement, and all of that class of doll-women who are content to remain dolls or 'caged birds,'—who have no souls above dress, flirtation, gadding, and gossip"—as those who were "bitter against the *Pioneer*." It endorsed Sojourner Truth, describing her as "an uneducated colored woman of great age, who has all the fire, force and enthusiasm of youth, and is withal a genius in her way," and reprinted part of her lecture on dress reform given in Detroit. Then, in a lengthy column titled, "Our White Slaves," the *Gazette* compared the enslavement of white women to household drudgery with the condition of black slaves.[49]

But the 1871 *Industrial Fair Gazette* also published less woman-friendly articles that not only contradicted but also contained its more progressive messages. Its August 10 issue featured a column that reprinted part and paraphrased some of a pastoral letter issued by Bishop Coxe of the Western Diocese of New York "in which he spoke in terms by no means flattering of 'The Women of America.'" It particularly emphasized the questionable morality of commercial amusements and indulgences. The column informed readers that "among other things, the Bishop inveighs against 'ungodly services,' 'crimes against social purity,' and the 'tawdry fashions, the costly vulgarity, and the wicked extravagance of the times.' The Bishop declares that the great majority of American women are 'strangers to the first law of refinement, simplicity in manners and attire.'" The bishop was quoted as saying, "When I see thousands of American women reading vile romances and degraded newspapers, and frequenting demoralizing dramatic representations, I feel that civilized heathenism is returning to the fields we have wrested from the Indians." While Bishop Coxe chastised American women for putting American civilization at risk through their participation in emergent forms of consumer culture, another account in the same issue focused on the racialized sexual availability of the women of Tahiti, whose less civilized status was implied in the reference to their lack of "proper" attire. "Prince Alfred, who has been cruising around the world for the last six years, studying the various forms of animated nature, says that the women of Tahiti are the most beautiful in the world. The poor unsophisticated youth is quite honest in this opinion. He saw more to admire in the women of Tahiti than he did in other women, because of their peculiar style of dress."[50]

As part of the social fabric of the city for five decades, the Mechanics' Institute fairs functioned as a cultural frontier that offered San Franciscans the materials to construct middle- and working-class identities at the same time that they effectively policed the meanings such identities could contain. In order to make factory work palatable, the fairs marshaled the producer ethic and the concept of the harmony of interests. Not only did this vision of the world help to create and sustain an industrial economy but it also advocated a working class identity that was not organized around radicalism but was about the quintessentially American desire to ascend into the middle class. Yet even as mechanics were honored in rhetoric, members of the working class often found themselves marginalized from the arena of the promenade unless they assumed the trappings of middle-class identity. At the fairs, the flirtatious sociability of the promenade created an environment in which the Mechanics' Institute's vision of harmonious class relations linked to a domestic ideal might be realized. Just as men were cautioned against being too radical, women were warned not to be too smart, too worldly, too domestic, or too desirous of equality with men. If, as a result of courtships begun around the fountain, hard-working men married respectable women, worked in honorable trades, and created stable family units, they laid the groundwork for a society organized around middle-class values and an industrializing economy that provided the foundation for making San Francisco an American place.

CHAPTER FIVE

Imagining the City:
The California Midwinter
International Exposition

The California Midwinter International Exposition—also known as the Mid-winter Fair—was held in San Francisco's Golden Gate Park from January 27 to July 4, 1894. Following on the heels of the World's Columbian Exposition, it showcased selected exhibits from Chicago's spectacular commemoration of the 400th anniversary of Columbus's journey to America as well as an impressive number of new exhibits at its specially constructed fairground, Sunset City. The driving force behind this extravaganza was Michael H. de Young, the publisher of the *San Francisco Chronicle*, who had also been Commissioner of California Exhibits at the Chicago Fair. In Chicago, he determined that San Francisco could reap economic and social benefits from hosting a similar fair. The city, like the rest of the nation, was reeling from the effects of the economic depression of 1893.[1]

De Young envisioned staging a publicly funded venture that would rein-vigorate the local economy and advertise San Francisco by showcasing California's temperate winter climate and agricultural bounty to visitors and potential migrants alike. He called a meeting of the local businessmen with him in Chicago, pitched his idea, and despite some skepticism, he extracted pledges totaling over $40,000—enough to get the enterprise off the ground. Although it had taken seven years to bring the Columbian Exposition to frui-tion, in eight busy months fair organizers set up a corporate-style administra-tive structure and ran successful local fund-raising and publicity campaigns. They arranged for many of the exhibits from the Chicago Fair to be carried by rail to San Francisco, developed an impressive number of new exhibits, and designed and built Sunset City. While the rush to completion was evident in areas where landscaping was sparse as well as in the delayed opening of some exhibits, the Midwinter Fair was nevertheless even more of an economic success than its promoters had hoped. By the time the fair closed on July 4, 1894, nearly two-and-a-half million people had attended (see figure 33).[2]

As the first American international exposition ever held west of Chicago, the Midwinter Fair provided San Francisco elites with an opportunity to present an image of the city to local, national, and international audiences. While the Mechanics' Institute fairs were small and local, their long history as a ritual cultural frontier offered important lessons in how to coordinate an event like the Midwinter Fair and use it to convey an ordered vision. The leaders in business, finance, and industry who joined de Young in organizing the fair pursued their course with the blessings of the mayor, the governor, and other state and local officials. Although central, northern, and southern Californians all had their representatives on fair committees, the Midwinter Fair's leading organizers were drawn from San Francisco's political, economic, and intellectual elite. These men sat at the helm of a city that, although less than fifty years removed from conquest had become, by 1890, the largest city on the West Coast and the eighth largest in the country. In planning and designing Sunset City, they created a paean to America's landed empire that showcased San Francisco—the jewel in the crown of western expansion and a burgeoning yet still relatively new American place that had its roots in the formative crucible of the frontier. With the frontier having been deemed officially closed by the Census Bureau in 1890, many of the fair organizers believed it was time for San Francisco to shake off some of its boomtown reputation. As banker and civic leader James D. Phelan announced at the Midwinter Fair's inaugural ceremonies, "We celebrate to-day this great fact—a history-making fact in the annals of the world—that the American people have reached the Pacific Ocean, and that civilization, having sprung in the remote east and pursued its destined course, has reached the western edge of the American continent in California . . . 'The eastern nations sink, their glory ends, / An empire rises where the sun descends.'"[3]

The fair's displays that exhibited local progress in manufacturing, agriculture, industry, and technology captured one component of what the arrival of civilization meant in California. But another part of what civilization's presence on the continent's edge signified were the ways California, and especially San Francisco, had gone from the social disorder of the gold rush years to a society organized along lines that were much more in keeping with national

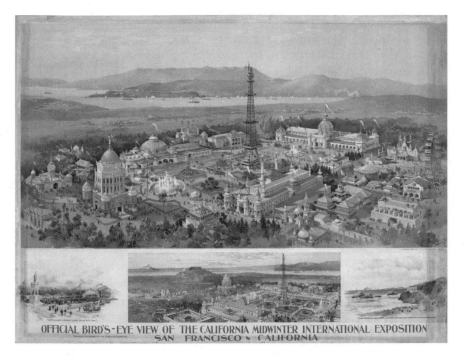

OFFICIAL BIRD'S-EYE VIEW OF THE CALIFORNIA MIDWINTER INTERNATIONAL EXPOSITION
SAN FRANCISCO ❧ CALIFORNIA

Figure 33. The California Midwinter International Exposition, 1894—the first international exposition held west of Chicago, which hosted the 1893 Columbian Exposition. (Robert B. Honeyman, Jr. Collection of Early California and Western American Pictorial Material, Bancroft Library, University of California, Berkeley)

norms. Through this process, this frontier region became recognizable as part of the nation. Through the fair, elites fashioned a story about the city as a distinctive place—with its own history and vision for the future—but placed squarely within the contours of the national story and central to the nation's development. On this level, the Midwinter Fair—as the elaborate fantasy of an anxious yet powerful elite—served as a cultural frontier that embodied the kind of ordering hierarchies that this elite had imagined, and had to some degree realized, for the city itself. Despite the fact of continual, stubborn social disorder, San Francisco in 1894 was not the socially fluid place that it had been in 1849. And, at the fair, just as in the city itself, the elite's ordered vision was at times successful, and at other times disrupted and undermined by people and forces beyond its control. Four aspects of the Midwinter Fair shed particular light on the connections between the social hierarchies this extravaganza represented and the vision of social order it promoted: the symbolic significance of its Orientalist architecture, the version of history articulated in its '49 Mining Camp exhibit, the gender politics of women at the fair as workers and as spectacle in the context of commercialized leisure, and the economic tensions disclosed at an event promoted as a balm for healing class divisions.

A central purpose of nineteenth-century expositions was to demonstrate the technological achievements and social hierarchies that constituted civilization. Although Chicago and San Francisco—and the eleven other international expositions held between 1876 and 1916—shared a vision of order and progress grounded in white racial dominance, patriarchal gender relations, and industrial class relations, they each chose different styles of architecture and design that fit with local and regional conditions. During the planning stages, San Francisco's Executive Committee operated under the assumption "that there was time enough, and artistic energy enough, for the development of a marked individuality" in the Midwinter Fair's architecture. Its members hoped that the buildings would capture "something of the characteristics of the locality and the people in whose midst the Exposition was to be built." De Young, as the fair's Director-General, had suggested that one way to avoid "the architectural reminiscences of Chicago" would be to "make their studies from the Japanese, Chinese, Indian, Egyptian, Moorish, and old Mission buildings." When the local architects who competed to design the buildings submitted their creations, it was found that de Young's suggestions "had been kindly received and largely acted upon." The architecture of the Chicago Fair was neoclassical; in San Francisco, it was broadly Orientalist.[4]

The Midwinter Fair's Orientalist theme was given its most spectacular expression in the five main buildings that formed Sunset City's Grand Court of Honor: Manufactures and Liberal Arts, Mechanical Arts, Horticulture and Agriculture, Fine Arts, and Administration. Each of the Grand Court's buildings combined a variety of Oriental styles and each possessed "an interesting individuality" and "unconventionality." As a whole, this turn toward the Orient presented a marked departure from the emphasis placed on balance, order, and architectural uniformity in Chicago's White City's expression of a hierarchically organized society in its imposing, symmetrical facades. A. Page Brown, the chief architect of the Midwinter Fair, designed the Administration Building using an eclectic mix that included both Moorish and East Indian influences. He was also the architect for the Manufactures and Liberal Arts Building, which had "something of the old Mission character in its architecture, with Moorish detail" and featured a much-noted turquoise blue dome and golden cupola. The Horticultural and Agricultural Building, the work of Samuel Newsom, was "distinctively characteristic of the early Spanish period in California." C. C. McDougall's Fine Arts Building was described as Egyptian and "covered with hieroglyphs" with "a suggestion of the temples of India in the pyramidal roof." The Mechanical Arts Building, the creation of Edmund R. Swain, was "East Indian in appearance" and was said to bring to mind "the Jumma Musjid at Delhi" and "the Pearl Mosque at Agra." Finally, the buildings of Sunset City were not white but painted colors chosen to evoke a sunset over the Pacific. Pink, turquoise, gold, vermilion, and greenish gray accents enlivened their creamy ivory facades (see figure 34).[5]

The literature of promoters and boosters—taken at face value—offers one way of reading the symbolic significance of Sunset City's Orientalist architecture. According to *The Official History*, "the marvelous city of towers, minarets, domes and castles" reflected "the spirit of California." This was defined as encompassing "the individuality of Californians" as well as their "dash and daring." This spirit likewise included "the freedom, the liberality, the open-handed hospitality, which are proverbially Californian characteristics." It also embodied "the strangely beautiful blending of the East and the West." Taken together, Sunset City exemplified "the most complete expression of a new civilization."[6]

But just below the surface, there were other less sanguine meanings suggested by the Midwinter Fair's Orientalist architecture. Although this particular style did not express the mastery of order and balance implied by neoclassicism, it nevertheless symbolized an ordered vision. By choosing Orientalist architecture, Sunset City's planners actively looked to the imaginings of a powerful, imperial Europe to symbolize the new civilization of the United States in the Pacific West. Sunset City's embrace of Orientalist styles was undergirded by an understanding of the Orient—known as Orientalism— that developed as Europe extended its imperial control over parts of Asia, India, and North Africa. Through the selective appropriation of cultural artifacts as well as styles of architecture and design, Europeans produced what came to be recognized as the authoritative representation of the Orient. In this representation, which was based upon a sense of ownership, Europe constructed "the Orient" as inferior to the "Occident." In doing so, Europe strengthened its own identity and reaffirmed its dominance over colonized peoples and places. Sunset City's Orientalism, although founded upon European precedent, was both more broadly and somewhat differently conceptualized as

Figure 34. The Manufactures Building. The Midwinter Fair's architecture was broadly Orientalist. This building, one of the five that constituted Sunset City's grand court of honor, was designed by A. Page Brown to convey both Mission and Moorish influences. (I. W. Taber, photographer. Souvenir of the California Midwinter International Exposition 1894, Bancroft Library, University of California, Berkeley)

a result of local conditions. In addition to encompassing East Indian, Egyptian, and Moorish qualities, it also claimed the power to represent Chinese, Japanese, and the related Mission and Spanish Colonial styles.[7]

The Columbian Exposition's White City had offered Americans a utopian vision of a well-ordered city. It emphasized the consolidation of the country's landed empire and displayed the United States as a country ready to dominate the other nations of the world. If some of the first ideological steps toward realizing the nation's nascent overseas imperial ambitions were taken at Chicago, the second steps were taken at the San Francisco fair. The Orientalist architecture of Sunset City represented San Francisco as "The Imperial City of the West" and communicated a more aggressive and targeted imperial position. Sunset City declared the United States—by way of San Francisco, its far Western commercial, financial, and military outpost—

a force actively reaching out toward and desiring dominance over Asia and Latin America. In this sense, Sunset City looked outward, to order places and people beyond the city. "It is through this ocean gateway," Taliesin Evans's popular guide to the fair reminded its readers, "that the commerce of the nation with the Orient, with the lands of the Pacific, with Australasia, the Russian and Asiatic Possessions, British Columbia, the western coasts of South and Central America and the bulk of the commerce of Mexico passes." Just four years later in 1898, the United States annexed Hawaii while troops en route to the Spanish American War—which resulted in further overseas imperial acquisitions—were stationed at San Francisco's Presidio precisely because of its strategic location as a base for American expansion into the Pacific.[8]

In extending and adapting Orientalism's formulation, Sunset City wove together a web of outward facing positions that expressed the kinds of relationships that the United States in the Pacific West desired with those beyond its borders and inward looking stances that reaffirmed local power relations. Sunset City's use of Orientalist architecture represented deep desires and anxieties connected to the local conditions and imperial ambitions of San Francisco and California vis-à-vis the American West, the American nation, and the Western Hemisphere. For example, following the logic of European Orientalism, the fair's promotional literature's renditions of Mission and Spanish Colonial styles created a "mythical architectural past" that echoed an equally mythical social history. The fair's *Official Guide* blithely suggested to readers that "whatever this Spanish period may have been to the people who actually lived in it, to modern Californians it is a heritage of legend and romance." Accordingly, the period was represented as one of "old grey Mission churches, with their tiled roofs, pillared corridors and high altars, crumbling into rust and dust;" "low, weather stained ranch houses where the haughty Dons lorded it in feudal fashion, and where the sound of the guitar and the castanets still seem to linger;" and "ruined presidios where swash-buckler soldiers passed their days in rough, careless gaiety." Remnants of this not-so-distant past could be seen "in many a suggestive bit of architecture or display of costume, custom or handiwork within the walls of the Midwinter Exposition." Through these kinds of representations of Mission and Colonial styles—that existed more in the imagination of Americans than they ever had in the reality of Mexican California—the Midwinter Fair, echoing mainstream histories of the region, presented conquest as an act of generosity, in which civilized Anglos lifted the lazy, yet romantic and colorful Californios out of the semi-barbaric state in which they had languished. This representation spoke to the position of Mexicans and Californios within the state's borders as dispossessed colonized peoples and manifested a powerful image of Latin American nations as decaying and primitive that worked to justify and encourage the United States' increasingly imperial and bellicose posture.[9]

The inward and outward looking ordering visions of the Orientalist architecture manifested in the quadrangle of buildings that formed Sunset City's Grand Court were reinforced by a number of concessional structures and exhibits that existed beyond the court's boundaries.[10] As the *Official History* explained, the fair's overall "arrangement assumed something of the character of an inner circle of purely expositional buildings with an outer concentric circle of concessional features."[11] It was along this outer ring that a visitor to the fair would find, among other things, the Chinese, Japanese, Hawaiian, and Esquimaux exhibits. According to the *Official Souvenir,* the purpose of the various buildings and village settings that made up these displays was purely educational. "The villages of Hawaii, Esquimaux, China, Japan and other localities are perfect reproductions of the originals in the lands they represent, and the whole is an object lesson which no book could teach. . . . a living and moving encyclopaedia." In a sense, this was true, as the reality these exhibits represented did have a pedagogical mission. More often than not, displays of Asians, Native Americans, and Pacific Islanders used Orientalist logic to instruct observers in the racial difference, strangeness, and barbarism of the exhibited groups. Although some of these exhibits had appeared at the Columbian Exposition, in San Francisco they were arrayed against a different local context. The social meanings derived from the exhibition of these peoples and cultures arose from the confluence of San Francisco's relatively high percentage of residents of Asian descent; its equally long history of anti-Asian racism; the conquest of the region's Native American inhabitants; and the nation's most recent imperial ambitions that necessitated the evaluation of the inhabitants of the Pacific as potential colonial subjects.[12]

The Chinese and Japanese exhibits created representations of these countries that had relevance for how China and Japan as distant nations were imagined as well as for the ways Chinese and Japanese residents in California were perceived. The Chinese Building, designed by a local architectural firm and financed by the city's Chinese merchants, allowed visitors to view and possibly purchase "the deft handiwork of Chinese artisans and the wonderful products of Chinese ingenuity" and provided "a curious and instructive object-lesson of the architectural ability of the inhabitants of the great Empire of the East." But the positive associations that could be derived from the Chinese Building about the achievements of Chinese culture were tempered by negative associations with Chinatown. Since the Chinese Building contained a restaurant, tea house, joss house, theater, and bazaar it not only replicated many of the standard sites of Chinatown's tourist terrain but also the racializing work done by them.[13] The fair's promotional literature even told visitors that all of the "attractive features" of Chinatown could be seen at the exposition's Chinese Village "under much pleasanter conditions"—thus playing on prevailing stereotypes of the neighborhood as filthy, malodorous, and teeming and conjuring up unfavorable images of Chinese immigrants willing to live in such an environment.[14]

Visitors to the fair's elaborate Japanese Tea Garden were told by Taliesin Evans's guidebook that with "one step" they would pass from "the grand plaza of this great achievement of Western civilization into a romantic scene faithfully depicting life in the ancient, but still semi-barbaric, 'Land of the Mikado.'" Conceptualized and designed by ardent Orientalist and local purveyor of Japanese goods George Turner Marsh and built by Japanese craftsmen, the Midwinter Fair's Tea Garden featured an impressive gateway, a thatch and wood tea room, and a three-story theater that hosted the performances of a troupe of Japanese jugglers. Japanese landscapers filled the grounds around the Tea Garden with various plants and bonsai trees, tranquil ponds, bridges, winding paths, restful benches, and colorful lanterns. Although Evans had initially described Japanese culture as "semi-barbaric," he also noted that the Japanese exhibit illustrated "the great regard of the Japanese people for cleanliness and fresh air in their homes, and public places, and their instinctive love for art and fine workmanship." *The Monarch Souvenir of Sunset City and Sunset Scenes* took a less charitable view and emphasized the religious and racial differences of the Japanese that could be inferred from the exhibit. It explained to readers that the "peculiar style of Japanese architecture" was "suggestive of all sorts of mysteries, to say nothing of idols and heathen rites" that were "a part and parcel of the home life of the 'little brown men.'" Here, even when the grandeur of a distant Asian civilization was invoked, it was double-edged and coupled with demeaning statements designed to highlight the inferior and less than fully civilized status of the Japanese and their culture vis-à-vis the West.[15]

The Midwinter Fair's exhibitions of Hawaiians and Inuits took place against a backdrop of heightened anxieties about the suitability of these colonized peoples for integration into the American nation. The *San Francisco Morning Call* described the Midwinter Fair's Hawaiian Village as displaying "a street of ancient Hawaiian straw cottages" in which "natives" made "mats, manufacture leis and poi and pursue other vocations." Taliesin Evans's guidebook noted its cyclorama that provided a "realistic representation of the burning crater of Kilauea." Visitors were also treated to an exhibition of "two empty 'throne' chairs that formerly were owned by Kamehamehali and Kalakaua, and that a little over a year ago were wrested from the possession of Liliukalani by the Provisional Government of Honolulu." The fact that the *Monarch Souvenir* deemed the Hawaiian Village "truly representative" was identified as being particularly important because "recent events" had "created a desire in the public mind for a more intimate knowledge of the Hawaiian people." "Recent events" was a euphemism for the United States' imperial maneuvers on the islands. As the reporter for the *Call* explained, "in permitting the transportation of these idle baubles of a deposed dynasty to a foreign land," the American sugar plantation owners who had taken control of the island "intended to give notice that these things would never again be needed at home." However, this account also noted that the "native islanders who serve as attendants in the Hawaiian Village" maintained "a different view." Instead of happily accepting the overthrow of their queen and agreeing that the chairs they were exhibited with symbolized her defeat, they looked "hopefully" to the time when she would "be re-enthroned" on one of the chairs. Hawaiians, seen from this vantage point, did not appear to be the kind of willing, passive subjects that would be easily assimilable into the American national fold. In fact, the issue of the desirability of Hawaiians as American citizens hovered over the subject of Hawaiian Annexation, which was debated at the inaugural meeting of the Midwinter Fair Congresses, on January 25, 1894, two days before the fair's official opening. Although the side opposing annexation in the debate was declared the winner, this—according to the judges—was "decided merely on the strength of the arguments and did not attempt to offer any suggestion in regard to the solution of the question of annexation."[16]

While the Hawaiian Village represented many of the ambiguities that surrounded the issue of American imperial adventures and conveyed an image of Hawaiians as possibly unwilling and probably undesirable Americans, the Inuit exhibits represented "Esquimauxs" as more thoroughly conquered, docile, physically weakened, and childlike. The Esquimaux Village occupied three acres at the fairgrounds and displayed the "mode of homelife" of Inuit people from both Labrador and Alaska. The exhibit featured igloos made from plaster staff, a lake, canoes, sealskin tents, and sled dogs. It offered, according to the *Monarch Souvenir*, an excellent way to learn about Inuits, "whose ways of living are so peculiar and whose race characteristics are so little known to the civilized nations of the world." The issue of integration in the American body politic was not as acute as in the Hawaiian case, in part, because Inuits at the fair conformed to prevalent understandings of Native Americans as, what the *Chronicle* termed, a "rapidly diminishing race of people." This image was reinforced by a tragically high infant mortality rate among the Inuits at both the Chicago Fair and the San Francisco Fair. All five of the children born to Inuits during the tenure of these two fairs died as infants.[17] Moreover, because Inuits were also perceived as childlike and thus naturally dependent and in need of protection, resistance to American dominance was not expected to be forthcoming. This image was reinforced by *Chronicle* reports of Inuits at the fair, who when left to their own devices were found "dropping dimes into the cocktail and rum slots of the automatic bar" and not attending educational exhibits geared more toward "the elevation of the race." Accounts in the *Chronicle* of their shopping trips downtown emphasized their attraction to shiny, childlike things: "gold watches and toys." Within three years, the Klondike gold rush would send Americans pouring into Alaska and thus add a new dimension to the conquest of the Inuits already well under way (see figure 35).[18]

Although the representations of Asians, Pacific Islanders, and Native Americans that emanated from these concessions were frequently negative, this did not stop exhibited peopled from partaking of aspects of some of these same Orientalist displays and participating in both the elaboration and disruption of the fair's ordered vision. On Sundays when the Esquimaux Village was closed, Inuit men explored the fairgrounds, taking in all the other shows, and both men and women traveled downtown on shopping expeditions. Special celebration days, like Chinese Day on June 17 and Japanese Day on June 9, complete with

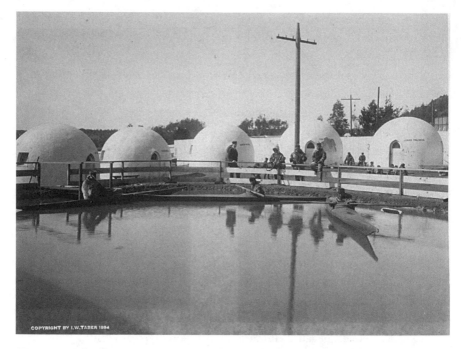

Figure 35. The Esquimaux Village. The Midwinter Fair's exhibits of Inuits and Hawaiians occurred in the context of debates about whether or not such newly colonized peoples would make suitable citizens. (I. W. Taber, photographer. Souvenir of the California Midwinter International Exposition 1894, Bancroft Library, University of California, Berkeley)

parades and pageants, drew large numbers of Asian patrons to the Midwinter Fair even though—or perhaps because—people of Asian descent had to struggle harder than other ethnic and fraternal groups to have these days set aside for them.[19] Numerous accounts drew attention to the wide-ranging participation of Chinese at the Midwinter Fair. *The Official History* remarked upon the "liberal patronage accorded the general features of the Exposition by the large Chinese population of San Francisco." The *Chronicle* reported that the young actors from the Chinese theater roamed the fairgrounds when not working and were apparently very fond of "the nickel-in-the-slot contrivance in Machinery Hall." During the fair's run, Chinese fair-goers regularly attended the Chinese theater, thoroughly enjoying an experience that many white patrons found educational but distasteful. On the day that the Chinese Building opened, a *Chronicle* report related, "The Chinese themselves took a huge interest in the exhibit and the place was thronged all day." This account noted that the merchants and tourist entrepreneurs "in charge" were "mightily proud of their building." They "conducted visitors to the joss house," while in the "reception room" a "cultured Chinese . . . explained the hidden meaning of the wondrous works of art which adorned the walls." These men aided and abetted the Midwinter Fair's Orientalist fantasy by presenting an image of the Orient that, to non-Asian visitors, likely came across as reinforcing the difference, strangeness, and barbarism of people of Asian descent. However they also created a space that San Francisco's Chinese could participate in and succeeded in representing Chinese culture in ways that this local community could respond to with enthusiasm and pride.[20]

The story of the jinrikishas at Sunset City, however, attests to the fact that there were limits beyond which people of Asian descent refused to go in the creation of an Orientalist version of their heritage. In the context of the Midwinter Fair, a "jirinkisha [sic]" was, according to Taliesin Evans's guidebook, "a conveyance used for the rapid transportation of visitors around the Fair grounds." It was "drawn by a human beast of burden at a fixed rate per trip or by the hour, at the pleasure of the person hiring the conveyance." The jinrikishas at Sunset City were acquired from Japan by George Marsh, the same Australian Orientalist who commissioned the Japanese Tea Garden. Mr. Marsh and others had hoped that jinrikishas would be pulled by Asian men and thus provide a form of transportation for fair-goers that would fit nicely with the Sunset City's Orientalist theme. To their dismay, they discovered that the jinrikisha was, as Evans related, "very unpopular with the natives of Japan" because it was "regarded as a dreadful degradation to be impelled to haul one." In fact, the *Examiner* published a portion of a petition that publicly articulated the extent of the Japanese community's opposition to the use of jinrikishas at the Fair. It had been "sent to the Midwinter Fair Executive Committee, the Supervisors and the Park Commissioners, signed by the Japanese residents of San Francisco and by M. C. Harris and E. A. Strong, in charge of the local Japanese missions." It read:

Gentlemen: We, the undersigned, desire respectfully to call your attention to a minor incident in connection with the Exposition, which is, however, of very considerable interest to the Japanese residents of San Francisco, and is also calculated to excite more or less discussion in Japan. We allude to the contemplated use of the jinrikisha.

There can be no valid objection urged to the mere exhibition of the jinrikisha at the Midwinter fair, but there are other circumstances in this connection of which in all probability you are not advised. . . .

The custom of requiring the jinrikisha to be drawn by men instead of animals is degrading and should not be encouraged in a civilized Christian country like America.

We, consequently, respectfully and earnestly protest against its use in this manner in the Park or upon public streets during the Fair.

"The petition," the *Examiner* continued, "then gives as reasons the fact that the practice is injurious to the health of the men who draw the vehicles; that it is a disgraceful and inhuman custom; that it is incompatible with the grand aims of the Midwinter Fair as an elevator of humanity." For Japanese immigrants, making such a statement was certainly a bold move. They had only recently begun to come to the mainland United States, settling primarily in California. As a group they possessed more education and were better-off financially than most European immigrants. Perhaps with guidance from their missionary friends, their use of the petition showed that they were not only unafraid to register their grievances but that they were politically savvy enough to do so in a form that smacked of Western traditions and played on notions of who, the Japanese or the Americans, was truly civilized.[21]

The petition, combined with the opinion of the Japanese community that it expressed, succeeded in keeping Japanese from manning the jinrikishas at Sunset City. It did not, however, dissuade Midwinter Fair officials from deploying jinrikishas at the Fair. Perhaps this was because jinrikishas were such a part of their Orientalist fantasy that exposition officials could not part with them. Maybe it had something to do with the contractual arrangements already made with Mr. Marsh. In any event, Sunset City had its fleet of jinrikishas and they were pulled by white men of various nationalities costumed in face-paint and Japanese garb. As the *Monarch Souvenir* explained, "The feeling of opposition to the introduction of man-power from Japan was so great that none except white men could be induced to do the work." An article in the *Overland Monthly* intimated that this was less than effective in achieving its desired objective, "At a distance of a half a mile a jinrikisha runner might be taken, possibly, for a Japanese, but at nearer view disenchantment must follow. The broad Hibernian face and the characteristic roll of the large figure are rendered grotesque by the tiny cap and skin-tight suit." The decision to

employ white men as jinrikisha drivers also had some unintended consequences. On Japanese Day many Japanese women rode in jinrikishas as did
both men and women of Chinese descent on Chinese Day. It "increased the
standing of a swell Mongol," the *Chronicle* reported, "to be seen scudding
along through the rain in the vehicle, smoking an Early Grave five-cent
cigar." Despite the derogatory language, it probably did increase the standing
of Asian men and women—or at least temporarily disrupt the racial hierarchy—to be pulled along in a hired jinrikisha by a white man dressed like a Japanese (see figure 36).[22]

Existing literally and symbolically outside of the Orientalist theme of Sunset City, the '49 Mining Camp was one of the most popular exhibits at the
Midwinter Fair. While Sunset City's Orientalist architecture expressed
dreams of a future filled with imperial grandeur grounded in white racial
dominance, the '49 Mining Camp transformed the history of the disordered
gold rush years into a nostalgic fantasy of a racially and economically simpler
past.[23] The concession sought to create a replica of a mining camp against a
"well constructed and artistically painted" panorama of Mount Shasta. It featured a gambling saloon, hotel, restaurant, "charming senoritas" dancing the
fandango, old cabins literally hauled down from the Gold Country, stagecoach rides, periodic gunfights, and a frontier press—the *Midwinter Appeal
and Journal of '49*—to name just a few of its attractions. The '49 Mining Camp
sat at the far western end of the exposition grounds at the base of Strawberry
Hill. Occupying 150,000 square feet, it was the largest single concession at
the fair. To reach it, visitors could either walk by way of North Drive, or "if
desiring to enter in the proper pioneer frame of mind," they could travel by a
stagecoach—purportedly the same one ridden in by Horace Greeley on his
visit to the West—which took hourly trips from the Administration Building
(see figure 37).[24]

A group of journalists and entertainment entrepreneurs created the '49
Mining Camp. A mining mogul provided most of its financing. Together,
these men, along with a few other investors, formed an incorporated company
"to establish the concession on business principles." One of the journalists
was Sam Davis, the editor of the Carson, Nevada, *Appeal*. His participation
explained both the name and the existence of the camp's frontier press. The
"well known theatrical manager and newspaper man" James H. Love, Esq.,
served as the '49 Mining Camp's manager and another journalist, Eugene
Hahn, assumed the duties of assistant manager and press agent. The president

Figure 36. White man pulling a jinrikisha at the Midwinter Fair. Despite fair organizers' hopes, Japanese men refused to pull jinrikishas at the fair because of the degrading nature of the work. White men in Japanese garb were employed to take on the task instead. (I. W. Taber, photographer. Souvenir of the California Midwinter International Exposition 1894, Bancroft Library, University of California, Berkeley)

of the '49 Mining Camp was Frank McLaughlin, a noted engineer who made "a fortune" pioneering the development of hydraulic mining techniques. He entered into the '49 Mining Camp project "with his whole heart and soul, and with the full power of his purse."[25]

At the '49 Mining Camp, promoters, performers, and visitors mobilized the refrain from a popular song—"The days of old, / The days of gold, / The days of '49"—as a memorable, catchy slogan. These lines, taken from *The Days of '49*, published by E. Zimmer in 1876, were repeated in association with the '49 Mining Camp in numerous guidebooks, souvenirs, and newspaper articles. "A jolly lot of seasoned miners and gentlemen of fortune in woolen shirts and slouch hats crowded the swaying coach inside and out," wrote one journalist in his description of the '49 Mining Camp. "There was

Figure 37. "Hold up" of the '49 stage. The '49 Mining Camp was one of the most popular exhibits at the Midwinter Fair. Its stagecoach was one of the features noted for making visitors feel that they had traveled fifty years back in time. (I. W. Taber, photographer. Souvenir of the California Midwinter International Exposition 1894, Bancroft Library, University of California, Berkeley)

an adventurer with a banjo on the coach top, and whenever the procession halted he struck up a ditty on 'the days of old and the days of gold, the days of '49.' Miners, gamblers, and the laughing throng joined in the chorus." The song looked back with longing to the gold rush years. It was narrated by an old pioneer, Tom Moore, who mourned the loss of that earlier time: "And I often grieve and pine, /" he confessed, "For the days of old, the days of gold, / The days of '49." The song took the listener through his fond memories. Part of what "old Tom Moore" missed from his younger days were his "comrades . . . a saucy set" who were rough but also "staunch and brave, as true as steel." Among the men he identified were the typical gold rush figures: gamblers, miners, and hard drinkers. "There was Kentuck Bill, one of the boys, / Who was always in for a game" and "New York Jake, the butcher boy, / So fond of getting tight." But another part of what Tom Moore lamented were social changes that he believed threatened both the American nation and his place in it as a white man. He made his sentiments clear in the song's final verse:

Since that time how things have changed
In this land of liberty.
Darkies didn't vote nor plead in court
Nor rule this country;
But the Chinese question, the worst of all,
In those days did not shine,
For the country was right and the boys all white.
In the days of '49."[26]

On February 17, 1894, *The Midwinter Appeal and Journal of Forty-nine* published an illustration that echoed the views expressed by Tom Moore in "The Days of '49." It featured Chinese miners working side-by-side with what looked like an Anglo miner. The Chinese appeared to have quite a bit of gold and a more sophisticated sifting system while the white miner panned for gold without, it seemed, much luck. The caption read: "Before Dennis Kearney's time." In the late 1870s, Dennis Kearney, a leader of the Workingman's Party, fomented support for violence against San Francisco's Chinese, and advocated policies prohibiting Chinese immigration. This illustration and its caption symbolized the belief held by some whites that before immigration restriction and restrictive mining laws, Chinese miners were getting more than their fair share. It also is suggestive of ways in which Chinese immigrants disrupted the nostalgic image of California as a white Jacksonian's paradise. The Chinese enjoyed, like other '49ers, a brief period in the earliest days of the gold rush in which it was possible for them to profitably work for themselves. But many also quickly and quite visibly became wage workers in the increasingly industrial enterprises of mining and railroad building in the West. In this capacity, the Chinese came to symbolize industrial capitalism—a system antithetical to an economy of small producers—and provided an easy scapegoat for what many men like Kearney believed they had lost.[27]

In a similar vein but with a different target, the *Midwinter Appeal*, in one of its typical pieces in which one of San Francisco's preeminent capitalists, sugar magnate Claus Spreckels, was spoofed as a Wild West Sheriff, reported that "Deputy Sheriff Spreckels went into Buckskin's saloon last evening and attempted to arrest Johnny Smoker while he was killing a Mexican." This action was not greeted with popular approval. Instead, the sheriff "was promptly thrown out and several citizens are talking of a mass meeting to ask him to resign his office." The problem, according to the *Midwinter Appeal*, was that Sheriff Spreckels had "a large idea of his duties, and when he enters a saloon without being invited and interferes with an American who is putting the quietus on a greaser it's time to inquire where our boasted land of freedom is tilting to." Here the category of American excluded people of Mexican descent and freedom meant white men's ability to guard their position atop the racial hierarchy without interference and with violent means if necessary. On one hand, in its rebuke of the sheriff, this historical vignette spoke nostalgically about non-elite whites' entitlement to democratic, egalitarian processes—even those that veered toward the extreme of vigilante justice. On the other, given the fact that the local citizenry meted out punishment to the sheriff for attempting to protect "a Mexican," this story, like Tom Moore's song, promoted the notion of a "herrenvolk democracy"—a society born out of fear from labor competition from below and loss of control from above in which democracy prevails for the dominant racial group while tyranny and inequality are the order of the day for subordinate groups.[28]

As these examples reveal, the basic story about the origins of the state of California that the '49 Mining Camp told is a familiar one. The primary purpose of the '49 Mining Camp was to provide profitable amusement. In conjunction with that, however, it was also in the business of proffering potent lessons about history, memory, and identity. At its core, the version of history presented in the '49 Mining Camp took the form of a creation myth that told a story about the origins of the state of California and its inhabitants that was as much about the present and the future as it was about the past. This creation myth was constructed through two distinct yet interwoven and overlapping stories. The first was a tale of nostalgia for a lost white republic that contained within it lessons about race relations in the West. The second was a story that celebrated the ideals of the independent, self-made man and rugged masculinity in the wake of the increasing dominance of bureaucracy and corporations in everyday life. Thus, although the fair as a whole was a celebration of the coming of civilization to the American West that contrasted San Francisco's disordered past to its current civilized state as an urban, industrial metropolis, the '49 Mining Camp looked back with longing to a romanticized notion of a less civilized time in California's history to construct meaningful identities for the present.

At the heart of this creation myth were the hardy pioneer miners, generally represented as young, white Anglo-Saxon Protestant men. The majority, as the Midwinter Fair's *Official Guide* told its readers, were "possessed of neither astonishing virtues or astonishing vices; they were simply honest, earnest men who in their own strong, rough way gradually curbed the vicious propensities of the criminal minority, forced law and order out of the turbulent chaos, and laid the foundations of the future State." These men were part of a larger contingent of nineteenth-century American expansionism embodied in sturdy, purified yeomanry spreading out over the accessible, undeveloped land of the frontier, supplanting savagery with civilization and blazing a fresh trail for egalitarian democracy and individual freedom along the way. One of the most coherent expressions of this ideology had occurred less than a year before at the Columbian Exposition. It was there that Frederick Jackson Turner articulated his theory of the formative role of the Western frontier on America's character and development and effectively marked this version of its history as integral to America's national identity.[29]

Despite the complicated multicultural terrain of many actual mining camps, this exhibit of California's founding moment made the white, American conquerors—otherwise known as pioneers—the central actors in its triumphal, progressive story. Other racial groups, when included, were relegated to the margins. This tactic of inclusion at the margins resonated in both the past and the present because it provided a way to incorporate yet simultaneously subordinate nonwhite groups in the historical record and, by extension, in California society. This story about California's origins offered solace to white Americans looking for order in the face of the racialized anxieties of the 1890s. Although the conquest of the Californios, Indian genocide, and Chinese exclusion were already history, in the 1890s issues of mixture and inclusion remained fractious in San Francisco—a city with the largest proportion of foreign-born residents in the United States.[30]

Although the *Midwinter Appeal* did not accord people of Mexican descent a place in the American body politic, an appropriated version of Mexican culture lived on in the dance hall—a telling indicator of the symbolic centrality of socially peripheral, racially subordinate groups to the '49 Mining Camp's representational goals.[31] The dance hall was a place, for both the miner of yore and the fair-going spectator of the 1890s, where gender and race came together in powerful ways. A visit to the dance hall, according to the *Monarch Souvenir*, provided an opportunity for "the unhappy lot of the argonautic goldseekers" to have some much-needed fun, providing "a ray of bright sun-shine athwart the gloom of an existence devoted to hard work, flapjacks, beans and bacon." Its promotional literature was laden with the language of con-quest and dominance. The *Official Guide* feminized and infantilized Mexicans as "dark-eyed, soft-voiced children of the South" and contrasted them to "a tribe of men only, bearded, rough of speech and manner, mighty in strength and endurance." A large part of the appeal and popularity of the dance hall re-volved around the prospect of the contact with "charming senoritas." The fe-male dancers at the '49 Mining Camp allowed white American men to partake of an exoticized sensuality and to indulge in fantasies of more "primitive" styles of masculinity. Such fantasies permitted white men to both transgress the constraints of allowable expression of middle-class masculinity and to re-affirm their own sense of gender and racial superiority. Some of the dancers, however, were men. Descriptions such as—"The pretty Spaniards, girls and men, were at the prettiest part of one of their graceful dances"—in which men were described as pretty and thus feminized bolstered the sense of superior masculinity of the white male spectators. In keeping with the nostalgic thread present in Tom Moore's song, here again the '49 Mining Camp represented a thoroughly conquered California in which white men's dominant racial posi-tion was unquestionably secure (see figure 38).[32]

Although Native Americans were marginal to the performance of the white man's West enacted at the '49 Mining Camp—included only as local color or as a component of the landscape—they were featured at two conces-sions located on the same side of the fairgrounds approximately the equiva-lent of a city block away. "One of these," the *Official History* explained, "was an encampment of Sioux Indians, where characteristic dances were given every day and evening." The other "was at the Arizona Indian Village, where a company of Yaqui Indians lived in huts similar to those they occupy at home, and made baskets and pottery." At the Sioux Village, which had also been exhibited at the Chicago Fair, a report in the *Chronicle* disclosed that the Native Americans "live just as they do in their native wilds where Govern-ment rations are given out." If one got to the fair early enough, the account continued, one could "gather in the rear of the Southern California Build-ing and watch the whole tribe garnering in oranges which went wrong in the citrus display the night before." Descriptions of the Arizona Indian Vil-lage tended to stress its inhabitants' barbarism, particularly evident in the descriptions of their dancing and the assumptions made about their gender

Figure 38. The dance hall at the '49 Mining Camp. Here, in the dancing of the fandango, argonauts mingled with charming señoritas, and an appropriated, racialized version of Mexican culture thrived. (I. W. Taber, photographer. Souvenir of the California Midwinter International Exposition 1894, Bancroft Library, University of California, Berkeley)

relations that, according to observers, positioned women as drudges and men as loafers. "Three Indians sit cross-legged inside the dance ring," an article in the *Overland Monthly* related, "their rude voices keeping time to the rubbing together of sticks and drumming on gourds . . . the barbaric play ends with . . . a general hubbub of cries and drumming." In general, when Native Americans were presented as active, their activities were scripted by negative stereotypes: dependent, barbaric, and drunk. When they served as part of the landscape or local color, Native Americans were represented as both passive and pacified, no longer part of the "wild" West. Tellingly, such representations were in keeping with the recent end of Native American resistance in the West, symbolized by the horrific massacre of Sioux men, women, and children by the U.S. Army four years earlier at Wounded Knee. Although these kinds of ethnographic representations of Native Americans obscured this recent history, they nevertheless succeeded in reinforcing the image of domesticated, dependent Native Americans that spoke to the kind of subordinate status that government policies frequently now relegated them.[33]

While the first part of the story of California's origins represented by the '49 Mining Camp offered lessons about race relations in the West told through the lens of nostalgia for a lost white republic, the second component told a story that celebrated the ideals of the self-made man and independent, rugged masculinity. At first glance, these two gender identities might appear to be a study in contrasts: the hard-scrabble life of pioneer miner as the epitome of independent, rugged masculinity versus the economic and political success and elite social standing that marked the self-made man. At the '49 Mining Camp, however, the two were interrelated. Independence and rugged masculinity were represented as preconditions for self-made manhood and self-made manhood often had its roots in independent, rugged masculinity. These gender identities, moreover, undergirded the racial ideology at the heart of the other strand of the '49 Mining Camp's creation myth—the nostalgia for a lost white republic. Reinvigorated for the 1890s, they continued to link white male power to white racial superiority. In addition, in the figure of the pioneer miner, Americans found a masculine image that was especially appealing in the wake of the increasing dominance of wage work, bureaucracies, and corporations—all of which could easily lead to a sense of compromised independence in everyday life.[34]

In the 1890s, middle-class Americans—especially those who were white and male—began to react against the constraints of both Victorian and industrial America: time discipline, carefully controlled emotions, parlor culture, urban living, and sexual restraint. One outcome of this reaction was the development of a new gender ideology—a rugged masculinity oriented around the ideal of the "strenuous life." This was set in contrast to what some viewed as the artificiality and effeteness of a different gender ideology—manliness— that had held sway since mid-century. Manliness was associated with possession of a solid character and exercising masterful control over one's interior and exterior self. The emergence of rugged masculinity was accompanied by an increased interest in sports and wilderness experiences; the elevation of science, business, and realism; and a desire for "authentic" experiences that sometimes drew upon premodern symbols such as the medieval craftsman, warrior, and saint. Theodore Roosevelt—the imperialist, capitalist, cowboy, athlete, and politician who feared "race suicide"—became the embodiment of this new construction of powerful white masculinity via the strenuous life.[35]

Displays at the '49 Mining Camp venerated the independent, rugged masculinity of the heroic pioneer miner. Its exhibits sought to capture "the rough-and-ready scenes when men were reckless and daring." Visitors to the office of the *Midwinter Appeal and the Journal of '49* were "invited to come into the sanctum, make free use of our corncob pipe, spit on the floor, and utilize the copy hook as they see fit." "If the gatekeeper gives you any palaver," they were told, "knock him down and walk in." At the barbershop customers could "indulge their inclination or have their whiskers either shot off or shaved off," and the saloons were "fitted up as saloons were when men were as likely to shoot the bartender as to take a drink." Even the food was tough. "After looking at the food of the ancients," wrote one account, "one need be told no more that the Argonauts were hardy people; the flapjacks show it."[36]

These miners were not only ruggedly masculine, they were also independent—free from wage work, bureaucracy, and the corporation. By choosing to represent a mining camp in the earliest days of the gold rush, the '49 Mining Camp focused its exhibit of life in the diggings on the very short span of time in which placer rather than hydraulic mining predominated. The exhibit proudly showcased "a placer mine showing the method of washing gold from gravel with sluice boxes, rockers, and all the primitive paraphernalia of the early prospector . . . in full operation." During the placer mining period, men could and did work independently, as the image of the lone miner with pan, pick, and shovel would suggest. For many of the men who flocked to California after gold was found at Sutter's Mill, mining offered a chance to return to an economy of small producers. It presented an opportunity to escape wage work in the industrial Northeast or farm work on the prairie. The halcyon days of placer mining, however, were quickly superseded by hydraulic mining, which came with a very different set of relations of production. Using the force of water to get at the gold deposits that the pan, pick, and shovel method could not reach, hydraulic mining required a large amount of start-up capital and large numbers of wage workers. It also concentrated the profits in the hands of the few and wreaked havoc on the natural environment. Ironically, the capital behind the representation of placer mining at the '49 Mining Camp came from Frank McLaughlin, renowned for developing the techniques of hydraulic mining on the Feather River.[37]

The '49 Mining Camp also mobilized the rugged masculine histories of numerous self-made men to challenge the commonplace associations of wealth and elite status with effeminacy and overcivilization. As these men had become increasingly successful—often amassing fortunes, political power, and social position—they also became increasingly removed from their roots in rugged masculinity. By emphasizing rugged pasts of these elites, the rightness and desirability of their economic, political, and social position—increasingly challenged not only by their effeteness but also by their capitalistic excesses—could be reaffirmed. One way rugged masculinity and self-made manhood were idealized and linked was through the displays of a number of cabins which "had actually been occupied in those 'days of gold'" by men "who, years ago, were unknown and poor, but who to-day are rich and powerful from their success in the mines." One was the cabin John W. Mackay had used "for six years as a home at Allegheny, Sierra County, in his humble mining days" long "before he became a bonanza king." Another cabin was that in which the U.S. senator from California, George C. Perkins, had been able "to make himself comfortable nearly forty years before he represented the State at Washington." The cabin of Major Downie, the founder of Downieville, whose name, one account declared, was "familiar in every mining camp on the Pacific Coast from the lower California line to Bering Strait" stood "in a recess in the hillside." The '49 Mining Camp also exhibited the cabins of some other men who had become "more than locally prominent"—Senator James G. Fair, Senator J. P. Jones of Nevada, Alvinza Hayward, and the early homes of writers Mark Twain and Bret Harte and John W. Marshall, the discoverer of gold at Sutter's Mill. Through these displays, the '49 Mining Camp provided a way for these elites to frame their biographies within California's creation myth.[38]

The '49 Mining Camp also functioned as a playground for numerous prominent men to indulge in fantasies of participation in the mythic Wild West. *The Midwinter Appeal and the Journal of '49* filled its pages with jovial yet fantastic spoofs on their supposed frontier antics. For example, not only did the paper report on Claus Spreckels as a racially misguided sugar magnate, it also reported that James G. Fair was the new Presbyterian minister at Jackass Hill, miner John Mackay wandered into Grizzly Gulch "half starved" and "dead broke," and "Adolph Sutro, a boy from Angel's Camp was in town yesterday on a big jag with Billy Sharon, one of the boys from Bobtail Canyon." In reality, James G. Fair was a railroad tycoon and a Comstock Lode

millionaire. John Mackay was also a Comstock Lode millionaire. William
Sharon was a banker, the owner of the Palace Hotel, and the U.S. senator
from Nevada. Adolph Sutro was a mining engineer on the Comstock Lode
who built Sutro baths in 1893 and would be elected mayor of San Francisco
later in 1894.[39]

Self-made men—many of them the epitome of corporate, elite manhood—also readily partook of the '49 Mining Camp exhibit. At one o'clock on
the exhibit's opening day, Director General de Young, the members of the Executive Committee, and a few invited guests boarded the old stagecoach at the
Administration Building. "There was little ceremony about it," the *Chronicle*
reported, "as they have none in connection with the camp. The driver cracked
his whip and the coach was off to the camp. It rumbled down the street and
stopped at the dance hall." In early February, the *Chronicle* reported another
visit: "Notice having been given that the pack train had got in, forty-two days
from 'Frisco, and that there was plenty of grub in the camp, the Director-
General, the executive committee and members of the press responded yesterday to an invitation to take lunch with Old Man Peakes at the Forty-nine
Mining Camp." They dined at the Rest for the Weary Hotel, where "Papa
Peakes and his assistants dispensed beans and other things." "Everything connected with the banquet," the reporter assured his readers, "was conducted in
the spirit which prevailed in the days of '49." Interestingly, much of what
passed for authenticity involved flagrant disregard for nineteenth-century
middle-class notions of proper etiquette and good manners—to some, surefire markers of feminization and overcivilization. "The guests kept their hats
on at table and the waiters wore pistols with which to resent criticisms on the
menu. Brown paper served as table-cloths and all the plate and china was of
tin" (see figure 39).[40]

A reporter for the Chronicle made clear the didactic intent of these displays. "The child of an investigating mind," he wrote, "will take much interest in the old cabins of the men who, since they lived in them, have become
famous." He explained that "these gentlemen attended strictly to business
when they went to sleep forty years ago" and "did not care whether the pil-
low had been aired or the mattress had been turned." Instead, "they went
right to off to sleep, as soon as they laid down." The result, he told readers,
was that "to-day they are rich and famous." The reporter further advised
good conduct and a little endurance at home as a recipe for prosperity in the
future: "Let little boys learn a moral from this and go to sleep just as soon as

Figure 39. The '49 Mining Camp with the Rest for the Weary Hotel and Restaurant on the left. Visitors, including elite businessmen and journalists, partook of flapjacks, beans, and bad manners here in order to capture the experience of the wild west. (I. W. Taber, photographer. Souvenir of the California Midwinter International Exposition 1894, Bancroft Library, University of California, Berkeley)

they get into bed. If they do, they will live long and prosper. There can be no hope, though, for the boy or girl who rolls around and always wants a drink of water. The Argonauts never asked for water. See the result—most of them are rich to-day and able to vote at the annual election of the Society of California Pioneers."[41]

While the didacticism presented above may appear a little silly, children—"the rising generations of the West"—were some of the primary consumers of the vision of social order served up at the '49 Mining Camp. The Midwinter Fair hosted a number of Children's Days on which youngsters were admitted without charge. On February 2, 1894, the Examiner reported, "Good news from the '49 Mining Camp. They cannot do enough for the children there! They were the first to throw open their concession to the children and they

seem to have spent every minute since trying to think up new kinds of fun."
On one such special day at the '49 Mining Camp, children were given "a bag
of candy and an orange apiece." In late March, "the sixty girls of the Maria
Kip Orphanage were special guests of the Forty-nine Mining Camp." They
"were conveyed to the Fair Grounds and back in the old-fashioned coaches"
that were a "feature of the camp" and while there, a "nice repast was spread
for them in the big private dining room of the manager." Moreover, it was the
belief of one journalist that: "A child can learn more about the . . . magnificent
life of the Argonauts by visiting this camp than his father, provided he is a pioneer, would ever tell him." In many respects, the '49 Mining Camp spoke for
itself, but on these special days, children and the adults that accompanied
them were "shown around by guides who will tell the 'tales of old, the days of
gold, the days of '49.'"[42]

Another audience viewed as particularly suited to visit the '49 Mining
Camp were the old pioneer miners themselves. "For the old pioneer who
spent a good portion of his life in just such a scene as this depicts, the camp
will arouse stirring memories," declared the Official Guide. "It is the Mecca
toward which every man who has at any time in his life been engaged in the
seductive occupation of gold-mining turns his footsteps," announced Taliesin
Evans's guide to the fair. With even greater clarity of the kind of memories the
'49 Mining Camp sought to evoke, it continued, "Here, the visitor finds himself in reality transported to a scene so realistic that, if he has at any time
mined, he lives over again the experiences of the free and independent life of
the past, all its trials and triumphs, all its hopes and pleasures being arrayed
before his mental vision."[43]

Visitors from the East or from abroad were also target audiences of the '49
Mining Camp. One of the camp's self-proclaimed goals was "to show visitors
from the East and elsewhere how the hardy California miner worked and lived."
The managers of the '49 Mining Camp hosted out-of-town journalists, many of
them from Chicago, and arranged special festivities for their benefit. "The life
of the camp was at its height when the guests of the day arrived in the old stage
coach," one account reported. "The keno game was in progress and the dance
hall presented its customary scene of rough gayety, with its pretty girls, miners,
gamblers, and Spaniards all in the hearty enjoyment of the fandango. . . . The
newspapermen enjoyed it all immensely. It was all new and strange to them."[44] A
writer for the Chronicle delineated at length the kind of coverage the '49 Mining
Camp was getting across the country and around the world:

The leading dailies, weeklies and monthly magazines in every country have for months past published extensive and profusely illustrated accounts of the quaint, unique, and realistic representations of early life in the mines to be found in the Midwinter Fair's Forty-nine Mining Camp. Harper's Weekly, Frank Leslie's, the New York Sun, the New York Herald, the Chicago Record, the Chicago Herald, and papers of Cincinnati, New Orleans, St. Louis, Omaha, Philadelphia and of nearly every other Eastern city of note have printed columns after columns about the Forty-nine Mining Camp, and the English, French and German exchanges, in mentioning the Midwinter Fair, never fail to speak of this special feature. To a Californian, this universal approval of a novel enterprise is more than a passing significance. It shows the great and mighty interest the people abroad take in the land of gold, immortalized by Mark Twain, Bret Harte, and Joaquin Miller and many others.[45]

In the literature generated to promote and commemorate the Midwinter Fair, the '49 Mining Camp was repeatedly praised for faithfully and literally capturing historical reality. Visitors, informed the *Monarch Souvenir*, "see presented the real life as it was in the first days of gold fever, and an exact reproduction of the surroundings of a pioneer mining camp." "The picture will be realistic to the last degree," the *Chronicle* assured its readers, "The life of almost fifty years ago will be lived again."[46] This notion of reconstituted reality persisted even as promotional material explicitly acknowledged that the exhibit was shaping its representation of history to mesh with literary fiction. Like the writer for the *Chronicle* quoted above, the *Official Guide* blatantly told its readers that the exhibition would be of particular interest to those "who have in imagination lost themselves in the Sierras with Bret Harte, crossed the Plains with Joaquin Miller or roughed it on the Comstock with Mark Twain."[47]

Joaquin Miller, Bret Harte, and Mark Twain were some of the most popular nineteenth-century myth-makers of the American West. Their stories—brought to life by the '49 Mining Camp—told the familiar tale of California's origins that revolved around nostalgia for a lost white republic and independent, rugged masculinity.[48] As the popularity of the '49 Mining Camp exhibit attested, its version of history—that echoed the mythological fiction of Miller, Harte, and Twain—possessed the cultural power it did because it represented the "reality" of a past that had incredible resonance in the present. In fact, in the 1890s, the relevance of this history had begun to take on a new intensity. It was during this decade that children of California pioneers—often organized in chapters of the Native Sons and Daughters of the Golden West, often having grown up on the work of Twain, Harte, and Miller, and often fearing that their forebears' history would be lost as the remaining material artifacts disappeared with time—began serious efforts to both revisit and preserve places associated with the California Gold Rush.[49]

While rugged, independent, white manhood was literally and symbolically displayed at the '49 Mining Camp, women workers constituted a significant part of the overall spectacle presented at the Midwinter Fair. As writer Elisabeth Bates put it in an article for the *Overland Monthly*, "Two distinct streams of people flow side by side at the Fair, namely, those who go to spend money and those who go to earn it."[50] Thousands of women in San Francisco faced unemployment and "destitute circumstances" during the five-year economic depression precipitated by the Panic of 1893. Nationally, this financial crisis devastated broad sectors of the economy and an unprecedented 15,252 American businesses went into receivership. By the winter of 1893, approximately 18 percent of the national workforce was without work while those who remained employed found their wages cut by an average of nearly 10 percent. The economic crisis hit the western United States especially hard. As eastern money receded, the already cash-starved banks of the debtor West collapsed. Of the national bank failures in 1893, only three institutions in the Northeast suspended operations while 115 banks went into receivership in the West. Of these, sixty-six were in the Pacific states and western territories. Since private charities and relief efforts largely ignored the plight of working women, many "suffered severely for food and clothing" during these years.[51] Within this context, many women hoped that employment at the Midwinter Fair would at least temporarily cure their economic troubles. The *Examiner* reported that "in every department" of the fair there was "the same story to tell." There was "a constant stream of applicants for work" with "girls not over twenty-two" making up "four out of every ten applicants." They seemed "to be pouring into the city from all over the coast" as well as "from the East." This, according to the journalist, was "a terrible mistake" as the city was "overrun with women and girls looking for work."[52]

The lucky few who found jobs at the Midwinter Fair formed a workforce of women that spread all over the fairgrounds. Gum girls, dressed in blue uniforms with scandalously short skirts, traversed the grounds—smiling, singing, and selling chewing gum. Exposition cash-girls collected the admission fees for various concessions and young women staffed booths in the fair's five main buildings. Other women found employment in the fair management's system of "paternal espionage" in which "real nice girls, with a knowledge of business methods" were "sent among the different concessions to keep tabs on the cash taken in." Almost all the exhibits of foreign nations and people of color employed women. Native American, Hawaiian, Samoan, and Dahomean women staffed living dioramas. At the Japanese Tea Garden, "Japanese maidens in their kimonos" served visitors "tea and sweetmeats." At the Vienna Prater, waiter girls served liquor and Austrian dishes. In the German Village, visitors found "a concert hall, a dancing hall, a restaurant, and, of course, Culmbacher and Wurzburger and other 'braus' and proper German girls to curtsy and serve it." At the Hungarian Csarda, one encountered "other girls and other beer and other things to eat," giving the impressions that all Austro-Hungary was "a vast eating place with feminine and drinkable incidents and an occasional park to give you exercise when you want to change your beer." Women of Mexican as well as Euro-American descent worked as dancers at the '49 Mining Camp while the Oriental Village maintained a troupe of young women as muscle-dancing Turkish Dancers. At the Tamale Cottage, the *Official Catalogue* informed its readers that "handsome, dark-eyed senoritas" could "be seen busily engaged in the manufacture of the delicious tamale" while "other equally charming beauties" worked "as serving maids."[53]

Since the Midwinter Fair brought men and women together in novel, sometimes promiscuous ways, it—like the promenades of the Mechanics' Institute's fairs—provided an arena in which emerging gender identities could be expressed and critiqued. Working women at the fair became vehicles through which various observers registered anxieties about women's more public roles and the fair's working women experienced for themselves both the perils and the pleasures of increased leisure time and new work-based peer groups. Nationally, during the final quarter of the nineteenth century, increasing numbers of middle-class women pushed into the public sphere and against the constraints of Victorian culture's dominant gender ideology that prescribed piety, purity, submissiveness, and domesticity. At the same time, many young working-class women shifted from working at various types of piece-work in their own homes, in domestic service in other people's homes, or in small, paternalistic factories to working in the more anonymous settings of large factories, offices, and retail stores. With a little money in their pockets in good economic times and new places to go for fun, some of these young women began to rebel against the gender ideologies of parents and society and to explore new identities and forms of sexual expression in part made possible by new, unchaperoned commercial spaces for heterosocial encounters. The turn of a significant proportion of middle-class men away from effete Victorian culture and their embrace of a new rugged masculinity—as seen in the '49 Mining Camp—was, in part, a response to anxiety aroused by women's more public identities.[54]

All women who worked at the fair were essentially on display and available for appraisal, fantasy, and flirtation in the exposition's climate of promiscuous mingling. As some of the stories that circulated around the fair's gum girls reveal, this public, sexualized persona treaded a thin line between representing a welcome freedom from social constraints and confirming a subordinate position vis-à-vis men for the women involved. That the fair was a place where men could gaze upon an international array of women was made clear from numerous articles that related the pleasant sights that other men had seen. Some of these even provided details of heterosocial encounters that perhaps their readers could hope for as well. An article published in the *Examiner* titled "Flirtations at the Fair: How Love Is Made and Unmade at Sunset City" advised male fair-goers that "for really enjoyable and promiscuous flirtations . . . the gum girls, so called, are better equipped than any other class of individuals as regards their duties, their skirts and their generally genial disposition." Not only could they roam the fairgrounds at will but "they may stop and talk pretty things with anybody under the pretext of vending gum."[55]

Sometimes flirtations were a source of heterosocial fun for the gum girls and their patrons. But with this kind of fun also came a certain amount of sexual danger. Giving one possible explanation for why they traveled in pairs, one gum girl said, "You see, there are two of us, and if you get badly gone on me and I don't want you to get too affectionate, Sally here stays close around all the time, and you don't have a show to tell a girl how much you love her or any of that sort of nonsense. But then, of course, if I give her a wink she understands and goes off to sell some gum." Sometimes, however, flirtations were anything but fun. One gum girl, Miss Violet Eilids, warded off the advances of a souvenir-machine man by deploying "her fists in a scientific manner." After he "sought to toy familiarly with Miss Eilids's necktie" while she was trying to sell him some gum, she punched him squarely in the nose, leaving him with "a barked proboscis." The paper that covered the story reported that, "She as well as the rest of the girls have to stand a great deal of guying from a class of men who think that because a girl peddles chewing gum she can endure all sorts of nonsense." Violet had learned boxing from her brother and after seeing how well it served her, the rest of the gum girls were "thinking of taking an immediate course in the manly art as a means of self-protection."[56]

Although ostensibly from Algeria, Morocco, Persia, and Egypt, the so-called Turkish Dancing Girls at the Midwinter Fair's Oriental Village presented even more of a sexually charged sensation than the gum girls. While undoubtedly alluring in their own right, the press definitely had a hand in the construction of the dancers' highly sexualized image that was based, in part, on notions of the heightened sensual appetites and sexual availability of colonized women of color that were part and parcel of Orientalist thinking. The *Examiner* described "the Oriental dames and damsels" as a "desperate class of flirts . . . who cast reciprocally amorous glances through ebony lashes" and make "callow youths feel the fire of those langorous looks and brag to one another about their conquests." These dancers had performed at the Chicago Fair to rave reviews. There they faced fewer questions about the morality of their dancing than in San Francisco where they were besieged by the Society for the Suppression of Vice as early as mid-December 1893. On January 4, 1894, the *Examiner* reported that "Catherina Dhaved and Marietta, the two dark-eyed daughters of Turkey who were compelled to desist from giving public dancing performances on Market street a few weeks ago by the Society for the Suppression of Vice, visited the officers of the society yesterday."[57]

Secretary Kane, who had witnessed the women's dancing, had no doubt of its "rank immorality." Nevertheless, the dancers had to endure a wait of several days before the society's directors could manage to convene for a viewing of their dances to determine if they were in fact immoral. The "sample dances" were performed in one of the rooms occupied by the women in the Ahlborn House on Grant Avenue. The "all-male audience," according to the *Examiner,* "was small, compact but interested from the start." It consisted of the five directors and Secretary Kane of the Society for the Suppression of Vice, two members of the Society for the Prevention of the Cruelty to Children and Animals, and Captain Holland of the Police Department. "We can judge better the morality or immorality of the dance by seeing it all, I think," said Director Morris, with no recognition that such private viewings might raise questions about the prurient interests of the audience. "The Directors," reported the *Examiner*, "leaned forward and watched the excited dancer with scrupulous interest. Unconscious of them the beautiful Catherina pirouetted in a dizzy circle, and falling to her knees bent far backwards half a dozen times. Her whole form quivered with the excitement of the moment." Director Goodkind concluded that the dance was "very picturesque but . . . hardly the thing for ladies and children to see," leaving unremarked upon the effect of such a performance on male audience members or the fact that such a spectacle may have been designed to be more appealing to male viewers to begin with.[58]

An earnest desire to rid the city of indecency—which included safeguarding the ordered environment created by Midwinter Fair organizers and cracking down on the Barbary Coast—motivated the Society for the Suppression of Vice. For the Turkish dancers, however, the Society's decree that deemed their dances to be beyond the bounds of respectability and prohibited their performance meant a disruption in their capacity to earn a living. "In Chicago everybody liked us," Catherina Dhaved told the *Examiner*, "We made a big hit in the Midway Plaisance; thirty-five an' forty dollar week; plenty to eat, plenty sleep, plenty everything—plenty money." Since coming to San Francisco, however, the girls had experienced "perilous times." By early January they had earned about $1,000 in the employ of two different leisure entrepreneurs in the weeks before the fair opened but had not "received a cent of it." "First an Armenian man hired us," Catherina continued, "Twenty-five dollars a week, on Market street. We work one, two three weeks, no money. Then an American man, Crosby, hired us. We work one, two, or three weeks more, no money. We owe plenty money at the hotel, and now we cannot dance and cannot pay what we owe." During the time they waited for the directors to convene in early January, the women lived on "short rations." When the dancers finally performed for the Society for the Suppression of Vice, the proprietor of their hotel was also present as "an interested witness." According to the *Examiner*, "He told the Directors that the girls owed him about $100 for back board and he did not propose to keep them any longer unless he was assured that they would be allowed to dance and make some money."[59]

Several days later after the "sample dances" at the Alhorn Hotel, on January 7, 1894, the Society for the Suppression of Vice paid a visit to the Turkish Dancing Girls performing at the Midwinter Fair. Although the fair did not officially open until later in the month, by early January so many concessions were open that thousands of people were paying to pass within its gates. Once again Secretary Kane expressed displeasure at what he saw, especially since "the dancers had received strict instructions to tone down their performance to suit Western audiences." A "sample" of the entire dance was again presented that same day for "the edification of the secretary." To guard against errors in either leniency or severity, two other agents of the society accompanied Secretary Kane as well as "a newspaperman or two, a company of Turks, and a few chosen friends." The *Examiner* reported Kane's findings on January 10, "In the muscular contortions of the majority of the ladies he found nothing to object to seriously; but in the closing measures of the *danse du ventre*, as rendered by the dusky Egyptian Hamede, he found grievous cause for complaint." Kane remained steadfast in his judgment even though the press cited the chief of the Midwinter Fair police as one among many admirers of the dance who did not object to it. The *Examiner's* reporter captured the way that Hamede's gyrations left Kane unnerved to the point of scrambling for words to describe what he had seen. "The muscular dances and the spinning exercises of the majority of the ladies can go on," he was reported as saying, "but the -er-er-er- the eccentric convolutions of the little brown lady must be curtailed."[60]

Three months later, on April 9, 1894, the Turkish Dancing Girls had their day in court. As the *Call* reported, "Under the glare of the gaslights and in the suffocating heat of Judge Conlan's courtroom the muscle-dancers of the Cairo village last night illustrated their peculiar dance for the benefit of the jury impaneled Friday last." Secretary Kane's testimony about the dance demonstrated that he "had studied it pretty thoroughly" and the description provided by Frank D. Gibson, a hardware clerk, likewise "showed keen powers of observation and perception, and that he had the dance down finer than even Secretary Kane." Nevertheless, despite the fact that the dance had been made familiar to officials through two sample performances as well as shows on Market Street and at the fair, the dancers' attorney requested that one of the dancers, Belle Baya, "give a representation of the dance." She agreed to perform to the packed courtroom despite the fact that she was not outfitted in her dancing costume but in a "lilac silk dress, lace fichu and white straw hat with green and white ostrich feathers." As the *Call* described, "Belle Baya followed in her dance, taking a silk handkerchief in each hand and the castanets on her fingers. The solitary fiddler mangled 'La Paloma' with frightful barbarity as an accompaniment. As the handsome Baya went through her dance the auditors went wild with excitement, and a clapping of hands was sternly rebuked by the court." Order was restored in the court in the wake of Belle Baya's dancing and proceedings in the dancers' case came to a close soon after. Her performance had apparently satisfied the jury that there was truly nothing immoral in her dance. "The case was submitted without argument," reported the *Call*, "and the jury retired at seven minutes past 11, returning five minutes later with a verdict of 'not guilty.'" The jury, it seems, had a much different opinion than the Society of what constituted the kind of indecency that would mar the city's image or detract from the glory of the fair.[61]

The Society for the Suppression of Vice's policing—combined with the dishonesty of a couple of leisure entrepreneurs—was more successful in impeding the Turkish dancers' ability to earn a living than in protecting them or their audiences from danger or immorality. Clearly, however, both the Turkish dancers and the gum girls were vulnerable to various forms of harassment as women working in the world of commercialized leisure. In July, the society turned its attention to another Midwinter Fair scandal that involved a woman worker who was so egregiously exploited by her male employers that she was actually in need of their efforts. On July 9, the *Examiner* reported that "the indecency of the danse du ventre and the grossness of the hula-hula were eclipsed last evening by an exhibition at the close of the Midwinter Fair which it is not permitted in the columns of a daily newspaper to describe further than by saying that the dancer was a nude woman."[62]

More than five hundred men had witnessed two such performances at Alexander Badlam's Aquarium on the Midway. The first evening the admission price was set at twenty-five cents "but there wasn't room in the Badlam building for the crowd that was willing to pay that price." As a result, the price on the second night was doubled "but the four-bit rate made little difference in the patronage." Spielers on the Midway had openly announced the upcoming events and apparently fair officials not only knew about the performances, but a number of them, including Colonel T. P. Robinson, the director of amusements, were in attendance. In fact, at the performances, "every class was represented. The majority of those on the benches were well-dressed attorneys, merchants and clerks." Also present were "concessionaires, sports, hoodlums, and men about town." While the press reported that the "room was dirty and the atmosphere stifling," the arena was also strategically equipped with an emergency door and a number of portholes that allowed for all but a few of the men present to escape arrest when the show was raided.[63]

Moreover, the *Examiner's* account of Jennie Johnson's dance and her subsequent arrest suggests that she was not operating under her own free will but was coerced by the manager of the event, Al Morris. "The sound of a violin drew attention . . . to the curtain which at the same moment was pulled aside revealing a woman seated in a chair enveloped in a dark cloak," the newspaper explained. "At the sound of the music she sprang to her feet revealing herself perfectly nude. Her head and face were veiled in a black scarf. She thus displayed herself for a few moments. Suddenly the sound of the violin ceased and the 'dancer' sank into her chair." As this account suggested and the press later confirmed, Jennie Johnson was not a professional dancer. Her performance did not even involve anything that could really be considered dancing. That she veiled her head and face with a dark scarf suggests she was ashamed enough of what she was doing that she did not want to be recognized. It is likely that she was also fearful of the arrest that might follow if she revealed her identity.[64]

Soon after Jennie Johnson returned to her chair, she was arrested by an officer of the Society for the Suppression of Vice who "sprang upon the stage." Although initially quite calm, soon, amid a flood of tears, she exclaimed, "I was forced into it. The man said I would be arrested if I did not give this dance." Apparently, the manager of the show, Al Morris, had convinced Jennie Johnson that if she did not perform she would be arrested for breach of contract. He had also "made her drink a liquor" before her performance. Morris also had refused to be specific about how much he would pay her, promising only "to make it all right with her" after she "danced." Jennie Johnson was about twenty years old and a resident of the Tenderloin district, one of San Francisco's rougher and poorer neighborhoods. It is possible that she was one of the many working-class and poor women facing exceptionally dire straits as a result of the economic depression. In such circumstances, the threat of a lawsuit might have been especially terrifying to her and maybe whatever Morris was willing to pay her was better than nothing. It is also possible than Jennie Johnson worked as a prostitute and perhaps she felt that displaying herself nude was a better job than having sex for money. Whatever the answers to these questions might have been, Jennie Johnson confessed that she had been "duped by an enterprising spieler—that his promise was as deceptive as any fake on the Midway."[65]

The same confluence of economic conditions that paved the way for Jennie Johnson's plight and sent women flocking to the fair to find work also

affected men. The financial panic of 1893 and the economic upheaval that
followed had made it clear that the economy of ruggedly masculine small
producers idealized in the '49 Mining Camp was truly a thing of the past.
The rampant economic ruin, unemployment, and class conflict that ravaged
the city and the nation presented an ironic, mocking contrast to the celebrations of capitalist progress and imperial grandiosity at the center of both the
Columbian Exposition and the Midwinter Fair. Cognizant of this the *Examiner* had noted that "starvation would not be an agreeable Midwinter Fair
exhibit." Yet at the same time, the economic crisis emphasized the centrality
of manufacturing, finance capitalism, and business consolidation to the
American economy. These developments—part of the transition from an
agricultural to an industrial economy—had far-reaching consequences for
the growing number of Americans—male and female—who made a living
working for wages. By the end of the nineteenth century, the United States
may have been the world's leading industrial power as well as its richest, but
it was also a place where a few benefited from the labor of many. As corporate strength grew through consolidation and novel managerial techniques,
not only did worker control over production decrease but workers, buffeted
along by the ebb and flow of the industrial business cycle, found themselves
in increasingly insecure economic straits. The panic's impact in San Francisco signaled the city's ties to the national economy. Its effects forced residents to confront conditions at home. While the Midwinter Fair put forth a
carefully constructed image of San Francisco suitable for outside consumption, the fair itself had been launched, in part, to generate jobs and revenue
for a city in economic trouble.[66]

Organizers heralded San Francisco's Midwinter Fair as an event that
would revive the local economy by creating jobs and heal growing class divisions by providing a unifying civic project for all of the city's residents. "These
were hard times," W.H.L. Barnes told the crowd that packed Metropolitan
Hall at a "monster mass-meeting" held to promote the fair on July 27, 1893.
"We shall build no souphouses," he declared, "no beggars shall be driven from
house to house. But out on the silver sands fringing the Pacific will be built at
a cost, I believe, of over a million dollars, buildings that will be the deposito-
ries of the hope of the world." The fair did provide work for some, although
as was the case for many women, the number of male applicants quickly over-
ran the available jobs. Promoters were faced with the fact that the migration
of the unemployed from other areas would only aggravate the condition of

the thousands of workingmen looking for employment in San Francisco. Many unemployed men did flock to Golden Gate Park but not always in search of work at the fair. Not far from the Midwinter Fair, a coalition of workingmen, merchants, ministers, and rabbis—known as the Citizens' Executive Committee for the Relief of the Unemployed—had launched a huge, city-wide relief project that raised money to pay out-of-work men to labor in the park. Just as this visible reminder of economic upheaval existed in the same geographic space as the Midwinter Fair's celebration of economic progress, coverage of this story in the press was often placed adjacent to coverage of the fair. Moreover, while the community support necessary for both of these efforts—the Midwinter Fair and the Citizens' Executive Committee— was the result of cross-class alliances, at the same time these projects actually made class divisions more visible. Coverage in local newspapers of how the fair and the relief committee fared in face of the social fallout of the economic crisis provided a vehicle for the representation of class identities that stood in stark contrast to the images of independent, self-made men depicted at the '49 Mining Camp and served to highlight how far the nation had moved from that ideal by presenting images that graphically showcased the conditions of everyday life in the nation's new industrial economy.[67]

One of the ways both the Midwinter Fair and The Citizens' Executive Committee for the Relief of the Unemployed generated representations of the working classes was by requiring the registration and enumeration of local unemployed. These people, dependent upon employers and wages, were the antithesis of Jacksonian producers. At the Midwinter Fair, this deployment of scrutinizing practices—akin to those associated with new scientific management techniques used by employers to keep a watchful eye over employees— was ostensibly instituted to insure that unemployed residents of the city were given work before outsiders.[68] It is likely that it was also used as a way to exert some control over large numbers of disgruntled and desperate men. "For the protection of the unemployed among the inhabitants of San Francisco, their names are being registered in the order in which they make application for work," the *Call* announced. "Only those mechanics and laborers who now reside here will be given employment in connection with the exposition." But press coverage of the numbers and characteristics of the unemployed seeking work at the Midwinter Fair that reporters garnered from registration rosters also disclosed information about the composition and condition of the working classes to a city-wide readership. By August 2, 1893, the press reported that from 300 to 400 employment applications were being received daily at the Midwinter Fair's headquarters and the total had already reached 4,000. "About 10 per cent are carpenters," the *Call* informed its readers, "as many more are other mechanics, including engineers, gardeners, teamsters, painters, watchmen and timekeepers. The majority are laborers, although a number are clerks and salesmen out of work and willing to take a pick and shovel and commence grading for the buildings." By August 9, 1893, the registration of applicants for work at the Midwinter Fair grounds was closed. Within five weeks, 5,000 men had registered their applications for employment. "The committee will not be able to use the services of half that number," the same paper disclosed, "and it was decided that it would be unfair to the applicants to still further increase their number." Press coverage of the registration process at the Midwinter Fair had made it unquestionably clear to city residents that ordinary men, many from respectable trades, were out of work in staggering numbers.[69]

The Citizens' Executive Committee for the Relief of the Unemployed engaged in similar registration practices when it began putting men to work in Golden Gate Park on January 4, 1894. At a meeting held in the rooms of the Merchants' Club on January 2, "It was unanimously agreed that the funds raised by the citizens for the aid of the unemployed should be used to improve and beautify Golden Gate Park." "While trees will be put out, plants placed in beds, lawns spaded up and sown, no experience in gardening will be needed by the unemployed," an article in the *Examiner* informed its readers, "as most of them will be given work in grading and preparing new grounds." Although Park Commissioner Stow initially assured the committee that "there was virtually no limit to the work to be done in the Park and that he would put to work all the men the committee would send to him" by the end of the month the number of men had to be pared back from a high of 2,800 to between 1,200 and 1,400. In part this was due to the rapid depletion of funds needed to pay so many workers, but it was also motivated by the concern that the park was becoming crowded with "more men than could be made useful by the Park Commission." Each employed man was assigned a ticket that entitled him to ten days of work for which he was paid one dollar per day. Throughout the period of relief, men who had worked more than ten days were often required to relinquish their jobs so that other unemployed men could work.[70]

Registration of the unemployed for park work was systematic and involved careful examination and evaluation of the men who applied. The relief committee scrutinized men to screen out "the bum element" and to make sure employment was given "only to those considered worthy." Married men with wives and families were also generally given preference over single men without dependents. As was the case with workers at the Midwinter Fair, San Francisco residents were given priority over the unemployed from outside the city. In fact, enough people in search of work were arriving in the city that after January 10, work tickets were only given to men who presented "letters from former employers or from business men stating that the applicant is known to be deserving and has resided in this city for some time." On January 4, 1894, the *Examiner* described the registration process for the 1,100 unemployed men who had gathered on Leidesdorff Street on the morning of the previous day. In groups they were "escorted by a special policeman through the side entrance of the Merchants' Exchange to be examined as to their eligibility for employment." "Detachments of fourteen men each were brought up the stairs and one by one examined by the selecting committee, consisting of Father Montgomery and M. P. Jones, while a third member of the executive committee kept a list and a fourth made out the employment cards." The recipient of the first work ticket was Jerry Sullivan, a San Francisco resident for twenty-one years who "had a wife and six children" and was described as "utterly without means and hungry."[71]

The press, in its coverage of the Citizens' Executive Committee's activities, also described and ran stories about the unemployed men. Most often, it represented the unemployed as ordinary but hardworking and dutiful men facing poverty despite their best efforts. Reports also tended to stress the diversity of the workforce in the park—showing, like the Midwinter Fair coverage, that economic hard times did not discriminate when it can to age, ethnicity, or the respectability or skill level of one's occupation. "Jewelers, piano-makers, cooks, drug clerks, book canvassers and sewing machine agents work side by side with the commonest of laborers glad to get an opportunity to earn $1 a day," one account in the *Chronicle* reported. "The men were of all nationalities, ages and physical conditions. Some were mere youths, while others were gray and bent with age," informed another.[72]

Some newspaper accounts profiled individual members of the unemployed. One of these related the story of a man "who asked that his name be withheld" because he did not "want all his friends to know that he has become one of the great army of unemployed." The abstract for the story read: "A man who had been standing in Pauper alley all night waiting for a chance for a work ticket wrote his story for the *Examiner* yesterday. He is an American, sober and industrious, born and brought up in San Francisco, and yet he has slept out of doors for weeks, and for weeks he has been on the verge of starvation." The man related that while he was "working on a building on sixteenth street last May" he "fell from the second story to the ground floor." This fall resulted in an injury to his left foot that rendered him unable to work for thirteen weeks. After he recovered he was unable to find work as a plasterer, his usual trade, or much of anything else. Between the bills for the doctor and living expenses for himself and his mother, he was soon insolvent without his regular wage of $3 a day. He sold all the furniture he owned to buy his mother a ticket to Oregon where his sister lived. Then, he disclosed, "I went to a cheap lodging house, but I soon had to take to the streets. I managed to earn a few cents here and there by cleaning up yards and such like. I was treated well in some places and called a lazy brute in others." Another article delineated for its readers what a wage of one dollar a day would buy by telling the stories of three park workers and providing examples of their household budgets. "One is the provider for a family of four—himself, his wife and two small children. The second is the sole supporter of his aged mother and his little brother. A third can spend all his dollar on himself, for no others are dependent on him, although he has a family in the East."[73]

Press coverage not only described the poor, it also disclosed notions about poverty and the deserving and undeserving poor, and thus formed the basis for the development of a civic discourse about class identity and economic inequality. In its favorable reports of the park relief project and its calls for increased charitable generosity, the press often emphasized the structural causes of poverty, challenging common attitudes that held that poverty was a result of personal moral failings. The *Chronicle* featured the partial text of a sermon given by Rev. Thomas Filben, pastor of the California Street Methodist Episcopal Church, which "took the present condition of the laboring classes in this city" as its subject. "Ordinarily poverty presupposes improvidence or vice," Filben explained, "and misfortune is usually the minor cause. The poverty among us now is unlike this. . . . Many of the best workmen in town are out of employment and utterly unable to find it . . . this city has a veritable army that must be provided for or else be compelled to great suffering and want."[74]

Even with the turn away from moral explanations to structural causes of poverty, a key element in the press's portrayal was the representation of the unemployed men as worthy poor—hardworking, victims of circumstance, well-mannered, temperate, and appropriately grateful for charity. The process of registering the unemployed was, in part, designed to separate the worthy from the unworthy poor and to assure donors to both the Midwinter Fair and park relief that aid was only going to the right sort of men. "There is plenty of work to be done and there are plenty of honest, sober men to do it, as the line before the door witnesses," intoned William M. Bunker, Chairman of the Citizen's Executive Committee. "I say honest, sober men, because each one of them bears a good recommendation from a reliable firm in this city." In the early stages of the park relief project, the *Chronicle* praised the men's industry: "This vast army of workingmen are literally making the dust fly at the Park . . . They are a conscientious lot of toilers and do not seem inclined to take it easy because they are working for less than it usually costs to have such work performed." The men's appropriate gratitude for relief was also lauded. Newspapers even reprinted their thank-you letters. William E. Lippert, of 748 Brannan Street wrote: "The men in my gang who were discharged on Wednesday requested me to tender their sincere thanks to the Executive Committee, churches, and schools for their assistance when a helping hand was much needed in the families of many of my gang." Similarly, the park workers were also represented as men of honesty and integrity. "The workingmen thus far have shown remarkably good faith in more ways than one," the *Chronicle* reported. "Four men yesterday returned their tickets for work with the explanation that they had found other employment, and requesting that the tickets be given to somebody out of a job."[75]

The press, in its coverage of the fundraising drives for both the Midwinter Fair and the Citizen's Executive Committee's enterprises, enthusiastically remarked upon the general climate of generosity in the city. "Subscriptions continue to come in freely," reported the *Chronicle*. "The cheerfulness with which the public are contributing to the fund makes the committee hopeful that work may be provided for San Francisco's suffering laborers long enough to enable them to get in better circumstances."[76] However, in its reportage of charitable participation, the press constructed an image of the upper classes that contrasted sharply with the image it presented of the working and middle classes. On March 1, 1894, the *Chronicle* published a resolution that had been adopted the day before by the Citizens' Executive Committee urging "banks, insurance companies and other wealthy corporations and the capitalists of the city to duplicate their original subscriptions to the relief fund." The pace of donations from these groups had slowed, the relief fund for the unemployed was being "rapidly exhausted," and the committee's resolution suggested that they did not believe it would quicken without considerable prodding.[77] Ferdinand Haber, head of the Viticulture Department at the Midwinter Fair, told the *Call* that "the real supports of the exhibition are the middle classes—retail merchants, mechanics, and laboring classes." "The capitalists and large real estate owners have done comparatively nothing. Some of these big men don't look beyond the threshold of their own doors."[78]

Within this context of economic crisis and disparate donation, the charitable acts of the poorest members of society were deemed especially impressive. The generosity of newsboys—working children often described as "ragged urchins"—received particular attention. On February 3, the *Chronicle* reported that Jimmy Collins, a newsboy, had paid a visit to treasurer Daniel Meyer's office shortly before two o'clock. He "sauntered into the place" and shouted, "Hey, dere, there's dat dime." Ever since the Citizen's Executive Committee had begun collecting subscriptions, Jimmy Collins had made it a practice to contribute ten cents a day, and usually he was accompanied by three other newsboys who did the same. He'd confided to one of the clerks who worked in the office that the reason he made this donation was that "when he was a few years younger his father was out of work for a long time and consequently he knew just what it was to be hard up." Also newsworthy were the charitable efforts of the city's newsboys on behalf of the Midwinter Fair. Abe Bienkowski—"a plain everyday newsboy, cast upon the world alone"—put out a call to "every newsboy in San Francisco" that several fundraising meetings for the Midwinter Fair were to be held at the Irish-American Hall. He was also "furnished with a subscription paper and authorized to collect from all newsboys who desired to contribute." Donations ranged from five to fifty cents. By August 9, the contribution of the newsboys was nearly $12 and on August 10 the subscription list published in the *Call* indicated "newsboys subscribed (additional) $3.70." One explanation offered for the charitable acts of the poor was that they gave because they knew what it was like to be in want while the elite and the middle classes needed to be educated about the poor in order to be motivated to generosity.[79]

In fact, as a form of exposé journalism, the press coverage of these two fundraising efforts did a considerable amount of public education and service in a time of crisis. In its routine chastisement of capitalists for their stinginess, it not only presented a stark contrast to the virtue of capitalist entrepreneurs lauded at the '49 Mining Camp, but also safely channeled and gave voice to local anger at growing social inequities. Its depictions of the worthy poor may very well have been a way to mollify readers who could identify with such a plight at the same time that they served to educate the middle and upper classes about the less fortunate. Through its coverage, local newspapers allowed middle-class readers to "know" the poor. The press also reported stories of middle-class "discovery" of the poor. While these generally occurred in "real life" and were reported in the pages of the press, they mirrored the kind of experiences and charitable actions such stories were designed to inspire in their readers.

The *Examiner* generated this kind of tale in its coverage of the Lincoln School boys who provided lunches for over 2,300 men in the park in mid-January. "A lady who noticed the scene from a carriage beckoned to one of the boys. 'I'll make up a box of lunches for to-morrow,' she said. 'I never dreamed such things could exist here in San Francisco. . . . I have been driving around after these wagons all morning, and I have seen these men eating like starving animals. To-morrow I shall do what little I can to help." The idea of having the children from various schools rotate the responsibility for providing lunches to the men in the park actually originated with one middle-class fifteen-year-old girl from Golden Gate Avenue, Lillie Meyer, in a moment of middle-class "discovery" of the poor. Upon their return from a buggy ride in Golden Gate Park, Lillie's older sister and little brother related that in the course of their ride they had came upon some of the park workers toiling on the roadways. It was lunch time but the men had nothing to eat. Well-stocked with cookies, the two Meyer children offered them to the men and they were gratefully received. After hearing this story, Lillie Meyer had an idea that "solved a question that had puzzled a lot of older heads." She said, "I'll speak to Miss Strauss, our teacher, and ask her to speak to all the scholars, and we'll each one of us bring a lunch and send them out to the poor men in the Park." While this episode conveniently conformed to images of children that stressed their innocence and viewed them as especially appropriate vehicles of charity, it also launched a huge community effort to help the less fortunate. The *Chronicle* even went so far as to encourage its readers to go out to the park and see the work of the unemployed men first hand, "If the hundreds who drive out to the Park to-day, before or after visiting the Midwinter Fair, will continue their journey a few yards beyond the fenced inclosure either on the north or the south, they will obtain some idea of the extent and value of the work which the dollar-a-day men are doing."[80]

But even as the depictions of the poor in the press made them visible and constructed them as worthy, hardworking, appropriately grateful, and honorable, this ostensibly favorable image designed to provoke charity also contained within it less savory elements. The poor did not represent themselves and stepping outside the image constructed for them meant risking being labeled unworthy and therefore undeserving of charity. Throughout the fundraising effort, concerns were raised about "bummers" and "loafers" receiving aid, that the poor would become dependent upon relief, and that the wage of one dollar a day was too much of a luxury for some. Moreover, a flyer circulated by the United Brotherhood of Labor in early September 1893 titled "Facts Concerning the Midwinter Fair" urged the public to refuse to fund the Midwinter Fair because it had failed to uphold its promise to give work to the unemployed. This flyer also made reference to the fact that the unemployed had "camped upon the Postoffice site nearly two months, and have had numerous street parades" yet were still waiting for their situation to be openly discussed in the *Chronicle*, Michael de Young's newspaper. These rumblings of discontent suggest that the city's widespread efforts to aid the unemployed emerged, in part, from the need for some gesture of appeasement to keep an increasingly volatile situation under control. [81] Through the provision of work and a little direct aid, combined with press coverage that channeled working-class anger and taught middle-class San Franciscans about the less fortunate in their midst at the same time that it moved them to charity, elites successfully weathered a crisis that had the potential to disrupt order not only at the fair, but in the city at large.

In July 1893, when the Midwinter Fair was still just a sparkle in de Young's eye, Clara S. Feliz had told a crowd assembled at a mass meeting to generate enthusiasm for the exposition that it would "attract the attention of the civilized world." After such a display, she explained "people elsewhere" would "not look at you as if you carried a pistol in your belt and a bowie-knife in your boot when you tell them you come from California."[82] For its six-month duration, the Midwinter Fair served as a cultural frontier on which San Francisco elites presented an image of the city to "the civilized world" that revealed a carefully ordered vision. Fair organizers packaged many of the these things that made San Francisco its own unique place—its gold rush history, its disorderly Wild West legacy, its diversity, and its position on the Pacific Rim—within an overarching framework that stressed the containment of class, race, and gender-based disorder in the city and the ascendance of locally inflected forms of nationally dominant social hierarchies. Sunset City offered to the world a picture of San Francisco as a civilized, conquered, and thus fully American place. Claiming this mantle reflected the city's position as a far-western urban center that, having gotten its own house in order, was not only ready for incorporation into the fabric of the nation, but was poised to be in-strumental in furthering the nation's growing imperial goals.

Conclusion:
Creating an American Place:
Cultural Ordering's Broader Implications

This book began with a description of the disorder of San Francisco's gold rush years. Nascent elites came to define their vision of an orderly city against the racial and ethnic mixture, class fluidity, and gender imbalances of those formative years. Many scholars and writers have adopted this vision as their own, narrating the city's history as a celebration of its transformation from a disordered boomtown to a well-ordered metropolis. Yet this work has argued that behind that triumphal narrative exists a different story about the process of ordering the disorderly city—one that shows both the costs, as well as the benefits, of this process and that makes central the ways San Franciscans understood, constructed, and translated difference into social power. Apprehending that new narrative has required recognizing two previously underappreciated aspects of nineteenth-century San Francisco: the role of imperial, nation-making processes in shaping categories of identity and the importance of the city's cultural frontiers in shaping processes of nation-making. From these insights, the concept of cultural ordering developed here emerged. Simply put, cultural ordering involved efforts to establish a distinctly American society built on nationally dominant hierarchies of race, class, and gender by way of the discourses, practices, and places generated on the city's cultural frontiers. While the initial military conquest and the subsequent establishment of legal and political authority in San Francisco were fairly straightforward, the extension and consolidation of nation-making through the inscription of race, class, and gender-based hierarchies—the foundation of social order in the city—was a much more complicated, contested, ongoing, and unevenly successful project. Although this story began with the disorder of the gold rush, as we have seen, just over four decades later at the Midwinter Fair's '49 Mining Camp, through cultural ordering, local elites had reconfigured and transformed the disordered history of those years into a narrative designed to contain the city's diversity through the assertion of race, class, and gender hierarchies.

In between the actual gold rush and its representation at the '49 Mining Camp, this study has charted the process of cultural ordering on five cultural frontiers of particular significance in the development of the city: restaurants, hotels, and boardinghouses; places of amusement; Chinatown; the fairs of the Mechanics' Institute; and the California Midwinter International Exposition. The first chapter revealed how as San Francisco grew from pueblo to metropolis, restaurants, hotels, and boardinghouses, reflective of the development of cultural ordering in the city, became increasingly spatially and socially segregated. Chapter 2 explored how the Barbary Coast, Woodward's Gardens, and the Pacific Museum of Anatomy and Science emerged in the 1860s as three varying strains of orderly and disorderly places of amusement that—as designed by leisure entrepreneurs, experienced by patrons, and labored in by employees—contributed to cultural ordering through their assertion, and sometimes contestation of, dominant categories of identity and visions of social order. Chapter 3 identified the ways the construction of Chinatown as a tourist attraction contributed to cultural ordering by representing the Chinese as exotic yet vilified and by directing racial anxieties among the city's diverse inhabitants toward the Chinese and the space of Chinatown. Chapter 4 analyzed how the annual Mechanics' Institute's fairs furthered cultural ordering through their dissemination of a vision for social order organized around particular configurations of labor, the economy, gender, and the family. Lastly, Chapter 5 assessed the elite-driven fantasy of a culturally ordered city presented at the California Midwinter International Exposition. In complex and contested ways, the Midwinter Fair articulated San Francisco's desire to be considered a thoroughly civilized and American place. Claiming this identity was linked to both the containment of San Francisco's heterogeneity and the promotion of a vision of this western city that was domesticated enough to be considered American yet wild enough to be regionally distinct.

While cultural ordering played a vital role in structuring categories of identity and social order on nineteenth-century San Francisco's cultural frontiers, this approach has implications that extend beyond its application to this one place and time. In particular, the concept of cultural frontiers deepens our understanding of westward expansion by making the link between empire-building and nation-making in the United States explicit rather than implicit and by positioning these two processes as "historically coterminous and mutually defining." As literary historian Amy Kaplan has argued, "United States continental expansion is often treated as an entirely separate phenomenon from European colonialism of the nineteenth century, rather than as an interrelated form of imperial expansion. The divorce between these two histories mirrors the American historiographical tradition of viewing empire as a twentieth-century aberration, rather than as part of an expansionist continuum." Seen from this vantage point, an important part of the story of America becomes one of conquest on military and political fronts combined with and linked to processes of nation-making on cultural ground working their way across all the varied places on the continent—hand in hand with landed expansion—from Plymouth Rock to the Pacific Coast. Moreover, rather than make invisible or marginal the histories and realities of the diverse groups of people that inhabited distinct regions, this joining of empire-building, nation-making, and cultural ordering is premised on a recognition of the relations of unequal social power that have long tied these groups into the same story.[1]

By keeping issues of social power and inequality at the fore, understanding the process of cultural ordering also contributes to our knowledge of how places are constituted as American in large measure through the construction of race, class, and gender hierarchies. Thinking about the way American places are defined through hierarchy allows for a different way of viewing some of Frederick Jackson Turner's conclusions about the significance of the frontier, as well as his assertions about its closing in 1890. In his ordering narrative, the "Frontier Thesis," Turner conceptualized the frontier as the meeting place of civilization and savagery that forged a unified American national character, which he characterized as independent, rugged, democratic, egalitarian, and masculine. He based his determination that the frontier was closed upon the 1890 census, which showed that the "population of the West had reached the figure of at least two persons per square mile, the basis for calling an area settled." While his reliance on this calculation had numerous conceptual problems, nevertheless, in Turner's formulation, settlement connoted the end of the frontier for a reason—it symbolized the establishment, however precarious, of a distinctly American social order organized around the largely positive and optimistic qualities he ascribed to the American national character. But, from the standpoint of groups other than whites or ethnic groups that fell less easily into the category of white, the kind of social order that indicated the establishment of an American place was unequal and hierarchical. All the same, it was just as, if not more, distinctly American—although the force that was necessary to secure it did not become obsolete in the 1890s. In other words, by shifting the focus it becomes apparent that when Turner wrote about the importance of settlement and population density on the frontier, he was also referring to processes of nation-making through hierarchy building. In a sense, the two phenomena are really just two very different sides of the same coin.[2]

One of the most notable departures from other recent studies on U.S. empire is that this work looks at imperial, nation-making processes in an urban, largely immigrant society. Most of the time, conquest and empire-building are seen as taking place vis-à-vis indigenous groups, usually Native Americans or Mexicans or Hispanos—not immigrants—and this construction leads it to be conceptualized as something that happens in the West, or on what used to be the frontier—not in the East and not usually in cities. Part of Turner's Frontier Thesis posited an evolutionary development of the American West—and, by association, the nation—that moved steadily from rural, agricultural settlements to towns to cities. Subsequent historians proved this not only to be in error but actually to be the reverse of what occurred. Writing in 1933, thirty years after Turner, Arthur Schlesinger countered one of Turner's central assumptions with the contention that towns actually preceded rural settlements in the development in the trans-Missouri West. In 1959, Schlesinger's student, Richard C. Wade, put forth the complementary argument that "towns were the spearheads of the frontier." "Planted far in advance of the line of settlement," he argued, "they held the West for the approaching population." In 1979, John W. Reps echoed these sentiments in his assertion that the "establishment of urban communities, whatever their origins, stimulated rather than followed the opening of the West to agriculture."[3]

These urban historians, however, did not push their analysis quite far enough. After all, if cities really were the spearheads of the frontier, they were also the engines of conquest. Although immigrant cities tend to be thought of as an eastern rather than western phenomenon, explicating the process of cultural ordering in San Francisco, the premier city of the nineteenth-century American West, with an immigrant society even more diverse than most eastern cities, allows for links to be made among the structuring of social power, hierarchies, and nation-making across the continent. The large numbers of immigrants that arrived on American shores in the nineteenth century were generally greeted with a combination of apprehension and hostility. Their new nation subjected them to a process of ordering that determined whether or not they were suitable for integration in the body politic and how they would be situated in the nation's social hierarchies in relation to other groups. Tempered by local conditions, the hierarchies that ordered immigrants in the East were similar to those that were brought to bear on immigrants in San Francisco. Cities in the East and West were thus linked in a reciprocal relationship through processes of empire-building and nation-making—which included aspects of assimilation and acculturation—that helped retool social hierarchies and categories of identity to accommodate new immigrant groups while perpetuating elite control.

The way this work conceptualizes cultural spaces also has implications beyond nineteenth-century San Francisco. The emphasis placed on the intersection of cultural frontiers and nation-making by this study is not only a departure from other works on U.S. empire but also makes it clear that it is no longer enough to talk about cultural processes and spaces in New York or the East Coast and have them be viewed as adequate stand-ins for the rest of the nation. Instead, the argument here is that the focus must shift to figuring out the interrelationships between the function of cultural spaces in different localities in varied regions and how those spaces were reflective of or resistant to the kinds of social hierarchies that were integral to nation-making. This approach, for example, offers a new way of interpreting the telling argument made by a number of historians that although western cities were often poor replicas of eastern cities, imitation proved to be a far stronger force than innovation in the urbanization of the nineteenth-century West. "Original achievements," wrote Gunther Barth of San Francisco, "disappeared in the flood of made-to-order imitations of eastern and European models that served the daily needs much more readily than did genuine creations that consumed time." Yet the emphasis on the imitative tendencies of western cities like San Francisco has not only oversimplified their cultural contours but also obscured the fact that perhaps some of the desire for imitation came from the kinds of social hierarchies embodied in eastern—already defined as distinctly American—cultural forms: city plans, architecture, restaurants, parades, fairs, hotels, and parks.[4] Clearly, we can learn new things about nation-making and empire-building by interrogating the reasons behind the regional differences and similarities of urban cultural forms.

This work ends with the imagined city of the 1894 Midwinter Fair. Just twelve years later, the metropolis that San Francisco had become came to an abrupt but temporary end as a result of the earthquake and fire of 1906. Neither of these endpoints—the hopeful yet anxious imaginings of 1894 nor the devastation and rebirth of 1906—offer sufficiently meaningful markers of a definitive end of the process of cultural ordering. They were, however, emblematic of telling transformations that signified both uneven, contested success and the completion of its most violent and extreme period—the formation of a new, American society. The imagined city of the California Midwinter International Exposition symbolized elite success in the real city of constructing race, class, and gender hierarchies in line with nationally dominant trends in the face of continuing resistance. The fact that elites chose not to implement Daniel Burnham's already existing city plan after 1906 suggests that the kind of order and hierarchy it sought to effect had already been established and could be maintained, at least in part, independent of such forms. As we have seen, in the 1890s, San Francisco remained an incredibly diverse city—one with proportionately more foreign-born residents than nearly any other city in the nation—but its diversity and continuing disorderliness were increasingly contained by spatial and social segregation. Yet even though cultural frontiers reinforced social hierarchies with increasing frequency, maintaining the always tenuous social order the city had achieved required continual cultural ordering. Just as subsequent historians have shown that Turner's formulation was too neat and that the frontier never really closed because frontier processes that were supposed to be contained by the nineteenth century bled deeply into the twentieth, processes of nation-making on the city's cultural ground did not come to a complete halt even once the structures and hierarchies that connoted an American place were established. As Patricia Limerick has argued, "Conquest basically involved the drawing of lines on a map, the definition and allocation of ownership . . . and the evolution of land from matter to property. The process had two stages: the initial drawing of the lines (which we have generally called the frontier stage) and the subsequent giving of meaning and power to those lines, which is still underway." The "giving of meaning and power" is at the heart of the intersection of nation-making and cultural frontiers described here. Once the structures and hierarchies that connoted an American place had been fairly well established, its primary directive had been achieved, and the intensity of cultural ordering definitely diminished, but its effects did

not. Episodes of cultural ordering—integrally related to processes of assimilation and acculturation yet distinct from the ground-up style of place-
making seen in nineteenth-century San Francisco—occur every time cultural
spaces and forms are deployed in debates about how a new immigrant group
or an existing minority group is situated in the American body politic in
terms of gender, race, and class.[5]

The story that has been told in these pages is not a particularly happy one
for either San Francisco or the United States, but it is a necessary and useful
one. As Gray Brechin has pointed out, "World-famed for the beauty of its
setting and for its romantic history, San Francisco has largely escaped the
harsh judgments to which less lovable cities are subject." San Francisco's
reputation as an especially tolerant, still somewhat wild city has shielded
popular conceptions of its history from critical scrutiny. Undoubtedly, it is
more open and tolerant in some—perhaps many—respects than other cities
in the nation. But the tolerance for which the city became and continues to
be known has revolved around labor radicalism and sexuality—both of which
have been largely white and frequently male-dominated movements. In
terms of race, San Francisco was never an especially tolerant city. That
whiteness was a more inclusive category in the city was not so much a sign of
racial tolerance as a reaction against its diversity. And while scholars have
agreed that blacks had it better in San Francisco than in much of the rest of
the nation, that was largely because the Chinese bore the brunt of racial hostility. As one of America's first truly multiracial cities, San Francisco be-
queaths a mixed legacy. The point is not so much that the idea of San Francisco as a liberal city is a myth. Rather, the aim here is to decenter San
Francisco's sense of its own unique history—which has to a great extent been
constructed around its reputation for tolerance—and to reemphasize its con-
nectedness to national and global processes of imperialism, to the hegemonic
categories of identity and social order associated with nation-making, and to
other places—both eastern cities like New York, as well as western cities like
Los Angeles.[6]

Despite sharing the same state, scholars and residents alike have frequently positioned San Francisco and Los Angeles as social, cultural, and
economic rivals and opposites—as distinct from one another in terms of
their images and the processes that shaped them as San Francisco and New
York. The regional rivalries between San Francisco and Los Angeles were,
and still are, very real—as are some of their social and cultural differences. In

part because of the 1906 earthquake and fire, by 1920 Los Angeles—already fast on San Francisco's heels by the 1880s—superseded San Francisco as the economically dominant city in the region. In terms of patterns of settlement and immigration, Los Angeles emerged as both whiter—with more domestic migration from the Midwest—and more Latino than San Francisco. In terms of urban design, planners created a Los Angeles that was sprawling, decentralized, yet still spatially segregated—in contrast to the different kinds of geographic limitations imposed upon San Francisco's social geography by its location on a peninsula. In recent years, the result of these differences has been that scholars have come to view Los Angeles as the trademark twentieth-century western city—along with other Sunbelt cities—while cities like San Francisco and Seattle are frequently dismissed as relics of the nineteenth century. For instance, in 1991, John Findlay, echoing a long historiographical trajectory, asserted, "In the nineteenth-century, the westerner's imitative state of mind had produced San Francisco. In the twentieth century the quest to diverge from eastern cities and midwestern farm towns resulted in a different type of city, exemplified by Los Angeles."[7] Although addressing this question is beyond the scope of this book, it seems likely that just as new insights into processes of nation-making and empire-building emerge when eastern and western immigrant cities are compared, similar benefits could come from examining San Francisco and Los Angeles's similarities instead of their differences. If this remnant of the divide between the nineteenth- and twentieth-century Wests that Turner erected could be traversed, perhaps we could get a clearer picture of why urban design as well as urban cultural spaces changed in the twentieth century in new places like Los Angeles with different populations and ordering imperatives, and how old spaces and places in nineteenth-century cities were made to serve new social and cultural purposes. A richer, more complex national narrative would surely result from making these kinds of connections between San Francisco, the premier city of the nineteenth-century West, and Los Angeles, the premier city of the twentieth, and tying them into the broader histories of nation-making and empire-building.[8]

What kind of national narrative would emerge? Viewing American history in this way requires recognizing the workings of social power through control of key cultural sites to erect hierarchies and shape society. It requires acknowledging America's imperial past as well as its democratic past, its social conformity as well as rugged individualism, its hierarchy as well as egalitarianism. In doing so, it would not negate what may be seen as more positive American virtues, but it does temper and contextualize them. And by making struggles over cultural authority central—by taking the politics of everyday life seriously—it would show how ordinary people both affect and are affected by the elite-driven, contested, and ongoing ordering processes that take place on America's cultural frontiers.

Notes

Introduction: Ordering the Disorderly City

1. For the divergent patterns of race relations in California see Tomás Almaguer, *Racial Faultlines: The Historical Origins of White Supremacy in California* (Berkeley: University of California Press, 1994), 1–2.

2. James O'Meara, "San Francisco in Early Days," *Overland Monthly*, 2nd ser., 1 (February 1883): 130.

3. This discussion draws on the "contact zone" concept developed by Mary Louise Pratt, *Imperial Eyes: Travel Writing and Transculturation* (New York: Routledge, 1992), 6 and 7; and John Kuo Wei Tchen, *New York before Chinatown: Orientalism and the Shaping of American Culture, 1776–1882* (Baltimore, MD: Johns Hopkins University Press, 1999), xix.

4. Most studies of restaurants, hotels and boardinghouses, fairs and expositions, and places of amusement in nineteenth-century San Francisco tend to be primarily descriptive rather than analytical. See, for example, Frances de Talavera Berger, *Sumptuous Dining in Gaslight San Francisco, 1875–1915* (New York: Doubleday, 1985) and Arthur Chandler and Marvin Nathan, *The Fantastic Fair: The Story of the California Midwinter International Exposition, Golden Gate Park, San Francisco, 1894* (Saint Paul, MN: Pogo Press, 1993). Important exceptions that deal with the inscription of race-, class-, and gender-based hierarchies in San Francisco's cultural spaces are Mary Ryan, *Women in Public: Between Banners and Ballots, 1825–1880* (Berkeley: University of California Press, 1990), and *Civic Wars: Democracy and Public Life in the American City during the Nineteenth Century* (Berkeley: University of California Press, 1997). Yet, while studies of cultural spaces in San Francisco and other cities of the American West are limited, the East Coast–centered literature is vast. Scholars have identified sites of leisure and consumption as arenas of class contestation and class formation. See, for example, Francis G. Couvares, "The Triumph of Commerce: Class Culture and Mass Culture in Pittsburgh," in Michael Frisch and Daniel Walkowitz, eds., *Working-Class America: Essays on Labor, Community, and American Society* (Chicago: University of Illinois Press, 1983); John F. Kasson, *Amusing the Million: Coney Island at the Turn of the Century* (New York: Hill and Wang, 1978); Roy Rosenzweig, *Eight Hours for What We Will: Workers and Leisure in an Industrial City, 1870–1920* (New York: Cambridge University Press, 1983); and Lawrence Levine, *Highbrow/Lowbrow: The Emergence of Cultural Hierarchy in America* (Cambridge, MA: Harvard University Press, 1988). Scholars

have also found that urban cultural spaces were profoundly gendered. See Kathy Peiss, *Cheap Amusements: Working Women and Leisure in Turn-of-the-Century New York* (Philadelphia: Temple University Press, 1986); Christine Stansell, *City of Women: Sex and Class in New York, 1789–1860* (Chicago: University of Illinois Press, 1987); and Elizabeth Ewen, *Immigrant Women in the Land of Dollars: Life and Culture on the Lower East Side, 1890–1925* (New York: Monthly Review Press, 1985). Studies have also determined that cultural spaces were key sites of racialization. See, for example, David R. Roediger, *The Wages of Whiteness: Race and the Making of the American Working Class* (New York: Verso, 1991); Eric Lott, *Love and Theft: Blackface Minstrelsy and the American Working Class* (New York: Oxford University Press, 1993); and Grace Elizabeth Hale, *Making Whiteness: The Culture of Segregation in the South, 1890–1940* (New York: Random House, 1998).

5. In this work, the concept of space functions on several different levels. It refers to specific restaurants, hotels, boardinghouses, places of amusement, fairs, and expositions as well as to the spatial geography of the city that provided the social context in which they existed. It also encompasses the processes by which such spaces were imbued with cultural meaning by discrete social groups that transformed them into locally significant places. The way cultural space has been conceptualized in this work draws upon the efforts of a number of theorists who point to the ways spaces constitute and are constituted through social relationships. Foremost among these is Henri Lefebvre, whose work has been foundational in linking the production of space to social and economic relations and thus to issues of identity formation and power. See Henri Lefebvre, *The Production of Space*, trans. Donald Nicholson-Smith (Cambridge, MA: Blackwell, 1991). A number of scholars have further explored the interaction of capitalism, power, and space and have complicated this basic formulation to include race, gender, sexuality, disease, the body, and various other markers of difference under the rubric of social relations. See, for example, Thomas C. Holt, "Marking: Race, Race-making, and the Writing of History," *American Historical Review* 100, no. 1 (February 1995): 1–20; Edward Soja, *Postmodern Geographies: The Reassertion of Space in Critical Social Theory* (New York: Verso, 1989); Doreen Massey, *Space, Place, and Gender* (Minneapolis: University of Minnesota Press, 1994); Susan Stanford Friedman, *Mappings: Feminism and the Cultural Geographies of Encounter* (Princeton, NJ: Princeton University Press, 1998); Sarah Deutsch, *Women and the City: Gender, Space, and Power in Boston, 1870–1940* (New York: Oxford University Press, 2000); and Susan Craddock, *City of Plagues: Disease, Poverty, and Deviance in San Francisco* (Minneapolis: University of Minnesota Press, 2000).

6. A.H.B., "Impressions on Arriving in San Francisco," *Pioneer, or California Monthly Magazine* (September 1854): 156; Bayard Taylor, *El Dorado, Or Adventures in the Path of Empire*, vol. 1 (New Mexico: Rio Grande Press, 1967 [first published 1850]), 54–57; Richard Henry Dana, *Two Years before the Mast*, rev. ed. published in 1869, as excerpted in Malcolm E. Barker, ed., *More San Francisco Memoirs, 1852–1899: The Ripening Years* (San Francisco: Londonborn Publications, 1996), 117.

7. Frank Soulé, John H. Gihon, and James Nisbet, *The Annals of San Francisco* (Berkeley, CA: Berkeley Hills Books, 1999 [originally published in 1855]), 246; Taylor, *El Dorado*, 68.

8. Taylor, *El Dorado*, 55. A creese (or kris) was a kind of dagger. See also Taylor, *El Dorado*, 113, for another description of this kind and Alonzo Delano, "On 'Long Wharf,'" in Joseph Henry Jackson, ed., *The Western Gate Reader* (New York: Farrar, Straus and Young, 1952), 181. Frank Marryat, *Mountains and Molehills or Recollections of a Burnt Journal*, with Introduction and Notes by Marguerite Wilbur (Stanford, CA: Stanford University Press, 1952 [originally published 1855]), 38.

9. William Issel and Robert W. Cherny, *San Francisco, 1865–1932: Politics, Power, and Urban Development* (Berkeley: University of California Press, 1986), 14; Gunther Barth, *Instant Cities: Urbanization and the Rise of San Francisco and Denver* (New York: Oxford University Press, 1975), 169.

10. Ryan, *Women in Public*, 15.

11. Judd Kahn, *Imperial San Francisco: Politics and Planning in an American City, 1897–1906* (Lincoln: University of Nebraska Press, 1979), 25.

12. In 1852 there were 464 African Americans in San Francisco; in 1900, 1,654. Douglas Henry Daniels, *Pioneer Urbanites: A Social and Cultural History of Black San Francisco* (Philadelphia: Temple University Press, 1980), 13. For information about the dwindling Indian population see Roger W. Lotchin, *San Francisco, 1846–1856: From Hamlet to City* (Lincoln: University of Nebraska Press, 1974), 104.

13. Issel and Cherny, *San Francisco, 1865–1932*, 14; Barth, *Instant Cities*, 169.

14. This description of Yerba Buena and its conquest is taken from Lotchin, *San Francisco: 1846–1856*, 7–8. Louis Laurent Simonin, from an article published in the French Magazine, *Le Tour du Monde*, excerpted in Malcolm E. Barker, ed., *More San Francisco Memoirs, 1852–1899: The Ripening Years* (San Francisco: Londonborn Publications, 1996), 108.

15. Lotchin, *San Francisco: 1846–1856*, 7–8. The conquest of Yerba Buena is treated as such a fait accompli in San Francisco historiography that very little has been written about its inhabitants immediately before, during, or after the American occupation. See Lisbeth Haas, "War in California, 1846–1848," in *Contested Eden: California Before the Gold Rush*, eds. Ramón Gutiérrez and Richard J. Orsi (Berkeley: University of California Press, 1998), 331–355, for a much-needed discussion of the neglect of the study of conquest in California, the ways conquest was resisted by Californios and indigenous peoples, and how it reorganized California society.

16. Almaguer, *Racial Faultlines*, 9–11. Key works that have influenced my approach to empire-building and nation-making include Amy Kaplan, "'Left Alone with America': The Absence of Empire in the Study of American Culture," in Amy Kaplan and Donald Pease, eds., *Cultures of United States Imperialism* (Durham: Duke University Press, 1993); Anne McClintock, *Imperial Leather: Race, Gender, and Sexuality in the Colonial Contest* (New York: Routledge, 1995); and Edward Said, *Orientalism* (New York: Vintage Books, 1979) and *Culture and Imperialism* (New York: Vintage Books, 1993).

17. Conceptualizing social order in the context of this study has meant invoking theories of social power. Power here is conceptualized in a way that combines Foucauldian and Gramscian approaches. The insight of Foucault that power is diffuse

and constituted through discourse tempers Gramsci and aids in the full appreciation of the significance of the micro-workings of power in the cultural spaces of everyday urban life. Gramsci's analysis of hegemony provides a framework that recognizes that not all power is equally powerful. Power—in its discursive forms—permeates and constitutes the most intimate aspects of lived experience. But, power, however diffuse, also has top-down qualities through which it is asserted by dominant cultural groups to control subordinate groups. Hegemony refers to the process by which the dominant culture asserts a vision of the social world to which subordinate cultures consent and participate in because it appears natural and normal. However, because the hegemonic vision is neither natural or normal, it is always unstable and must be continually asserted in novel ways, frequently through cultural forms that are embedded in processes of capitalist development. At the same time, in a dialectical process, subordinate groups routinely talk back to hegemonic culture and in the process generate counterhegemonic discourses—some of which are then co-opted and incorporated into the hegemonic vision. See Michel Foucault, *Discipline and Punish: The Birth of the Prison* (New York: Vintage Books, 1979) and Antonio Gramsci, *The Modern Prince and Other Writings* (New York: International Publishers, 1957, 1987). For works that have deployed similar conceptualizations of the intersection of power and culture see Stuart Hall, "Notes on Deconstructing the 'Popular,'" in Raphael Samuel, ed., *People's History and Socialist Theory* (London: Routledge, 1981), 227–239, and Richard Butsch, "Introduction: Leisure and Hegemony in America," in Richard Butsch, ed., *For Fun and Profit: The Transformation of Leisure in Consumption* (Philadelphia: Temple University Press, 1990), 3–27.

18. With regard to identity, Stuart Hall's work has been particularly useful in analyzing the ways the discourses and representations generated by and through the kinds of semipublic commercial spaces examined here impact identity formation. See Stuart Hall, "Introduction: Who Needs 'Identity'?" in *Questions of Cultural Identity*, Stuart Hall and Paul du Gay, eds. (London: Sage Publications, 1996), 1–17. Joan W. Scott's work has also been instrumental in shaping the way I think about categories of identity. "The story," she writes, "is no longer about the things that have happened to women and men and how they have reacted to them; instead it is about how the subjective and collective meanings of women and men as categories of identity have been constructed." Joan Wallach Scott, *Gender and the Politics of History* (New York: Columbia University Press, 1988), 6.

19. This recognition of the power of the market in shaping the culture of everyday life is a shift from the focus of three important works on San Francisco that examine the ways different social groups made claims to the political culture of the Habermasian public sphere. These are Philip Ethington, *The Public City: The Political Construction of Urban Life in San Francisco, 1850–1900* (Cambridge: Cambridge University Press, 1994) and Ryan, *Women in Public* and *Civic Wars*.

20. Frederick Jackson Turner, "The Significance of the Frontier in American History," *Proceedings of the Forty-First Meeting of the State Historical Society of Wisconsin* (Madison, Wisconsin, 1894), 79–112.

21. Simonin, from an article published in the French magazine *Le Tour du Monde*, 1862, 107–108.

22. Racial and ethnic relations in San Francisco have been documented by a number of fine social histories focused on one particular group. See Robert A. Burchell, *The San Francisco Irish: 1846–1880* (Manchester, UK: Manchester University Press, 1979); Daniels, *Pioneer Urbanites*; Albert S. Broussard, *Black San Francisco: The Struggle for Racial Equality in the West, 1900–1954* (Lawrence: University Press of Kansas, 1993); Deanna Paoli Gumina, *The Italians of San Francisco, 1850–1930* (New York: Center for Migration Studies, 1978); and Judy Yung, *Unbound Feet: A Social History of Chinese Women in San Francisco* (Berkeley: University of California Press, 1995). See also Alexander Saxton, *The Indispensable Enemy: Labor and the Anti-Chinese Movement in California* (Berkeley: University of California Press, 1971); Andrew Gyory, *Closing the Gate: Race, Politics, and the Chinese Exclusion Act* (Chapel Hill: University of North Carolina Press, 1998); and Robert F. Heizer and Alan J. Almquist, *The Other Californians: Prejudice and Discrimination under Spain, Mexico and the United States to 1920* (Berkeley: University of California Press, 1971).

23. For the centrality of frontier processes to the making of America, see Patricia Nelson Limerick, *The Legacy of Conquest: The Unbroken Past of the American West* (New York: W. W. Norton, 1987); William Cronon, George Miles, and Jay Gitlin, "Becoming West: Toward a New Meaning for Western History," in *Under an Open Sky: Rethinking America's Western Past*, William Cronon, George Miles, and Jay Gitlin, eds. (New York: W. W. Norton, 1992), 3–27; and Kerwin Lee Klein, *Frontiers of Historical Imagination: Narrating the European Conquest of Native America, 1890–1990* (Berkeley: University of California Press, 1997).

24. Lotchin, *San Francisco, 1846–1856*, 31; Issel and Cherny, *San Francisco, 1865–1932*, 117; Gray Brechin, *Imperial San Francisco: Urban Power, Earthly Ruin* (Berkeley: University of California Press, 1999), xxiv–xxv.

25. This approach to San Francisco's transformation from a walking city to an industrial metropolis is from William Bullough, *The Blind Boss and His City: Christopher Augustine Buckley and Nineteenth-Century San Francisco* (Berkeley: University of California Press, 1979), 27. While Bullough did not coin the term *walking city* and is not the only scholar to deploy it, his use of it vis-à-vis San Francisco has particular relevance here. For the origins of the term, see Sam Bass Warner, *Streetcar Suburbs: The Process of Growth in Boston, 1870–1900* (Cambridge: Harvard University Press, 1962). Lotchin, *San Francisco, 1846–1856*, 83–84; 36–42; Issel and Cherny, *San Francisco, 1865–1932*, 80–82, and Bullough, *Blind Boss and His City*, 117–131.

26. Edith Sparks, *Capital Intentions: Female Proprietors in San Francisco, 1850–1920* (Chapel Hill: University of North Carolina Press), 216, Bullough, *Blind Boss and His City*, 100–101 and 233.

27. Issel and Cherny, *San Francisco, 1865–1932*, 80–82; Ronald Takaki, *Strangers from a Different Shore: A History of Asian Americans* (New York: Penguin Books, 1989), 110–112; Issel and Cherny, *San Francisco, 1865–1932*, 139, 140, 154.

Chapter 1. Living in the City: Everyday Cultures of
Restaurants, Hotels, and Boardinghouses

1. John S. Hittell, *A History of the City of San Francisco and Incidentally of the State of California* (San Francisco: A. L. Bancroft, 1878), 447; Robert A. Burchell, *The San Francisco Irish: 1846–1880* (Manchester, UK: Manchester University Press, 1979), 46. See also "A California Caravansary," *Harper's New Monthly Magazine* 24, no. 203 (April 1867): 603–606; "Caravansaries of San Francisco," *Overland Monthly*, 1st ser., 5 (August 1870): 176–181; and William Bullough, *The Blind Boss and His City: Christopher Augustine Buckley and Nineteenth-Century San Francisco* (Berkeley: University of California Press, 1979), 9–10. Regarding the shortage of servants, see Jessie Benton Fremont, *A Year of American Travel*, as excerpted in Oscar Lewis, ed., *This Was San Francisco: Being First-hand Accounts of the Evolution of One of America's Favorite Cities* (New York: David McKay, 1962), 99, and Hubert Howe Bancroft, *History of California*, vol. 5, 1846–1848 (San Francisco: History Company, 1886), 236.

2. Bayard Taylor, *El Dorado, Or Adventures in the Path of Empire*, vol. 1 (New Mexico: Rio Grande Press, 1967 [first published in 1850]), 116–117.

3. Samuel Williams, "The City of the Golden Gate," *Scribner's Monthly*, July 1875, as excerpted in *This Was San Francisco*, 186. See also Richard Pillsbury, *From Boarding House to Bistro: The American Restaurant Then and Now* (Boston: Unwin Hyman, 1990), 33; Will Irwin, *The City That Was: A Requiem of Old San Francisco* (New York: B. W. Huebsch, 1906), 32; and Charles Keeler, *San Francisco and Thereabouts* (San Francisco: California Promotional Committee, 1903), 45.

4. "Restaurants and Their Function," *Nation* (November 2, 1865): 561. For information about the development of nineteenth-century restaurants, see Pillsbury, *From Boarding House to Bistro*. Pillsbury points out that even the term *restaurant* came into general use in America in the nineteenth century, supplanting a variety of regional names for dining establishments. For information about the development of nineteenth-century hotels, see Jefferson Williamson, *The American Hotel: An Anecdotal History* (New York: Alfred. A. Knopf, 1930). For an explication of civilization discourses, see Gail Bederman, *Manliness and Civilization: A Cultural History of Gender and Race in the United States, 1880–1917* (Chicago: University of Chicago Press, 1995), 24–26.

5. John Kasson, *Rudeness and Civility: Manners in Nineteenth-Century Urban America* (New York: Hill and Wang, 1990), especially 117. Other works that have influenced my thinking on the ways middle-class Americans apprehended and grappled with the rituals of private life and urban public culture, as well as their intersections, include Lawrence Levine, *Highbrow/Lowbrow: The Emergence of Cultural Hierarchy in America* (Cambridge: Harvard University Press, 1988); Richard L. Bushman, *The Refinement of America: Persons, Houses, Cities* (New York: Random House, 1992); Harvey A. Levenstein, *Revolution at the Table: The Transformation of the American Diet* (New York: Oxford University Press, 1988); and Norbert Elias, *The Civilizing Process: The History of Manners and State Formation and Civilization*, trans. Edmund Jephcott (London: Blackwell, 1994, originally published 1939). See also Mary Douglas, *Purity and Danger: An*

Analysis of the Concepts of Pollution and Taboo (London: Routledge, 1966) for how the choices individuals or groups make or the constraints they face about food and eating are political, in the broad sense of the word, and rehearse some of the most basic ways in which order and value are maintained in a society.

6. Kasson, *Rudeness and Civility*, especially 183–214.

7. Gunter Barth, *Instant Cities: Urbanization and the Rise of San Francisco and Denver* (New York: Oxford University Press, 1975), 168. For how middle-class culture was disrupted and asserted during the gold rush see, Brian Roberts, *American Alchemy: The California Gold Rush and Middle-Class Culture* (Chapel Hill: University of North Carolina Press, 2000).

8. Data regarding the state of things in these early years has been drawn from Malcolm E. Barker, ed., *San Francisco Memoirs, 1835–1851: Eyewitness Accounts of the Birth of a City* (San Francisco: Londonborn Publications, 1994), 41–45. Information about the buildings in the city as of April 1848 is from Frank Soulé, John H. Gihon, and James Nisbet, *The Annals of San Francisco* (Berkeley, CA: Berkeley Hills Books, 1999 [originally published in 1855], 174. The description of the City Hotel is from Hittell, *History of the City*, 447. It is worth noting that recreating an exact record of hotels, restaurants, and boardinghouses during these early years is next to impossible because of the fires and the fluidity of the community. Such was the conclusion drawn by Bancroft, *History of California*, 172–173.

9. Quotes about the bunkhouses and clipper ships are from Williamson, *American Hotel*, 85 and 84. Taylor, *Eldorado*, vol. 2, 55–56. Data about the amenities in the city in 1853 from Soulé et al., *Annals of San Francisco*, 492.

10. William Shaw, *Golden Dreams and Waking Realities* (first published in 1851), as excerpted in *San Francisco Memoirs, 1835–1851*, 169. For corroborating descriptions see, Taylor, *Eldorado*, vol. 1, 54–57 and James O'Meara, "San Francisco in Early Days," *Overland Monthly*, 2nd ser., 1 (February 1883): 129–136.

11. Shaw, *Golden Dreams and Waking Realities*, 170–172. Other accounts that similarly describe restaurant life during this period include, Albert Benard de Russailh, *Last Adventure* (San Francisco: Westgate Press, 1931), excerpted in *This Was San Francisco*, 186; Frank Marryat, *Mountains and Molehills or Recollections of a Burnt Journal*, with Introduction and Notes by Marguerite Wilbur (Stanford, CA: Stanford University Press, 1952 [originally published 1855]), 311; and Richard Henry Dana, *Two Years before the Mast*, as excerpted in Malcolm E. Barker, ed., *More San Francisco Memoirs, 1852–1899: The Ripening Years* (San Francisco: Londonborn Publications, 1996), 117.

12. Amelia Ransome Neville, *The Fantastic City: Memoirs of the Social and Romantic Life of Old San Francisco* (Boston and New York: Houghton Mifflin, 1932), 38–39.

13. Information about different styles of hotel dining has been drawn from Williamson, *American Hotel*, 192–199 and Kasson, *Rudeness and Civility*, 205–207.

14. Regarding tilting, see Kenneth Ames, *Death in the Dining Room and Other Tales of Victorian Culture* (Philadelphia: Temple University Press, 1992), 209.

15. John Henry Brown, *His Reminiscences and Incidents of the Early Days of San Francisco, 1845–1850* [first published in 1886], as excerpted in *San Francisco Memoirs*,

1835–1851, 128–129; Taylor, *Eldorado*, vol. 1, 55–56; Soulé et al., *Annals of San Francisco*, 245. For an analysis of the ways racial and gender hierarchies were established and enacted through types of labor see, Susan Lee Johnson, *Roaring Camp: The Social World of the California Gold Rush* (New York: W. W. Norton, 2000).

16. Taylor, *Eldorado*, vol. 1, 117; O'Meara, "San Francisco in Early Days," 134; James J. Ayers, *Gold and Sunshine*, published in 1922, as excerpted in *San Francisco Memoirs, 1835–1851*, 198. See also Shaw, *Golden Dreams and Waking Realities*, 172.

17. Sarah Royce, *A Frontier Lady: Recollections of the Gold Rush and Early California* (New Haven, CT: Yale University Press, 1932), 98–102. My understanding of the significance of the spatial organization of middle-class homes and the importance of the parlor in Victorian culture is derived from Karen Halttunen, "From Parlour to Living Room: Domestic Space, Interior Decoration, and the Culture of Personality," in Simon J. Bronner, ed., *Consuming Visions: Accumulation and Display of Goods in America, 1880–1920* (New York: W. W. Norton, 1989), 157–189.

18. Royce, *Frontier Lady*, 98–102.

19. Ibid.

20. Taylor, *Eldorado*, vol. 2, 59; F. P. Wierzbicki, *California as It Is and It May Be: Or, a Guide to the Gold Fields*, as excerpted in *This Was San Francisco*, 80. See also Bancroft, *History of California*, 236–237.

21. A.H.B., "Impressions on Arriving in San Francisco," *The Pioneer, or California Monthly Magazine*, September 1854, 157–158.

22. Hubert Howe Bancroft, *The Works of Hubert Howe Bancroft*, The History Co., San Francisco, 1888, as excerpted in *The Western Gate: A San Francisco Reader*, Joseph Henry Jackson, ed. (New York: Farrar, Straus, and Young, 1952), 239–241; Taylor, *Eldorado*, vol. 1, 118. See also Ayers, *Gold and Sunshine*, 198; Soulé et al., *Annals of San Francisco*, 216; and Maria Knight, "Early Days in San Francisco: A Near View of Vigilante Times," *Overland Monthly*, 2nd ser., 30 (July 1897): 253–322.

23. J. Philip Gruen, "Manifest Destinations: Tourist Encounters in the Late-Nineteenth-Century Urban American West" (unpublished manuscript in author's possession) provides a perceptive discussion of how "elites considered a harmonious ethnic diversity and a collection of high cultural institutions tantamount to a progressive, cosmopolitan city" (p. 3, Chapter 5). For a more sanguine view of San Francisco's cosmopolitanism, see Glenna Matthews, "Forging a Cosmopolitan Civic Culture: The Regional Identity of San Francisco and Northern California," in David M. Wrobel and Michael C. Steiner, eds., *Many Wests: Place, Culture, and Regional Identity* (Lawrence: University Press of Kansas, 1997), 211–234.

24. Bullough, *Blind Boss and His City*, 31 and 42. For the construction and patronage of finer hotels in the 1860s and 1870s, see Hittell, *History of the City*, 450. For a discussion of the increase of civilized mannerliness in the city, see Timothy J. Haggerty, "The San Francisco Gentleman," *California History* 65 (June 1986): 96–103. My thinking about urban danger has been influenced by Judith R. Walkowitz, *City of Dreadful Delight: Narratives of Sexual Danger in Late-Victorian London* (Chicago: University of Chicago Press, 1992); Paul Boyer, *Urban Masses and Moral Order in America,*

1820–1920 (Cambridge, MA: Harvard University Press, 1978); and William Cronon, *Nature's Metropolis: Chicago and the Great West* (New York: W. W. Norton, 1991).

25. Samuel Williams, "The City of the Golden Gate," *Scribner's Monthly*, July 1875, as excerpted in *This Was San Francisco*, 192.

26. *The San Francisco Directory, For the Year Commencing October 1864*, compiled by Henry G. Langley (San Francisco: Excelsior Steam Presses: Towne and Bacon, Book and Job Printers, 1864); Noah Brooks, "Restaurant Life in San Francisco," *Overland Monthly*, 1st ser., 1 (November 1868): 466–467; Hittell, *History of the City*, 450; B. E. Lloyd, *Lights and Shades in San Francisco* (San Francisco: A. L. Bancroft, 1876), 62–63. See also "Two Great Cities, by an American," *Cornhill Magazine* 17 (June 1868): 493–512.

27. For stories of disorderliness in restaurants, hotels, and boardinghouses see, for example, *San Francisco Call*, January 14, 1875, theft from a lodging house and robbery at the Continental Hotel; *Daily Alta California*, March 7, 1870, a suspicious death at the Wisconsin Hotel; *Call*, March 18, 1875, proprietor assaulted with a brick by patron who tried to sneak out without paying for his meal and report of an encounter with a disorderly drunk at a lodging house on Washington and Kearny; *Call*, January 16, 1875, suspicious, unattended death in a boardinghouse on Minna Street; *Call*, January 17, 1875, "Thirty impecunious individuals were accommodated with 'lodgings' in the city Hotel last evening. A number of drunks were also brought in"; *Alta*, August 6, 1877, "Henry Raymond, a colored porter employed at the St. Cloud Hotel, on Sutter street, was arrested yesterday . . . on a charge of grand larceny;" *Alta*, August 16, 1877, possible murder-suicide at the International Hotel; *Call*, January 22, 1875, "Exciting Adventure of a Delirium tremens Victim," at the Alta Lodging House; *Alta*, August 13, 1877, attempted suicide at the Avenue House; *Call*, January 8, 1875, keeper of a Chinese boardinghouse accused of "having made a murderous assault upon one of his boarders;" *Call*, March 27, 1875, suspicious, unattended death at the Avenue House; *Call*, March 24, 1875, suspicious death at boardinghouse; *Alta*, March 10, 1870, "A Married Man Blows His Brains Out" at Meyer's Hotel.

28. The story of the Stevenson-MacDonald rape case has been culled from generally corroborating and frequently identical accounts in the *Call*, January 19, 21, 22, 23 24, 25, 26, 29; *San Francisco Examiner*, January 20, 21, 23, 25, 27, and February 8, 1868; *Alta*, January 30, 1868, and the *California Police Gazette*, January 25, 1868, and February 1, 1868. The citations that follow will refer only to directly quoted material. Quotations describing the crowd are from the *Call*, January 22 and 23, 1868. Those describing MacDonald and Stevenson are from the *Call*, January 19, 1868. For a discussion of nineteenth-century fears about counterfeit identities see Karen Halttunen, *Confidence Men and Painted Women: A Study of Middle-Class Culture in America, 1830–1870* (New Haven, CT: Yale University Press, 1982).

29. *Call*, January 19, 1868.

30. Ibid.

31. Ibid.

32. Ibid.

33. *Call*, January 19, 1868; *San Francisco Examiner*, January 20, 1868, also omitted details of a sexual nature; *California Police Gazette*, January 25, 1868.

34. *Examiner*, January 20, 1868.

35. *Call*, January 20 and 25, 1868.

36. *California Police Gazette*, January 25, 1868; *Call*, January 21, 1868; *California Police Gazette*, February 1, 1868. Apparently, while in Portland, under the care of Dr. Robert La Mert—the half brother of San Francisco's Dr. L. J. Jordan, proprietor of its Anatomical Museum—Martha alleged that she was given chloroform by the doctor, seduced, had a child by him, and that he subsequently supported her. It was unclear whether this actually happened or not—Martha did tell Police Chief Crowley about it in an attempt to secure redress—but La Mert, although subpoenaed, made himself unavailable for testimony.

37. *Call*, January 28, 1868; *Alta*, January 30, 1868.

38. Bullough, *Blind Boss and His City*, 30; William Issel and Robert W. Cherny, *San Francisco, 1865–1932: Politics, Power, and Urban Development* (Berkeley: University of California Press, 1986), 124–125; Neville, *Fantastic City*, 190; *Springfield Daily Republican*, August 31, 1875, as reproduced in Robert Mayer, ed. and comp., *San Francisco: A Chronological and Documentary History, 1542–1970* (New York: Oceana Press, 1974); Oscar Lewis and Carroll D. Hall, *Bonanza Inn: America's First Luxury Hotel* (New York: Alfred A. Knopf, 1939), 20, 25; and *The Palace Hotel, San Francisco* (Prospectus, Signed: A. D. Sharon and G. Schonewald, lessees, 1875). Descriptions of the Palace Hotel have been culled from Lewis and Hall, *Bonanza Inn*, 3–35; Williamson, *American Hotel*, 91–94; Lloyd, *Lights and Shades*, 50–57 and 71–77; Mary Goodrich, *The Palace Hotel* (San Francisco: Crandall Press, 1930); and a description printed in the *Springfield Daily Republican*, August 31, 1875.

39. William Laird MacGregor, *Hotels and Hotel Life at San Francisco California, in 1876* (San Francisco: S.F. News Company, 1877), 9–15; *Springfield Daily Republican*, August 31, 1875; Lewis and Hall, *Bonanza Inn*, 28, 20.

40. Although it takes a different tack, my analysis of the intended significance of the Palace Hotel has its starting point in Lewis and Hall; see *Bonanza Inn*, 15. This character sketch of William Chapman Ralston has been drawn from Bullough, *Blind Boss and His City*, 40–42, and Lewis and Hall, *Bonanza Inn*, 10–15.

41. Evelyn Wells, *Champagne Days of San Francisco* (New York; D. Appleton-Century, 1939), 81; Goodrich, *Palace Hotel*, 32; Issel and Cherny, *San Francisco, 1865–1932*, 63.

42. This description of the hotel's dining style and facilities is from Lewis and Hall, *Bonanza Inn*, and MacGregor, *Hotels and Hotel Life*.

43. Lewis and Hall, *Bonanza Inn*, 37, 38, 78, called my attention to these celebrations and their work was used in this description. Quotations are from Goodrich, *Palace Hotel*, 32; *Call*, October 15, 1875, as excerpted in *Western Gate*, 336; Goodrich, 30, and 32; *Call*, October 15, 1875; Goodrich, 32; *Call*, October 15, 1875; Goodrich, 30.

44. Quotations are from Julia Cooley Altrocchi, *The Spectacular San Franciscans* (New York: E. P. Dutton, 1949), 211; Lucius Beebe and Charles Clegg, *San Francisco's Golden Era: A Picture Story of San Francisco before the Fire* (Berkeley, CA: Howell-North Books, 1960), 175; Lewis and Hall, *Bonanza Inn*, 85. For the way the event brought San Franciscans together, see Altrocchi, *Spectacular San Franciscans*, 211. For general description, see also Lewis and Hall, *Bonanza Inn*, 82.

45. *Call*, October 15, 1875, as excerpted in *Western Gate*, 336; Douglas Henry Daniels, *Pioneer Urbanites: A Social and Cultural History of Black San Francisco* (Philadelphia: Temple University Press, 1980), 35–40; Lewis and Hall, *Bonanza Inn*, 31.

46. *The San Francisco Illustrated Directory for Hotels and Steamers* (San Francisco: Amos Currier, 1878).

47. For examples of mixture and disorder located in lower-end eateries and hostelries, see "Stabbed to Death, A French Cook Kills His Employer," *San Francisco Chronicle*, November 21, 1893; "Lost His Whiskers: How He Committed Arson on Himself," *Chronicle*, January 2, 1894; "Norman Schuler Is Arrested—Found in a Seventh-Street Lodging House," *Call*, September 1, 1896; "S. S. Conley Found in a Pool of Blood [in a Market Street Lodging-House]," *Call*, January 1, 1894; "An Early Morning Shooting Affray Awakens Roomers in a Howard-Street Lodging-House," *Call*, August 23, 1893; "Death Claims a Fair Victim, Susie Pinkerton Passes Away in a Lodging-House," *Call*, July 24, 1896; "An Explosion in a Lodging House," *Chronicle*, November 16, 1893; "Stole Silk Dresses. Smooth Work in a Lodging House," *Chronicle*, June 9, 1894. Even tony establishments did not completely escape association with urban dangers. See, for example, "Tragic Occurrence in the Grand Hotel. Suicide of a Prominent Clergyman's Son," *Call*, August 24, 1893.

48. Works that emphasized the city's first-class eateries include Will Irwin, *The City That Was: A Requiem of Old San Francisco* (New York: B. W. Huebsch, 1906), 34; Charles Keeler, *San Francisco and Thereabout* (San Francisco: California Promotional Committee, 1903), 45; and Daniel O'Connell, *The Inner Man: Good Things to Eat and Drink and Where to Get Them* (San Francisco: Bancroft, 1891). Mary Watson, writing in 1887, noted the growing tendency of the San Francisco elite to define itself through increasingly elaborate dining rituals. See Mary Watson, *San Francisco Society: Its Characters and Its Characteristics* (San Francisco: Francis, Valentine, 1887), 9.

49. O'Connell, *Inner Man*, iv, 43, 94.

50. Irwin, *City That Was*, 32, as well as 35–37. See also Keeler, *San Francisco and Thereabout*, 42–47, and Roland White, "The Humbler Restaurants of San Francisco," *Overland Monthly*, 2nd ser., 41 (May 1903): 363–367.

51. Charles S. Greene, "The Restaurants of San Francisco," *Overland Monthly*, 2nd ser., 20 (December 1892): 561–572; 561.

52. Greene, "Restaurants of San Francisco," 561, 563, 565.

53. Elinor Croudace, "Noon Hour in the Café," *San Francisco Evening Bulletin*, May 23, 1896.

54. Ibid.

55. Ibid. Similar themes are explored in Alice S. Wolf, "Two Gourmets of Bloom-field," *Overland Monthly*, 2nd ser., 20 (September 1892): 299–310.

56. *San Francisco Classified Business Directory*, 1906; Rudyard Kipling, "How I Got to San Francisco and Took Tea with the Natives There," excerpted in Barker, ed., *More San Francisco Memoirs, 1852–1899*, 273; and *Chronicle*, November 30, 1893.

57. Figures regarding the increase in trade unions were found in Bullough, *Blind Boss and His City*, 97; Edward Paul Eaves, "A History of the Cooks' and Waiters' Unions of San Francisco," M.A. thesis, University of California, 1930, 2, iii–iv. With regard to the name of this union, Eaves refers to it as the Cooks and Waiters' Anti-Chinese Club while Daniels, *Pioneer Urbanites*, 35–40, calls it the Cooks' and Waiters' Anti-Coolie Association. I have decided to go with Daniels's terminology as Eaves tends to take racial strife for granted and thus downplay its significance.

58. Eaves, "History of the Cooks' and Waiters' Unions," 3, 4.

59. Ibid., 4, 6, 8.

60. *Alta*, March 21, 1887; *Chronicle*, March 22, 1887; and *Call*, January 18, 1888, as quoted in Eaves, "History of the Cooks' and Waiters' Unions," 9, 10.

61. Eaves, "History of the Cooks' and Waiters' Unions," 11–20.

62. Lewis and Hall, *Bonanza Inn*, 31; Lewis and Hall offer a brief discussion of the African American workers at the Palace and their eventual dismissal. A more substantive and critical look at these workers is provided by Daniels, *Pioneer Urbanites*, 35–40. I have derived the account presented here from these sources.

63. Both the *Alta* and the black workers' response is quoted from Lewis and Hall, *Bonanza Inn*, 58–59, more specific citation information not provided; Daniels, *Pioneer Urbanites*, 35–38.

64. Daniels, *Pioneer Urbanites*, 35.

Chapter 2. Playing in the City: Vicious and Virtuous Amusement

1. John S. Hittell, *A History of the City of San Francisco and Incidentally of the State of California* (San Francisco: A. L. Bancroft, 1878), 443.

2. Information about the city's early circuses was drawn from Frank Soulé, John H. Gihon, and James Nisbet, *The Annals of San Francisco* (Berkeley, CA: Berkeley Hills Books, 1999 (originally published in 1855), 248, and Herbert Asbury, *The Barbary Coast: An Informal History of the San Francisco Underworld* (New York: Capricorn Books, 1933), 17–18. Information about early theaters was culled from Soulé et al., *Annals of San Francisco*; Asbury, *Barbary Coast*, 17–18; and the *Daily Alta California*, September 11, 1850. Facts about Russ Gardens were taken from Hittell, *History of the City*, 444, and the *Alta*, May 2, 1859. The tally of the city's amusements in 1853 is from Soulé et al., *Annals of San Francisco*, 493. The quote about the prevalence of gambling is from ibid., 248.

3. Asbury, *Barbary Coast*, 3; B. E. Lloyd, *Lights and Shades in San Francisco* (San Francisco: A. L. Bancroft, 1876), 124.

4. This historical trajectory of the Barbary Coast is drawn from Asbury, *Barbary Coast*, 49–50. Quotations are from 102, 49, and 50.

5. The exact reason why the Barbary Coast was chosen as the name for the city's vice district is unclear, although it purportedly had something to do with similarities, probably found by sailors, with the Barbary Coast in Africa. Asbury, *Barbary Coast*, 98–102. Quotation from 99. Similar mappings of the geography of the Barbary Coast were found in "City Life. Barbary Coast Surveyed," *San Francisco Chronicle*, November 28, 1869; Lloyd, *Lights and Shades*, 78; William Issel and Robert W. Cherny, *San Francisco, 1865–1932: Power, Politics, and Urban Development* (University of California Press, 1986), 75.

6. *California Police Gazette*, "A Night on Pacific Street," August 14, 1869.

7. "The Pretty Waiter Girl Saloons," *California Police Gazette*, March 21, 1868. For discussions of sporting culture, see Howard P. Chudacoff, *The Age of the Bachelor: Creating an American Subculture* (Princeton, NJ: Princeton University Press, 1999); David Nasaw, *Going Out: The Rise and Fall of Public Amusements* (Cambridge, MA: Harvard University Press, 1993); Timothy J. Gilfoyle, *City of Eros: New York City, Prostitution, and the Commercialization of Sex, 1790–1920* (New York: W. W. Norton, 1992); and Helen Lefkowitz Horowitz, *Rereading Sex: Battles over Sexual Knowledge and Suppression in Nineteenth-Century America* (New York: Alfred A. Knopf, 2002).

8. During the 1850s, prostitution was centered around Portsmouth Square and, according to Asbury, in the community of Chilenos near Telegraph Hill. In the early twentieth century, the upper Tenderloin emerged as an area where prostitution was also concentrated in addition to the Barbary Coast. Asbury, *Barbary Coast*, 232–234.

9. Asbury, *Barbary Coast*, 104-105; Don Hugo, "The Demi-Monde of San Francisco," *California Police Gazette*, January 9, 1869; and *California Police Gazette*, August 15 and 22, 1868. For a discussion of the rise of these types of amusement in a larger context, see Gilfoyle, *City of Eros*, 129–131 and 224–232, and Nasaw, *Going Out*, 10–18.

10. Asbury, *Barbary Coast*, 125; *California Police Gazette*, "Low Places of Amusement: Subjects for the Next Grand Jury," January 11, 1868. For similar descriptions see also, "City Life. Barbary Coast Surveyed," *Chronicle*, November 28, 1869, and "Cesspools of Indecency on the Barbary Coast," *San Francisco Call*, April 10, 1900. Minstrelsy was as popular in San Francisco as it was in the rest of the country. The first minstrel show in the city was presented at the Bella Union in 1849. For discussions of minstrelsy and its significance in the formation of racialized class identities, see David Roediger, *The Wages of Whiteness: Race and the Making of the American Working Class* (New York: Verso, 1991), and Eric Lott, *Love and Theft: Blackface Minstrelsy and the American Working Class* (New York; Oxford University Press, 1993).

11. *California Police Gazette*, March 20, 1859; *California Police Gazette*, January 4, 1868; *California Police Gazette*, August 15, 1868.

12. "City Life. Barbary Coast Surveyed"; "Night on Pacific Street"; "Pretty Waiter Girl Saloons." See also Lloyd, *Lights and Shades*, 83; and Don Hugo, "The Demi-Monde of San Francisco," *California Police Gazette*, January 16, 1869, and February 13, 1869.

13. Don Hugo, "The Demi-Monde of San Francisco," *California Police Gazette*, January 2 and 16, 1869; Asbury, *Barbary Coast*, 115, 176, 242-246; Lloyd, *Lights and Shades*, 83; and "Trial of Eugene Tucker for the Murder of Celina Bouclet," *California Police Gazette*, February 8, May 9, 16, and 23, 1868.

14. For the presence of black maids, see Asbury, *Barbary Coast*, 255-259. For prostitution in San Francisco and the West, see also Jacqueline Baker Barnhart, *The Fair but Frail: Prostitution in San Francisco, 1849-1900* (Reno: University of Nevada Press, 1986); Benson Tong, *Unsubmissive Women: Chinese Prostitutes in Nineteenth-Century San Francisco* (Norman: University of Oklahoma Press, 1994); Anne Butler, *Daughters of Joy: Sisters of Misery: Prostitutes in the American West, 1865-1890* (Urbana: University of Illinois Press, 1985); and Judy Yung, *Unbound Feet: A Social History of Chinese Women in San Francisco* (Berkeley: University of California Press, 1995).

15. Yung, *Unbound Feet*, 27-28. See also Peggy Pascoe, *Relations of Rescue: The Search for Female Moral Authority in the American West, 1874-1939* (New York: Oxford University Press, 1990), 14-15.

16. For a discussion of the racialization of Chinese immigrants as pollutants, see Robert Lee, *Orientals: Asian Americans in Popular Culture* (Philadelphia: Temple University Press, 1999). Hugo, "The Demi-Monde of San Francisco," and "The Chinese Dens," *California Police Gazette*, March 21, 1868. For further evidence of patronage by white men, see Asbury, 168, 172-173, 175.

17. "Chinese Immigration," *California Police Gazette*, May 16, 1868.

18. Yung, *Unbound Feet*, 29.

19. *California Police Gazette*, January 2, 1869; Asbury, *Barbary Coast*, 19, 106-107, 130; *Call*, November 28, 1897; and *San Francisco News*, February 22, 1934. For a discussion of this change in attitude, see Ruth Rosen, *The Lost Sisterhood: Prostitution in America, 1900-1918* (Baltimore, MD: Johns Hopkins University Press, 1982).

20. *Chronicle*, October 24, 1935; "Ornamental Gardening," *Pacific Rural Press*, January 7, 1871. See also *Alta*, April 23, 1871, and Lloyd, *Lights and Shades*, 325.

21. Lloyd, *Lights and Shades*, 325; *Illustrated Guide and Catalogue of Woodward's Gardens* (San Francisco: Francis and Valentine, 1873), back cover. See also *Pacific Rural Press*, January 7, 1871.

22. Ethel Malone Brown, "Woodward's Gardens," from *Vignettes of Early San Francisco Homes and Gardens*, Mrs. Silas H. Palmer, ed. (December 1935 program of the San Francisco Garden Club), 1. See also *Chronicle*, September 25, 1932, and Charles Lockwood, "Woodward's Natural Wonders," *California Living Magazine, San Francisco Sunday Examiner and Chronicle*, November 20, 1977, 41-45.

23. Lockwood, "Woodward's Natural Wonders"; *Illustrated Guide and Catalogue of Woodward's Gardens*, 1873; *Pacific Rural Press*, January 7, 1871; and Brown, "Woodward's Gardens," 2. See also *Alta*, June 28, 1861.

24. *Pacific Rural Press*, January 7, 1871; Brown, "Woodward's Gardens," 2-3; Lockwood, "Woodward's Natural Wonders."

25. *Pacific Rural Press*, January 7, 1871; Lawrence Levine, *Highbrow/Lowbrow: The Emergence of Cultural Hierarchy in America* (Cambridge, MA: Harvard University Press, 1988), 202-204. See also Lockwood, "Woodward's Natural Wonders." Other descriptions of the gardens that stress their pastoral qualities can be found in Lloyd, *Lights and Shades*, 325-326; *Illustrated Guide and Catalogue of Woodward's Gardens*, F. Gruber, comp. (San Francisco: Francis Valentine and Co., 1879), 3.

26. This motto was prominently displayed on the *Illustrated Guide and Catalogue of Woodward's Gardens*, 1873, 1875, and 1879. Brown, "Woodward's Gardens," 3.

27. Brown, "Woodward's Gardens," 4-6, and *Pacific Rural Press*, January 7, 1871.

28. For discussion in the changing nature of nineteenth-century museums and amusements see Levine, *Highbrow/Lowbrow*; Nasaw, *Going Out*; Andrea Stulman Dennett, *Weird and Wonderful: The Dime Museum in America* (New York: New York University Press, 1997); Charles Coleman Sellers, *Mr. Peale's Museum: Charles Wilson Peale and the First Popular Museum of Natural Science and Art* (New York: W. W. Norton, 1980); David R. Brigham, *Public Culture in the Early Republic: Peale's Museum and Its Audience* (Washington, D.C.: Smithsonian Institution Press, 1995); and Neil Harris, *Cultural Excursions: Marketing Appetites and Cultural Tastes in Modern America* (Chicago, University of Chicago Press, 1990).

29. *Pacific Rural Press*, January 7, 1871; See also Lloyd, *Lights and Shades*, 327-328. Information about the aquarium is from *Illustrated Guide and Catalogue of Woodward's Gardens*, 1879, 67-70.

30. *Illustrated Guide and Catalogue of Woodward's Gardens*, 1879, 67. See also Lloyd, *Lights and Shades*, 325-331.

31. Price of educational guides found in *Programme of Woodward's Gardens*, 1885. Data on beavers taken from *Illustrated Guide and Catalogue of Woodward's Gardens*, 1875, 24.

32. This connection was not lost on B. E. Lloyd, who described, "Man, in his Darwinian stage of early development—just at that period when the irregular pulse of reason is lulled into faint flutter by the strong throbs of instinct—scampers about his cage indulging in most ungentlemanly pranks, to the infinite delight of juvenile spectators, or retires in high dudgeon at any personal affront from his more favored and enlightened progeny." Lloyd, *Lights and Shades*, 327. For some of the social implications of nineteenth-century science, see Gail Bederman, *Manliness and Civilization: A Cultural History of Gender and Race in the United States, 1880–1917* (Chicago: University of Chicago Press, 1995); Michael Omi and Howard Winant, *Racial Formation in the United States: From the 1960s to the 1990s*, 2nd ed. (New York: Routledge, 1994); Cynthia Eagle Russett, *Sexual Science: The Victorian Construction of Womanhood* (Cambridge, MA: Harvard University Press, 1989); Paul Spickard and G. Reginald Daniel, eds., *Racial Thinking in the United States: Uncompleted Independence* (Notre Dame, IN: University of Notre Dame Press, 2004).

33. F. L. McKenney, "Where the 'Old-Timers' Frolicked," *Chronicle*, November 9, 1913.

34. I have found Woodward referred to as the Barnum of the West in McKenney, "Where the 'Old-Timers' Frolicked"; Walter J. Thompson, "With the Picnic Throngs of Other Days," *Chronicle*, July 9, 1916; and Lockwood, "Woodward's Natural Wonders." *Pacific Rural Press*, January 7, 1871; Brown, "Woodward's Gardens," 4–6; and *Alta*, March 23, 1875. See also Lloyd, *Lights and Shades*, 326–327. For a discussion of the way issues of Barnum's fraudulency fit into larger issues in nineteenth-century society see James W. Cook, *The Arts of Deception: Playing with Fraud in the Age of Barnum* (Cambridge, MA: Harvard University Press, 2001).

35. *Alta*, April 23, 1871; Lloyd, *Lights and Shades*, 327.

36. *Illustrated Guide and Catalogue of Woodward's Gardens*, 1873, 61; Lloyd, *Lights and Shades*, 330.

37. *Illustrated Guide and Catalogue*, 1873, 3; *Illustrated Guide and Catalogue*, 1879, 4.

38. McKenney, "Where the 'Old-Timers' Frolicked." See also Thompson, "With the Picnic Throngs of Other Days."

39. This move towards more stratified and sacralized cultural spaces in the last quarter of the nineteenth century is delineated in Levine, *Highbrow/Lowbrow*, 85–242.

40. See *Guidebook and Street Manual of San Francisco, California* (San Francisco: F. W. Warner, 1882), 17, 106; *The Pocket Exchange Guide of San Francisco* (San Francisco: Tiffany and MacDonald, 1875), 74; and *A Street and Avenue Guide of San Francisco* (San Francisco: Henry G. Langley, 1875), 94.

41. *California Police Gazette*, February 1 and April 18, 1868. For ads in other papers, see for example, *Daily Dramatic Chronicle*, January 2, 1868; *Alta*, November 3, 4, 6, 1867; *California Weekly Mercury*, February 9, 1868, and March 15, 1868. Extant runs of the *California Police Gazette* are limited. However, the Pacific Museum ran regular ads in it from January 1868 through July 1869.

42. *San Francisco Examiner*, December 9, 16, 23, 1913. For information about Gibbons, see E. Graeme Robertson, *Melbourne's Public Anatomical and Anthropological Museums, and the Jordans* (Glebe, New South Wales: Australasian Medical Publishing, 1956), 40.

43. *Examiner*, December 16, 1913, and June 22, 1915.

44. See Robertson, *Melbourne's Public Anatomical and Anthropological Museums*, 11–24. Information about Louis Jordan as Louis Kahn and about the existence of museums in New Orleans and Boston comes from correspondence with Michael Sappol, author of *A Traffic in Dead Bodies: Anatomy and Embedded Social Identity in Nineteenth-Century America* (Princeton, NJ: Princeton University Press, 2004). Dennett asserts that the New York Museum of Anatomy was founded by Dr. H. J. Jordan and a Dr. Beck in 1848. Other sources point to the Jordans' emergence in New York and elsewhere in the early 1860s. Dennett, *Weird and Wonderful*, 63.

45. Hugo, "The Demi-Monde of San Francisco," *California Police Gazette*, January 23, 1869. For sporting culture's relationship to male sexuality see also Gilfoyle, *City of Eros*, 92–116 and Horowitz, *Rereading Sex*, 125–158.

46. *Handbook of the Pacific Museum of Anatomy and Science* (San Francisco: 1865), front cover. The announcement for the move was found in an edition that did not give copyright information other than San Francisco, 1865, although the announcement for the move has an 1876 date. The cover is titled *The Philosophy of Marriage*; inside the front cover is the title page for the *Handbook and Descriptive Catalogue of the Pacific Museum of Anatomy and Science*. This combining of the two works was unusual. Louis J. Jordan, *The Philosophy of Marriage, Being Four Important Lectures on the Functions and Disorders of the Nervous System and Reproductive Organs* (San Francisco: Donald Bruce's Book and Job Printing House, 537 Sacramento Street), front cover, and *Guidebook and Street Manual of San Francisco, California* (San Francisco: F. W. Warner, 1882), 106.

47. See for example Jordan, *Philosophy of Marriage*, first unnumbered page after title page and last page of the *Handbook of the Pacific Museum of Anatomy and Science* (San Francisco: 1865). Information about the timing of Jordan's lectures was obtained from *The Handbook and Descriptive Catalogue of the Pacific Museum of Anatomy and Natural Science* (San Francisco: Commercial Steam Printing House, 1869), unnumbered last page.

48. *Handbook and Descriptive Catalogue*, 1869, npn. Advertising asserted that the museum was the product of a considerable amount of collecting. As an 1868 ad in the *California Police Gazette* explained, "During the proprietor's . . . recent trip to Europe, he [Jordan] collected some fifty thousand dollars' worth of works of science, natural history and art, which have been added to the immense collection with which his place is filled." *California Police Gazette*, March 21, 1868. This same trip was referred to in ads later that year that read, "Dr. L. J. Jordan, the proprietor, on his recent trip to Europe, collected an extensive assortment of all that is curious in nature and art, which he has added to the institution." See *California Police Gazette*, July 11, 1868; July 18, 1868; July 25, 1868; August 1, 1868; August 8, 1868.

49. *Handbook and Descriptive Catalogue*, 1869, 5–14. For a discussion of the social functions of freak shows and similar displays of nonnormative bodies, see Rosemarie Garland Thompson, *Extraordinary Bodies: Figuring Disability in American Culture and Literature* (New York: Columbia University Press, 1997), 55–80.

50. *Handbook and Descriptive Catalogue*, 1869, 51–56.

51. Jordan, *Philosophy of Marriage*, 1865. For the great demand for sexual advice literature in nineteenth-century America, see John D'Emilio and Estelle B. Freedman, *Intimate Matters: A History of Sexuality in America* (New York: Harper and Row, 1988), 68, and Horowitz, *Rereading Sex*, 86–102.

52. D'Emilio and Freedman, *Intimate Matters*, 66–68.

53. D'Emilio and Freedman, *Intimate Matters*, 68–69, and Bederman, *Manliness and Civilization*, 77–120.

54. Jordan, *Philosophy of Marriage*, 28; 7–26. Quotes, 26, 27. His discussion of the structure and function of the female organs was comparatively brief. In terms of misunderstanding female reproduction, Jordan equated menstruation and ovulation, putting ovulation at the time of menstruation, 18. He did, however, identify the significance of the clitoris in female sexual pleasure, 24.

55. Ibid., 36, 37–38.

56. Ibid., 41, 40, 45, 46, 47.

57. Ibid., 111.

58. Ibid., 51–54.

59. Ibid., 43–44, 40, 83–84, 86, 87, 90.

60. Faith Gibson, "Brief History and Theory of Physician Discipline in California, 1876–1998," http://www.marijuana.org/MedBdHistoryCal.htm, 1–2. See also Barbara Ehrenreich and Deidre English, *For Her Own Good: 150 Years of the Experts' Advice to Women* (Garden City, NY: Anchor Books, 1979), and Paul Boyer, *Urban Masses and Moral Order in America, 1820–1920* (Cambridge, MA: Harvard University Press, 1978). Allopathy refers to the style of medicine practiced by today's M.D.'s. It treats disease with remedies that produce effects different from those produced by the disease. The term was initially used to designate opposition to homeopathy. Homeopathy is a system of medical treatment that holds that certain diseases can by cured by giving very small doses of drugs that in larger doses would produce symptoms like the disease. Osteopathy places particular emphasis on the interrelationship of the musculoskeletal system to all other body systems. See *Webster's New World Dictionary of the American Language*, 2nd college ed. (Cleveland: William Collins and World Publishing), 1976.

61. D'Emilio and Freedman, *Intimate Matters*, 207–208.

62. Rosen, *Lost Sisterhood*; D'Emilio and Freedman, *Intimate Matters*, 203.

63. Carol Leigh, "A Brief History of Government Policies toward Prostitution in San Francisco," *San Francisco Task Force on Prostitution Final Report 1996*, 2–3; http://www.bayswan.org/sfhist.html.

64. Leigh, "Brief History," 4; Patricia O'Flinn, "Moral Purity Campaigns, Middle-Class Clubwomen, and the California Red Light Abatement Act," http://userwww.sfsu.edu/~epf/1996/redlight.html; and Issel and Cherny, *San Francisco, 1865–1932*, 107–108.

65. Leigh, "Brief History," 4, and O'Flinn, "Moral Purity Campaigns, Middle-Class Clubwomen," 11.

66. O'Flinn dates the clinic's opening as 1913. Leigh dates it as 1911.

Chapter 3. Making Race in the City: Chinatown's Tourist Terrain

1. E.G.H., *Surprise Land: A Girl's Letters from the West* (Boston: Cupples, Upham, 1887), 75, 94. San Francisco's Chinatown is the oldest and largest Chinese community in the United States. It has remained a popular tourist attraction for visitors to San Francisco as well as an essential component in the city's tourist industry. See Chalsa M. Loo, *Chinatown: Most Time, Hard Time* (New York: Praeger Publishers, 1991), 3–21.

2. E.G.H., *Surprise Land*, 76–80.

3. Ibid., 83.

4. Ibid., 96–99.

5. For histories of Chinese American communities and the struggles of Chinese Americans against racism and discrimination, see, for example, Sucheng Chan, ed., *Entry Denied: Exclusion and the Chinese Community in America, 1882–1943* (Philadelphia: Temple University Press, 1991); Gary Okihiro, *Margins and Mainstreams: Asians in American History and Culture* (Seattle: University of Washington Press, 1994); Ronald Takaki, *Strangers from a Different Shore: A History of Asian Americans* (New York: Penguin Books, 1989); Sucheng Chan, *Asian Americans: An Interpretive History* (Boston: Twayne, 1991); Charles J. McClain, *In Search of Equality: The Chinese Struggle against Discrimination in Nineteenth-Century America* (Berkeley: University of California Press, 1994); Yong Chen, *Chinese San Francisco, 1850–1943: A Trans-Pacific Community* (Stanford, CA: Stanford University Press, 2000); Erika Lee, *At America's Gates: Chinese Immigration during the Exclusion Era, 1882–1943* (Chapel Hill: University of North Carolina Press, 2003); Roger Daniels, *Asian America: Chinese and Japanese in the United States since 1850* (Seattle: University of Washington Press, 1988); and Judy Yung, *Unbound Feet: A Social History of Chinese Women in San Francisco* (Berkeley: University of California Press, 1995).

6. The workings of the process of racialization are delineated in Michael Omi and Howard Winant, *Racial Formation in the United States: From the 1960s to the 1980s*, 2nd ed. (New York: Routledge and Keegan Paul, 1986). See also Tomás Almaguer, *Racial Faultlines: The Historical Origins of White Supremacy in California* (Berkeley: University of California Press, 1994), and Matthew Frye Jacobson, *Whiteness of a Different Color: European Immigrants and the Alchemy of Race* (Cambridge, MA: Harvard University Press, 1998).

7. Several recent works have drawn on Edward Said's scholarship to explore American variants of Orientalism. See Edward Said, *Orientalism* (New York: Vintage Books, 1979); Robert G. Lee, *Orientals: Asian Americans in Popular Culture* (Philadelphia: Temple University Press, 1999); John Kuo Wei Tchen, *New York before Chinatown: Orientalism and the Shaping of American Culture, 1776–1882* (Baltimore, MD: Johns Hopkins University Press, 1999); Anthony Lee, *Picturing Chinatown: Art and Orientalism in San Francisco* (Berkeley: University of California Press, 2001); Malini Johar Schueller, *U.S. Orientalisms: Race, Nation, and Gender in Literature, 1790–1890* (Ann Arbor: University of Michigan Press, 1998); and David Palumbo-Liu, *Asian/American: Historical Crossings of a Racial Frontier* (Stanford, CA: Stanford University Press, 1999).

8. In many respects, Chinatown tourism defined tourists as "American" and "citizens" and the Chinese as squarely outside the bounds of those categories. For a discussion of the way tourism has functioned "as a ritual of citizenship" for white Americans, see Marguerite S. Schaffer, *See America First: Tourism and National Identity, 1880–1940* (Washington, D.C.: Smithsonian Institution Press, 2001), 225. See also David Wrobel and Patrick T. Long, eds., *Seeing and Being Seen: Tourism in the American West* (Lawrence: University Press of Kansas, 2001). For discussions of international tourism in postcolonial and colonial contexts, respectively, that have relevance

for the tourist–toured upon relationship in the internal colony of Chinatown, see Malcolm Crick, "Representations of International Tourism in the Social Sciences: Sun, Sex, Sights, Savings, and Servility," *Annual Review of Anthropology* 18 (1989), 307–344, and Mary Louise Pratt, *Imperial Eyes: Travel Writing and Transculturation* (New York: Routledge, 1992).

9. My understanding of the literature of urban exploration is informed by the discussion of urban spectatorship in Judith R. Walkowitz, *City of Dreadful Delight: Narratives of Sexual Danger in Late Victorian London* (Chicago: University of Chicago Press, 1992), 15–39. Both guides who led tourists around and the tourist literature that prepared tourists for what to expect to see facilitated the "collection of signs" that made up the detached, differentiating "tourist gaze" that tourists deployed in their consumption of Chinatown. See John Urry, *The Tourist Gaze: Leisure and Travel in Contemporary Societies* (London: Sage Publications, 1990), 3, and *Consuming Places* (London and New York: Routledge, 1995). Chinatown tourism was less about pleasure and leisure than many of the sites Urry identifies, but the gaze itself was similarly objectifying. For a compelling discussion of the way a "collection of signs" in the form of objects can manifest more claims on what is real than they actually possess, see Eric Gable, Richard Handler, and Anna Lawson, "On the Uses of Relativism; Fact, Conjecture, and Black and White Histories at Colonial Williamsburg," *American Ethnologist* 19, no.4 (November 1992): 791–805.

10. For the classic discussion of "staged authenticity," see Dean MacCanell, *The Tourist: A New Theory of the Leisure Class* (New York: Schocken Books, 1976). See also Raymond Rast, "Staging Chinatown: The Place of the Chinese in San Francisco's Tourist Industry" (unpublished paper in author's possession).

11. For works advocating or referring to the use of guides see, for example, Isaiah West Taber, *Hints to Strangers* (San Francisco: Taber, 188-), 3; *Disturnell's Strangers' Guide to San Francisco and Vicinity: A Complete and Reliable Book of Reference for Tourists and Other Strangers Visiting the Metropolis of the Pacific* (San Francisco: W. C. Disturnell, 1883), 108–109; "Seeing the Sights," *Century Illustrated Magazine* 65, no. 6 (April 1903): 101; B. E. Lloyd, *Lights and Shades in San Francisco* (San Francisco: A. L. Bancroft, 1876), 262–263; "San Francisco's Chinatown," in *Seen by the Spectator; Being a Selection of Rambling Papers First Published in the Outlook, under the Title The Spectator* (New York: Outlook, 1902); D. E. Kessler, "An Evening in Chinatown," *Overland Monthly and Out West Magazine* 49, no. 5 (May 1907): 445; Eleanor B. Caldwell, "The Picturesque in Chinatown," *Arthur's Home Magazine* 65, no. 8 (August 1895): 653, and *New Petersen Magazine* 4, no. 1 (July 1894): 595 (subsequent references to this source refer to *Arthur's Home Magazine*); Charles Warren Stoddard, *A Bit of Old China* (San Francisco: A. M. Robertson, 1912), as excerpted from *In the Footprints of the Padres* (San Francisco: A. M. Robertson, 1901); and *Bancroft's Tourist Guide* (San Francisco: A. L. Bancroft, 1871). While a number of sources suggest that there was some sort of licensing procedure for guides, the details of that system have not revealed themselves. See, for example, Joseph Carey, D.D., *By the Golden Gate or San Francisco, the Queen City of the Pacific Coast: With Scenes and Incidents Characteristic of Its Life* (Albany, New York:

Albany Diocesan Press, 1902), 138–140; William Bode, *Lights and Shadows of China-town* (San Francisco: H. S. Crocker, 1896); and Helen Throop Purdy, *San Francisco as It Was, as It Is, and How to See It* (San Francisco: Paul Elder, 1912).

12. W. H. Gleadell, "Night Scenes in Chinatown," *Eclectic Magazine* (September 1895): 378–383, quote from 379. For examples of other cautionary tales about what could happen if one ventured off the beaten path in Chinatown, see Rudyard Kipling, *Rudyard Kipling's Letters from San Francisco* (San Francisco: Colt Press, 1949), 31–32; Frank Norris, *The Third Circle* (New York: John Lane, 1909); and Emma Frances Dawson, "The Dramatic in My Destiny," *Californian* 1, no. 1 (January 1880): 1–11. If estimates were correct—from $1 per person to $2–$3 per hour—guides would have been affordable for the middle classes that made up the bulk of the tourist trade. See Carey, *By the Golden Gate*, 138–140 and John S. Hittell, *A Guidebook to San Francisco* (San Francisco: Bancroft, 1888), 50. For ways Chinese men were sexualized in relation to white women see Lee, *Orientals*, 83–105.

13. Will Irwin, ed. *Old Chinatown: A Book of Pictures by Arnold Genthe* (New York: Mitchell and Kennerly, 1980), 154–155; Bode, *Lights and Shadows*, npn. Writers have disagreed about the existence, or at least extent, of Chinatown's underground laby-rinths. For example, Louis Stellman contended that "as for the human *rabbit warrens* supposed to exist under Chinatown, the great fire of 1906 utterly disproved this ca-nard." See Louis J. Stellman, *Chinatown: A Pictorial Souvenir and Guide* (unpublished manuscript, 1917), 31, as well as Purdy, *San Francisco as It Was*, 137–138. Will Irwin, however, argued that the board of health had "filled in passage after passage" to pre-vent epidemics prior to the earthquake and fire. See Irwin, *Old Chinatown*, 153–155.

14. Caldwell, "Picturesque in Chinatown," 662.

15. Ernest C. Peixotto, *Ten Drawings in Chinatown with Certain Observations by Robert Howe Fletcher* (San Francisco: A. M. Robertson, 1898), 1–2.

16. Peixotto, *Ten Drawings*, 4–5.

17. J. W. Ames, "A Day in Chinatown," *Lippincott's Magazine* (October 1875): 499; *Bancroft's Tourist Guide*, 215; "'China Town' in San Francisco, by Day and by Night," *Cornhill Magazine*, 56.

18. For a brilliant discussion of the way the staged touristic presentations of the physical body construct difference, see Jane C. Desmond, *Staging Tourism: Bodies on Display from Waikiki to Sea World* (Chicago: University of Chicago Press, 1999). Quo-tation and Figures 19–22 are from a booklet of photos titled *Chinatown*, published by Henry R. Knapp, San Francisco, 1889. These same photos were pasted into A. E. Browne's unpublished, handwritten travel journal to illustrate her experiences. A. E. Browne, *A Trip to California, Alaska, and the Yellowstone Park*, vol. 1 (unpublished travel journal, ca. 1891). Photographs with a similar pedigree also accompanied "The 'Labor Question' on the Pacific Coast," *Harper's Weekly* (October 13, 1888): 778.

19. Stoddard, *Bit of Old China*, 7–8; Gleadell, "Night Scenes in Chinatown," 381. See also Lloyd, *Lights and Shades*, 262–263.

20. Rev. O. Gibson, A.M., *The Chinese in America* (Cincinnati: Hitchcock and Walden, 1877), 93–94.

21. Gibson, *Chinese in America*, 93-94. Gibson had established a Methodist Episcopal mission in Chinatown in 1868. He was involved, among other things, in the creation of a mission school and in activities to provide sanctuary for Chinese prostitutes. See Chen, *Chinese San Francisco*, 77, 131, 134, 140-141.

22. "Horrors of a Great City: Chinadom by Day and Night," *San Francisco Chronicle*, December 5, 1869; Walter Turnbull, scrapbook of clippings of San Francisco area affairs: telegrams, drawings, letters to and from Turnbull (1882-1885), Rare Book Department, California Scrapbook, 27, Huntington Library. Contains at least one letter from 1890. Newspaper clippings omit years, but have dates. Sunday, February 22, *Alta California Publishing Company/Daily Alta California*; J. Torrey Connor, "A Western View of the Chinese in the United States," *Chautauquan: A Weekly Newsmagazine* 32, no. 4 (January 1901): 378.

23. This understanding of "the Oriental" is drawn from Lee, *Orientals*, 8-9, 27-32. Lee identifies four aspects of "the Oriental" in nineteenth-century American culture—the pollutant, the coolie, the deviant, and the yellow peril—which are constructed around issues of unassimilability, public health and sanitation, labor competition, and vice.

24. Rev. J. C. Holbrook, "Chinadom in California," *Hutchings' Illustrated California Magazine* 4 (1859-1860): 130. For reference to the foreign-ness of Chinatown, see also Carey, *By the Golden Gate*, 136-137; Bode, *Lights and Shadows of Chinatown*, npn; Lucien Biart, *My Rambles in the New World*, trans. Mary de Hauteville (London: Sampson Low, Marston, Searle and Rivington, 1877), 83-84; G. B. Densmore, *The Chinese in California: Description of Chinese Life in San Francisco, Their Habits, Morals, and Manners*, illustrated by Voegtlin (San Francisco: Pettit and Russ, 1880), 21; William Doxey, *Doxey's Guide to San Francisco and the Pleasure Resorts of California* (San Francisco: At the Sign of the Lark, 1897), 116-117; "Chinese Highbinders," *Harper's Weekly* (February 13, 1890): 103; C. Baldwin, "A Celestial Colony," *Lippincott's Magazine* (February 1881): 123; "'China Town' in San Francisco," 50; Gleadell, "Night Scenes in Chinatown," 1895, 379; "The Chinese in San Francisco," *Harper's Weekly* (March 20, 1880): 182; "Lenz's World Tour," *Outing, An Illustrated Monthly Magazine of Recreation* 22, no. 5 (August 1893): 363; Connor, "Western View of the Chinese," 374; Kessler, "Evening in Chinatown," 445; Caldwell, "Picturesque in Chinatown," 653; Will Brooks, "Fragment of China," *Californian* 6, no. 31 (July 1882): 2; *New California Tourists' Guide to San Francisco and Vicinity* (San Francisco: Samuel Carson, 1886), 59; Mabel C. Craft, "Some Days and Nights in Little China," *National Magazine* (November 1897), 100, 109; Charles Keeler, *San Francisco and Thereabout* (San Francisco: California Promotion Committee, 1902), 65; George Hamlin Fitch, "The City by the Golden Gate" *Chautauquan* 23, no. 6 (September 1896): 666; Lloyd, *Lights and Shades*, 236; and A.M., "A Glimpse of San Francisco," *Lippincott's Magazine* (June 1870): 645.

25. For an extended analysis of the way public health and race came together in Chinatown, see Nyan Shah, *Contagious Divides: Epidemics and Race in San Francisco's Chinatown* (Berkeley: University of California Press, 2001). Densmore, *Chinese in California*, 1880. Also, Gibson, *Chinese in America*, 63-64; Willard B. Farwell, *The Chinese*

at Home And Abroad: Together with the Report of the Special Committee of the Board of Supervisors of San Francisco on the Condition of the Chinese Quarter of That City (San Francisco: A. L. Bancroft, 1885), 53–54, 59; and "Horrors of a Great City."

26. Carey, *By the Golden Gate*, 196; Gibson, *Chinese in America*, 71; Josephine Clifford, "Chinatown," *Potter's American Monthly* (May 1880): 354–364; Doxey, *Doxey's Guide to San Francisco*, 118; *Disturnell's Strangers' Guide*. It is worth noting as well that much of Gibson's description was reprinted in "Chinese in San Francisco," 182. For further description of the polluted quality of Chinese food, see also Ames, "Day in Chinatown," 500; Browne, *Trip to California*; Kessler, "Evening in Chinatown," 445; and Caldwell, "Picturesque in Chinatown," 657. Brooks, "Fragment of China," 4, also noted the possibilities for deception. Lee, *Orientals*, 38–39.

27. Craft, "Some Days and Nights in Little China," 102–103; E.G.H., *Surprise Land*, 80; Brooks, "Fragment of China," 3–4. See also, "'China Town' in San Francisco," 52; and Doxey, *Doxey's Guide to San Francisco*, 118.

28. Craft, "Some Days and Nights in Little China," 102–103. Doxey, *Doxey's Guide to San Francisco*, 118, also mentioned arranging a meal in advance in suspiciously similar language. Gibson, *Chinese in America*, 70–71.

29. Gibson, *Chinese in America*, 71–72.

30. Lloyd, *Lights and Shades*, 231 mentions these banquets. *Daily Alta California*, September 20, 1864; *San Francisco Examiner*, January 28, 1868. See also, for example, the *San Francisco Call*, March 1, 1896. Two of these banquets in the 1860s, as reported in the local papers, hosted high-ranking members of the police force and law enforcement at one and "members of the press, the Judiciary, the bar, the army" and the fire department at the other. Another in 1896, that fêted numerous city officials "at the Hang Fer Low restaurant, 713 Dupont street" was sponsored by "The Tinn Yee Quong Sow Benevolent Association of the Low Quong Chung Chew—a group organized specifically to smooth relations between whites and Chinese.

31. As Mary Douglas has shown, the specific ways people feed their physical bodies disclose and shed light on the needs and fears of the social body. See Mary Douglas, *Purity and Danger: An Analysis of the Concepts of Pollution and Taboo* (London: Routledge, 1966). See also John Kasson, *Rudeness and Civility* (New York: Hill and Wang, 1990), 182.

32. "Chinese in San Francisco," 182. This article was paraphrasing from Gibson, *Chinese in America*, 70. Doxey, *Doxey's Guide to San Francisco*, 118; Carey, *By the Golden Gate*, 187. See also Keeler, *San Francisco and Thereabout*, 62.

33. Clifford, "Chinatown," 354–355.

34. Keeler, *San Francisco and Thereabout*, 62; Gleadell, "Night Scenes in Chinatown," 379.

35. See Holbrook, "Chinadom in California," 131, for tourist interest in the 1860s. Doxey, *Doxey's Guide to San Francisco*, 118; *Disturnell's Strangers' Guide*, 107–108. Craft, "Some Days and Nights in Little China," 104, provides the same explanation for the etymology of the term *joss*.

36. Craft, "Some Days and Nights in Little China," 104–105; Iza Duffus Hardy, "In Chinatown," *Belgravia: An Illustrated London Magazine* (January 1881): 221; Kessler,

"Evening in Chinatown," 446–447; Browne, *Trip to California*, 99. For similar description, see also Clifford, "Chinatown," 362; Gleadell, "Night Scenes in Chinatown," 380; Keeler, *San Francisco and Thereabout*, 66; A.M., "Glimpse of San Francisco," 647; Connor, "Western View of Chinese," 373; L. A. Littleton, "Chinese Mythology in San Francisco," *Overland Monthly and Out West Magazine* vol. 1, no. 6 (June 1883): 615; Stoddard, *Bit of Old China*, 2; Caldwell, "Picturesque in Chinatown," 653; "A Chinese Miracle. A Strange Scene in a Joss House—A Reporter Takes a Peep behind the Scenes," undated article from the *San Francisco Chronicle* in *The Chinese Invasion: Revealing the Habits, Manners, and Customs of the Chinese, Political Social and Religious, on the Pacific Coast, Coming in Contact with the Free and Enlightened Citizens of America; Containing Careful Selections from the San Francisco Press*, comp. H. J. West (San Francisco: Excelsior Office, Bacon and Company Printers, 1873), 89.

37. "'China Town' in San Francisco," 52; Ames, "Day in Chinatown," 498–499. See also Hittell, *Guidebook to San Francisco*, 45–46.

38. Ames, "Day in Chinatown," 499; Kessler, "Evening in Chinatown," 446–447.

39. Craft, "Some Days and Nights in Little China," 104–105; Hittell, *Guidebook to San Francisco*, 45. See also Gibson, *Chinese in America*, 72–73; Browne, *Trip to California*, 99; Mrs. James Edwin (Ida Dorman) Morris, *A Pacific Coast Vacation—Illustrated from Photographs Taken en Route* (London: Abbey Press, 1901), 175.

40. Craft, "Some Days and Nights in Little China," 104–105.

41. Carey, *By the Golden Gate*, 206, 210, 214–215

42. Densmore, *Chinese in California*, 61; Gibson, *Chinese in America*, 71–73.

43. Regarding the significance of the theater in nineteenth-century American culture, see Lawrence Levine, *Highbrow/Lowbrow: The Emergence of Cultural Hierarchy in America* (Cambridge, MA: Harvard University Press, 1988). Carey, *By the Golden Gate*, 199.

44. *Disturnell's Strangers' Guide*, 107–108; "'China Town' in San Francisco," 58. For general information about location, times, and prices see also, Doxey, *Doxey's Guide to San Francisco*, 127; Gibson, *Chinese in America*, 74, 80–81; Ames, "Day in Chinatown," 501; Clifford, "Chinatown," 362; and E. M. Green, "The Chinese Theater," *Overland Monthly*, 2nd ser., 21 (February 1903): 119. Regarding decreasing attendance at the theater among the Chinese post–Exclusion Act, see Frederic J. Masters, D.D., "The Chinese Drama," *Chautauquan: A Weekly Newsmagazine* (July 1895): 21, 4, 436. For different prices for whites and Chinese, see Green, "Chinese Theater," 119; and Masters, "Chinese Drama," 439.

45. Lloyd, *Lights and Shades*, 264; Gleadell, "Night Scenes in Chinatown," 382; Masters, "Chinese Drama," 440; Gibson, *Chinese in America*, 78–79. See also Keeler, *San Francisco and Thereabout*, 65–66; Craft, "Some Days and Nights in Little China," 102–103, and Densmore, *Chinese in California*, 54–58.

46. Gibson, *Chinese in America*, 78–79; Biart, *My Rambles in the New World*, 80; E.G.H., *Surprise Land*, 78.

47. Henry Burden McDowell, "The Chinese Theater," *Century Illustrated Monthly Magazine* (November 1884): 27–44; quotes from 31 and 35.

48. Masters, "Chinese Drama," 436; Gibson, *Chinese in America*, 80–81; McDowell, "Chinese Theater," 28. For similar description, see also Gleadell, "Night Scenes in Chinatown," 382; Carey, *By the Golden Gate*, 199–202; Doxey, *Doxey's Guide to San Francisco*, 127; Ames, "Day in Chinatown," 501; Brooks, "Fragment of China," 4; and Browne, *Trip to California*, 102.

49. "'China Town' in San Francisco," 58–59; Lloyd, *Lights and Shades*, 264–265; Clifford, "Chinatown," 364. See also Doxey, *Doxey's Guide to San Francisco*, 127; Gibson, *Chinese in America*, 80–81; Ames, "Day in Chinatown," 501; Keeler, *San Francisco and Thereabout*, 65–66; and Craft, "Some Days and Nights in Little China," 102–103.

50. "Lenz's World Tour," 363; Carey, *By the Golden Gate*, 202; Browne, *Trip to California*, 104. For other accounts of tourists seated on the stage, see *Doxey's Guide to San Francisco*, 127; Craft, "Some Days and Nights in Little China," 102–103; Gleadell, "Night Scenes in Chinatown," 382–383; Keeler, *San Francisco and Thereabout*, 65; Masters, "Chinese Drama," 125; and Caldwell, "Picturesque in Chinatown," 660.

51. Craft, "Some Days and Nights in Little China," 102; Carey, *By the Golden Gate*, 201; Gleadell, "Night Scenes in Chinatown," 382 and 379.

52. See Lee, *Orientals*, 124. *San Francisco Chronicle*, February 18, 1894.

53. Lloyd, *Lights and Shades in San Francisco*, 260–261, and Hardy, "In Chinatown," 217. See also, Ames, "Day in Chinatown," 500; Keeler, *San Francisco and Thereabout*, 65; Gleadell, "Night Scenes in Chinatown," 381–382; Clifford, "Chinatown," 355; "Lenz's World Tour," 362; Browne, *Trip to California*, 104–105; Stoddard, *Bit of Old China*, 11; and Caldwell, "Picturesque in Chinatown," 660–661

54. Clifford, "Chinatown," 355; Gleadell, "Night Scenes in Chinatown," 381–382; and Hardy, "In Chinatown," 217. For similar descriptions, see also Carey, *By the Golden Gate*, 173–179; Ames, "Day in Chinatown," 500; Stoddard, *Bit of Old China*, 11; Morris, *Pacific Coast Vacation*, 176; and E.G.H., *Surprise Land*, 99.

55. Gleadell, "Night Scenes in Chinatown," 381–382, and Caldwell, "Picturesque in Chinatown," 661.

56. Caldwell, "Picturesque in Chinatown," 661; Stoddard, *Bit of Old China*, 12; and "'China Town' in San Francisco," 52–53.

57. I. W. Taber, "White Women in Opium Den, Chinatown S.F.," Copyrighted by I. W. Taber, May 31, 1892.

58. Lloyd, *Lights and Shades*, 262; E. W. Wood, *Life and Experience of Prof. E. W. Wood Appertaining to the Opium Habit of the Chinese* (New York: Dick's Publishing House, 18-), npn; and Connor, "Western View of the Chinese," 378. See also Carey, *By the Golden Gate*, 179.

59. For the illegality of opium smoking in public but not private in San Francisco, see *San Francisco Chronicle*, February 18, 1894, and C. P. Holden, "The Opium Industry in America," *Scientific American* 77, no. 10 (March 5, 1898): 147. For the common use of opium among the Chinese, see *San Francisco Chronicle*, February 18 and 19, 1894. *San Francisco Chronicle*, February 18, 1894; "Hitting the Pipe," *National Police Gazette* 38, no. 204 (August 20, 1881): 6; *San Francisco Chronicle*, February 19, 1894.

60. "John Chinaman in San Francisco," *Scribner's Monthly* 17, no. 6 (October 1876): 871; "Lenz's World Tour," 363; and Connor, "Western View of the Chinese," 375. See also Lloyd, *Lights and Shades,* 213–217; Gleadell, "Night Scenes in Chinatown," 378; Densmore, *Chinese in California,* 1, 117; "The Chinese at Home and Abroad," *Hutchings' Illustrated California Magazine,* 5 (1860–1861) 324–330; Fitch, "City by the Golden Gate," 659–668; Baldwin, "Celestial Colony," 128–129; Hardy, "In Chinatown," 226; Holbrook, "Chinadom in California," 129–132, 173–178; *Bancroft's Tourist Guide,* 217; and Craft, "Some Days and Nights in Little China," 100, 109.

Chapter 4. Celebrating the City: Labor, Progress, and the Promenade at the Mechanics' Institute Fairs

1. *Daily Alta California,* September 8, 1857.

2. *Alta,* September 8 and 9, 1857; *100 Years of the Mechanics' Institute of San Francisco, 1855–1955* (San Francisco: Mechanics' Institute of San Francisco, 1955), 8; *Alta,* September 21, 1857. Fair organizers had borrowed $7,000 to hold the fair and within ten days they had exceeded that amount in fair revenue.

3. For information about the number and timing of the fairs see Nora Leishman, "The Mechanics' Institute Fairs, 1857–1899," *Argonaut: Journal of the San Francisco Historical Society* 10, no. 2 (Fall 1999): 40–57. Attendance figures culled from *The Argonaut Sketchbook, Mechanics' Fair, 1877,* npn; *San Francisco Morning Call,* August 20, 1882; and letter from Lucy Alice Harrison Pownall Senger to her parents, August 26, 1877 (Letters from Lucy Alice Harrison Pownall Senger to her parents March 18, 1877–August 31, 1878, Huntington Library PW 851–922). The precise reasons for the cessation of the fairs are vague. One official account concluded that "when they were discontinued" it was "apparent . . . that they had served their purpose." See *100 Years of the Mechanics' Institute,* 18.

4. *Call,* August 20, 1882; *Mechanics' Fair Daily Press,* August 12, 1868.

5. *100 Years of the Mechanics' Institute,* 1–2, 7–8, 15.

6. These middle class and entrepreneurial tendencies prevailed at the Mechanics' Institutes in New York, Boston, and London as well. See Sean Wilentz, *Chants Democratic: New York City and the Rise of the American Working Class, 1788–1850* (New York: Oxford University Press, 1984), 272. See also James Hole, Esq., *An Essay on the History and Management of Literary, Scientific, and Mechanics' Institutes* (London: Longman, Brown, Green, and Longmans, 1853). Hole, the honorary secretary of the Yorkshire Union of Mechanics' Institutions, lamented the failure "to attract the mechanic classes" and that "the Mechanics' Institutes belong to Mechanics only in name." That the San Francisco Mechanics' Institute was modeling itself on its predecessors was clear from its activities as well as its outreach to its eastern kin. See *Alta,* February 9, 1855: "The purpose is, among other things, to collect a large library and secure courses of lectures, scientific, philosophic, and discursive, and render it similar in its uses and benefits to the Mechanics' Associations of Boston and New York." For the

proclivity to unionize among San Francisco's working classes see Carey McWilliams, *California: The Great Exception* (Berkeley: University of California Press, 1949, 1999), 128–133, and William Issel and Robert W. Cherny, *San Francisco, 1865–1932: Power, Politics, and Urban Development* (Berkeley: University of California Press, 1986), 80–82.

7. *Announcement of the Mechanics' Institute 28th Industrial Exhibition*, 1895, npn; John H. Wood, comp., *75 Years of History of the Mechanics' Institute* (San Francisco: Benham Printing, 1930), 7; *100 Years of the Mechanics' Institute of San Francisco*, 2, 13–16; *Constitution, By-Laws, Rules and Regulations of the Mechanics' Institute of the City of San Francisco*, 1855; and *Alta California*, February 9, 1855.

8. *100 Years of the Mechanics' Institute of San Francisco*, 4–5.

9. Ramon E. Wilson, Esq., inaugural oration, *Report of the 21st Industrial Exhibition*, 1886; Wood, comp., *75 Years of History of the Mechanics' Institute*, 7; *Constitution, By-Laws, Rules and Regulations of the Mechanics' Institute of the City of San Francisco*, 1855; *Alta*, September 8, 1857; and *Constitution, By-Laws, Rules and Regulations of the Mechanics' Institute of the City of San Francisco, California* (San Francisco: J. R. Brodie, 1885), 9. Membership records for the years before the fire and earthquake are not extant.

10. For an excellent distillation of the producer ethic, see Michael Kazin, *The Populist Persuasion: An American History* (Ithaca, NY: Cornell University Press, 1995 and 1998, rev ed), 13–17, and Wilentz, *Chants Democratic*, 273–275. For the harmony of interests, see Stephen P. Rice, *Minding the Machine: Languages of Class in Early Industrial America* (Berkeley: University of California Press, 2004), especially 42–68, and Martin J. Burke, *The Conundrum of Class: Public Discourse on the Social Order in America* (Chicago: University of Chicago Press, 1995), 108–132. For accounts of downward mobility see McWilliams, *California: The Great Exception*, 132; Roger W. Lotchin, *San Francisco, 1846–1856: From Hamlet to City* (Lincoln: University of Nebraska Press, 1974), 83.

11. *100 Years of the Mechanics' Institute of San Francisco*, 7–17. See also Wood, comp., *75 Years of History of the Mechanics' Institute*, 10–18.

12. For evidence that capital felt threatened by labor in California, see McWilliams, *California: The Great Exception*, 133. He asserts, "Labor's opportunity in California, was, of course, capital's special disability. From the outset employer groups felt compelled to experiment with strong-arm tactics in order to offset the advantage which labor possessed."

13. Hon. Milton S. Latham, at the opening exercises, as reported by the *Alta*, August 9, 1871. Anti-union views were also expressed in the *Mechanics' Fair Daily Press*, September 20, 1869. A few years later, on August 11, 1871, the *Industrial Fair Gazette* denounced both foreigners and radicals.

14. Opening oration by W. J. Winans, Esq., as reported in the *Alta*, August 14, 1878.

15. Inaugural address by P. B. Cornwall, *Report of the 23rd Industrial Exhibition*, 1888. In his address at the opening of the 1891 Fair, Hon. Thomas F. Barry similarly decried labor unrest and situated it terms of a society out of balance rather than an inevitable conflict. See *Report of the 26th Industrial Exposition*, 1891.

16. Closing address, Rev. A. H. Myers, September 23, 1858, *Report of the Second Industrial Exhibition*, 1858; Opening address by Hon. John Conness, as reported in the *Mechanics' Fair Daily Press*, September 5, 1864; inaugural address by P. B. Cornwall, *Report of the Twentieth Industrial Exhibition*, 1885. Labor's praises were sung in numerous addresses and poems. See, for example: opening address by President Irving M. Scott as reported by the *Alta*, August 14, 1878; *Mechanics' Fair Daily Press*, September 16 and 22, 1869; inaugural address by Senator Conness, *Alta*, September 3, 1864; *Address of Hon. Newton Booth at the Opening of the 6th Industrial Exhibition, August 8, 1868* (San Francisco: Dewey, 1868); Rev. Dr. Scott, *The Mechanics' Industrial Exhibition, or the Useful Arts Exponents of the Nature, Progress, and Hope of Christian Civilization*, A Discourse Delivered in Calvary Church, Sunday evening, August 23, 1857 (San Francisco: Hutchings and Rosenfield, 1857); Henry F. Williams, *Opening Address, Delivered at the Inauguration of the Fair of the Mechanics' Institute* (San Francisco: Whitton, Towne, 1857); address given by the president of the Mechanics' Institute at the close of the first fair, as reported by the *Alta*, September 29, 1857; inaugural remarks of Hon. Nathan Porter as covered in the *Alta*, March 27, 1867; *Mechanics' Fair Daily Press*, October 30, 1869; *Industrial Fair Gazette*, August 11, 1871; address by Vice President Starbird at opening exercises as covered in the *Call*, September 12, 1883; address by Captain C. A. Woodruff, opening exercises as covered in the *Call*, January 11, 1893; and opening exercises, oration by George H. Maxwell, *Report of the 25th Industrial Exposition*, 1890.

17. Williams, *Opening Address*, 1857. For similar constructions of the California mechanic, see also opening address by James A. Banks, September 1, 1858, *Report of the Second Industrial Exhibition*, 1858, and "Opening Poem," by Edward Pollock, Esq., *Alta*, September 8, 1857.

18. *Mechanics' Fair Daily Press*, August 14, 1868; Scott, opening address; *Industrial Fair Gazette*, August 18, 1871. See also *Mechanics' Fair Daily Press*, August 11 and August 14, 1868; *Mechanics' Fair Daily Press*, September 22, 1869; *Industrial Fair Gazette*, August 11, 1871; Wilson, inaugural oration, 1886.

19. *Industrial Fair Gazette*, August 28, 1875; *Mechanics' Fair Daily Press*, September 22, 1869; Williams, *Opening Address*, 1857. See also *Mechanics' Fair Daily Press*, August 16, 1868; *Mechanics' Fair Daily Press*, August 19, 1868; *Report of the Twentieth Industrial Exhibition*, 1885; *Mechanics' Fair Daily Press*, August 10, 1868; *Call*, August 20, 1882; Scott, *Mechanics' Industrial Exhibition*; *Alta*, September 2, 1865; *Call*, August 19, 1882; Myers, closing address, 1858.

20. Scott, *Mechanics' Industrial Exhibition*. See also *Industrial Fair Gazette*, August 18, 1871; *Call*, August 16, 1882; Myers, closing address, 1858.

21. *Alta*, February 7, 1858.

22. For accounts that stress the progress of the city and state see, Scott, *Mechanics' Industrial Exhibition*; *Address of Hon. Newton Booth at the Opening of the 6th Industrial Exhibition*; address given by the president of the Mechanics' Institute at the close of the first fair, as reported by the *Alta*, September 29, 1857; *Alta*, September 21, 1857; discussion of the Mechanics' Institute in *Hutchings' California Magazine* (1860–1861):

155–157; inaugural address by Senator Conness, as reported in the *Alta*, September 3, 1864; *Alta*, September 4, 1860; and "Address Delivered by Morris M. Este at the Opening of the 22nd Industrial Exposition," September 1st, *Report of the Twenty-Second Industrial Exhibition*, 1887.

23. Scott, *Mechanics' Industrial Exhibition*, 1857; *Alta*, August 9, 1868. For issues of self-sufficiency see also Henry F. Williams, *Opening Address*, 1857; *Alta*, September 8 and 29, 1857; *Alta*, October 3, 1864; and *Alta*, August 11, 1868; *Mechanics' Fair Daily Press*, September 9, 1868; *Mechanics' Fair Daily Press*, September 20, 1869; *Mechanics' Fair Daily Press*, August 17 and August 24, 1868.

24. Banks, opening address, 1858; inaugural oration by Irving M. Scott, as covered in the *Alta*, September 15, 1869. See also Latham, at the opening exercises; *Mechanics' Fair Daily Press*, August 10, 1868; *Mechanics' Fair Daily Press*, August 15, 1868; inaugural oration by Irving Scott, *Report of the 24th Industrial Exposition*, 1889; and *Mechanics' Fair Daily Press*, August 14, 1865.

25. *Alta*, September 9, 1857.

26. Banks, opening address, 1858; Myers, closing address, 1858; and Scott, *Mechanics' Industrial Exhibition*, 1857.

27. *Alta*, September 2, 1865; *Industrial Fair Gazette*, August 28, 1871; and *Call*, August 20, 1882. See also *Alta*, September 23 and October 3, 1864; *Mechanics' Fair Daily Press*, August 16, 1865; and *Alta*, August 11, 1868.

28. *Mechanics' Fair Daily Press*, September 7, 1858.

29. *Alta*, August 11, 1865; *Alta*, August 11, 1868; *Alta*, September 16, 1869; *The Argonaut Sketchbook*, Mechanics' Fair 1878, npn. For identification of the fairs as an important site of civic sociability, see also *Our Daily Circular*, August 17, 1878; *Mechanics' Fair Daily Press*, September 1, 1869; *Alta*, September 10, 1864; *Mechanics' Fair Daily Press*, August 19, 1868; Scott, *Mechanics' Industrial Exhibition*; and articles in the *Alta* on September 10, 1864, and August 11, 1865, as well as September 11, 1881. For further mention of the significance of the fountain, see *Alta*, August 9, 1868, and September 16, 1869, and *Our Daily Circular*, August 26, 1878. For the importance of the ritual of promenade to middle-class identities, see David Scobey, "Anatomy of the Promenade: The Politics of Bourgeois Sociability in Nineteenth-Century New York," *Social History* 17, no. 2 (May 1992): 203–227.

30. *Alta*, August 14, 1882 and *Call*, August 18, 1891.

31. For an insightful discussion of the emergence of semi-public commercial spaces for women, see Ryan, *Women in Public*, 58–94. Scott, *Mechanics' Industrial Exhibition*.

32. Demographic data is from Edith Sparks, *Capital Intentions: Female Proprietors in San Francisco, 1850 to 1920* (Chapel Hill: University of North Carolina Press, 1974) 216, and Roger W. Lotchin, *San Francisco, 1846–1856: From Hamlet to City* (Lincoln: University of Nebraska Press, 1974), 103–104. For further discussion of the connections between gender, family, and the state, see Mary P. Ryan, *Cradle of the Middle Class: The Family in Oneida County, New York, 1790–1865* (New York: Cambridge University Press, 1981), and Carole Pateman, *The Sexual Contract* (Stanford, CA: Stanford University Press, 1988).

33. *Mechanics' Fair Daily Press*, August 14, 1868. See also *Our Daily Circular*, August 17, 1878. "Young men of the middle class are getting so shy and hard to catch, that parents will have to begin to offer a copy of *The Mechanics Fair* [a farcical play with the fair at its center] along with their marriageable daughters."

34. *Industrial Fair Gazette*, August 18, 1871.

35. *Mechanics' Fair Daily Press*, September 20, 1869; *Industrial Fair Gazette*, August 23, 1871. For other evidence of bachelors seemingly in retreat, see *Industrial Fair Gazette*, August 19, 1871.

36. *Argonaut Sketchbook*, 1878, npn.

37. *Industrial Fair Gazette*, August 23, 1871; *Argonaut Sketchbook*, 1878, npn.

38. *Industrial Fair Gazette*, August 23, 1871; *Industrial Fair Gazette*, August 26, 1871; *Industrial Fair Gazette*, August 18, 1871; *Industrial Fair Gazette*, August 28, 1871; *Industrial Fair Gazette*, August 26, 1871.

39. *Industrial Fair Gazette*, August 18, 1871; *Our Daily Circular*, August 27, 1878; *Industrial Fair Gazette*, August 21, 1871.

40. *Industrial Fair Gazette*, August 30, 1871; *Industrial Fair Gazette*, August 18, 1871.

41. *Mechanics' Fair Daily Press*, August 17, 1868, and August 22, 1868.

42. *Argonaut Sketchbook*, 1878, npn.

43. *Industrial Fair Gazette*, August 23, 1871. The *Argonaut Sketchbook*, 1878, also made note of "the omnipresent sewing machine girls, who are always adept enough in the art, to entertain the few masculines in the hall at this hour."

44. *Industrial Fair Gazette*, August 21, 1871; *Industrial Fair Gazette*, August 31. 1871; *Industrial Fair Gazette*, August 25, 1871.

45. Ryan, *Women in Public*, and Karen Halttunen, *Confidence Men and Painted Women: A Study of Middle-Class Culture in America, 1830–1870* (New Haven, CT: Yale University Press, 1982). *Industrial Fair Gazette*, August 11, 1871.

46. *Industrial Fair Gazette*, August 18, 1871.

47. *Industrial Fair Gazette*, August 26, 1871.

48. *Industrial Fair Gazette*, August 30, 1871; *Mechanics' Fair Daily Press*, September 18 and 25, 1869.

49. *Industrial Fair Gazette*, August 23, 1871; *Industrial Fair Gazette*, August 24, 1871; *Industrial Fair Gazette*, August 19, 1871; *Industrial Fair Gazette*, August 31, 1871. See also a column that featured the accomplishments of individual women, *Industrial Fair Gazette*, August 26, 1871.

50. *Industrial Fair Gazette*, August 10, 1871.

Chapter 5. Imagining the City: The California Midwinter International Exposition

1. See Arthur Chandler and Marvin Nathan, *The Fantastic Fair: The Story of the California Midwinter International Exposition, Golden Gate Park, San Francisco, 1894* (St.

Paul, MN: Pogo Press, 1993). De Young's motives are further elaborated in the *Official Guide to the California Midwinter Exposition*, 1st ed., Compiled from Official Sources under the Direct Supervision of the Exposition Management (San Francisco: George Spalding, 1894), 19; *The Official History of the California Midwinter International Exposition: A Descriptive Record of the Origin, Development and Success of the Great Industrial Expositional Enterprise, Held in San Francisco from January to July 1894* (San Francisco: H. S. Crocker, 1895), 11–24; and James D. Phelan, "Is the Midwinter Fair a Benefit?" *Overland Monthly*, 2nd ser., 23 (April 1894): 390–392.

2. According to Chandler and Nathan's calculations the exposition netted a profit of $66,851.49. See *Fantastic Fair*, 67. Funding of the Midwinter Fair was based solely on popular subscription. Contributions from ordinary San Franciscans were comparatively more generous than those from wealthy firms and individuals. In the midst of the economic crisis, federal, state, or municipal financing was an impossibility. See *Official History*, 11–22. Attendance figures are based on Chandler and Nathan, *Fantastic Fair*, 77. To provide a sense of scale, 27,529,400 people attended the Columbian Exposition. See Robert Rydell, *All the World's a Fair: Visions of Empire at American International Expositions, 1876–1916* (Chicago: University of Chicago Press, 1984), 40.

3. *Official History*, 11–24; Phelan's speech was reprinted in *Official History*, 74–75. San Francisco native James Duval Phelan was a prominent banker, civic leader, and proponent of the City Beautiful movement. In 1897, he was elected mayor of San Francisco and served three two-year terms. In his opening remarks, he quoted Social Gospel Movement founder Josiah Strong's "Anglo-Saxon Predominance" from 1891. Strong was quoting John Adams.

4. *Official History*, 48 and 47. See also *Official Guide*, 25. When the Midwinter Fair is mentioned in the historical literature at all, it is routinely dismissed as being "largely imitative" of the Chicago Fair. See Rydell, *All the World's a Fair*, 51. Although the Midwinter Fair did import many exhibits from Chicago, the idiom of exposition design was already well articulated prior to the Chicago Fair. Moving exhibits to San Francisco, a different setting with distinctive architecture, changed local conditions, plus novel added exhibits made for a decidedly distinct exposition experience. My understanding of nineteenth-century expositions has been shaped by: James Gilbert, *Perfect Cities: Chicago's Utopias of 1893* (Chicago: University of Chicago Press, 1991); Alan Trachtenberg, *The Incorporation of America: Culture and Society in the Gilded Age* (New York: Hill and Wang, 1982); Gail Bederman, *Manliness and Civilization: A Cultural History of Gender and Race in the United States, 1880–1917* (Chicago: University of Chicago Press, 1995); Rydell, *All the World's a Fair*; and William Cronon, *Nature's Metropolis: Chicago and the Great West* (New York: W. W. Norton, 1991).

5. Descriptions of the buildings come from *The Monarch Souvenir of Sunset City and Sunset Scenes: Being Views of California Midwinter Fair and Famous Scenes in the Golden State* (San Francisco: H. S. Crocker, 1894) and *Official Guide*, 43, 55, 67. For more detail about the architects and architecture of the Midwinter Fair, see Chandler and Nathan, *Fantastic Fair* and Kevin Starr, *Inventing the Dream: California through the Progressive Era* (New York: Oxford University Press, 1985), 190–193.

6. *Official History*, 47.

7. The seminal work on Orientalism remains Edward W. Said, *Orientalism* (New York: Pantheon Books, 1978).

8. Taliesin Evans, *All about the Midwinter Fair, San Francisco, and Interesting Facts Concerning California*, 1st ed. (San Francisco: W. B. Bancroft, 1894), 24. The city had also long been secure in its imperial dominance of its regional hinterlands. See Gray Brechin, *Imperial San Francisco: Urban Power, Earthly Ruin* (Berkeley: University of California Press, 1999). As a result of the Spanish American War the United States acquired varying levels of dominion over Cuba, the Philippines, Puerto Rico, and Guam.

9. David Gebhard, "One Hundred Years of California Architecture," in David Gebhard and Harriette Von Breton, eds., *1868–1968, Architecture in California, An Exhibition Organized by David Gebhard and Harriette Von Breton to Celebrate the Centennial of the University of California, The Art Galleries, University of California, Santa Barbara, April 16 to May 12, 1968* (The Regents, University of California, 1968), 7, 16; and *Official Guide*, 16. See also David G. Gutiérrez , "Significant to Whom?: Mexican Americans and the History of the American West," *Western Historical Quarterly* 44, no. 4 (November 1993): 519–539, and Carey McWilliams, *North from Mexico: The Spanish-Speaking People of the United States* (Philadelphia: J. B. Lippincott, 1949), 36, who coined the term "Spanish Fantasy Heritage" to describe this kind of appropriation.

10. The outline of the Midwinter Fair's Grand Court of Honor exists today as the Music Concourse in Golden Gate Park. Until 1921, the Fine Arts Building served as San Francisco's first public art museum, the De Young Memorial Museum, in memory of the Midwinter Fair.

11. Evans, *All about the Midwinter Fair*, 1st ed., 75, and *Official History*, 146, 47.

12. *California Midwinter Exposition Illustrated, Official Souvenir: Illustrations and Descriptions of All Prominent Buildings, Biographical Sketches, Synoptical History of Early California, Notice of Concessions, etc.* (San Francisco: Robert A. Irving, 1894), npn.

13. *Official History*, 150, and *Official Guide*, 100–101. See also *San Francisco Chronicle*, March 22, 1894, and Nathan and Chandler, *Fantastic Fair*, 46. The Chinese government refused to set up an official exhibit at either the Columbian Exposition or the Midwinter Fair in protest over renewed restrictions on Chinese immigration.

14. This concept of differential racialization based on distance or proximity is developed by Robert G. Lee, *Orientals: Asian Americans in Popular Culture* (Philadelphia: Temple University Press, 1999), 27–28; *Official Guide*, 100–101. See also *San Francisco Examiner*, January 28, 1894.

15. Evans, *All about the Midwinter Fair*, 2nd ed., 168, 175; and *Monarch Souvenir of Sunset City*. This description is also drawn in part from Chandler and Nathan, *Fantastic Fair*, 42. They note that "The Japanese Tea Garden was so popular an attraction at the exposition that the Golden Gate Park Commissioners purchased it from Marsh at the Fair's end and it has since remained one of San Francisco's most beloved possessions," 42.

16. *San Francisco Morning Call*, October 31, 1893; Evans, *All about the Midwinter Fair*, 2nd ed., 150; *Monarch Souvenir of Sunset City*, npn. See also Chandler and Nathan,

Fantastic Fair, 19. For debate over Hawaiian Annexation, see *Chronicle*, January 26, 1894; *Official History*, 256; *Chronicle*, February 26 and 28, 1894.

17. *Official History*, 162; *Monarch Souvenir of Sunset City*; and *Chronicle*, March 24, 1894. On February 10, 1894, Francisca Tehama Deer had been born in the Esquimaux Village. She died in early April. Four Inuit children had been born at the Columbian Exposition and all but one had died within a week of their birth. The surviving baby, Christopher Columbus Poliseer, died in San Francisco on April 10, 1894. At least one of these children was reported to have died of hereditary syphilis. See *Chronicle*, March 10, 1894; *Call*, April 11, 1894.

18. I have chosen to use the term *Inuit* rather than *Eskimo* since it is the current and, I hope, most respectful designation. I use *Esquimaux* when referring specifically to the village, since it was called the "Esquimaux Village," or when citing specific sources that used that term. *Chronicle*, February 26 and 28, 1894.

19. *Chronicle*, June 18, June 17, June 9, 1894. Chinese Day was announced in May, while the special days of other groups were announced in the press on January 8, 1894, and were published in guidebooks and other fair literature. Its initial announcement stated that it would take place on June 7, but it was actually held the last Sunday of the fair, June 17. These facts suggest that Chinese Day was awarded not only belatedly but also reluctantly. Similarly, Japanese Day was only listed in one guidebook and there it was assigned the wrong date, March 9. The Midwinter Fair did not feature a special day for Native Americans. It did host a Hawaiian Day that was, however, as much if not more about the United States' imperial ambitions than about native culture. The Midwinter Fair hosted an African American day that seems to have been awarded without the struggles of the Chicago Fair. Perhaps the Executive Committee had learned a lesson from the Columbian Exposition or perhaps African Americans—a small population in San Francisco compared to Asians—did not pose the same kind of threat to whites. See *Chronicle*, May 1, 1894; Evans, *All about the Midwinter Fair*, 1st ed., 85.

20. *Chronicle*, February 28, 1894; *Official History*, 150; *Chronicle*, April 1, 1894; and *Chronicle*, February 18, 1894.

21. Evans, *All about the Midwinter Fair*, 2nd ed., 153; *Examiner*, January 20, 1894; *Monarch Souvenir of Sunset City*, npn. In 1889, Article 30 of the Constitution of the Empire of Japan gave citizens the right of petition during a period in which Japan adopted new forms of Western-style governance. Voting rights for all men were not granted until 1925. See Arthur Tiedemann, *Modern Japan: A Brief History*, rev. ed. (Princeton, NJ: D. Van Nostrand, 1962). For information about Japanese immigrants, see Ronald Takaki, *Strangers from a Different Shore: A History of Asian Americans* (New York: Penguin Books, 1989), 42–53.

22. Elisabeth S. Bates, "Some Breadwinners of the Fair," *Overland Monthly*, 2nd ser., 23 (April 1894), 374–384; and *Chronicle*, June 17, 1894.

23. Although Susan Johnson has argued that communities of color frequently kept alive counter-hegemonic memories and histories of the gold rush period, the storytellers who crafted the '49 Mining Camp chose to perpetuate a strain of what came to be the culturally dominant narrative—tailored to the concerns of the

1890s—that operated in the interests of white, often elite, males. As Johnson asserts, "After the decline of California's surface diggings in the 1850s, the Gold Rush increasingly came to be remembered as the historical property of Anglo Americans, especially Anglo American men." See Susan Lee Johnson, *Roaring Camp: The Social World of the California Gold Rush* (New York: W. W. Norton, 2000), 11.

24. For testimonials to the '49 Mining Camp's popularity, see *Official History*, 152; and *California Midwinter Exposition Illustrated*, npn. Mention of "charming senoritas," can be found in Evans, *All about the Midwinter Fair*, 2nd. ed., 155–161. Data about the size and the location of the '49 Mining Camp comes from Evans, *All about the Midwinter Fair*, 1st ed.; *Official Guide*, 106; and *Chronicle*, November 24, 1893. In 1859, the newspaper editor and reformer Horace Greeley traveled overland to California, sending dispatches back to his paper, the *New York Tribune*, in support of a railroad to the Pacific. The words "go West, young man" are often attributed to him but were actually written by an Indiana editor, John Soule. Greeley, however, was a staunch proponent of organized settlement and did express many similarly phrased versions of this sentiment.

25. The incorporation of the '49 Mining Camp Company is mentioned in the *Chronicle*, November 24, 1893. The *California Midwinter Exposition Illustrated*, npn, contains information about the '49 Mining Camp Company's officers and managers.

26. The description of men at the '49 Mining Camp singing the "Days of '49" is from the *Examiner*, January 28, 1894. Robert G. Lee's work on racialization and popular songs called my attention to the significance of the recurrence of this tune. See *Orientals*, 50. For some examples of its repetition see Lee, *Monarch Souvenir of Sunset City*, npn; *Official Guide*, 106–107; *California Midwinter Exposition Illustrated*, npn; *San Francisco Examiner*, January 6, 1894; *Examiner*, January 28, 1894; and *Chronicle*, March 25, 1894. Full text of the lyrics to *The Days of '49* can be found in Richard E. Lingenfelter, comp, *Songs of the American West* (Berkeley: University of California Press, 1968), 558–559.

27. *Midwinter Appeal and the Journal of '49*, February 17, 1894. As Lee has shown, "In the 1850s, California was constructed in the popular mind as a Jacksonian community of independent small producers, miners, and pioneers. These men imagined California as a place where a lost American organic community could be reconstructed and their own identities remade." See Lee, *Orientals*, 15–31. See also Alexander Saxton, *The Indispensable Enemy: Labor and the Anti-Chinese Movement in California* (Berkeley: University of California Press, 1971), 116–121.

28. *Midwinter Appeal and the Journal of '49*, January 7, 1894. The concept of *herrenvolk* democracy is drawn from George M. Fredrickson, *The Black Image in the White Mind: The Debate on Afro-American Character and Destiny, 1817–1914* (New York: Harper and Row, 1971), 61. Fredrickson draws upon the ideas of Pierre L. van den Berghe, *Race and Racism: A Comparative Perspective* (New York: Wiley, 1967), 17–18. See also Lee, *Orientals*, 47.

29. *Official Guide*, 16–17. See also *Chronicle*, January 15, 1894; *Chronicle*, January 30, 1894; *Chronicle*, January 14, 1894; *Examiner*, January 28, 1894. Frederick Jackson Turner, "The Significance of the Frontier in American History," *Proceedings of the*

Forty-First Meeting of the State Historical Society of Wisconsin (Madison, Wisconsin, 1894), 79–112. Three important correctives to this history of gold rush society that actively grapple with and disclose its diversity and complexity are Johnson, *Roaring Camp*; Albert L. Hurtado, *Intimate Frontiers: Sex, Gender, and Culture in Old California* (Albuquerque: University of New Mexico Press, 1999); and Malcolm J. Rohrbough, *Days of Gold: The California Gold Rush and the American Nation* (Berkeley: University of California Press, 1997).

30. Curtis Hinsely has aptly termed this strategy "representation containment." See Curtis Hinsely, "Strolling through the Colonies," in Michael P. Sternberg, ed., *Walter Benjamin and the Demands of History* (Ithaca, NY: Cornell University Press, 1996) 119–140.

31. See Peter Stallybrass and Allon White, *The Politics and Poetics of Transgression* (Ithaca, NY: Cornell University Press, 1986). As they point out, "The low-Other is despised and denied at the level of political organization and social being whilst it is instrumentally constitutive of the shared imaginary repertoires of the dominant culture," 5–6.

32. Evans, *All about the Midwinter Fair*, 2nd ed., 155–161; *Monarch Souvenir of Sunset City*, npn; and *Official Guide*, 16–17. The ways in which white middle-class men of the late nineteenth century projected themselves into more "primitive" styles of masculinity has been developed by Bederman, *Manliness and Civilization*, and E. Anthony Rotundo, *American Manhood: Transformations in Masculinity from the Revolution to the Modern Era* (New York: Basic Books, 1993). Male dancers were described in the *Examiner*, January 15, 1894. While the dancers were understood to be Mexican or Spanish—the two terms were used interchangeably—it is likely that some of them were not what they appeared to be. Some names, like Miss Mamie Davidson, Señorita Amalia Monroy, Señor Edward Abrams, and Señorita Irene Hubbard are suggestive of racial masquerading and/or mixed-race descent. The names of some of the other dancers were less ambiguous: Señorita Carmen Martinez, Jose Vincent, Señorita Christina Lopez, and Francisco G. Valenzuela. It is also possible that all of these names were stage names and thus connoted nothing other than the choice of the performer. The names of performers were found in the *Chronicle*, January 14, 1894.

33. *Official History*, 162; Ninetta Eames, "The Wild and Woolly at the Fair," *Overland Monthly*, 2nd ser., 23 (April 1894): 356–373. For evidence of Native Americans as local color and landscape, see *Official Guide*, 106–107; *Call*, November 24, 1893.

34. Bederman, *Manliness and Civilization*, 20–22.

35. See Bederman, *Manliness and Civilization*, 1–44, 170–215; John Higham, "The Reorientation of American Culture in the 1890s," in John Weiss, ed., *The Origins of Modern Consciousness* (Detroit: Wayne State University Press, 1965); Jackson Lears, *No Place of Grace: Antimodernism and the Transformation of American Culture, 1880–1920* (Chicago: University of Chicago Press, 1981); Warren I. Susman, *Culture as History: The Transformation of American Society in the Twentieth Century* (New York: Pantheon Books, 1984); Peter Filene, *Him/Her/Self: Gender Identities in Modern America*, 3rd ed.

(Baltimore, MD: Johns Hopkins University Press, 1998). While the migrants to the gold fields came from a variety of areas inside and outside the nation, within San Francisco the nascent elite class was dominated by already middle-class if not elite migrants from the East, especially from eastern cities like New York and Boston. See Peter R. Decker, *Fortunes and Failures: White-Collar Mobility in Nineteenth-Century San Francisco* (Cambridge, MA: Harvard University Press, 1978).

36. *Chronicle*, January 14, 1894; *Chronicle*, November 24, 1893; and March 25, 1894. See also *Examiner*, January 28, 1894.

37. *Official Guide*, 106–107. Mining's relationship to an economy of small producers is further developed by Lee, *Orientals*, 19. Details about Frank McLaughlin can be found in *California Midwinter Exposition Illustrated*, npn.

38. *Official History*, 153, and *Chronicle*, January 8, 1894. Information on John W. Mackay, George C. Perkins, and Major Downie from Evans, *All about the Midwinter Fair*, 2nd ed., 155–161, and *Official History*, 153. As Peter Filene has pointed out, biographies in popular magazines in the 1890s frequently positioned businessmen as Napoleonic heroes embodying the militarism, physicality, and individualism of the "strenuous life." See Filene, *Him/Her/Self*, 76.

39. *Midwinter Appeal and the Journal of '49*, January 17, 1894.

40. *Chronicle*, January 15, 1894, and February 4, 1894.

41. *Chronicle*, January 15, 1894, and February 4, 1894.

42. *Chronicle*, January 15, 1894, and February 4, 1894.

43. *Chronicle*, January 15, 1894, and February 4, 1894.

44. *Chronicle*, January 15, 1894, and February 4, 1894.

45. *Chronicle*, January 15, 1894, and February 4, 1894.

46. *Chronicle*, January 15, 1894, and February 4, 1894.

47. *Official Guide*, 106–107; *Chronicle*, April 22, 1894. See also *Official Catalogue of the California Midwinter International Exposition*, 154.

48. Mark Twain needs little in the way of introduction but Joaquin Miller and Bret Harte are less well known. Joaquin Miller, known as "the poet of the Sierras," migrated to Oregon from Ohio when he was an adolescent. He adopted his name from the legendary California bandit, Joaquin Murietta, and became a colorful character who dressed in a buckskin coat and red shirt and wore his hair in long, blonde tresses. On his visits to Europe he personified the rugged American West and in fact set the prototype for the "Man of the Wild West" whom Buffalo Bill imitated. As a poet he used embellished episodes from his own life—and sometimes even outright fabricated events—to create and sustain an image of the mythic West. Francis Bret Harte was born in Albany, New York, in 1839 and migrated to California at the age of fifteen. In 1868, he became the first editor of the *Overland Monthly* and for it he wrote most of his best-known frontier literature and local color stories although he only had limited experiences in gold rush mining camps.

49. For the development of this trend in preservation, see David Glassberg, *Sense of History: The Place of the Past in American Life* (Amherst: University of Massachusetts Press, 2001), 173–175. Some pioneers also participated in these efforts.

50. Bates, "Some Breadwinners at the Fair," 374–384.

51. These figures on the Panic of 1893 are from the Utah History Encyclopedia located at: http://eddy.media.utah.edu/medsol/UCME/p/PANIC1893.html; *Chronicle*, January 10, 1894.

52. *Examiner*, January 6, 1894 and *Call*, July 13, 1893.

53. Chandler and Nathan, *Fantastic Fair*, 21, briefly discuss the gum girls; *Examiner*, February 11, 1894; *Examiner*, January 28, 1894; *Official Catalogue of the California Midwinter International Exposition*, npn. Dahomean women were from Dahomey, Africa.

54. For discussion of places of amusement as sites of gender politics see: Kathy Peiss, *Cheap Amusements: Working Women and Leisure in Turn-of-the-Century New York* (Philadelphia: Temple University Press, 1986); Elaine Tyler May, *Great Expectations: Marriage and Divorce in Post-Victorian America* (Chicago: University of Chicago Press, 1980); and John Kasson, *Amusing the Million: Coney Island at the Turn-of-the-Century* (New York: Hill and Wang, 1978).

55. *Examiner*, February 11, 1894. See also *Examiner*, January 28, 1894.

56. *Examiner*, February 11, 1894; *Chronicle*, May 6, 1894. The women who worked at the Tamale Cottage were also said to "flirt coquettishly with the patrons who sit around the tables eating tamales," *Official Catalogue of the California Midwinter International Exposition*, npn. That the climate of heterosociability could proved dangerous was attested to by the results of a contest, run by The Irish Whiskey, in which one of the "young ladies employed in various capacities in the Agriculture building" was judged the "Most Popular Lady, Midwinter Fair, '94," *Chronicle*, June 21, 1894. Mrs. Bessie Findlay, the winner, was subsequently shot and wounded by her abusive, idle, and alcoholic husband in a fit of jealousy prompted by her victory as well as the fact that she and a girlfriend were escorted home by two boys they had met in the Manufactures Building, *Examiner*, July 9, 1894.

57. *Examiner*, February 11, 1894; *Chronicle*, November 29, 1893; and *Examiner*, January 4, 1894.

58. *Examiner*, January 4, 1894 and *Examiner*, January 6, 1894. See also Nathan and Chandler, *Fantastic Fair*, 22–23.

59. *Examiner*, January 4 and January 6, 1894.

60. *Chronicle*, January 8, 1894, and *Examiner*, January 10, 1894. The *danse du ventre* is also known as belly dancing.

61. *Call*, April 10, 1894.

62. *Examiner*, July 9, 1894. See also Chandler and Nathan, *Fantastic Fair*, 63–65.

63. *Examiner*, July 9 and July 10, 1894.

64. *Examiner*, July 9 and 10, 1894.

65. *Examiner*, July 9 and 10, 1894. On July 10, 1894, the *Examiner* reported that there may have been a different dancer for the first performance and thus cast doubt on the credibility of Jennie Johnson's assertions that "Al Morris, the spieler who had charge of the exhibition, threatened to have her arrested for taking part in the dance on Saturday night." Although the press suggested that Miss Johnson may have been

trying to "evade some portion of the responsibility resting upon her," the evidence still points to coercion. This was not an example of an empowered sex worker.

66. Historian David Montgomery has identified the period from 1873 to 1897 as one of an ongoing deflationary crisis with "endemic conflicts over wages and the costs of production." Two key strikes of the 1890s framed the financial panic of 1893—the Homestead Strike of 1892 and the Pullman Strike of 1894. Both were viewed by many Americans fearful of the ways society was changing as profound manifestations of social disorder. In San Francisco, while the depression and an employer-led city-wide open-shop drive of the early 1890s squelched many of the gains labor had made in the 1880s, by the late 1890s labor activism and union membership was at an unprecedented high. See David Montgomery, *The Fall of the House of Labor: The Workplace, the State, and American Labor Activism, 1865–1925* (New York: Cambridge University Press, 1987), 5, and Issel and Cherny, *San Francisco, 1865–1932: Politics, Power, and Urban Development* (Berkeley: University of California Press, 1986), 80–82.

67. *Call*, July 27, 1893. See also *Call*, July 27, 1893; *Call*, August 10, 1893. See *Call*, July 13, 1893, and *Call*, July 30, 1893, for the deluge of unemployed that besieged the offices of the Midwinter Fair's secretary, Alexander Badlam. This name was used in the *Examiner*, January 24, 1893. The relief effort was also referred to as "The Unemployed Movement" and "the Relief Committee." Adjacent coverage was especially true in the *Examiner*.

68. Alan Trachtenberg, in *The Incorporation of America*, has shown that at Chicago's Columbian Exposition, the laborers who built the fairgrounds were both carefully controlled and concealed. Workers at the Midwinter Fair were undoubtedly subject to various controls. For example, the *Call* rather cryptically reported on July 18, 1893 that "At the regular meeting of the executive committee a complete set of bylaws and rules were adopted for the government of the committee, and giving the director-general full power over the operations and employees of the exposition 'to assume and employ all such executive powers as shall be necessary to secure promptness, efficiency, and good faith in every department of the work.'" In early September 1893, a group called the United Brotherhood of Labor circulated a flyer titled, "Facts Concerning the Midwinter Fair" that alleged that Buckman and Warren, a team of contractors, "compel you to board in their camp, work you like a convict, give you food that many dogs would not touch, pay $1 per day at the expiration of 30 days, or discount you ten percent." However, the large numbers of unemployed made it impossible and undesirable for them to be completely concealed, in part because publicity about employing the unemployed reflected favorably on the fair management.

69. *Call*, July 30, 1893. For similar sentiments about preferential employment of city residents, see the *Call*, July 27, 1893, *Call*, November 26, 1893; *Call*, August 1, 1893; *Call*, August 2, 1893; *Call*, August 10, 1893. It is also worth noting that organized labor was craft-based at this time and more involved with securing work for its skilled membership than aiding the unemployed. For example, the Building Trades Union offered one day's pay to the fair fund from "every man engaged in building or whose work brings him in contact with builders and who is a member of

a labor organization" in exchange for limiting work on fair buildings to local labor, *Call*, July 17, 1893. Similarly, the Carpenters' and Joiners' Union of Stockton submitted a petition to the managers of the Midwinter Fair asking for work on the buildings to be erected, promising to give one day's labor each month for the benefit of the fair, *Call*, August 2, 1893.

70. *Examiner*, January 3, 1894; *Examiner*, January 1, 1894; *Examiner*, January 6, 1894; *Chronicle*, January 30, 1894 and *Chronicle*, February 3, 1894. These lay-offs were unwelcome news for the men who depended on the dollar-a-day wage provided by work in the park. *Chronicle*, January 26, 1894.

71. *Chronicle*, January 1, 1894; *Examiner*, January 3, 1894. For the practice of requiring letters to confirm, see *Examiner*, January 4 and 16, 1894, and *Chronicle*, January 10, 1894.

72. *Chronicle*, January 6 and January 28, 1894.

73. *Examiner*, January 13 and 14, 1894.

74. *Chronicle*, January 1, 1894.

75. *Chronicle*, February 4, 1894; *Examiner*, January 26, 1894; *Chronicle*, January 10, 1894. The Committee for the Relief of the Unemployed limited its relief efforts to aiding unemployed men. In part, this was due to common attitudes that viewed women workers as superfluous because their wages supposedly did not support families. See Alice Kessler Harris, *Out to Work: A History of Wage-Earning Women in the United States* (New York: Oxford University Press, 1982). For similar representations of the worthy poor, see *Chronicle*, January 17, 1894; *Examiner*, January 17, 1894; *Chronicle*, January 2, 22, 26, 27, 1894; and *Examiner*, January 29, 1894. For other examples of the park workers' industry, see *Examiner*, January 27, 1894 and *Chronicle*, January 27, 1894; *Chronicle*, March 1, 1894; and *Chronicle*, March 4, 1894. For other examples of appropriate gratitude, see *Chronicle*, January 9 and January 15, 1894; *Examiner*, January 18, 23, 24, 1894, and February 10, 1894.

76. *Chronicle*, January 10, 1894.

77. *Chronicle*, Thursday, March 1, 1894.

78. *Call*, August 2, 1893. The same sentiments were expressed in the *Call*, July 30, 1893; August 10, 1893; July 27, 1893; July 18, 1893; *Call*, August 30, 1893; *Call*, August 6, 1893; and *Call*, August 9 and 10, 1893; and *Chronicle*, March 14, 1894.

79. *Chronicle*, February 3, 1894; *Call*, August 2, 1893, and August 10, 1893. In return for their generosity, newsboys and other working children were admitted to the fair without charge on Saturday, March 31, 1894—*Chronicle* Day. A week later, 1,500 newsboys were given an additional day at the fair that was sponsored by the *Daily Report* and the concessionaires. However, while the executive committee of the Midwinter Exposition was willing to demonstrate its charitable generosity by throwing its doors open to the city's children, it was less willing to readily make the fair affordable for working adults—admittedly the backbone of the fair's financial support. After numerous contentious meetings, members of the committee did agree to drop the admission fee from fifty cents to twenty-five cents on the weekends and after five o'clock in the evening on weekdays. Although it took them until mid-May to adopt this plan that

was initially proposed in January, it met with great public approval and considerably increased attendance at the fair. See *Chronicle*, March 16, 1894; *Chronicle*, March 23, 1894; *Chronicle*, March 28 and 29, 1894; *Chronicle*, January 5, 1894; *Chronicle*, March 6, 1894; *Chronicle*, April 11, 1894; *Call*, May 6, 1894; *Call*, May 13, 1894; and *Call*, May 14, 1894.

80. *Examiner*, January 19, 1894; *Examiner*, January 14 and 15, 1894; and *Chronicle*, March 4, 1894. For other community-lead relief efforts, see *Chronicle*, January 9, 1894; *Examiner*, January 20, 1894; and *Chronicle*, January 6, 1894.

81. *Chronicle*, January 22, 1894; United Brotherhood of Labor, "Facts Concerning the Midwinter Fair."

82. *Call*, July 27, 1893.

Conclusion: Creating An American Place: Cultural Ordering's Broader Implications

1. Amy Kaplan, "'Left Alone with America': The Absence of Empire in the Study of American Culture," in Amy Kaplan and Donald Pease, eds., *Cultures of United States Imperialism* (Durham, NC: Duke University Press, 1993), 17. The idea of this formulation tying groups together in the same story is drawn from Patricia Nelson Limerick, *Legacy of Conquest: The Unbroken Past of the American West* (New York: W. W. Norton, 1987), 27.

2. Frederick Jackson Turner, "The Significance of the Frontier in American History," *Proceedings of the Forty-First Meeting of the State Historical Society of Wisconsin* (Madison, Wisconsin, 1894), 79–112. Quotation about population density from Harold P. Simonson, Introduction to Frederick Jackson Turner, *The Significance of the Frontier in American History*, Harold P. Simonson, ed. (New York: Frederick Ungar, 1963), 8, as quoted in Limerick, *Legacy of Conquest*, 23. The population figures Turner used privileged private property in ways that failed to account for large tracts of unoccupied federal lands and the less clear-cut kinds of property claims of grazing and mining rights.

3. Arthur M. Schlesinger, Sr., *The Rise of the City, 1878–1898* (New York: Macmillan, 1933); Richard C. Wade, *The Urban Frontier: Pioneer Life in Early Pittsburgh, Cincinnati, Lexington, Louisville, and St. Louis* (Cambridge, MA: Harvard University Press, 1959), 1; John W. Reps, *Cities of the American West: A History of Frontier Urban Planning* (Princeton, NJ: Princeton University Press, 1979), 667. See also John. M. Findlay, "Far Western Cityscapes and American Culture Since 1940," *Western Historical Quarterly* 22 (February 1991): 21.

4. Gunther Barth, *Instant Cities: Urbanization and the Rise of San Francisco and Denver* (New York: Oxford University Press, 1975), 185–186. Lawrence Larsen contended that by 1880, a city life familiar to easterners was plainly visible in the West. This was because "Americans built cities west of the ninety-fifth meridian that were carbon copies of those constructed earlier in the older parts of the country." John Reps, echoing

these sentiments, wrote that "Western cities by 1890 closely resembled older communities east of the Great Plains." Earl Pomeroy, writing about the Far West, was one of the few to capture some of the complexity of western cities. He wrote, "The Pacific Slope is both the most Western and, after the East itself, the most Eastern part of America. No other section is more like the Atlantic seaboard and Western Europe; no part is more different; and no part has wished more to be both." See Lawrence Larsen, *The Urban West at the End of the Frontier* (Lawrence, KS: Regents Press of Kansas, 1978), xi; Reps, *Cities of the American West*, 667; and Earl Pomeroy, *The Pacific Slope: A History of California, Oregon, Washington, Idaho, Utah, and Nevada* (New York: Alfred A. Knopf, 1965), 3.

5. Limerick, *Legacy of Conquest*, 27.

6. Gray Brechin, *Imperial San Francisco: Urban Power, Earthly Ruin* (Berkeley: University of California Press, 1999), xxiii. See also William Issel, "Liberalism and Urban Policy in San Francisco from the 1930s to the 1960s," *Western Historical Quarterly* 22 (November 1991): 431–450, and Robert W. Cherny, "Patterns of Toleration and Discrimination in San Francisco: The Civil War to World War I," *California History* 73 (Summer 1994): 130–141.

7. Findlay, "Far Western Cityscapes," 41.

8. For a work that masterfully analyzes the intersection of physical spaces, cultural production, and social power in twentieth-century Los Angeles in just this way, see Eric Avila, *Popular Culture in the Age of White Flight: Fear and Fantasy in Suburban Los Angeles* (Berkeley: University of California, 2004).

Bibliography

Primary Sources

Address of Hon. Newton Booth at the Opening of the 6th Industrial Exhibition, August 8, 1868. San Francisco: Dewey, 1868.

A.H.B. "Impressions on Arriving in San Francisco" *Pioneer, or California Monthly Magazine,* September 1854.

A.M. "A Glimpse of San Francisco," *Lippincott's Magazine* (June 1870).

Ames, J. W. "A Day in Chinatown." *Lippincott's Magazine* (October 1875).

Announcement of the Mechanics' Institute 28th Industrial Exhibition, 1895.

The Argonaut Sketchbook, Mechanics' Fair, 1877.

The Argonaut Sketchbook, Mechanics' Fair, 1878.

Avila, Eric. *Popular Culture in the Age of White Flight: Fear and Fantasy in Suburban Los Angeles.* Berkeley: University of California, 2004.

Ayers, James J. *Gold and Sunshine,* published in 1922. Excerpted in *San Francisco Memoirs, 1835–1851: Eyewitness Accounts of the Birth of a City,* edited by Malcolm E. Barker. San Francisco: Londonborn Publications, 1994.

Baldwin, C. "A Celestial Colony," *Lippincott's Magazine,* February 1881.

Bancroft, Hubert Howe. *History of California,* vol. 5, 1846–1848. San Francisco: History Company, 1886.

———. *The Works of Hubert Howe Bancroft.* San Francisco: History Company, 1888. Excerpted in *The Western Gate: A San Francisco Reader,* edited by Joseph Henry Jackson. New York: Farrar, Straus, and Young, 1952.

Bancroft's Tourist Guide. San Francisco: A. L. Bancroft, 1871.

Bates, Elisabeth S. "Some Breadwinners of the Fair." *Overland Monthly,* 2nd ser., 23 (April 1894).

Biart, Lucien. *My Rambles in the New World,* translated by Mary de Hauteville. London: Sampson Low, Marston, Searle and Rivington, 1877.

Bode, William Walter. *Lights and Shadows of Chinatown.* San Francisco: H. S. Crocker, 1896.

Brooks, Noah. "Restaurant Life in San Francisco." *Overland Monthly,* 1st ser., 1 (November 1868).

Brooks, Will. "A Fragment of China." *Californian* 6, no. 31 (July 1882).

Browne, A. E. *A Trip to California, Alaska, and the Yellowstone Park,* vol. 1. Unpublished travel journal, ca. 1891 Beinecke Library, Yale University.

Brown, Ethel Malone. "Woodward's Gardens." In *Vignettes of Early San Francisco Homes and Gardens*, edited by Mrs. Silas H. Palmer. December 1935 Program of the San Francisco Garden Club.

Brown, John Henry. *His Reminiscences and Incidents of the Early Days of San Francisco 1845–1850* (first published in 1886). Excerpted in *San Francisco Memoirs, 1835–1851: Eyewitness Accounts of the Birth of a City*, edited by Malcolm E. Barker. San Francisco: Londonborn Publications, 1994.

Caldwell, Eleanor B. "The Picturesque in Chinatown." *Arthur's Home Magazine* 65, no. 8 (August 1895), and *New Petersen Magazine* 4, no. 1 (July 1894).

"A California Caravansary." *Harper's New Monthly Magazine* 24, no. 203 (April 1867).

California Midwinter Exposition Illustrated, Official Souvenir: Illustrations and Descriptions of All Prominent Buildings, Biographical Sketches, Synoptical History of Early California, Notice of Concessions, etc. San Francisco: Robert A. Irving, 1894.

"Caravansaries of San Francisco" *Overland Monthly*, 1st ser., 5 (August 1870).

Carey, D.D., Joseph. *By the Golden Gate or San Francisco, the Queen City of the Pacific Coast: With Scenes and Incidents Characteristic of Its Life*. Albany, New York: Albany Diocesan Press, 1902.

" 'China Town' in San Francisco, by Day and By Night." *Cornhill Magazine*, July 1886.

"The Chinese at Home and Abroad." *Hutchings' Illustrated California Magazine*, vol. 5, 1860–1861.

"Chinese Highbinders." *Harper's Weekly*, February 13, 1890.

"The Chinese in San Francisco." *Harper's Weekly*, March 20, 1880.

"A Chinese Miracle. A Strange Scene in a Joss House—A Reporter Takes a Peep behind the Scenes." Undated article from the *San Francisco Chronicle* in *The Chinese Invasion: Revealing the Habits, Manners, and Customs of the Chinese, Political Social and Religious, on the Pacific Coast, Coming in Contact with the Free and Enlightened Citizens of America; Containing Careful Selections from the San Francisco Press*, compiled by H. J. West. San Francisco: Excelsior Office, Bacon and Company Printers, 1873.

Clifford, Josephine. "Chinatown" *Potter's American Monthly* (May 1880).

Connor, J. Torrey. "A Western View of the Chinese in the United States." *Chautauquan: A Weekly Newsmagazine*, Vol. 32, No. 4, January 1901.

Constitution, By-Laws, Rules and Regulations of the Mechanics' Institute of the City of San Francisco, 1855.

Constitution, By-Laws, Rules and Regulations of the Mechanics' Institute of the City of San Francisco, California. San Francisco: J. R. Brodie, 1885.

Craft, Mabel C. "Some Days and Nights in Little China" *National Magazine* (November 1897).

Dana, Richard Henry. *Two Years before the Mast*, rev. ed., 1869. Excerpted in *More San Francisco Memoirs, 1852–1899: The Ripening Years*, edited by Malcolm E. Barker. San Francisco: Londonborn Publications, 1996.

Dawson, Emma Frances. "The Dramatic in My Destiny." *Californian* 1, no. 1 (January 1880).

de Russailh, Albert Benard. *Last Adventure*. San Francisco: Westgate Press, 1931. Excerpted in *This Was San Francisco: Being First-hand Accounts of the Evolution of One of America's Favorite Cities*, edited by Oscar Lewis. New York: David McKay, 1962.

Delano, Alonzo. "On 'Long Wharf'" In *The Western Gate Reader*, edited by Joseph Henry Jackson. New York: Farrar, Straus, and Young, 1952.

Densmore, G. B. *The Chinese in California: Description of Chinese Life in San Francisco, Their Habits, Morals, and Manners*, illustrated by Voegtlin. San Francisco: Pettit and Russ, 1880.

Disturnell's Strangers' Guide to San Francisco and Vicinity: A Complete and Reliable Book of Reference for Tourists and Other Strangers Visiting the Metropolis of the Pacific. San Francisco: W. C. Disturnell, 1883.

Doxey, William. *Doxey's Guide to San Francisco and the Pleasure Resorts of California*. San Francisco: At the Sign of the Lark, 1897.

Eames, Ninetta. "The Wild and Woolly at the Fair." *Overland Monthly*, 2nd ser., 23 (April 1894).

E.G.H. *Surprise Land: A Girl's Letters from the West*. Boston: Cupples, Upham, 1887.

Evans, Taliesin. *All about the Midwinter Fair, San Francisco, and Interesting Facts Concerning California*. 1st ed. San Francisco: W. B. Bancroft, 1894.

——. *All about the Midwinter Fair, San Francisco, and Interesting Facts Concerning California*. 2nd ed. San Francisco: W. B. Bancroft, 1894.

Farwell, Willard B. *The Chinese at Home and Abroad: Together with the Report of the Special Committee of the Board of Supervisors of San Francisco on the Condition of the Chinese Quarter of That City*. San Francisco: A. L. Bancroft, 1885.

Fitch, George Hamlin. "The City by the Golden Gate." *Chautauquan* 23, no. 6 (September 1896).

Fremont, Jessie Benton. *A Year of American Travel*. Excerpted in *This Was San Francisco: Being First-hand Accounts of the Evolution of One of America's Favorite Cities*, edited by Oscar Lewis. New York: David McKay, 1962.

Gibson, A. M., Rev. O. *The Chinese in America*. Cincinnati: Hitchcock and Walden, 1877.

Gleadell, W. H. "Night Scenes in Chinatown." *Eclectic Magazine* (September 1895).

Green, E. M. "The Chinese Theater" *Overland Monthly*, 2nd ser., 21 (February 1903).

Greene, Charles S. "The Restaurants of San Francisco" *Overland Monthly*, 2nd ser., 20 (December 1892).

Guidebook and Street Manual of San Francisco, California. San Francisco: F. W. Warner, 1882.

Handbook of the Pacific Museum of Anatomy and Science. San Francisco: 1865.

The Handbook and Descriptive Catalogue of the Pacific Museum of Anatomy and Natural Science. San Francisco: Commercial Steam Printing House, 1869 and 1874.

Hardy, Iza Duffus. "In China Town" *Belgravia: An Illustrated London Magazine* (January 1881).

Hittell, John S. *A History of the City of San Francisco and Incidentally of the State of California*. San Francisco: A. L. Bancroft, 1878.

———. *A Guidebook to San Francisco*. San Francisco: Bancroft, 1888.

Holbrook, Rev. J. C. "Chinadom in California." *Hutchings' Illustrated California Magazine* 4, 1859–1860.

Holden, C. P. "The Opium Industry in America," *Scientific American* 77, no. 10 (March 5, 1898).

Hole, James, Esq. *An Essay on the History and Management of Literary, Scientific, and Mechanics' Institutes*. London: Longman, Brown, Green, and Longmans, 1853.

Illustrated Guide and Catalogue of Woodward's Gardens. San Francisco: Francis and Valentine, 1873.

Illustrated Guide and Catalogue of Woodward's Gardens. San Francisco: Francis and Valentine, 1875.

Illustrated Guide and Catalogue of Woodward's Gardens, compiled by F. Gruber. San Francisco: Francis Valentine and Co., 1879.

Irwin, Will. *The City That Was: A Requiem of Old San Francisco*. New York: B. W. Huebsch, 1906.

———, ed. *Old Chinatown: A Book of Pictures by Arnold Genthe*. New York: Mitchell and Kennerly, 1908.

"John Chinaman in San Francisco." *Scribner's Monthly* 17, no. 6 (October 1876).

Jordan, Dr. Louis J. *The Philosophy of Marriage, Being Four Important Lectures on the Functions and Disorders of the Nervous System and Reproductive Organs, Illustrated with Cases*. San Francisco: Donald Bruce's Book and Job Printing House, 1865.

Keeler, Charles. *San Francisco and Thereabout*. San Francisco: California Promotional Committee, 1903.

Kessler, D. E. "An Evening in Chinatown." *Overland Monthly and Out West Magazine* 49, no. 5 (May 1907).

Kipling, Rudyard. "How I Got to San Francisco and Took Tea with the Natives There." Excerpted in *More San Francisco Memoirs, 1852–1899: The Ripening Years*, edited by Malcolm E. Barker. San Francisco: Londonborn Publications, 1996.

———. *Rudyard Kipling's Letters from San Francisco*. San Francisco: Colt Press, 1949.

Knapp, Henry R. *Chinatown*. San Francisco, 1889.

Knight, Maria. "Early Days in San Francisco: A Near View of Vigilante Times." *Overland Monthly*, 2nd ser., 30 (July 1897).

"The 'Labor Question' on the Pacific Coast," *Harper's Weekly* (October 13, 1888).

Langley, Henry G., compiler. *The San Francisco Directory, For the Year Commencing October 1864*. San Francisco: Excelsior Steam Presses, Towne and Bacon, Book and Job Printers, 1864.

"Lenz's World Tour." *Outing, An Illustrated Monthly Magazine of Recreation* 22, no. 5 (August 1893).

Littleton, L. A. "Chinese Mythology in San Francisco." *Overland Monthly and Out West Magazine* 1, no. 6 (June 1883).

Lloyd, B. E. *Lights and Shades in San Francisco* San Francisco: A. L. Bancroft, 1876.

MacGregor, William Laird. *Hotels and Hotel Life at San Francisco California, in 1876*. San Francisco: S.F. News, 1877.

Marryat, Frank. *Mountains and Molehills or Recollections of a Burnt Journal*, with Introduction and Notes by Marguerite Wilbur. Stanford, CA: Stanford University Press, 1952 (originally published 1855).

Masters, Frederic J., D.D. "The Chinese Drama." *Chautauquan: A Weekly Newsmagazine* (July 1895).

McDowell, Henry Burden. "The Chinese Theater." *Century Illustrated Monthly Magazine* (November 1884).

The Monarch Souvenir of Sunset City and Sunset Scenes: Being Views of California Midwinter Fair and Famous Scenes in the Golden State. San Francisco: H. S. Crocker, 1894.

Morris, Mrs. James Edwin (Ida Dorman). *A Pacific Coast Vacation—Illustrated from Photographs Taken En Route*. London: Abbey Press, 1901.

Neville, Amelia Ransome. *The Fantastic City: Memoirs of the Social and Romantic Life of Old San Francisco*. Boston and New York: Houghton Mifflin, 1932.

New California Tourists' Guide to San Francisco and Vicinity. San Francisco: Samuel Carson, 1886.

Norris, Frank. *The Third Circle*. New York: John Lane, 1909.

O'Connell, Daniel. *The Inner Man: Good Things to Eat and Drink and Where to Get Them*. San Francisco: Bancroft, 1891.

The Official Catalogue of the California Midwinter International Exposition: A Reference Book of Exhibitors and Exhibits, Officers and Members of the California Midwinter International Exposition, Together with Descriptions of all General, State, and Other Buildings, Etc. San Francisco: Harvey, Whitcher and Allen, 1894.

Official Guide to the California Midwinter Exposition, 1st ed., Compiled from Official Sources under the Direct Supervision of the Exposition Management. San Francisco: George Spalding, 1894.

The Official History of the California Midwinter International Exposition: A Descriptive Record of the Origin, Development and Success of the Great Industrial Expositional Enterprise, Held in San Francisco from January to July 1894. San Francisco: H. S. Crocker, 1895.

O'Meara, James. "San Francisco in Early Days." *Overland Monthly*, 2nd ser., 1 (February 1883).

The Palace Hotel, San Francisco. Prospectus, Signed: A. D. Sharon and G. Schonewald, lessees, 1875.

Peixotto, Ernest C. *Ten Drawings in Chinatown with Certain Observations by Robert Howe Fletcher*. San Francisco: A. M. Robertson, 1898.

Phelan, James D. "Is the Midwinter Fair a Benefit?" *Overland Monthly*, 2nd ser., 23 (April 1894).

The Pocket Exchange Guide of San Francisco. San Francisco: Tiffany and MacDonald, 1875.

Programme of Woodward's Gardens, 1885.

Purdy, Helen Throop. *San Francisco as It Was, as It Is, and How to See It*. San Francisco: Paul Elder, 1912.

Report of the Second Industrial Exhibition, 1858.

Report of the 20th Industrial Exhibition, 1885.

Report of the 21st Industrial Exhibition, 1886.

Report of the 23rd Industrial Exhibition, 1888.

Report of the 24th Industrial Exposition, 1889.

Report of the 25th Industrial Exposition, 1890.

Report of the 26th Industrial Exposition, 1891.

"Restaurants and Their Function." *Nation,* November 2, 1865.

Royce, Sarah. *A Frontier Lady: Recollections of the Gold Rush and Early California.* New Haven, CT: Yale University Press, 1932.

San Francisco Classified Business Directory, 1906.

The San Francisco Illustrated Directory for Hotels and Steamers. San Francisco: Amos Currier, 1878.

"San Francisco's Chinatown," in *Seen by the Spectator; Being a Selection of Rambling Papers First Published in the Outlook, under the Title The Spectator.* New York: Outlook, 1902.

Scott, Rev. Dr. *The Mechanics' Industrial Exhibition, or the Useful Arts Exponents of the Nature, Progress, and Hope of Christian Civilization.* A Discourse Delivered in Calvary Church, Sunday evening, August 23, 1857. San Francisco: Hutchings and Rosenfield, 1857.

"Seeing the Sights." *Century Illustrated Magazine* 65, no. 6 (April 1903).

Senger, Lucy Alice Harrison Pownall. Letters to her parents, March 18, 1877–August 31, 1878. [Huntington Library PW 851–922].

Shaw, William. *Golden Dreams and Waking Realities,* published in 1851. Excerpted in *San Francisco Memoirs, 1835–1851: Eyewitness Accounts of the Birth of a City,* edited by Malcolm E. Barker. San Francisco: Londonborn Publications, 1994.

Simonin, Louis Laurent, from an article published in the French magazine *Le Tour du Monde.* Excerpted in *More San Francisco Memoirs, 1852–1899: The Ripening Years,* edited by Malcolm E. Barker. San Francisco: Londonborn Publications, 1996.

Soulé, Frank, John H. Gihon, and James Nisbet. *The Annals of San Francisco.* Berkeley, CA: Berkeley Hills Books, 1999 (originally published in 1855).

Springfield Daily Republican, August 31, 1875. In *San Francisco: A Chronological and Documentary History, 1542–1970,* edited and compiled by Robert Mayer. New York: Oceana Press, 1974.

Stellman, Louis J. *Chinatown: A Pictorial Souvenir and Guide.* Unpublished manuscript, 1917.

Stoddard, Charles Warren. *A Bit of Old China.* San Francisco: A. M. Robertson, 1912. Excerpted from *In the Footprints of the Padres.* San Francisco: A. M. Robertson, 1901.

A Street and Avenue Guide of San Francisco. San Francisco: Henry G. Langley, 1875.

Taber, Isaiah West. *Hints to Strangers.* San Francisco: Taber, 188-.

Taylor, Bayard. *El Dorado, Or Adventures in the Path of Empire.* New Mexico: Rio Grande Press, 1967 (first published 1850).

Turnbull, Walter. Scrapbook of clippings of San Francisco area affairs: telegrams, drawings, letters to and from Turnbull (1882–1885), California Scrapbook, 27, Huntington Library.

"Two Great Cities, by an American." *Cornhill Magazine* 17 (June 1868).

United Brotherhood of Labor, "Facts Concerning the Midwinter Fair."

Watson, Mary. *San Francisco Society: Its Characters and Its Characteristics.* San Francisco: Francis, Valentine, 1887.

White, Roland. "The Humbler Restaurants of San Francisco," *Overland Monthly,* 2nd ser, 41 (May 1903).

Wierzbicki, F. P. *California as It Is and It May Be: Or, a Guide to the Gold Fields.* Excerpted in *This Was San Francisco: Being First-hand Accounts of the Evolution of One of America's Favorite Cities,* edited by Oscar Lewis. New York: David McKay, 1962.

Williams, Henry F. *Opening Address, Delivered at the Inauguration of the Fair of the Mechanics' Institute.* San Francisco: Whitton, Towne, 1857.

Williams, Samuel. "The City of the Golden Gate." *Scribner's Monthly,* July 1875. Excerpted in *This Was San Francisco: Being First-hand Accounts of the Evolution of One of America's Favorite Cities,* edited by Oscar Lewis. New York: David McKay, 1962.

Wolf, Alice S. "Two Gourmets of Bloomfield." *Overland Monthly,* Vol. 20, 2nd Series, September 1892.

Wood, E. W. *Life and Experience of Prof. E. W. Wood Appertaining to the Opium Habit of the Chinese.* New York: Dick's Publishing House, 18 –.

Local Newspapers

California Police Gazette
California Weekly Mercury
Daily Alta California
Daily Dramatic Chronicle
Industrial Fair Gazette
Mechanics' Fair Daily Press
Midwinter Appeal and the Journal of '49
Our Daily Circular
Pacific Rural Press
San Francisco Call
San Francisco Chronicle
San Francisco Evening Bulletin
San Francisco Examiner
San Francisco News

Secondary Sources

Almaguer, Tomás. *Racial Faultlines: The Historical Origins of White Supremacy in California.* Berkeley: University of California Press, 1994.

Altrocchi, Julia Cooley. *The Spectacular San Franciscans.* New York: E. P. Dutton, 1949.

Ames, Kenneth. *Death in the Dining Room and Other Tales of Victorian Culture.* Philadelphia: Temple University Press, 1992.

Asbury, Herbert. *The Barbary Coast: An Informal History of the San Francisco Underworld.* New York: Capricorn Books, 1933.

Barker, Malcolm E., ed. *San Francisco Memoirs, 1835–1851: Eyewitness Accounts of the Birth of a City.* San Francisco: Londonborn Publications, 1994.

Barnhart, Jacqueline Baker. *The Fair but Frail: Prostitution in San Francisco, 1849–1900.* Reno: University of Nevada Press, 1986.

Barth, Gunther. *Instant Cities: Urbanization and the Rise of San Francisco and Denver.* New York: Oxford University Press, 1975.

Bederman, Gail. *Manliness and Civilization: A Cultural History of Gender and Race in the United States, 1880–1917.* Chicago: University of Chicago Press, 1996.

Beebe, Lucius, and Charles Clegg. *San Francisco's Golden Era: A Picture Story of San Francisco before the Fire.* Berkeley, CA: Howell-North Books, 1960.

Berger, Frances de Talavera. *Sumptuous Dining in Gaslight San Francisco, 1875–1915.* New York: Doubleday, 1985.

Blumin, Stuart. *The Emergence of the Middle Class: Social Experience in the American City, 1760–1900.* New York: Cambridge University Press, 1989.

Boyer, Paul. *Urban Masses and Moral Order in America, 1820–1920.* Cambridge, MA: Harvard University Press, 1978.

Brechin, Gray. *Imperial San Francisco: Urban Power, Earthly Ruin.* Berkeley: University of California Press, 1999.

Brigham, David R. *Public Culture in the Early Republic: Peale's Museum and Its Audience.* Washington, D.C.: Smithsonian Institution Press, 1995.

Broussard, Albert S. *Black San Francisco: The Struggle for Racial Equality in the West, 1900–1954.* Lawrence: University Press of Kansas, 1993.

Bullough, William. *The Blind Boss and His City: Christopher Augustine Buckley and Nineteenth-Century San Francisco.* Berkeley: University of California Press, 1979.

Burchell, Robert A. *The San Francisco Irish: 1846–1880.* Manchester, UK: Manchester University Press, 1979.

Burke, Martin J. *The Conundrum of Class: Public Discourse on the Social Order in America.* Chicago: University of Chicago Press, 1995.

Bushman, Richard L. *The Refinement of America: Persons, Houses, Cities.* New York: Random House, 1992.

Butler, Anne. *Daughters of Joy: Sisters of Misery: Prostitutes in the American West, 1865–1890.* Urbana: University of Illinois Press, 1985.

Butsch, Richard. "Introduction: Leisure and Hegemony in America." In *For Fun and Profit: The Transformation of Leisure in Consumption,* edited by Richard Butsch. Philadelphia: Temple University Press, 1990.

Chan, Sucheng. *Asian Americans: An Interpretive History.* Boston: Twayne, 1991.

———, ed. *Entry Denied: Exclusion and the Chinese Community in America, 1882–1943.* Philadelphia: Temple University Press, 1991.

Chandler, Arthur, and Marvin Nathan. *The Fantastic Fair: The Story of the California Midwinter International Exposition, Golden Gate Park, San Francisco, 1894*. St. Paul, MN: Pogo Press, 1993.

Chen, Yong. *Chinese San Francisco, 1850–1943: A Trans-Pacific Community*. Stanford, CA: Stanford University Press, 2000.

Cherny, Robert W., "Patterns of Toleration and Discrimination in San Francisco: The Civil War to World War I." *California History* 73 (Summer 1994): 130–141.

Choy, Philip P.; Dong, Lorraine; and Hong, Marlon K., eds. *The Coming Man: Nineteenth-Century American Perceptions of the Chinese*. Seattle: University of Washington Press, 1994.

Chudacoff, Howard P. *The Age of the Bachelor: Creating an American Subculture*. Princeton, NJ: Princeton University Press, 1999.

Cook, James W. *The Arts of Deception: Playing with Fraud in the Age of Barnum*. Cambridge, MA: Harvard University Press, 2001.

Couvares, Francis G. "The Triumph of Commerce: Class Culture and Mass Culture in Pittsburgh." In *Working-Class America: Essays on Labor, Community, and American Society*, edited by Michael Frisch and Daniel Walkowitz. Chicago: University of Illinois Press, 1983.

Craddock, Susan. *City of Plagues: Disease, Poverty, and Deviance in San Francisco*. Minneapolis: University of Minnesota Press, 2000.

Crick, Malcolm. "Representations of International Tourism in the Social Sciences: Sun, Sex, Sights, Savings, and Servility." *Annual Review of Anthropology* 18 (1989): 307–344.

Cronon, William. *Nature's Metropolis: Chicago and the Great West*. New York: W. W. Norton, 1991.

Cronon, William, George Miles, and Jay Gitlin. "Becoming West: Toward a New Meaning for Western History." In *Under an Open Sky: Rethinking America's Western Past*, edited by William Cronon, George Miles, and Jay Gitlin. New York: W. W. Norton, 1992.

Daniels, Douglas Henry. *Pioneer Urbanites: A Social and Cultural History of Black San Francisco*. Philadelphia: Temple University Press, 1980.

Daniels, Roger. *Asian America: Chinese and Japanese in the United States since 1850*. Seattle: University of Washington Press, 1988.

Decker, Peter R. *Fortunes and Failures: White-Collar Mobility in Nineteenth-Century San Francisco*. Cambridge, MA: Harvard University Press, 1978.

D'Emilio, John, and Estelle B. Freedman *Intimate Matters: A History of Sexuality in America*. New York: Harper and Row, 1988.

Dennett, Andrea Stulman. *Weird and Wonderful: The Dime Museum in America*. New York: New York University Press, 1997.

Desmond, Jane C. *Staging Tourism: Bodies on Display from Waikiki to Sea World*. Chicago: University of Chicago Press, 1999.

Deutsch, Sarah. *Women and the City: Gender, Space, and Power in Boston, 1870–1940*. New York: Oxford University Press, 2000.

————. *No Separate Refuge: Culture, Class, and Gender on an Anglo-Hispanic Frontier in the American Southwest.* New York: Oxford University Press, 1987.

Douglas, Mary. *Purity and Danger: An Analysis of the Concepts of Pollution and Taboo.* London: Routledge, 1966.

Eaves, Edward Paul. *A History of the Cooks' and Waiters' Unions of San Francisco.* Thesis, Master of Arts, Economics, University of California, 1930.

Ehrenreich, Barbara, and Deidre English. *For Her Own Good: 150 Years of the Experts' Advice to Women.* Garden City, NY: Anchor Books, 1979.

Elias, Norbert. *The Civilizing Process: The History of Manners and State Formation and Civilization,* translated by Edmund Jephcott. London: Blackwell, 1994, originally published 1939.

Ethington, Philip. *The Public City: The Political Construction of Urban Life in San Francisco, 1850–1900.* Cambridge: Cambridge University Press, 1994.

Ewen, Elizabeth. *Immigrant Women in the Land of Dollars: Life and Culture on the Lower East Side, 1890–1925.* New York: Monthly Review Press, 1985.

Filene, Peter. *Him/Her/Self: Gender Identities in Modern America.* 3rd ed. Baltimore: Johns Hopkins University Press, 1998.

Findlay, John. M. "Far Western Cityscapes and American Culture since 1940." *Western Historical Quarterly* 22 (February 1991).

Foucault, Michel. *Discipline and Punish: The Birth of the Prison.* New York: Vintage Books, 1979.

Fredrickson, George M. *The Black Image in the White Mind: The Debate on Afro-American Character and Destiny, 1817–1914.* New York: Harper and Row, 1971.

Friedman, Susan Stanford. *Mappings: Feminism and the Cultural Geographies of Encounter.* Princeton, NJ: Princeton University Press, 1998.

Gable, Eric; Richard Handler, and Anna Lawson. "On the Uses of Relativism; Fact, Conjecture, and Black and White Histories at Colonial Williamsburg." *American Ethnologist* 19, no.4 (November 1992): 791–805.

Gebhard, David. "One Hundred Years of California Architecture." In *1868–1968, Architecture in California, An Exhibition Organized by David Gebhard and Harriette Von Breton to Celebrate the Centennial of the University of California, The Art Galleries, University of California, Santa Barbara, April 16 to May 12, 1968,* edited by David Gebhard and Harriette Von Breton. The Regents, University of California, 1968.

Gibson, Faith. "Brief History and Theory of Physician Discipline in California, 1876–1998." http://www.marijuana.org/MedBdHistoryCal.htm.

Gilbert, James. *Perfect Cities: Chicago's Utopias of 1893.* Chicago: University of Chicago Press, 1991.

Gilfoyle, Timothy J. *City of Eros: New York City, Prostitution, and the Commercialization of Sex, 1790–1920.* New York: W. W. Norton, 1992.

Glassberg, David. *Sense of History: The Place of the Past in American Life.* Amherst: University of Masachusetts Press, 2001.

Goodrich, Mary. *The Palace Hotel.* San Francisco: Crandall Press, 1930.

Gramsci, Antonio. *The Modern Prince and Other Writings*. New York: International Publishers, 1957, 1987.

Gruen, J. Philip. "Manifest Destinations: Tourist Encounters in the Late-Nineteenth-Century Urban American West." Unpublished manuscript in author's possession.

Gumina, Deanna Paoli. *The Italians of San Francisco, 1850–1930*. New York: Center for Migration Studies, 1978.

Gutiérrez, David G. "Significant to Whom? Mexican Americans and the History of the American West," *Western Historical Quarterly* 44, no. 4 (November 1993): 519–539.

Gyory, Andrew. *Closing the Gate: Race, Politics, and the Chinese Exclusion Act*. Chapel Hill: University of North Carolina Press, 1998.

Haas, Lisbeth. "War in California, 1846–1848," in *Contested Eden: California before the Gold Rush*, edited by Ramón Gutiérrez and Richard J. Orsi. Berkeley: University of California Press, 1998.

Haggerty, Timothy J. "The San Francisco Gentleman," *California History* 65 (June 1986): 96–103.

Hale, Grace Elizabeth. *Making Whiteness: The Culture of Segregation in the South, 1890–1940*. New York: Random House, 1998.

Hall, Stuart. "Introduction: Who Needs 'Identity'?" In *Questions of Cultural Identity*, edited by Stuart Hall and Paul du Gay. London: Sage Publications, 1996.

———. "Notes on Deconstructing the 'Popular.'" In *People's History and Socialist Theory*, edited by Raphael Samuel. London: Routledge, 1981.

Halttunen, Karen. "From Parlour to Living Room: Domestic Space, Interior Decoration, and the Culture of Personality." In *Consuming Visions: Accumulation and Display of Goods in America, 1880–1920*, edited by Simon J. Bronner. New York: W. W. Norton, 1989.

———. *Confidence Men and Painted Women: A Study of Middle-Class Culture in America, 1830–1870*. New Haven, CT: Yale University Press, 1982.

Harris, Alice Kessler. *Out to Work: A History of Wage-Earning Women in the United States*. New York: Oxford University Press, 1982.

Harris, Neil. *Cultural Excursions: Marketing Appetites and Cultural Tastes in Modern America*. Chicago: University of Chicago Press, 1990.

Higham, John. "The Reorientation of American Culture in the 1890s." In *The Origins of Modern Consciousness*, edited by John Weiss. Detroit: Wayne State University Press, 1965.

Heizer, Robert F., and Almquist, Alan J. *The Other Californians: Prejudice and Discrimination under Spain, Mexico and the United States to 1920*. Berkeley: University of California Press, 1971.

Hinsely, Curtis. "Strolling through the Colonies." In *Walter Benjamin and the Demands of History*, edited by Michael P. Sternberg. Ithaca, NY: Cornell University Press, 1996.

Holt, Thomas C. "Marking: Race, Race-making, and the Writing of History." *American Historical Review* 100, no. 1 (February 1995), 1–20.

Horowitz, Helen Lefkowitz. *Rereading Sex: Battles over Sexual Knowledge and Supression in Nineteenth-Century America*. New York: Alfred A. Knopf, 2002.

Hurtado, Albert L. *Intimate Frontiers: Sex, Gender, and Culture in Old California*. Albuquerque: University of New Mexico Press, 1999.

Issel, William. "Liberalism and Urban Policy in San Francisco from the 1930s to the 1960s." *Western Historical Quarterly* 22 (November 1991): 431–450.

Issel, William, and Robert W. Cherny. *San Francisco, 1865–1932: Politics, Power, and Urban Development*. Berkeley: University of California Press, 1986.

Jacobson, Matthew Frye. *Whiteness of a Different Color: European Immigrants and the Alchemy of Race*. Cambridge, MA: Harvard University Press, 1998.

Johnson, Susan Lee. *Roaring Camp: The Social World of the California Gold Rush*. New York: W. W. Norton, 2000.

Kahn, Judd. *Imperial San Francisco: Politics and Planning in an American City, 1897–1906*. Lincoln: University of Nebraska Press, 1979.

Kaplan, Amy. "'Left Alone with America': The Absence of Empire in the Study of American Culture." In *Cultures of United States Imperialism*, edited by Amy Kaplan and Donald Pease. Durham, NC: Duke University Press, 1993.

Kasson, John F. *Rudeness and Civility: Manners in Nineteenth-Century Urban America*. New York: Hill and Wang, 1990.

———. *Amusing the Million: Coney Island at the Turn of the Century*. New York: Hill and Wang, 1978.

———. *Civilizing the Machine: Technology and Republican Values in America, 1760–1900*. New York: Hill and Wang, 1976.

Kazin, Michael. *The Populist Persuasion: An American History*. Ithaca, NY: Cornell University Press, 1995 and 1998, rev. ed.

Klein, Kerwin Lee. *Frontiers of Historical Imagination: Narrating the European Conquest of Native America, 1890–1990*. Berkeley: University of California Press, 1997.

Larsen, Lawrence. *The Urban West at the End of the Frontier*. Lawrence, KS: Regents Press of Kansas, 1978.

Lears, Jackson. *No Place of Grace: Antimodernism and the Transformation of American Culture, 1880–1920*. Chicago: University of Chicago Press, 1981.

Lee, Anthony. *Picturing Chinatown: Art and Orientalism in San Francisco*. Berkeley: University of California Press, 2001.

Lee, Erika. *At America's Gates: Chinese Immigration during the Exclusion Era, 1882–1943*. Chapel Hill: University of North Carolina Press, 2003.

Lee, Robert G. *Orientals: Asian Americans in Popular Culture*. Philadelphia: Temple University Press, 1999.

Lefebvre, Henri. *The Production of Space*, translated by Donald Nicholson-Smith. Cambridge, MA: Blackwell, 1991.

Leishman, Nora. "The Mechanics' Institute Fairs, 1857–1899." *Argonaut: Journal of the San Francisco Historical Society* 10, no. 2 (Fall 1999): 40–57.

Leigh, Carol. "A Brief History of Government Policies toward Prostitution in San Francisco." *San Francisco Task Force on Prostitution Final Report 1996*. http://www.bay swan.org/sfhist.html.

Levenstein, Harvey A. *Revolution at the Table: The Transformation of the American Diet*. New York: Oxford University Press, 1988.

Levine, Lawrence. *Highbrow/Lowbrow: The Emergence of Cultural Hierarchy in America*. Cambridge, MA: Harvard University Press, 1988.

Lewis, Oscar, and Carroll D. Hall. *Bonanza Inn: America's First Luxury Hotel*. New York: Alfred A. Knopf, 1939.

Limerick, Patricia Nelson. *The Legacy of Conquest: The Unbroken Past of the American West*. New York: W. W. Norton, 1987.

Lingenfelter, Richard E., compiler. *Songs of the American West*. Berkeley: University of California Press, 1968

Lockwood, Charles. "Woodward's Natural Wonders," *California Living Magazine*, San Francisco Sunday *Examiner & Chronicle*, November 20, 1977.

Loo, Chalsa M. *Chinatown: Most Time, Hard Time*. New York: Praeger Publishers, 1991.

Lotchin, Roger W. *San Francisco, 1846–1856: From Hamlet to City*. Lincoln: University of Nebraska Press, 1974.

Lott, Eric. *Love and Theft: Blackface Minstrelsy and the American Working Class*. New York: Oxford University Press, 1993.

MacCanell, Dean. *The Tourist: A New Theory of the Leisure Class*. New York: Schocken Books, 1976.

Massey, Doreen. *Space, Place, and Gender*. Minneapolis: University of Minnesota Press, 1994.

Matthews, Glenna. "Forging a Cosmopolitan Civic Culture: The Regional Identity of San Francisco and Northern California." In *Many Wests: Place, Culture, and Regional Identity*, edited by David M. Wrobel and Michael C. Steiner. Lawrence: University Press of Kansas, 1997.

May, Elaine Tyler. *Great Expectations: Marriage and Divorce in Post-Victorian America* Chicago: University of Chicago Press, 1980.

McClain, Charles J. *In Search of Equality: The Chinese Struggle against Discrimination in Nineteenth-Century America*. Berkeley: University of California Press, 1994.

McClintock, Anne. *Imperial Leather: Race, Gender, and Sexuality in the Colonial Contest*. New York: Routledge, 1995.

McWilliams, Carey. *California: The Great Exception*. Berkeley: University of California Press, 1949, 1999.

———. *North from Mexico: The Spanish-Speaking People of the United States*. Philadelphia: J. B. Lippincott, 1949.

Montgomery, David. *The Fall of the House of Labor: The Workplace, the State, and American Labor Activism, 1865–1925*. New York: Cambridge University Press, 1987.

Nasaw, David. *Going Out: The Rise and Fall of Public Amusements*. Cambridge, MA: Harvard University Press, 1993.

O'Flinn, Patricia. "Moral Purity Campaigns, Middle-Class Clubwomen, and the California Red Light Abatement Act." http://userwww.sfsu.edu/~epf/1996/redlight.html.

Okihiro, Gary. *Margins and Mainstreams: Asians in American History and Culture.* Seattle: University of Washington Press, 1994.

Omi, Michael, and Howard Winant. *Racial Formation in the United States: From the 1960s to the 1990s.* 2nd ed. New York: Routledge, 1994.

100 Years of the Mechanics' Institute of San Francisco, 1855–1955. San Francisco: Mechanics' Institute of San Francisco, 1955.

Palumbo-Liu, David. *Asian/American: Historical Crossings of a Racial Frontier.* Stanford, CA: Stanford University Press, 1999.

Pascoe, Peggy. *Relations of Rescue: The Search for Female Moral Authority in the American West,* 1874–1939. New York: Oxford University Press, 1990.

Pateman, Carole. *The Sexual Contract.* Stanford, CA: Stanford University Press, 1988.

Peiss, Kathy. *Cheap Amusements: Working Women and Leisure in Turn-of-the-Century New York.* Philadelphia: Temple University Press, 1986.

Pillsbury, Richard. *From Boarding House to Bistro: The American Restaurant Then and Now.* Boston: Unwin Hyman, 1990.

Pomeroy, Earl. *The Pacific Slope: A History of California, Oregon, Washington, Idaho, Utah, and Nevada.* New York: Alfred A. Knopf, 1965.

Pratt, Mary Louise. *Imperial Eyes: Travel Writing and Transculturation.* New York: Routledge, 1992.

Rast, Raymond. "Staging Chinatown: The Place of the Chinese in San Francisco's Tourist Industry." Unpublished paper in author's possession.

Reps, John W. *Cities of the American West: A History of Frontier Urban Planning* Princeton, NJ: Princeton University Press, 1979.

Rice, Stephen P. *Minding the Machine: Languages of Class in Early Industrial America* Berkeley: University of California Press, 2004.

Roberts, Brian. *American Alchemy: The California Gold Rush and Middle-Class Culture.* Chapel Hill: University of North Carolina Press, 2000.

Robertson, E. Graeme. *Melbourne's Public Anatomical and Anthropological Museums, and the Jordans.* Glebe, New South Wales: Australasian Medical Publishing, 1956.

Roediger, David R. *The Wages of Whiteness: Race and the Making of the American Working Class.* New York: Verso, 1991.

Rohrbough, Malcolm J. *Days of Gold: The California Gold Rush and the American Nation.* Berkeley: University of California Press, 1997.

Rosen, Ruth. *The Lost Sisterhood: Prostitution in America, 1900–1918.* Baltimore: Johns Hopkins University Press, 1982.

Rosenzweig, Roy. *Eight Hours for What We Will: Workers and Leisure in an Industrial City, 1870–1920.* New York: Cambridge University Press, 1983.

Rotundo, E. Anthony. *American Manhood: Transformations in Masculinity from the Revolution to the Modern Era.* New York: Basic Books, 1993.

Russett, Cynthia Eagle. *Sexual Science: The Victorian Construction of Womanhood.* Cambridge, MA: Harvard University Press, 1989.

Ryan, Mary. *Civic Wars: Democracy and Public Life in the American City during the Nineteenth Century*. Berkeley: University of California Press, 1997.

———. *Women in Public: Between Banners and Ballots, 1825–1880*. Berkeley: University of California Press, 1990.

———. *Cradle of the Middle Class: The Family in Oneida County, New York, 1790–1865*. New York: Cambridge University Press, 1981.

Rydell, Robert. *All the World's a Fair: Visions of Empire at American International Expositions, 1876–1916*. Chicago: University of Chicago Press, 1984.

Said, Edward. *Orientalism*. New York: Vintage Books, 1979.

———. *Culture and Imperialism*. New York: Vintage Books, 1993.

Sappol, Michael. *A Traffic in Dead Bodies: Anatomy and Embedded Social Identity in Nineteenth-Century America*. Princeton, NJ: Princeton University Press, 2004.

Saxton, Alexander. *The Indispensable Enemy: Labor and the Anti-Chinese Movement in California*. Berkeley: University of California Press, 1971.

Schaffer, Marguerite S. *See America First: Tourism and National Identity, 1880–1940*. Washington, DC: Smithsonian Institution Press, 2001.

Schlesinger, Arthur M., Sr., *The Rise of the City, 1878–1898*. New York: Macmillan, 1933.

Schueller, Malini Johar. *U.S. Orientalisms: Race, Nation, and Gender in Literature, 1790–1890*. Ann Arbor: University of Michigan Press, 1998.

Scobey, David. "Anatomy of the Promenade: The Politics of Bourgeois Sociability in Nineteenth-Century New York." *Social History* 17 (May, 1992): 203–227.

Scott, Joan Wallach. *Gender and the Politics of History*. New York: Columbia University Press, 1988.

Sellers, Charles Coleman. *Mr. Peale's Museum: Charles Wilson Peale and the First Popular Museum of Natural Science and Art*. New York: W. W. Norton, 1980.

Shah, Nyan. *Contagious Divides: Epidemics and Race in San Francisco's Chinatown*. Berkeley: University of California Press, 2001.

Soja, Edward. *Postmodern Geographies: The Reassertion of Space in Critical Social Theory*. New York: Verso, 1989.

Sparks, Edith. *Capital Intentions: Female Proprietors in San Francisco, 1850–1920* (Chapel Hill: University of North Carolina Press, 2006).

Spickard, Paul, and G. Reginald Daniel, eds. *Racial Thinking in the United States: Uncompleted Independence*. Notre Dame, IN: University of Notre Dame Press, 2004.

Stallybrass, Peter, and Allon White. *The Politics and Poetics of Transgression*. Ithaca, NY: Cornell University Press, 1986.

Stansell, Christine. *City of Women: Sex and Class in New York, 1789–1860*. Chicago: University of Illinois Press, 1987.

Starr, Kevin. *Inventing the Dream: California through the Progressive Era*. New York: Oxford University Press, 1985.

Susman, Warren I. *Culture as History: The Transformation of American Society in the Twentieth Century*. New York: Pantheon Books, 1984.

Takaki, Ronald. *Strangers from a Different Shore: A History of Asian Americans*. New York: Penguin Books, 1989.

Tchen, John Kuo Wei. *New York before Chinatown: Orientalism and the Shaping of American Culture, 1776–1882.* Baltimore: Johns Hopkins University Press, 1999.

——, ed. *Genthe's Photographs of San Francisco's Old Chinatown.* New York: Dover, 1984.

Tiedemann, Arthur. *Modern Japan: A Brief History.* Rev. ed. Princeton, NJ: D. Van Nostrand, 1962.

Thompson, Rosemarie Garland. *Extraordinary Bodies: Figuring Disability in American Culture and Literature.* New York: Columbia University Press, 1997.

Tong, Benson. *Unsubmissive Women: Chinese Prostitutes in Nineteenth-Century San Francisco.* Norman: University of Oklahoma Press, 1994.

Trachtenberg, Alan. *The Incorporation of America: Culture and Society in the Gilded Age.* New York: Hill and Wang, 1982.

Turner, Frederick Jackson. "The Significance of the Frontier in American History." *Proceedings of the Forty-First Meeting of the State Historical Society of Wisconsin.* Madison, Wisconsin, 1894: 79–112.

Urry, John. *The Tourist Gaze: Leisure and Travel in Contemporary Societies.* London: Sage Publications, 1990.

——. *Consuming Places.* London and New York: Routledge, 1995.

Wade, Richard C. *The Urban Frontier: Pioneer Life in Early Pittsburgh, Cincinnati, Lexington, Louisville, and St. Louis.* Cambridge, MA: Harvard University Press, 1959.

Walkowitz, Judith R. *City of Dreadful Delight: Narratives of Sexual Danger in Late-Victorian London.* Chicago: University of Chicago Press, 1992.

Warner, Sam Bass. *Streetcar Suburbs: The Process of Growth in Boston, 1870–1900.* Cambridge, MA: Harvard University Press, 1962.

Wells, Evelyn. *Champagne Days of San Francisco.* New York: D. Appleton-Century, 1939.

Welter, Barbara. "The Cult of True Womanhood: 1820–1860." In *Our American Sisters: Women in American Life and Thought,* edited by Jean E. Friedman and William G. Shade. Boston: Allyn and Bacon, Inc., 1973.

Wilentz, Sean. *Chants Democratic: New York City and the Rise of the American Working Class, 1788–1850.* New York: Oxford University Press, 1984.

Williamson, Jefferson. *The American Hotel: An Anecdotal History.* New York: Alfred. A. Knopf, 1930.

Wood, John H., compiler. *75 Years of History of the Mechanics' Institute.* San Francisco: Benham Printing, 1930.

Wrobel, David, and Patrick T. Long, eds., *Seeing and Being Seen: Tourism in the American West.* Lawrence: University Press of Kansas, 2001.

Yung, Judy. *Unbound Feet: A Social History of Chinese Women in San Francisco.* Berkeley: University of California Press, 1995.

Index